Classical Music

CLASSICAL MUSIC

A Reader's Digest Book
Edited and designed by Mitchell Beazley,
an imprint of Reed Consumer Books Limited

Copyright © 1994 Reed International Books Limited
Text copyright © 1994 John Stanley
Illustrations copyright © 1994 Reed International Books Limited

The acknowledgments that appear on page 272 are hereby made
a part of this copyright page.

Project Editor Kirsty Seymour-Ure
Art Editor Rozelle Bentheim
Editors Christopher Wood, Katherine Martin-Doyle
Designers Blânche-Adrienne Harper, Vivienne Cherry
Editorial Assistant Michelle Pickering
Researcher Katherine Fry
Picture Researchers Jenny Faithfull, Emily Hedges,
Anne Hobart, Julia Ruxton, Sally Ryall
Production Controller Michelle Thomas
Indexer Hilary Bird

Executive Editor Sarah Polden
Art Directors Tim Foster, Jacqui Small

Instruments illustrations Grundy Northedge
Contents illustration Dan Davis

10 9 8 7 6 5 4 3 2 1

Library of Congress Cataloging in Publication Data

Stanley, John.
    Classical Music : an introduction to classical music through
the great composers and their masterworks / John Stanley.
        p.   cm.
    Includes index.
    ISBN 0-89577-606-5
    I. Music—History and criticism.   2. Music appreciation.
I. Title.
ML160.S82   1994
780' .9—dc20   94-1931

CD Edition ISBN 0-89577-947-1

Printed in China

**The publisher would like to thank the following people
for their invaluable contributions to the book:**
Dr. A. V. Antonovics, Christopher Atkinson, John Bailie,
Andrew Ball, Alan Blyth, Meurig Bowen, Ian Chilvers,
Paul Collen, Rosemary Fforbes-Butler, Andrew Herbert,
Stephen Jackson, Clare Le Fort, Thadeus Parsons, Al Roots,
Simeon Shoul, Mark Wiggins and Iain Zaczek.
We are greatly indebted to them.

Classical Music

AN INTRODUCTION
TO CLASSICAL MUSIC
THROUGH THE
GREAT COMPOSERS
& THEIR
MASTERWORKS

JOHN STANLEY

FOREWORD BY
SIR GEORG SOLTI

THE READER'S DIGEST ASSOCIATION, INC.
Pleasantville, New York • Montreal

Contents

Introduction 10

The Middle Ages and the Renaissance 38

The Baroque Era 64

The Classical Era 96

Foreword

I have watched with close interest the development of this book from its very early stages of planning, as I was extremely sympathetic to John Stanley's intention, to set the lives of great composers in the broadest possible context. All too often we read about them with reference only to their fellow musicians and to their own world of music. How much more interesting it is, therefore, to see the effect upon them of the other arts and disciplines of their times.

Virtually all great composers have left us evidence, in letters and writings, of their interest in and often passion for these other art forms. Many of them have written works specifically influenced by great buildings, wonderful paintings or works of literature, political actions or religious celebrations. Events of history as well as changes in fashion and thinking can all be witnessed in music, once it is examined in the context of the world at large at the time it was written.

In this way, classical music can be seen as an integral part of our history and I am sure that the book will arouse the interest of music and art lovers everywhere.

Preface

Today, we often use the term classical as the musical opposite of 'popular.' But in fact, these great works are 'classics' because they have demonstrated a timeless quality, an enduring appeal that has survived the changing musical ages. They have stood the test of time.

But why do some works find a place in the canon of great music while others disappear into obscurity? We can pick out with relative ease works that exhibit lasting value and so deserve to be called classics, if they were written before the mid-twentieth century. But more recent music is far more difficult to judge, because the test of time cannot help us. We need to identify qualities that define the earlier classics and look for the same qualities in recent or contemporary music.

Scholars have developed a complex if inexact science of musicology, seeking to evaluate many of the classics. The great theorist Heinrich Schenker (1868–1935), a pupil of Bruckner, developed an influential system of analysis that has given insights into music from Bach through to Mahler. But the system is of virtually no use when applied to works by composers who did not fit his system, although they are now established classics.

However, no classic was ever established by the judgment of a musicologist. A potential classic must first find an audience, and in this respect critics, patrons, performers, and other composers have exercised considerable influence. This 'musical establishment' has largely trusted its instincts — often informed instincts, certainly — in reaching a verdict on new music. How successful have they been in the past in assessing classic potential?

Their track record is mixed. Schumann was a discerning critic, heaping praise on Chopin and the young Brahms after only a token acquaintance with their music. He even had a few good words for the then much-maligned Berlioz. Mendelssohn deserves much of the credit for rescuing Bach from semi-obscurity when, in 1829, he mounted the first performance of the St. Matthew Passion since Bach's death in 1750. The Vienna Philharmonic pronounced Bruckner's symphonies unplayable, compositions that were also attacked by the Viennese critic Eduard Hanslick. Hanslick's own record is mixed; he detested Wagner and Liszt and approved of Brahms and Richard Strauss. And of course the Viennese imperial court made the celebrated error of judgment in preferring Salieri to Mozart. Such ambiguous results do not inspire confidence in the ability of a modern-day musical establishment to select a contemporary classic.

In reality, both scholars and the listening public will choose their own best-loved contemporary compositions in much the way they chose favorites in the past. The works may or may not prove to be classics. It will be for another generation to judge whether they embody that elusive timeless quality that characterizes the works — true classics — recommended in the following pages.

In this book, the place of music in Western society and the changing role of the composer over the centuries are introduced, along with the basic tools of classical music — the instruments — and how they have appeared in groups and ensembles — and of course the human voice.

The main body of the book consists of studies of the lives and works of some 150 composers selected by *Gramophone* magazine, the internationally renowned classical music authority. They appear in approximate chronological order, based on their dates of major compositional activity, and cover the period from 1100 to the present. Recent scholarship has shed much new light on the music and composers of the Middle Ages and the early renaissance, and their inclusion reflects their proper place in a majestic span of classical music history over nearly a thousand years. Similarly, the increasing interest in and popularity of composers of our time led to the inclusion of a selection of important contemporary movements and composers who are among their leading exponents.

The composers are grouped into distinct eras. The categories are meaningful in that they correspond to periods in history characterized by well-known cultural and artistic movements. Inevitably there is some overlap, and many composers could arguably fit into more than one category. You will find the lives and works of these composers related to their more general cultural context.

The choice of the composers themselves reflects careful consideration. There is a relatively small body of true, undisputed giants of classical music, among them such figures as Palestrina, Bach, Mozart, Beethoven, Wagner, Mahler, and Stravinsky. Some 150 composers are included in order to present a much fuller picture of the whole of the classical tradition. Beyond the first core fifty or one hundred, there could be much justified debate as to who should be included, particularly from the twentieth century, where reputations are still being forged and cannot be judged with the benefit of hindsight. Some were chosen because of the developmental role they played, although their ideas and innovations may have reached fruition in the work of another, perhaps greater composer. We hope that, in bringing the works of such lesser-known composers to light, they will find a new, enthusiastic audience.

For each composer you will find several works selected as representative of that composer's output, chosen to illustrate the main characteristics and virtues of the composer's style as a basis for further exploration. In each case a particular recording is recommended, chosen by *Gramophone* with the benefit of 70 years of experience in selecting the highest quality performances available to the home listener. CD information (name of work, artists, record company, and catalog number) has been given and the details should enable the CD to be easily found in a store, or to be ordered.

It is richly rewarding to explore any or all of these composers, their works, and their eras, to form an individual opinion, and to look beyond the composers and works cited. Time may see the emergence of contemporary classics from as yet unknown composers.

Introduction

Human beings have been inspired to make music from the very earliest times. This most sophisticated of arts is also the most fundamental. There is something in us that responds to sound and to rhythm, and in producing our own music we have taken our inspiration from nature, be it the wind in the trees, the pounding of waves, or the calling of birds. We have developed methods of imbuing sound with meaning, combining notes, pitches, and rhythms to make melody, and using music as an intricate means of expression on infinitely varied levels.

It was late in history that music was written down; until the Middle Ages it was passed down orally from generation to generation. The voice was the most primitive instrument, with songs — often wordless — used in all cultures as far back as prehistoric times for prayer and ritual, for celebration, exhortation, and lament. The first written music was the plainchant of medieval monks, who were also the first composers; their simple vocal lines celebrated the glory of God. Basic pre-Christian instruments such as reed pipes, bone flutes, and pottery drums were refined through the ages, and during the Renaissance were incorporated fully into sacred as well as secular music. The role of the composer developed as western society became ever more complex, and music reflected the sometimes radical changes of a constantly evolving culture.

With the lessening influence of both church and royal court as artistic patrons in the nineteenth century, composers were freed from the inevitable restrictions that patronage imposed. Public concerts and publication became important sources of income, a trend that continues today with broadcast fees and recordings. Classical music has become in some areas almost dauntingly experimental, but, paradoxically, is now in many ways more accessible to a broader public than ever before.

Overview of an orchestra
The world of classical music is starting to shed its elitist image and open its doors to everyone. Traditional orchestras exist alongside a great diversity of other means of making and enjoying music.

The Composer in Society

Music has been a vital part of human society since time immemorial. In the West, what we now call classical music evolved over centuries, though its documentation did not begin until around the ninth century, with the first systems of musical notation. Because the church and court effectively dominated classical music until the nineteenth century, the art and culture of these institutions have left the clearest record. The composer's position in society has also evolved, as our expectations of music have changed and grown.

The Medieval period

The first composers probably did not consider themselves composers as we think of them today. They composed as a way of glorifying God, often in the context of monasteries, such as that at Cluny in the eleventh century. These monasteries became the first great musical centers, and one of their members, the Abbess Hildegard of Bingen, was among the earliest recognized composers. Their form of expression was plainchant (or plainsong) — a single, clear line of vocal music — used in religious services and devised primarily to convey the words and meaning of the sacred texts.

Outside the church, twelfth-century French troubadours and their successors created a demand for secular music that rivaled the sacred. With the Crusades came a rediscovery of ancient Greek culture, knowledge, and philosophy. At the same time, the first universities such as those at Bologna, Paris, and Oxford came into existence. Against this background, church composers expanded their music into an art of its own, with grammar and rules of construction that did not depend on religious texts or functions. The new musical techniques drew inspiration as well from the great new cathedrals that were being built around Europe at the time, especially Notre Dame in Paris, with its vast soaring vaults that virtually demanded equally soaring, celebratory music.

In the early 1300's the composer and churchman Philippe de Vitry dubbed the new music Ars Nova: New Art. Pope John XXII, in his *Edict Docta Sanctorum* (1324–25), described it as 'a multitude of notes so confusing that the seemly rise and decorous fall of the plainsong melody, which should be the distinguishing feature of the music, is entirely obscured.' Negative reaction to modern music is not unique to our own times, but in this case it revealed papal recognition that the leading com-

posers had begun to consider themselves not merely servants of the liturgy but also artists.

The major composers continued to combine the functions of churchman and musician (often as chapel or cathedral singers) until the Renaissance and beyond, but they also increasingly served in the courts of the ruling classes, writing both sacred and secular music. The fourteenth-century composer Guillaume de Machaut, though better known for his complete musical setting of the Mass, actually wrote more secular music, and held positions at the courts of Luxembourg and Normandy as well as at Rheims Cathedral.

The Renaissance

With the Renaissance came a shift in music's center of gravity in Europe. The great new bastions of culture were not the monasteries of northern France but rather the city-states of Italy. Music now depended on the patronage of various dukes and princes. Within the aristocratic courts themselves, music — like all the other arts — was still focused largely on religion, and the pope remained a leading patron. The composer Josquin Desprez, although he was born and died in the French-speaking Netherlands, found his varied career in the service of the powerful Sforza family of Milan, Duke Hercules of Ferrara, and the pope, among others.

Josquin's importance is reflected in how much of his music was published from the beginning of the sixteenth century by the Venetian pioneer of music printing, Ottaviano dei Petrucci. The advent of printing had an enormous influence on the music world, enabling the widespread distribution of sheet music for the first time, and doubtless contributing to Josquin's fame throughout western Europe. It fed the first commercial demands for music coming from an emerging middle class of traders and merchants, who gathered informally to sing madrigals or chansons (two forms of secular song). The

A concert given by angels, painted by Paolo Veneziano

Medieval composers viewed their art as a means of glorifying God. Often working in monasteries, they composed in plainchant, using a single clear vocal line.

new secular forms pervaded church music too; composers increasingly turned to secular melodies for their sacred compositions, the Masses, Passions, and Magnificats.

The Catholic church could not significantly influence the new musical developments of the secular world. But in the Council of Trent (1545–63), convened principally in reaction to the Protestant Reformation, it attempted to curb what it regarded as dangerous elements in religious music, still the principal focus of leading composers. The greatest composer of the time, Palestrina, and his followers were instructed to re-address themselves to a clear, unadorned setting of the sacred texts, free from all emotional or artistic extravagances. In fact they achieved a musical style of great beauty and artistry, but one that still deferred to the authority of the church.

The Baroque period

With opera — perhaps the single most important development of the Baroque period — secular music finally acquired a form that was sufficiently popular, expressive, and large-scale to tip the balance of patronage away from the church to the princely courts, and eventually to the general public. Monteverdi, whose *La favola d'Orfeo* (1607) is credited as the first true opera, spent the first half of his professional life at the courts of Cremona and Mantua, and then, from 1613 until his death, as director of music at St. Mark's in Venice.

The circumstances of *Orfeo* dispel the notion, however, that aristocratic (rather than church) patronage meant artistic emancipation. Monteverdi was required to alter his original version to provide a happy ending suitable for the occasion of its performance — probably part of an attempt to arrange a politically advantageous marriage. The first public opera house, the Teatro San Cassiano in Venice, opened in 1637, and Monteverdi wrote music for some of

the competing establishments that soon appeared in its wake. The phenomenon reflected an increasing appetite not only for opera but also for public access to music in general.

The public concert also appeared in an early form in the Baroque period. In private academies — learned societies for the promotion of science and the arts, including music — performances were given for the local aristocracy as well as upper-class outsiders. The Accademia Filarmonica in Verona (founded in 1543) was probably the first to promote music, but accademias spread rapidly in the seventeenth century until every major town had one, and sometimes several. The Accademia dei Filarmonici, founded in Bologna in 1666, counted Mozart and Rossini among its later members.

The Venetian *ospedali*, or orphanages, also fulfilled a function as embryonic music conservatories. Virtually all the major seventeenth- and eighteenth-century Italian composers spent time as either pupils or teachers at these establishments, which also mounted frequent public concerts. Vivaldi — who had trained as a priest — was for 36 years in charge of music at the Ospedale della Pietà for girls.

In England, the period of the Commonwealth, after the Civil War, left music predominantly in the hands of the middle classes, who mounted semi-private performances in private houses, colleges, and taverns. Roger North, Attorney-General and author of *Memoires of Musick* (1728), cites a 1664 performance at the Mitre Inn, London, as the first public concert. In 1678, Thomas Mace converted a room in the York Buildings near Charing Cross in London into a specialist concert venue, and by 1700 a number of such enterprises existed, not only in the capital. Concerts proliferated in eighteenth-century England, promoted by music societies in all the major towns. The success of Handel's 1733 concerts in Oxford prompted the foundation there of the Holywell Music Room — supposedly the first venue built specifically for the holding of concerts.

But it would be a long time before composers could live on the income from such ventures. Unless they appeared themselves as performers, they usually earned nothing from performances of their music. Without performing rights protection, and with the first (hopelessly inadequate) copyright legislation not appearing until 1709, composers still relied on salaries from their wealthy patrons, supplemented by payments for works accepted by often exploitative publishers. Handel fell out with his unscrupulous publisher, John Walsh, over the publication of his opera *Rinaldo* in 1711; he did not return to the company until Walsh's son took over ten years later.

Church music flourished for a while in Protestant England particularly with the anthems of Henry Purcell, whose versatility also led him to compose music for the theater and the royal court. Religious music enjoyed even more importance in Lutheran north Germany, where both the clear, simple congregational hymns or chorales and more complex cantatas and Passion settings could be found. Such options attracted skilled musicians, including

Johann Sebastian Bach, to the larger, well-endowed churches. Bach was probably the last of the great composers to devote most of his musical efforts to the church. His employment at Leipzig required him to write a cantata every week for the Sunday services; although he was effectively writing to order, his devotional works represent some of the most sublime music he produced.

The Classical era

After Bach, the more puritan Pietist movement successfully replaced the semi-operatic cantata of the Lutheran service with the sermon. Once again the focus of religious music shifted south, this time to Catholic Austria, where the Masses of Haydn, Mozart, Beethoven, and Schubert appeared.

But by now, for these composers and most others, the growth of interest in orchestral music — particularly with the development of the symphony — pushed religious music to the sideline. The cost of maintaining the necessary large body of musicians initially concentrated such music in Mannheim, Paris, Berlin, Dresden, and Vienna, and with Haydn's long-time employers at Esterháza. There it could be underwritten by a handful of European ruling establishments with sufficient inclination and resources.

By the 1790's, though, Haydn had won recognition throughout western Europe. He also earned a sizable freelance income, notably from his final 12 *London Symphonies* for the public concerts organized by the London impresario J. P. Salomon from 1791 to 1795. Haydn was shrewd in his dealings with publishers, transferring to Breitkopf and Härtel in Leipzig when he became dissatisfied with Artaria in Vienna. Breitkopf's pioneering methods produced elegant sheet music which, with larger print runs, could be sold cheaply and distributed widely. Haydn may not have reaped the income from royalties that he might under today's copyright laws, but Breitkopf's publications brought him widespread fame, and with it lucrative commissions for new works. By contrast, Mozart, who for want of a permanent salaried court position also attempted a freelance existence, failed to get his works published in his lifetime and suffered a stunning lack of professional success.

The Romantic age

Beethoven ranks as the first great composer to lead a successful freelance career, though it may have been his unique personal characteristics that enabled him to do so. He was the first musical figure to whom the Romantic image of the tortured artist-hero, struggling in isolation with his muse, applies with any accuracy. Such an existence initially grew from his habit of wooing the aristocracy for private commissions, rather than from the public cult following that he only later attracted.

Beethoven's career nevertheless made the notion of a professional composer, freed from all except artistic considerations, seem a real possibility for the first time, and this matched the spirit of the new subjective and emotionally liberated Romantic age. In reality, with few exceptions, composers fulfilled a variety of musical and nonmusical roles out of economic necessity, until the public recognized their artistic stature — if it ever did. Liszt and Paganini toured widely as virtuoso solo performers, for whom there was a huge public demand; Berlioz and Schumann were music critics; Bruckner was a cathedral organist; and Borodin taught chemistry. Most, at some stage, played or conducted their own and others' music.

Artistic greatness has never been a guarantee of public recognition and still less of financial success. Conversely, some

Performance of an 18th-century oratorio, possibly with Handel conducting

The oratorio was structured similarly to the opera, but with a greater stress on the chorus. Handel's oratorios on sacred themes are some of the greatest ever written.

Beethoven's study in the Schwarzspanierhaus, Vienna, just after his death in 1827

Beethoven, the first great composer to have enjoyed a successful freelance career, is the exemplar of the Romantic artist.

composers whose music proved of no great lasting value were extremely popular in their day. But for those who won enduring fame, a rapidly growing audience awaited — the urban and middle-class populations that expanded dramatically during the industrial revolution. As the great age of amateur music-making dawned in the nineteenth century, composers for the first time earned a significant income from publication of their work in the form of printed sheet music.

Classical music became recreation for the middle classes, from informal concerts in private homes to soirées such as those that took place in the well-heeled Mendelssohn household. On a larger scale, music societies, now freed from aristocratic control, sponsored public orchestral concerts as a feature of city life throughout Europe and the United States. Beethoven's *Ninth Symphony* was written partly in response to a £50 commission in 1822 from the recently founded London Philharmonic Society (1813). Similar societies appeared in Vienna (1812), Berlin (1826), and Paris (*c.*1828), and in the latter half of the century, many of the world's great independent and municipal orchestras and concert halls were established.

Orchestral concerts and opera performances were often organized as part of musical festivals, such as on the Lower Rhine from 1817 (under Mendelssohn's directorship from 1833 to 1847), and from 1876 at Bayreuth, where Wagner built a festival theater for annual performances of his own operas. Bayreuth remains a major event in the opera calendar today.

The twentieth century

Many of the features of nineteenth-century musical life continued into the twentieth century. The orchestral concert and opera remain the principal focal points. Societies and festivals have proliferated; annual events at such places as Darmstadt in Germany and Tanglewood in the United States have played a vital role, from the 1940's on, in music education and in the commissioning and dissemination of new works. But a number of technological developments in this century have transformed the musical world at least as radically as the evolution of notation and printing in earlier eras.

World War I accelerated the development of broadcasting technology, and by 1920 a number of competing radio stations, particularly in the United States, scheduled daily programs. The BBC was set up in Britain in 1922 as a government monopoly and had sold 4.5 million licenses for 'wireless' sets by 1931, enabling it to provide generous sponsorship for music. The BBC founded its own symphony orchestra in 1930, and in 1927 it took over the Henry Wood Promenade Concerts (founded in 1895), which have grown to become one of the world's major festivals, responsible for several new commissions each year. In Germany, the state Rundfunk companies support symphony orchestras in each of the provinces and major cities. But the main impact of broadcasting (even more so in the age of satellites) was that classical music finally became available to a mass audience.

Through the purchase of recordings, this audience was next able to select the music it wanted to hear. Beginning with Edison's cylinder phonograph in 1877, recorded sound developed through disc and magnetic tape in the late 1920's, Columbia Records' Long-Playing disc in 1948, stereophonic reproduction in 1957, Philips' compact cassette in 1963, to the arrival of digital recording and compact discs in the early 1980's. Each innovation has represented an improvement in convenience and the fidelity of the recording to the original performance, which has boosted sales and demanded the re-recording of anything on obsolete formats.

Broadcasts and recordings, requiring no great musical skill for their appreciation, have now replaced sheet music as the main distributors (and also sponsors) of classical music, and have dramatically expanded the overall market. Recent startling successes for artists such as Pavarotti, composers such as Górecki, and the British radio station Classic FM have even rivaled those of the normally far more lucrative pop industry. But many classical composers agree that they are seeking a more elusive artistic or spiritual end, for which financial reward is welcome but of secondary importance.

Despite the growth of their potential audience, today's composers may or may not stand a better chance of earning a living from their music than their Romantic counterparts. Composers are certainly acknowledged in society as creative artists, writing from a subjective viewpoint and inspired by personal beliefs. But they have found new and often better ways of supporting themselves in related areas, particularly in the film industry and education. Most modern composers have made contributions in either or both of these areas, which therefore deserve some credit as twentieth-century patrons.

The needs of the film soundtrack have, with a few notable exceptions, rarely coincided with those of great classical music, and yet a host of composers, from Prokofiev, through Britten and Copland, to Pärt and Takemitsu, have supplemented their income by writing film scores. Schoenberg, Shostakovich, Messiaen, Cage, Carter, Berio, and others have held teaching posts in universities and conservatories, few of which are more than a century old. In most cases these composers probably enjoyed the opportunity to share their knowledge with the next musical generation, since the life of a composer can be an isolated one.

Leonard Bernstein conducting the New York Philharmonic for German television (main picture) and (inset) arriving in Berlin, 1960

Leonard Bernstein's career coincided with a period when his charisma and star appeal could be exploited by the burgeoning broadcast industry.

Conclusion

Classical music has diversified and developed over the centuries in response to changes in society; composers, like anyone else, have depended on society to earn their living. They began with practically the sole option of a monastic career, writing music for the church, of an appropriately limited nature. Most have striven ever since for greater variety and freedom of expression, restrained by the type and degree of patronage that society granted them. Sources of patronage today have become almost as varied as the music they support, coming from governments (especially in the countries of the former Soviet Bloc), universities, film, broadcasting and recording companies, wealthy societies, foundations and individuals, and the musical public. All these patrons impose far fewer rules than the church and aristocracy of previous ages, but according to the extent of their economic resources, they still limit what proportion of a composer's output will be performed. And yet, as is the case with all art forms, there is no limiting the artistic drive itself, and composers are perhaps freer today than ever before.

The Voice: The First Instrument

The capacity of the human voice for communication — one of the most extraordinary aspects of our being — distinguishes us from all other creatures on earth. Through the ability to cause controlled changes of pitch — to sing — the voice is the most ancient, universal, and sophisticated of all musical instruments.

Singing is as old as the earliest civilized cultures. According to the Old Testament Book of Exodus, Moses and the Israelites sang their praises to God on being delivered from the Egyptians — believed to have been in the thirteenth century B.C. The Ancient Greeks sang in worship and in the theater, as did the Romans; and with the advent of Christianity, the ancient Jewish tradition of chanting the Psalms of David passed into Christian worship too. This link with Judeo-Christian worship binds many strands of vocal musical history in the Western world, from plainchant to oratorio, from chanting monks to church choirs and choral societies.

Monks, troubadours, and Paris polyphony

It was the monks of the Middle Ages who first wrote music down in a form that could be transmitted accurately over generations. They committed to paper the previously purely oral tradition, the practice of chanting plainchant. The earliest vocal music to survive as notation is religious music; church authorities did not encourage notation of nonreligious music; and secular music — folk songs, ballads, courtly ditties — was in any case predominantly improvised.

Until the ninth century, every mode of singing was monophonic — meaning, literally, a single line of sound. The earliest known reference to the coming together of two separate voices dates to about A.D. 860 in northeastern France. Referred to as organum, it coupled a line of plainchant with another

Illumination from a 15th-century Book of Hours for John, Duke of Berry

During the Middle Ages, vocal music reached its zenith, and the singer was celebrated as the foremost musician of the day.

voice at a different pitch. A major stage in the development of this multi-voiced music ('polyphony') came at the end of the twelfth century when the French composer Pérotin, based in Paris at the time the great cathedral of Notre Dame was built, wrote the first music for three and four separate voices. From this came the glories of medieval and Renaissance church music, and the rise of the singer as pre-eminent musician.

The growth of the choir

The singers who were given the task of performing this early polyphony were, of necessity, specialists. Almost certainly, therefore, each part was performed by a single singer. In large monastic establishments, with singing 'clerks' numbering 50, the majority sang only the monophonic plainchant. By the beginning of the fourteenth century, a polyphonic choral style had developed in England and northern Europe to the point where the complexities of this multi-lined music had become familiar, and small choirs began to perform it instead of soloists.

The wealth and influence of the church in late medieval society remain apparent all over Europe in the grandeur of its cathedrals, abbeys, and monasteries. As buildings became more architecturally ambitious, so the provision for music became more generous. Choirs increased steadily in size throughout the fifteenth and sixteenth centuries, and the music written for them became more elaborate — as demonstrated by Thomas

Illumination from *The Romance of King Meliadus*, written for Louis II of Naples

This fourteenth-century illumination shows singers accompanying themselves on a psaltery and mandora.

Tallis's motet for 40 voices (eight choirs of five parts), *Spem in Alium*. In England, especially, many choral foundations were established during this time in cathedrals and collegiate chapels, establishments still renowned for choral music, such as Westminster Abbey, Canterbury Cathedral, and King's College, Cambridge.

In medieval and Renaissance times it was singers from the Low Countries and France whose expertise was most admired; in fact many were specially employed in court chapels and cathedrals all over Europe, particularly in Italy. It was not uncommon for this new type of traveling professional singer to compose as well, and the most distinguished of them included Ockeghem, Dufay, Brumel, Obrecht, and Josquin Desprez. No period of musical history since has tied singing and composing so closely to one another.

Late 16th-century French painting of a singing group

The three women singers in this group reflect the new appreciation of the female voice that emerged in the late sixteenth century.

Madrigals, opera, and castrati

The following generation of Franco-Flemish composers in Italy — Verdelot, Willaert, and Jannequin — introduced the earliest madrigals, the major secular vocal form of the sixteenth century. Settings of both the elevated courtly love poetry of Petrarch and more emotional, down-to-earth verse created a style of music that was at once highly accessible, expressive, and changeable in mood. Such need for musical drama was one of the reasons why the vocal ranges in this genre became greatly extended. Medieval plainchant had required of its male singers a range of merely one octave, and the polyphonic writing of subsequent centuries rarely asked its performers — boy sopranos, adult male altos, tenors, and basses — to sing particularly high or low. Through the late sixteenth-century madrigal, the high female voice found appreciation for the first time. This was particularly so in Italy, and at the noble court of Ferrara a specially trained ensemble of female singers became famous for its virtuosity.

This new taste for the high voice posed problems for the church, which forbade women to sing in acts of worship. Choirs in the English post-Reformation church relied on pre-pubescent boys to sing the top line; the Roman Catholic church in sixteenth-century Italy used falsettists from Spain, specializing in the soprano register. Falsetto, a means of voice production for the adult male, whereby an artificially high voice is created, is inevitably limited in its range and flexibility. Another solution — perhaps the most extraordinary phenomenon in the history of music — was the castrato, a male singer castrated before puberty to preserve his high voice. The first acknowledgment of a castrated male on the payroll of the Sistine Choir in Rome was in 1599, and despite the serious moral questions that this operation raised, such singers became a crucial element of Catholic choirs in Europe over the next two centuries. (In the churches of Rome alone, more than 200 castrati were employed in 1780; the last eunuch singer retired from the Sistine Chapel in 1913.)

Castrati were not confined to ecclesiastical environments; they became a mainstay of the fastest-growing and most influential secular genre of the seventeenth century: opera. Opera required a more conspicuous, virtuoso type of singer, and the castrato was particularly suited to this new mode of vocal performance. Although the vocal apparatus remained immature as a result of emasculation, the rest of the body — in particular the chest — grew to a great size. Thus the main area of vocal production and support, the lungs and diaphragm, developed great power and stamina, enabling the singer to produce sounds of unprecedented volume, intensity, and control. The castrati became the first real singing stars. The finest, such as Farinelli, Senesino, and Guadagni, enjoyed international careers in the manner of modern opera stars. Despite their unusual sexuality, they were adored on and off stage.

Detail of *Musical Portrait Group* by Jacopo Amigoni, c.1750, showing the castrato Farinelli (center)

Castrati were prized for their powerful, virtuosic vocal production.

Oratorio and the choral society

Sacred music in the seventeenth and eighteenth centuries was greatly influenced by opera, the most notable development being the oratorio. With origins in early seventeenth-century Rome, the oratorio dealt with religious subjects, and took full advantage of a new form of sung storytelling, the recitative. As opera developed into a systematic interplay of recitative and the more lyrical aria, so too did the sacred oratorio, culminating in the works of Alessandro Scarlatti at the beginning of the eighteenth century. The young Handel heard such works in Rome, and it was this influence, together with English church music and a background in Lutheran Passion music, that he later fused in such glorious works as the *Messiah* and *Jephtha*.

Meanwhile, in Germany, sacred music in the Protestant Lutheran Church emphasized congregational singing (chorales, the immediate ancestors of hymns) and the composition of Passion settings. The dramatic nature of the Italian oratorio did not really affect German religious music until an opera house opened in Hamburg in the 1670's. Choral interjections were added to the recitative-aria pattern — an influence drawn from the Passion settings — and this style reached its most sophisticated and sublime form in the Passions and church cantatas of J. S. Bach, written primarily in Leipzig.

Bach's sacred music was intended for performance as worship. Handel's oratorios, with their operatic roots, were invariably performed in theaters. The tendency for sacred music to be performed outside its 'natural' environment became more and more pronounced in the following decades, as religious music steadily became an important part of the late eighteenth- and nineteenth-century phenomenon of concertgoing.

The advance of the public concert was made possible by the rise of the middle classes and the resulting emancipation of music from the confines of religion and the nobility. With this came the development of music-making in a broader context, involving nonspecialist amateurs. The greatest example of this, which still influences musical life today, is the choral society. These developed first in Germany and Britain, and had their origins in workers' cooperatives and the choirs of parish churches and nonconformist chapels. During the nineteenth century, a distinction grew between the highly trained professional solo singer and the ranks of enthusiastic amateur choral singers. In this environment the descendant of Handel's oratorios — the large-scale concert oratorio — flourished. A succession of works, from Mozart's *Requiem*, Haydn's *Creation*, Beethoven's *Missa Solemnis*, and Mendelssohn's *Elijah*, to the hugely scored and unashamedly dramatic *Requiems* of Berlioz and Verdi, has provided the modern choral society with a cor-

Concert featuring a choir, soloists, and orchestra, Munich, by R. Reinicke, 1893
Concerts with a choir and soloists became popular among both the middle class and high society in the nineteenth century.

pus of masterpieces. In the twentieth century, perhaps influenced by Handel's pioneering work in this genre, the oratorio has been most extensively developed in Britain, with notable contributions by Elgar, Walton, Britten, and Tippett.

The voice as agent of change

The phenomenal vocal feats of the castrato had created an entirely new awareness of the mechanics of voice production. Until the seventeenth century, it is likely that the technical aspects of singing were undeveloped, and relied on production only from the throat and the head. From around 1600, with the dawn of opera, the process of developing greater power, projection, and stamina, different colors, and extended ranges had been constant, concentrating in the nineteenth century on diaphragmatic support and the use of resonating spaces in the head and chest. As singers achieved this, composers inevitably wrote music to exploit such skills. This is nowhere more apparent than in the renowned role of Queen of the Night in Mozart's *Magic Flute*, in which the soprano singer is required to

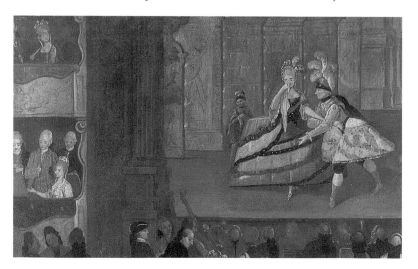

Italian painting showing a performance of an *opera seria*, by G. de Albertis
The audience in this eighteenth-century painting pay little attention to the performers on stage; a night at the opera was as much an opportunity to chat with friends as to hear music.

repertory; it features a deeply recessed orchestra pit, with the loud brass instruments set way back from the conductor and far beneath the singers on stage.

Italian opera in the early nineteenth century placed great demands not so much on the size of a singer's voice as on its agility. The coloratura writing of Rossini, Bellini, and Donizetti requires extraordinary virtuosity, asking the voice to alter pitch with great speed and deftness. With the operas of Verdi, the emphasis shifted from athletic vocal display to expressive intensity and dramatic power: such roles require heavier and brighter voices. For the first time, different voice types were named according to their suitability for the demands of a particular role. The German term *Heldentenor*, for example, refers to the voice required for most of Wagner's tenor roles (such as Lohengrin, Tristan, Siegmund, and Siegfried), stipulating power, substantial range, and a stamina able to withstand the demands of Wagner's long scores.

The use of the singing voice has further diversified in our own century. The advent of Enrico Caruso brought a change in operatic voice production, caused partly by the growing size of the-

negotiate a stratospherically high line featuring several high F's.

The reverse process has also occurred, with certain musical developments causing singers to adapt their technique accordingly. Examples in the late eighteenth and nineteenth centuries include the gradual heightening of 'concert' pitch (making notes higher for the singer); the technological developments in instrument-making, making instruments louder and brighter; the steady increase in the size of the orchestra; and the increase in size of opera houses and concert halls. All had a crucial bearing on the development of singing technique: consider the vast difference between being a choir member singing Renaissance church music, unaccompanied and in a church acoustic with generous reverberation, and a soloist pitched against a full-sized symphony orchestra in a large concert hall with a variable acoustic.

The latter problem was tackled in opera by moving the orchestra into a 'pit,' sunk below the level of the audience (early opera orchestras had generally been placed at the side of the stage). The huge orchestras of Wagner's and Richard Strauss's operas necessitated extreme treatment to allow the singers — selected for the weight and color of their voices — to be heard. Wagner's opera house at Bayreuth is the finest example of a performance hall built specifically for a certain

aters, with a new emphasis on power. The tendency has continued to the present day with such tenors as Gigli, Domingo, and Pavarotti, and sopranos such as Maria Callas. Most recently, the voice has had to acquire new disciplines, such as *Sprechgesang* (a type of vocal performance between speech and song) in Schoenberg's *Pierrot Lunaire*, and in the works of avant-garde composers has adapted to even wider interpretations of the word 'singing' — from screaming, humming, and coughing to generating harmonics and microtones (pitches lying in between the notes of the traditional scale). All these fall under the heading 'extended vocal techniques.' And, crucially, the voice has been recorded, allowing the individual voice to live on after the decline and death of the vocalist.

Today, choral societies exist alongside specialist chamber choirs. The music of the Roman Catholic church, with a few notable exceptions, is now a mere shadow of its former glory, while the Anglican choral tradition continues to flourish, despite an increasingly secular society. A modern opera star may record chart toppers in duets with pop singers and perform to thousands in parks and stadiums. And yet, amid all the evidence of immense change over the centuries, one can travel to the monasteries of Europe and still hear monks singing plainchant, hardly altered since the Middle Ages.

Instruments Through the Ages
1100–1750

Ever since prehistoric times, when humans found they could produce agreeable sounds by striking pieces of wood, blowing through an animal horn, or twanging the gut strings of their hunting bows, they have sought to improve these sounds by refining the tools — the instruments — that produce them. This process of refinement has been far from consistent. It has depended on the changing pressures and demands of society, especially the ways people use music, and on the people who make music — composers and performers.

In Europe before 1100, the Christian church presided over all formal music. The church decreed that music be sung, with no accompaniment except the organ. The rise of instrumental music in Europe largely awaited the import of Middle Eastern instruments via the Moorish conquest of Spain (eighth century) and the twelfth- and thirteenth-century Crusades. Nearly all our modern orchestral instruments have distant ancestors in central Asia and distant cousins that survive there.

With the Renaissance came ideals that greatly increased the scope of instruments. The church no longer held exclusive rights to literacy, knowledge, or formal music. Composers began to use instruments to double or replace human voices in polyphonic music. Instrument makers varied the sizes and shapes of instruments to create sounds from bass to soprano, to match vocal ranges. During the later Baroque period, the burgeoning orchestras demanded instruments that could blend with each other and satisfy the subtle tastes of an increasingly sophisticated audience. Instrument makers became skilled artists in their own right, and the fame of some, such as Antonio Stradivari, even rivaled that of the greatest composers.

Stringed Instruments–bowed

Viol Family

This family of bowed instruments first appeared in the late fifteenth century in the Valencia region of Spain. Viols were probably carried to Italy by the famous Borgia family, two of whom became popes, and their use is recorded at the wedding of Lucrezia Borgia in 1502. Their delicate, slightly nasal sound soon made them popular as chamber instruments, though they lacked the percussive quality useful for dance music. Viols were eventually overshadowed by the louder and more expressive violin family, but Bach was still using the bass viol in his Passions and in the last *Brandenburg Concerto* in the early eighteenth century. Also known as the viola da gamba, the bass viol was held body downward between the legs like a cello. Unlike violins, smaller viols were also held body downward, on the lap.

Baryton Family

Joseph Haydn brought the baryton to its high point in musical history when he composed 175 works for the instrument for his patron Prince Nicolaus Joseph Esterházy, himself an enthusiastic player. Otherwise, the instrument played a minor role in music and was little known outside Austria and southern Germany. Mozart's father Leopold admired both the baryton and its shoulder-held relative, the viola d'amore, for their loveliness of tone. Developed from viols, they have additional strings that vibrate in sympathy with the bowed strings — a feature that points to possible Islamic origins. The great violin maker Stradivari planned to make a viola d'amore in 1716 (though if he did, it has not survived), and Bach made expressive use of the instrument in solo parts in the *St. John Passion*.

Bass Viol
c.1500–c.1730

Tenor Viol
c.1500–c.1730

Treble Viol
c.1500–c.1730

Treble Viol
from c.1500–1525

Baryton
c.1650–c.1800

Viola d'amore
c.1660–c.1800

Baryton
from c.1720

Stringed Instruments—plucked

Violin Family

The development of the violin family was a triumph for instrument making. The violin offered an unprecedented range of expression, intensity, and nuance, and inspired great music and great performers. It derived from various medieval bowed instruments, descendants of central Asian models brought into tenth-century Spain and southern Italy by the Arabs. The rebec was popular at dances and later evolved into the kit, while the fiddle was widely used by troubadours and developed into the lira da braccia (the violin's closest ancestor). Northern Italy, the cradle of violin making, remained the major center until the eighteenth century, especially under the Amati family of Cremona. The family's last and most distinguished member, Nicolò, also taught Antonio Stradivari, perhaps the greatest violin maker ever.

Guitar Family

The guitar (also gittern) developed as an offshoot of the lute family, distinguishable by its flat back and incurved sides. The earliest guitar shapes are again found in central Asian sources, from the first to the fourth century A.D., reappearing in twelfth-century carvings at Santiago de Compostela in northern Spain. Chaucer mentions gitterns in his *Canterbury Tales*, describing their use in a boisterous dance and noting elsewhere their soft and gentle sound. The Spanish guitar and its Italian relation, the chitarra battente, superseded the gittern in southern Europe in the sixteenth century, and the guitar became the national instrument of Spain. Its popularity spread during the seventeenth and eighteenth centuries, partly because people found it easier to play than the lute, and Boccherini used it in some of his chamber music.

Lute Family

The earliest known lutes are represented on Mesopotamian figurines from before 2000 B.C., and since then various kinds of lute have spread throughout the world. The European lute developed from the Arabian ud, introduced into Europe during the Moorish occupation of Spain (A.D. 711–1492). Illustrations show non-Moors using it from the thirteenth century on, and records from 1396 list a lute player in the service of the Duke of Orleans. During the Renaissance the lute, like other instruments, evolved into a family of different sizes and pitch ranges corresponding to those of the human voice, as well as a number of variants such as the theorbo. Its heyday came in the sixteenth and seventeenth centuries, particularly through the intimate and expressive song accompaniments of John Dowland.

Rebec
c.1300–c.1700

Kit
c.1550–c.1800

Double bass
c.1600 onward

Violoncello
c.1600 onward

Viola
c.1600 onward

Violin
c.1600 onward

Violin
from c.1700

Gittern
c.1100–c.1500

Guitar
c.1500 onward

Chitarra battente
c.1550–c.1750

Guitar
from c.1550
(modern reproduction)

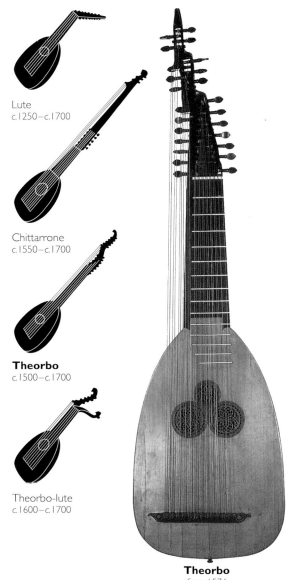

Lute
c.1250–c.1700

Chittarrone
c.1550–c.1700

Theorbo
c.1500–c.1700

Theorbo-lute
c.1600–c.1700

Theorbo
from 1576

Strings–plucked

Harp Family

The harp's history in Europe could be roughly traced through a succession of illustrations and paintings of the biblical King David: continually updated versions of the instrument appear from the eleventh century on. Spreading from Ireland and Wales to the European continent during the twelfth century, it was highly regarded by the troubadours. The double harp, first described by Vincenzo Galilei in 1581, and the triple harp that soon followed, added second and third rows of strings that gave the harpist the full range of notes in all keys. Jakob Hochbrucker of Bavaria invented a pedal action in 1697 that could change the pitch of the strings, enabling a return to the more convenient single row of strings, and Sébastien Érard's double-action pedal harp of 1810 perfected the system.

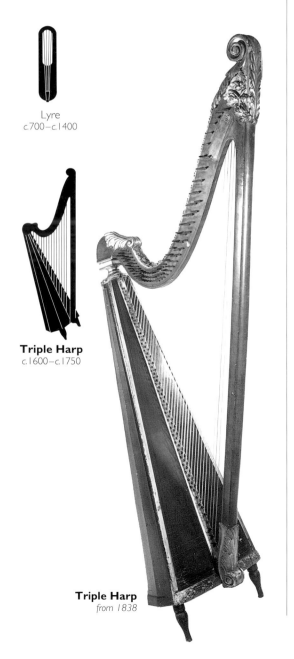

Lyre
c.700–c.1400

Triple Harp
c.1600–c.1750

Triple Harp
from 1838

Stringed Instruments–plucked and struck

Harpsichord Family

The invention of the harpsichord is credited to Hermann Poll, according to a record of 1397. Its earliest depiction appears in a 1425 altarpiece sculpture at Minden in northern Germany. Improvements to the instrument made in Italy around 1500 increased its effectiveness and popularity. Within a century, Flemish Antwerp became the focus of harpsichord development. Prominent members of the keyboard instrument makers' Guild of St. Luke, the Ruckers family, dominated harpsichord making in the Netherlands until 1700. The instrument's mechanism limits how varied a sound it can make. When a key is depressed, a piece of wood is thrown up and an attached quill plucks the string. Clean tone and precise attack, however, made the harpsichord a favorite among some composers, including Byrd, Scarlatti, and Rameau, in solo and chamber works. It continued in use in opera orchestras until Mozart's time. Smaller versions of the harpsichord, more suitable for private use, were made by placing the strings parallel to the keyboard (the virginal) or diagonal to it (the spinet). The clavichord used a different mechanism, by which the depression of a key pressed a small brass plate onto the string. This produced a delicate, subtly variable tone.

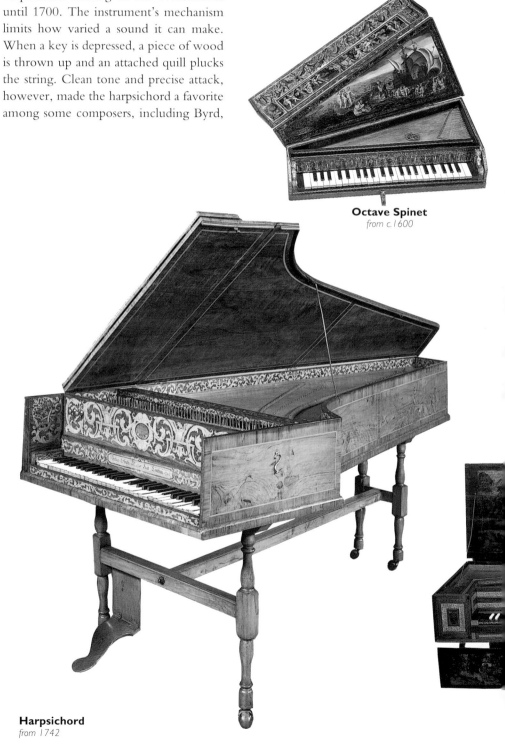

Octave Spinet
from c.1600

Harpsichord
from 1742

Zither Family

The medieval zither was normally known as the psaltery, from the Greek word *psalterion* for both 'harp' and the Book of Psalms. The psaltery was a trapezoid or rectangular soundbox with the strings stretched across it and plucked to produce the sound. The addition of a keyboard with plucking mechanism gave rise to the harpsichord. In the same way, the dulcimer, similar in shape but played with light wooden beaters, is an ancestor of the piano. Originating in Persia and Assyria, the psaltery spread to Europe with the Moorish conquest of Spain, appearing in reliefs at Santiago de Compostela from 1184, and also through Turkey as the forerunner of the Hungarian *cimbalom*. The term 'zither' usually refers to the Bavarian or Austrian instrument, little different from the psaltery, that was current in folk music until the 19th century.

Harpsichord
c.1450–c.1800

Spinet
c.1500–c.1800

Clavichord
c.1450–c.1800

Virginal
c.1500–c.1750

Virginal
from 1664

Psaltery
c.1200–c.1500

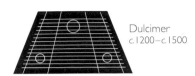

Dulcimer
c.1200–c.1500

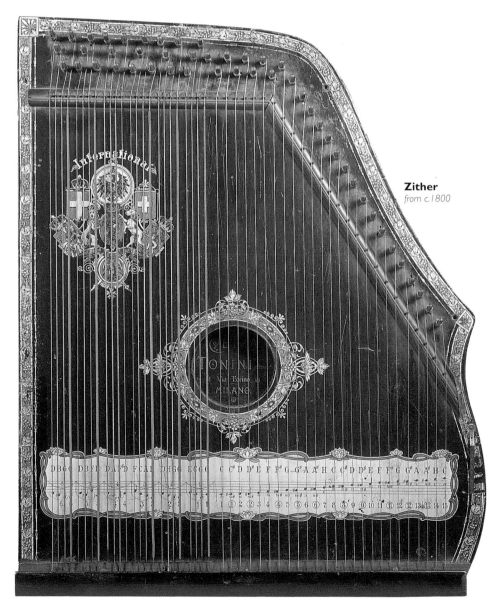

Zither
c.1200–c.1500

Zither
from c.1800

Wind Instruments—pipes

Recorder Family

Thought to have originated in northern Italy in the fourteenth century, the recorder became popular throughout Europe. A recorder from as early as 1350 was found at a house in Dordrecht in the Netherlands. Henry VIII of England, himself an accomplished player, had 76 recorders of various sizes as well as 72 flutes. The two differ in that the recorder works like a whistle, whereas the far older and more widespread flute is played by blowing over a hole as one might over the top of a bottle. The transverse or sideways flute became the standard in Europe but for a long time remained a relatively coarse-sounding instrument compared with the sweeter-toned recorders. The flute gradually superseded the recorder during the eighteenth century, although Bach continued to use both.

Shawm Family

Shawm-like instruments are thought to have entered Italy at the time of the fifth Crusade (1217–21) and were used in outdoor ceremonial or dance music. In the fifteenth century, shawms and trumpets became the main instruments of the so-called 'high,' or loud, outdoor ensembles, and appear in paintings by Hieronymus Bosch. In France after 1500, they were known as 'hautbois' (meaning high or loud woodwind), and this name was eventually transferred to their more refined descendant, the oboe, in the late seventeenth century. During the sixteenth century, the rough-sounding shawm became less popular in ensemble music, giving way to a mellower blend of strings, cornetts, and trombones. Although the shawm was Middle Eastern in origin, the later development of its two vibrating reeds probably

owes a debt to the indigenous European bagpipe. Air supply distinguishes the shawm and the bagpipe — the shawm is blown, its double reed held between the lips, while the bagpipe's windbag acts as a bellows operated under the player's arm. A number of other instruments developed in Europe using the double-reed principle. The racket, which appeared in the mid-sixteenth century and was similar to the shawm, was made of tubes folded several times to fit inside a compact cylinder. In Michael Praetorius's 1619 compendium of early seventeenth-century musical knowledge, the *Syntagma Musicum*, the racket's sound is described as 'quiet, almost like blowing through a comb.' Another variant, the curtal, with its U-shaped tube within a single piece of wood, was the forerunner of the modern bassoon.

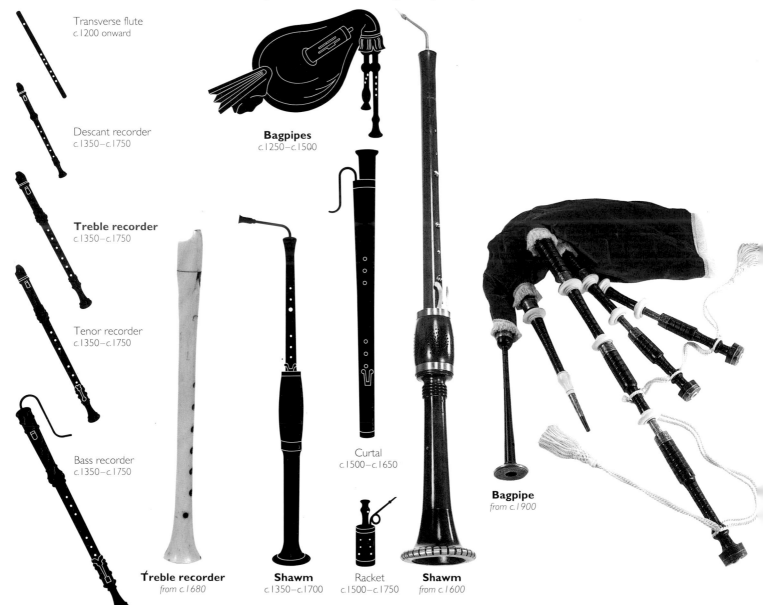

Transverse flute
c.1200 onward

Descant recorder
c.1350–c.1750

Treble recorder
c.1350–c.1750

Tenor recorder
c.1350–c.1750

Bass recorder
c.1350–c.1750

Bagpipes
c.1250–c.1500

Curtal
c.1500–c.1650

Bagpipe
from c.1900

Treble recorder
from c.1680

Shawm
c.1350–c.1700

Racket
c.1500–c.1750

Shawm
from c.1600

Organ Family

The organ originated from the ancient panpipes principle of using a row of pipes, one for each note, rather than a single pipe with finger holes. The first instance of a true organ is a keyboard instrument with mechanical air supply made by Ktesibios of Alexandria in about 250 B.C. By the Middle Ages the organ was highly developed. An organ in Winchester Cathedral installed under Bishop Elphege (died 951) reportedly had 400 pipes, 26 bellows, and two keyboards. The organ was the only instrument the church did not prohibit during the so-called dark ages; as the uses of classical music broadened, it remained largely in church use. Because of its cumbersome size, a smaller version, the positive (or chamber) organ, was developed in the fourteenth century, along with the more portable portative, depicted in paintings with Dufay as performer. The different tone qualities of these smaller instruments (the regal organ used reed rather than flue pipes) were later incorporated into larger organs, eventually with mechanical 'stops' that could divert the airflow to a different sets of pipes. By the sixteenth century the organ had almost reached its final form, and enjoyed a golden age during the next two centuries that culminated in the great corpus of organ works by Bach.

Portative organ
c.1100–c.1650

Positive organ
c.1100–c.1650

Regal organ
c.1400–c.1650

Positive organ
from c.1600

Regal organ
from c.1630

Wind Instruments–brass

Brass Family

Pipe instruments whose sound is produced by the player's vibrating lips date from prehistoric times, but only relatively recently did they evolve into instruments capable of playing sophisticated classical music. The horn and trumpet, which began as simple animal horns, remained coarse-sounding instruments even in their brass form. They were used mainly for hunting, military, or ceremonial purposes until the late seventeenth century. Monteverdi used trumpets in his opera *La favola d'Orfeo* in 1607, and by the late Baroque period, skilled musicians could play complicated melodies. In the instrument's high range, the natural resonances are close together, so players had to attach 'crooks' (brass tubing of different lengths) to achieve all the notes they wanted. Purcell and Bach wrote trumpet parts for choral sections of their cantatas, and Bach gave the instrument a virtuoso role in his *Brandenburg Concerto No. 2*. The sackbut, a lower-pitched version of the trumpet, entered classical music much earlier, appreciated for its mellow tone and a slide that could lengthen or shorten the tube, allowing all the notes of the scale to be played. It was used to accompany motets by Dufay and others, and by the end of the fifteenth century, it had taken on the appearance of its modern successor, the trombone. The cornett belongs in the brass family because of how its sound is produced; but it was actually made of wood and had a gentle sound that worked well with strings and voices. Its bass relative, the serpent, dates from the sixteenth century and was used until the mid-nineteenth in works by Rossini, Wagner, and Verdi.

Trumpet
c.1300–c.1750

Sackbut
c.1400–c.1750

Serpent
from c.1725

Serpent
c.1550–c.1850

Horn
c.1100–c.1700

Percussion

The percussion family includes the oldest instruments in the world. The most numerous, the hundreds of types of drum, are usually made by stretching an animal skin over a wooden rim, forming a taut surface that is hit with a beater. Common during the Middle Ages, the Arabic tabor — a two-headed cylindrical drum — was used by early troubadours to accompany rhythmic dances. The kettledrum had a single skin stretched over a large metal pot, producing a deep, resonant tone, which people eventually learned how to tune to give a definite note. It gradually came into orchestra use in the seventeenth century and may have been used in Monteverdi's *Orfeo* in 1607. Instruments using vibrating metal such as bells and cymbals are most likely as old as metal itself and were used in Europe after the thirteenth century.

Kettledrum
c.1100 onward

Tabor
c.1100–c.1750

Tambourine
c.1100 onward

Triangle
c.1100 onward

Cymbal
c.1100 onward

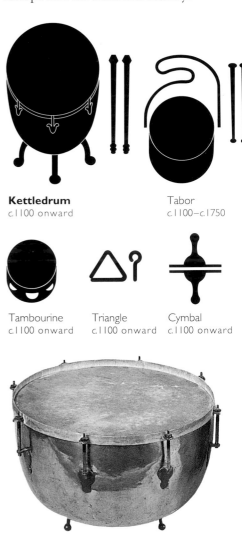

Kettledrum
from c.1600

Instruments Through the Ages

1750 onward

By 1750, the piano and most of our modern orchestral instruments already existed, though many were still far from their final form. The violin family, already established as the main body within the orchestra, was the most clearly defined. But in the Romantic era, composers wanted greater volume and increased expressiveness, and even the violin family went through further changes. In addition, public concerts in large concert halls became common, which increased the need to make instruments louder.

Musicians themselves were looking for technical improvements. Pianists, harpists, and woodwind and brass players wanted to play faster and with easier access to all the notes in every key. They wanted improved tuning, tone quality, and consistency. Sébastien Érard responded with critical additions to the piano and harp, Theobald Böhm invented an elaborate keywork system for the woodwinds, and Blühmel and Stölzel developed the valve for the brass instruments, all within the first 30 years of the nineteenth century. The age of virtuoso performers soon followed, and instrument makers and composers responded variously to their demands.

In the twentieth century, composers continue to experiment with an increasing variety of instruments and have once again turned to non-Western musical traditions, particularly in search of new percussion effects. Using electronic computers and synthesizers they have added mathematical precision and a new range of colors to the composer's musical palette. A revival in early music has also prompted musicians to take up the instruments of earlier ages again, both for 'authentic' performances of older music and to provide ever more resources for the new.

Wind Instruments – pipes

Flute Family

The transverse flute replaced the recorder (see page 26) as an orchestral instrument, largely because of its ability to play louder. Some credit is due to the virtuoso flautist Quantz (1697–1773), whose treatise *The True Art of Flute Playing* is still used for teaching. He was in the service of Frederick the Great of Prussia (1712–1786), himself an able player and composer for whom Quantz wrote over 300 concertos. During Haydn's time, the flute became a permanent member of the orchestra. Mozart wrote several works for the instrument including two solo concertos and one with harp. The modern flute dates from developments introduced by Theobald Böhm around 1830. Böhm's system used a series of pads to cover the finger holes, allowing them to be better placed acoustically, and enabling the player to perform in any key.

Oboe Family

The oboe developed during the mid-seventeenth century as a more refined version of the shawm. In the eighteenth century it was still a relatively loud and coarse instrument, but Bach, at least, recognized its potential for subtlety and it became one of the first wind instruments to win a permanent place in the Classical orchestra. During the nineteenth century oboe makers added the Böhm keywork system (see flute), bringing it close to its modern form. The oboe's alto cousin, the cor anglais, is not a full member of the orchestra but is used frequently for its expressive, mournful sound. The bass of the family, the bassoon, developed as a short step from the curtal, and quickly became the bass woodwind instrument in Haydn's orchestra. Mozart considered it expressive enough to deserve a concerto.

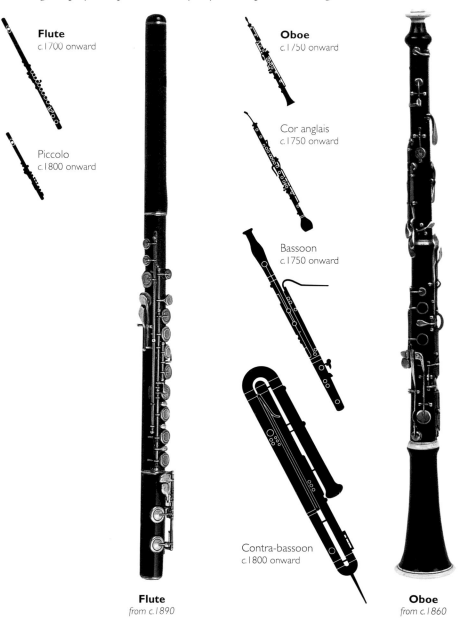

Flute
c.1700 onward

Piccolo
c.1800 onward

Flute
from c.1890

Oboe
c.1750 onward

Cor anglais
c.1750 onward

Bassoon
c.1750 onward

Contra-bassoon
c.1800 onward

Oboe
from c.1860

Wind Instruments—brass

Clarinet Family

Much of the clarinet's development was the work of Johann Denner and his son at Nuremberg from 1690 to 1720. With its single reed it belongs to a far smaller and younger family of instruments than the double reeds, and has only one possible ancestor, the chalumeau. It rapidly became popular, though, because it possessed a smoother, fuller (some might say blander) tone than the oboe. Haydn barely used it, but Mozart was deeply impressed with the instrument, particularly in the hands of the virtuoso, Anton Stadler, for whom he wrote his final concerto. Mozart also wrote for the basset horn — the lower, mellower cousin of the clarinet — in his *Requiem*. But apart from its use in a few works by Beethoven and Mendelssohn, the basset horn went quickly out of fashion, replaced by the alto clarinet.

Brass Family

By 1750, horn makers had significantly mellowed the horn's sound, though to achieve all necessary notes they still used inconvenient crooks (see early brass family). Soon after, horns became permanent members of Haydn's orchestra. Then in around 1815, the valve was invented simultaneously by Blühmel in Silesia and Stölzel in Berlin. By pressing a key, the player could divert the airflow through extra tubing, as if adding a crook. The valve was also added to the trumpet. Experiments with key-covered holes and slides, as on a trombone, resulted in compromised tone; but with valves, the trumpet became an agile melody instrument. The trombone, little altered since the 1500's, entered the orchestra in Beethoven's *Fifth Symphony*. The serpent was eventually replaced by the tuba.

Stringed Instruments—

Piano Family

In around 1700, interest developed in the idea of a hammer-action (rather than plucked) harpsichord, inspired by Pantaleon Hebenstreit (1669–1750) and his enlarged dulcimer. Credit for the invention of the piano, however, goes to Bartolomeo Cristofori (1655–1730) of Florence. His *gravicembalo col pian'e forte* was the first instrument to use a hammer mechanism to produce a soft (*piano*) or loud (*forte*) sound, depending on how hard the player depressed the key. He refined the mechanism, and it remained basically unaltered until 1821, when Sébastien Érard introduced the 'double-escapement' action for more rapid repetition of notes. Stein in Vienna and Broadwood in England developed rival piano designs during the 1770's. These coincided with the first true piano compositions in the

Clarinet
c.1840 onward

Basset horn
c.1840 onward

French horn
c.1750 onward

Trumpet
c.1770 onward

Trombone
c.1790 onward

Tuba
c.1850 onward

Clarinet
from c.1857

French horn
from c.1880

Grand piano
from c.1900

struck

sonatas of Haydn and Mozart. Soon the piano replaced the harpsichord as the composers' preferred keyboard instrument. It has since attracted a huge and rich repertoire through its wide expressive and dynamic range. The last major development came in 1825 with Alpheus Babcock's one-piece cast-iron frame. Much heavier strings under far greater tension (18 tons on a modern grand) could be used, allowing the piano to compete in volume with large orchestras in concertos by Brahms, Liszt, and Rachmaninov. As music making in the home became more popular, various space-saving adaptations were explored. The giraffe piano from the early 1800's simply up-ended the concert grand, but this idea was improved by lowering the string frame to floor level, forming the basis for the modern upright piano.

Grand piano
c.1775 onward

Giraffe piano
c.1800–c.1830

Giraffe piano
from c.1800

Percussion

Composers continue to use an increasing variety of drums and other untuned percussion instruments that have become louder and more resonant with the use of modern materials under higher tensions. But their most significant expansion has been in the realm of tuned percussion. The kettledrums, now more commonly called timpani, have pedal mechanisms that change the note by altering the tension of the skin. Bartók explored the possibility of glissando effects in *Music for Strings, Percussion and Celeste*. The xylophone, known in Europe since 1500, finally took an orchestral role as a set of musical rattling bones in Saint-Saëns's *Danse Macabre* (1874). The glockenspiel and its keyboard version, the celeste, won respect after they featured in dances from Tchaikovsky's *Nutcracker* ballet of 1892.

Timpani
c.1650 onward

Xylophone
c.1875 onward

Glockenspiel
c.1875 onward

Ensembles and Orchestras

Early religious music

The earliest musical instruments date from prehistoric times. In the classical Greek and Roman cultures, more sophisticated instruments took form; yet their development in the West stagnated after the fall of the Roman Empire. The early Christian church strongly discouraged the use of instruments in religious music, owing to their pagan associations, and consequently the system of chant used by the church, known as plainchant, made no provision for them.

But the situation began to change with the advent of polyphony in church music. Polyphony, which combined several separate lines of music rather than using the single line of plainchant, became prevalent from around the twelfth century. To achieve richer textures, composers gradually introduced organs, doubling plainchant lines. As more complex forms developed, the long-held notes of the vocal bass line almost certainly were doubled at times by string or wind instruments. Many surviving manuscripts also show textless polyphonic introductions or interludes that could have been played by an unspecified combination of instruments without voices.

During the fifteenth and sixteenth centuries, extensive use of instruments in church music, at least on ceremonial occasions, became standard. A chronicler of the time reports the use of trumpets, vielles (a precursor to the violin), and other instruments during the consecration of Florence Cathedral in 1436. In 1569, Massimo Troiano reported that the musical accompaniment at a Bavarian court marriage included eight trombones, eight viols, eight flutes, a harpsichord, and a large lute.

Secular music in the Middle Ages

In secular music too, composers gradually introduced instruments to augment existing vocal forms. The troubadours of twelfth- and thirteenth-century southern France were accompanied in their love songs by jongleurs on vielles, citterns (an early guitar), or harps. These versatile entertainers could usually play several instruments as well as act and perform acrobatics. They found their way into court life as *ménestrels* (minstrels) and increased their status by organizing themselves into guilds.

The courts had the necessary resources to organize and support larger groups, referred to as 'high' or 'low' ensembles, so called not on the basis of pitch but on their generally 'loud' or 'soft' nature. High ensembles, including pipes, shawms (a forerunner of the oboe), and various percussion instruments, accompanied hunting, warfare, and certain kinds of dance. Low ensembles, using harps, lutes, recorders, psalteries, small organs, bells, and cymbals, accompanied the festivities of the nobility in dances or interludes to other entertainments.

Dance music was largely improvisatory, requiring little more than characteristic rhythms and meters. Consequently, the leading composers of the day concerned themselves mainly with vocal forms. But instruments figured prominently in accompaniments to the secular songs that later developed into the chansons (three-part songs) of Machaut and the Burgundian School in the fifteenth century; the popularity of the chanson ensured its place among the earliest printed musical editions. The first fully printed music book was the *Harmonice Musices Odhecaton* (Hundred Pieces of Harmony Music), published in Venice in 1501 by Ottaviano dei Petrucci. Most of the collection's chansons have no text, probably because their performance was wholly instrumental.

The High Renaissance

At the start of the sixteenth century, composers still did not specify the combination of instruments required to play a piece; this began with the aesthetic developments of the High Renaissance.

In both sacred and secular music, the various lines in a polyphonic piece had hitherto served distinct functions — supplying melody, bass line, or accompaniment. It was therefore an asset to have

1 Plainchant Detail from 15th-century manuscript showing singers of Gregorian chant.
2 Voices and instruments Detail from German manuscript, *c.*1650: singers with organ and horn.
3 Low ensemble Detail from English painted frieze, *c.*1585, showing musicians with 'low' or 'soft' instruments.

4 High ensemble Medieval Irish musicians with various 'high' or 'loud' instruments.
5 Whole consort 17th-century consort of viols at the court of Louis XIII.
6 Broken consort Detail of palace musicians, *c.*1596, playing different types of instruments, including an organ, lutes, a viol, and a flute.

an ensemble of instruments of contrasting timbres to avoid confusion — a rebec (an early bowed string instrument), a psaltery, a harp, and a flute, for example — as there was little difference among most instruments in terms of their pitch range. But with the new Renaissance ideals of clarity and balance came polyphonic music, particularly by Josquin Desprez, in which all lines or parts were equally important. This prompted the development of different-sized versions of the same instrument. By varying the size of such instruments as lutes, viols, and recorders, it was possible to make up ensembles of standardized timber and extended range of pitch.

In England in the seventeenth century, these single-family ensembles of three to eight instruments became known as 'whole consorts,' as opposed to the 'broken consorts' that retained the older mix of different types. Thomas Morley's *First Booke of Consort Lessons* (1599) was written for a broken consort of treble lute, pandora (a large lutelike instrument), cittern, bass viol, flute, recorder, and treble viol.

The growing body of exclusively instrumental music reflected the growing status of instruments. But such

33

compositions as the new keyboard toccata (a form that could not be sung), though written for a particular type of instrument, still avoided more specific instrumentation indications. Such indications were probably first made in Giovanni Gabrieli's *Sacrae Symphoniae* of 1597, which were written expressly for various combinations of cornetts, trombones, and violins.

In one of these compositions, the *Sonata pian' e forte*, Gabrieli also explored for the first time the possible contrasts between 'soft' and 'loud' groupings of instruments in a single ensemble. More often these two options were still confined to separate ensembles performing in differing circumstances. The louder, high ensembles were used for open-air performances by town musicians playing horns, sackbuts, shawms, and early violins during public festivities, while the low ensembles had developed into a variety of chamber groups consisting of softer, more intimate flutes, viols, and other instruments, for the entertainment of wealthy patrons.

The Baroque era

Monteverdi's opera *La favola d'Orfeo* of 1607 (an example of socially exclusive entertainment) signaled the Baroque period's departure from the harmony of the Renaissance in favor of a richer, more sophisticated form of expression. Novel use of instrumentation became crucial, and in *Orfeo* the term 'orchestra' began to acquire its modern meaning. The orchestra had its roots in the sixteenth-century intermedio — a musical interlude that was an important part of Renaissance court entertainment. Intermedi involved harpsichords, viols, trombones, tenor recorders, cornetts, flutes, and lutes, among others. Monteverdi innovated by adding violins to lead a body of bowed stringed instruments (with viols), and the careful selection of instruments for particular dramatic effects. In the Underworld scenes, for example, he used the mellow, somber timbers of a small organ, sackbuts, and cornetts.

After *Orfeo* composers downgraded the operatic orchestra to provide an unassuming background to increasing vocal virtuosity, mainly using strings rather than wind instruments. The louder, more expressive violin gradually superseded the viol, and the leading seventeenth-century orchestra, established by Jean-Baptiste Lully, actually went under the name 'Les vingt-quatre violons du Roi' (the King's 24 violins). By 1700 it included a wind section of flutes, oboes, and horns, as well as the lower-pitched members of the violin family.

The developing orchestra soon gained a role in religious music, accompanying the opera-related genres of oratorio, Passion, and cantata, notably in the works of Schütz, Purcell, Handel, and Bach. Handel's opera orchestras were limited by the size of orchestra pits in London theaters, but in his oratorios — effectively sacred operas for concert performance — the orchestra took its place on the stage and expanded to 15 violins, 5 violas, 3 cellos, 3 double basses, various wind instruments, and kettledrums. Such an ensemble was, however, still a rarity, and composers wrote for a variety of forces, depending upon the resources available to them.

In all these operatic genres, composers used their instrumental forces fairly sparingly and tended to restrict the full orchestra to instrumental overtures or sinfonias, and to large chorus numbers. During solo arias, a small group of strings and perhaps a few solo wind instruments accompanied the singers; instrumentation was even further reduced in the recitatives to a bass-dominated accompaniment known as the basso continuo. This consisted of one or two bass instruments (lute, theorbo, gamba, or later on, cello, double bass, or bassoon) and a keyboard instrument (generally a harpsichord or organ) to fill out the harmony.

The continuo was an important element in the growing number of purely instrumental forms. In both chamber and orchestral music, it provided the consistent foundation of a bass

7 Early orchestra Detail from a 1560 manuscript: Bavarian court orchestra.
8 Mid-18th-century orchestra Detail of a 1740 watercolor of a festive evening with musical entertainment.

line and harmony. In chamber music, it provided the third part in the trio sonata format (the first two being solo violins or wind instruments), which therefore often, somewhat confusingly, comprised four instruments in all.

Some of the new instrumental forms developed from dance music, and the names of the various dances persisted long after they had evolved into purely concert works. Gigues, sarabandes, minuets, courantes, bourrées, and gavottes were arranged into suites and could be scored for orchestra (Handel's *Water Music* and Bach's *Orchestral Suites*), for keyboard instruments (works by Couperin and Rameau), or even for a solo melody instrument (notably for cello and violin by Bach).

But instruments really began to come into their own in concertos, where increasing technical skill was required. Gabrieli's experiments with contrasting groups of instruments were furthered in 1620 in works that juxtaposed a solo or concertino group with the full orchestra or ripieno ensemble. These developed into the concerto grosso works of Corelli and Handel, reaching a high point in Bach's *Brandenburg Concertos*. Vivaldi and others reduced the concertino group to a single instrument (most commonly the violin, but also cello, harpsichord, trumpet, flute, oboe, bassoon, or others), and the virtuoso solo concerto was born.

The Classical era

During the eighteenth century, the orchestra was gradually standardized, although its total size, and the composition of the wind section, still varied according to available resources. In 1756, the Mannheim court orchestra, the leading ensemble of the day, consisted of 20 violins, 4 each of violas, cellos, and double basses, 2 each of flutes, oboes, bassoons, and timpani, 4 horns, and a trumpet.

This kind of ensemble became the standard accompanying group for operas, oratorios, and concertos, but it found its ideal

expression in the symphony. Developed initially by Haydn from the earlier orchestral sinfonias, and later by Mozart and Beethoven, this was the largest instrumental form so far, and a showpiece for coloristic orchestral effects. The continuo gradually disappeared (and the harpsichord with it) as the distinction between solo and accompaniment blurred. The functions of melody and harmony were spread among various instruments as composers searched for novel timbers and sonorities. In pursuit of these goals, larger, more versatile orchestras came into being. The chamber orchestra thus grew into the symphony orchestra. Haydn began writing symphonies for the Esterházy court orchestra, which in 1766 numbered only 17 players; by the 1790's he was writing for a London orchestra of over 50. Mozart added clarinets to the symphonic configuration, while Beethoven added trombones, piccolo, contrabassoon, and various percussion instruments. Orchestras that had once been directed from the harpsichord, or by the first violinist, began from about 1800 to need specialist, baton-wielding conductors.

The demise of the continuo combination coincided roughly with the arrival of the piano. As well as possessing the ability shared by all keyboard instruments to render a number of parts simultaneously, the piano had a much stronger, more flexible, and therefore more expressive sound than the harpsichord. It soon became the most popular solo instrument in both concertos and sonatas. In trio sonatas it not only replaced the harpsichord but also took over much of the melodic role. Composers even wrote sonatas for the solo piano with the accompaniment of a violin or cello. Mozart's and Beethoven's solo keyboard sonatas were probably all written for the new instrument, and their violin and cello sonatas included pianos as equal partners.

The increasing use of a variety of instruments for supplying melody and accompaniment meant that the harpsichord in a trio sonata configuration could be replaced by a viola to form a string quartet of two violins, viola, and cello. This combination proved immensely successful and became the vehicle for some of the greatest music of Haydn and Beethoven, while Mozart seemed equally inspired by the addition of another viola to form a string quintet. Piano trios (with violin and cello), wind octets, and single wind instruments with strings were also popular, but the string quartet reigned supreme and has held a special attraction for composers ever since.

The symphony orchestra

The orchestra for which Beethoven wrote is recognizable as a relative of the modern-day symphony orchestra, but there were still further changes in store. The Romantic era ushered in a desire for an even greater range of expression. New forms such as the symphonic poem, with its inclusion of elements inspired by literature, gave freer rein to the composer's imagination.

Berlioz's 1830 *Symphonie Fantastique* set the tone, creating brilliant orchestral effects with harps, enlarged brass and percussion sections, and the shrill E flat clarinet to depict a Ball, the March to the Scaffold, and a Witches' Sabbath. In his 1844 *Treatise on Instrumentation*, Berlioz listed a 'finest orchestra,' consisting of 21 first violins, 20 second violins, 18 violas, 8 first cellos, 7 second cellos, 10 double basses, 4 harps, 2 piccolos, 2 flutes, 2 oboes, 1 cor anglais, 2 clarinets, 1 basset horn or bass clarinet, 4 bassoons, 4 French horns, 2 trumpets, 2 cornets, 3 trombones, 1 bass trombone, 1 tuba, 4 timpani, 1 bass drum, and a pair of cymbals. This closely approximates to the modern symphony orchestra, though such an orchestra was rare in Berlioz's day.

Most of Berlioz's aspirations for the orchestra were realized later in the nineteenth century, particularly with the growth of public concerts, giving composers and impresarios greater influence over instrumental forces than under their previous aristocratic or church patronage. Around this time many of today's famous orchestras were founded, including the Berlin Philharmonic (1882), the Chicago Symphony (1891), and the London Symphony Orchestra (1904). With them the specialist conductor was firmly established, not only coordinating large numbers of performers but also playing a crucial role in the artistic interpretation of the music.

Composers such as Wagner, Mahler, and Richard Strauss continued to write for ever larger forces. Mahler scored his *Eighth Symphony* (1907) for a combined woodwind and brass section of 45 players plus timpani, bells, mandolin, organ, piano, and celeste, as well as the normal strings, a huge chorus, and eight solo singers. Debussy and Ravel achieved breathtaking and subtle effects through virtuoso orchestrations for a slightly more modest ensemble, to which Ravel added saxophones in some of his larger works.

During the twentieth century, professional orchestras have developed into virtuoso ensembles, particularly with the advent of high-definition recorded sound. Bartók, Lutoslawski, Carter, and others have written 'concertos for orchestra,' recognizing the solo capabilities of instruments and their players throughout the orchestra. Ever new possibilities for the symphony orchestra were signaled in Messiaen's massive *Turangalîla Symphony* of 1948, which added a solo piano, vibraphone, glockenspiel, celeste, the electronic ondes martenot, and Indonesian gamelan gongs to an already inflated orchestra.

Chamber ensembles

The works of the Classical period were (and still are) frequently performed, and chamber orchestras were formed parallel to the symphony orchestras with the aim of specializing in such repertoire. They also found a role in more recent works, such as Stravinsky's neoclassical compositions. Composers such as Tchaikovsky and Elgar explored more deeply the rich resonances of stringed instruments in works for string orchestra.

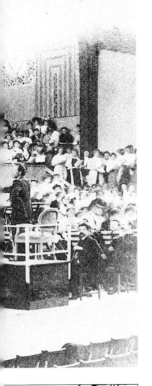

9 Early 19th-century orchestra A London promenade concert in 1849.
10 Late 19th-century orchestra Mahler rehearsing his *Eighth Symphony*, Munich, 1910.
11 20th-century orchestra The City of Birmingham Symphony Orchestra.
12 Chamber group Rehearsal of Berg's *Lyric Suite* with Berg and Schoenberg, 1927.
13 Electronic ensemble The computer as musical instrument, late 20th century.

The range of instruments used in smaller chamber ensembles continued to grow during the nineteenth century, with compositions for anything from one to more than ten players. A wealth of solo piano music was written by Chopin, Schumann, Liszt, and many others, and sonatas for other instruments still called for a more or less equal piano part. The more successful larger groups continued to feature a core of strings, particularly in Brahms's majestic trios, quartets, quintets, and sextets for strings alone, or with piano.

All these combinations live on into the present, though none more robustly than the string quartet. Bartók gave the combination new impetus in the earlier part of this century, and notable contributions followed, in particular from Shostakovich and Carter.

The twentieth-century ensemble

Generally speaking, the twentieth century has witnessed the development of an 'anything goes' approach to scoring for chamber groups, as well as a narrowing of the gap between chamber and orchestral music. The dividing line is now hard to draw. Part of the impetus came from a desire to achieve a clearer definition of the individual timbers of the instruments, as opposed to overblown orchestral effects.

Stravinsky largely abandoned traditional combinations and geared his choice of instruments precisely to the particular colors and effects that he sought. In *Ragtime* (1918) he used an ensemble of 11 contrasted instruments including a cimbalom; he scored the *Ebony Concerto* (1946) for jazz band with solo clarinet; and in *Les Noces* (1923) he created an ensemble of four pianos and percussion for an impersonal and mechanical counterpart to the chorus and solo singers.

Folk, non-Western, and jazz instruments, particularly percussion, were early additions to the twentieth-century ensemble. From Africa came a variety of drums and other unpitched instruments, and the marimba — a deeper version of the xylophone — which contributed to the development of the vibraphone. From Indonesia came the gamelan gongs used by Messiaen and others.

Since World War II, most composers, especially the avant-garde, have experimented with a variety of nontraditional instrumental combinations. Boulez scored his *Éclat* (1965) for piano, celeste, harp, glockenspiel, vibraphone, mandolin, guitar, cimbalom, tubular bells, alto flute, cor anglais, trumpet, trombone, viola, and cello. In an age of such choice, no single work can be described as typical, but this example gives some indication of the possibilities. To perform this repertoire, various groups have been formed, with a variable personnel from which the necessary combinations can be drawn.

Electronic music and beyond

Around the middle of the century, composers began to explore the possibilities of electronic instruments such as the ondes martenot, the electric organ, and later, tape machines, synthesizers, modulators, amplifiers, oscillators, and computers. Stockhausen, Babbitt, and others worked in electronic studios and became composer-engineer-performers, synthesizing and modifying sounds in performance or for recordings. Such resources have also been combined with natural instruments to produce sounds that may be electronically modified.

John Cage, more than anyone else, opened the door to using as a musical instrument just about any object capable of producing a sound, or even nothing at all. He began with the 'prepared piano,' inserting various items among its strings to produce a theoretically unlimited range of sounds, and later moved on to radios, food processors, plant materials, and fire.

The 'original instrument' revival

With the inventive spirit in the realms of modern music thriving, more attention has turned in recent years to the ways in which the music of previous ages was originally performed. Research has led to the rediscovery, restoration, and reconstruction of so-called period instruments, and the formation of a number of specialist ensembles, using as near to the original forces as can be determined. Coincidental or not, it is interesting to reflect that this stage in music history of apparently limitless possibilities for new instruments is also a time of vigorously renewed interest in old ones.

The Middle Ages and the Renaissance

12th to 16th century

Throughout the Middle Ages, though western Europe was a patchwork of separate kingdoms, it was held together by a shared religion and strict hierarchies. Eventually, however, the secular rulers would not abide a rich and powerful church that challenged their local sovereignty. Conflict between church and state left the pope's authority weakened, and over time, led to the Protestant Reformation. With the end of the Catholic church's dominance, kingdoms became nation-states, and religion became cause for war. Nation fought nation, and peasants took up arms against their lords. At the same time, the Black Death was ravaging the population. Yet kings sought to extend their domains into vast empires. European influence soon extended around the globe.

Soaring cathedral spires that marked the power and centrality of the church, and cathedral schools, in which learning and the arts were intended first and foremost to glorify God, gave birth to universities. A strong tradition of nonreligious literature grew, including Arthurian romances and masterpieces, among them Dante's *Divine Comedy* and Chaucer's *Canterbury Tales*. Artists, such as Leonardo da Vinci and Michelangelo, looked back to ancient Greece for inspiration. Meanwhile, the printing press made it possible for the ideas of the dawning Renaissance to reach an ever wider audience.

The music of the period kept pace with changes in society. To the early Gregorian chants, church composers added new melodic lines. Troubadours traveled and sang secular songs of love's joys and sorrows, and by the sixteenth century, musicians had joined voice and instruments in complex multi-part compositions that would lead the way to a more elaborate and sophisticated age.

Featured Composers

The Last Judgment by Stefan Lochner, c.1440

The church was the center of existence for most people during this age, when chaos seemed to prevail and people's lives were subject to forces beyond their control, whether flood, plague, famine, or war.

For people living during the period from 1100 to 1600, and even earlier, life contained a great deal to fear. Shortages of food and money, constant fighting, illness and disease, and political instability posed ever-present threats. The one constant factor was religion. The church stood at the center of people's lives, and of their everyday rituals of existence: it was powerful, rich, and the provider to many. A close association between religion, music, and all other significant aspects of culture was therefore entirely natural.

Pre-medieval culture

Early music used regularly in religious services was committed to memory, in the oral tradition, and was passed down through the centuries in this way, until notation was devised to record it in the ninth century. The word 'mousike' comes from ancient Greece, where music played a vital role. The body of musical ideas evolved by the Greeks (among them Plato, Aristotle, and Pythagoras) formed the basis for music's development in western Europe in later times, after Greek culture was transmitted throughout the west by the Romans. Instruments used in ancient Greece included lyres and flutes, which were generally used in songs to accompany poetry. The absence of instruments in early western Christian music can be partly understood as a reaction against their perceived pagan origins.

Christianity spread through the Roman Empire, and by the fourth century AD was the official religion. The church grew in influence as it established land ownership and wealth. Many people were disillusioned with the material nature of prosperous Roman society, and this led to the development of the first monasteries, dedicated to self-denial and religious worship. Christianity in its Orthodox form was growing in the east (around present-day Greece and Turkey). Rome and the west suffered continual turmoil, but the eastern part of the Empire

Picture from a 15th-century Book of Hours

Music was an integral part of the Christian ritual; here, monks are singing a funeral Mass.

remained intact. This became the Byzantine Empire, with Constantinople (Istanbul) as its capital: it would flourish for the next thousand years.

During the 'Dark Ages' (the name given by Renaissance thinkers to the Middle Ages [c.AD 1000–1400] and before), the vital classical heritage of the ancient Greeks was safeguarded in the eastern Empire. In the west, as the Roman world declined, monasteries provided the only safe haven for classical knowledge and arts. Against a general backdrop of unrest and insecurity, they were more than just secure retreats. As they accumulated gifts from devout followers, they became rich and substantial landowning bodies, which could commission work from the best architects, artists, sculptors, and composers. They became the main patrons of the arts. Except in Italy, they were virtually the only providers of schools and education. Altogether, it is not surprising that culture was strongly flavored by religion.

Early Christian music

Early Christian music was characterized by various types of chant, with different places developing their own styles. Ambrosian chant grew up in Milan, named after the fourth-century bishop Ambrose, who first recorded them. Spain and France evolved separate bodies of liturgical (church-service) music. It was the church music of the city of Rome, however, that laid the substantial foundations on which later western music was built. The many traditional chants (called PLAINCHANT or PLAINSONG) were gathered into an ordered system by Pope Gregory I in the sixth century, and hence are often referred to as Gregorian chant. This collection became the standard music of the Roman Catholic Church. In the ninth century the repertory began to develop and expand, with extra material — both words and music — being incorporated into the chants to give a richer, more complex sound. A radical new concept was also gradually introduced into music at this time,

---

MUSICAL DEFINITIONS

PLAINCHANT or PLAINSONG Sung chant that accompanied the services and Offices of the Christian church from the earliest times. It consisted of a single line of text and melody, sung by a single voice (the priest) or by several voices in unison (the choir).

Right: Miniature from the Pontifical of Bishop Erasmus Ciolek, Cracow, 1510

The many strata of society are apparent here, from the bishop at the center, nobles to his left and right, and lower classes in the foreground. Pipers are seen in the high gallery to the left.

which would further enrich it as well as take it in a dramatic new direction that would last for centuries. The new style was known as POLYPHONY, and was distinguished by its use of several separate musical lines (contrasting with the single line of plainchant). The main form of early polyphony was ORGANUM.

The Holy Roman Empire

On Christmas Day in the year 800, Charlemagne, King of the Franks, was crowned Emperor of the Romans by Pope Leo III. This revival of the Roman imperial title, which had not been used in western Europe since the fifth century, heralded the birth of what would come to be known, much later, as the Holy Roman Empire. This vast, shifting political and military empire would stretch for a thousand years across what are now, broadly speaking, Germany, northern Italy, and part of France. Its chief lands were mostly German, and its ruler was usually the German king. Throughout the Middle Ages the ruling dynasty was closely allied with the Roman papacy in its leadership of Christian Europe. Such a political and religious alliance accentuated the increasing gap between the western and eastern (Byzantine) sides of the Roman Empire. Early in the eleventh century, there was a fatal deterioration in the relationship between the western Church of Rome and the eastern Orthodox (Byzantine) Church. In 1054 a state of schism was declared, and the two increasingly went their separate ways.

In the ninth and tenth centuries a revival occurred in the classical arts, encouraged by the Emperor Charlemagne at the Frankish court and subsequently by the Ottonian German Emperors (whose dynasty followed that of Charlemagne). In the late eleventh century a new style in architecture and manuscript illumination reached its pinnacle in western Europe. Known as Romanesque (because of its indebtedness to the classical Roman past), this movement fused local traditions with Roman, Germanic, and Byzantine influences. Resulting from

---

MUSICAL DEFINITIONS

POLYPHONY Greek, 'many-sounded.' The style of music that developed from increasing the number of independent melodic lines from one (as with chant) to two, three, or even four, giving greater depth and complexity. The style evolved over many centuries, flourishing from the 13th to the 16th.

ORGANUM Form of early polyphony, mainly choral but sometimes accompanied by the organ. Initially, the separate musical lines moved in parallel and in the same rhythm. As the style evolved, the lower voice (tenor) retained the basic, stable plainchant melody while the other parts moved more freely above it, allowing room for some rhythmic inventiveness. Later still, the upper parts even used nonreligious texts, which the church appears to have accepted provided that the sacred music of the tenor line was not obscured. Organum reached its most developed state with Pérotin in the 12th century.

MOTET A polyphonic composition, initially based on plainchant, classically in three parts. Each part was sung at a different speed and using different words, not always Latin (the language of the church). At first religious, by the 13th century it had adapted to secular functions too. In later medieval times the motet was the main form of musical composition, often accompanied by the organ.

a widespread religious revival at this time and seen most clearly in the building of monasteries and churches, the style touched on all the decorative arts of the period, and was characterized by a confidence and grandeur in buildings, and exuberant freedom in monumental sculpture.

Medieval Europe: the expansion of culture

By the twelfth century, society in western Europe was becoming more complex and more cultured. As teachers set up schools separate from the monasteries (for example, those attached to new cathedrals such as Chartres in northern France), they created new opportunities for education. Opportunities outside the church also increased; art, architecture, music, and literature began to expand to meet wider needs. An era was dawning that would see universities appear and courts become influential patrons. Yet, for music and all the arts, the patronage of the church remained vital.

By the mid-twelfth century, Romanesque was superseded by Gothic, the second major European art movement of the Middle Ages, lasting several hundred years. Gothic architecture used the principle of converging arches, with ornate stone ceilings and vast decorated windows. After the heavy Romanesque style, the Gothic constructions, with their slim columns and tremendous sense of height, were truly buildings of celebration. Their proportions and their very fabric amplified sound — a special inspiration to composers, who developed techniques to fill the space with glorious, soaring music.

The Notre Dame school of music

The church of Notre Dame in Paris now became the main center of musical influence in western Europe. The great Gothic cathedral was commissioned in 1160 to replace the old Romanesque building: it took 80 years to build, during which time much sacred polyphonic music was composed. The French poet and musician Léonin, a canon of the cathedral, wrote his *Magnus liber organi* (Great Book of Organum), a major collection of material for the church year. His successor, Pérotin, took the work further, expanding the organum form (adding, for example, aspects of rhythm taken from secular — nonreligious — music), and creating new forms. It was at the Notre Dame school that the MOTET (essentially a composition for more than one voice) developed, encouraged in large part by Pérotin's innovations.

Secular music: the troubadour tradition

The development through the Middle Ages of liturgical, as opposed to secular, music was relatively well documented. Secular music, though not chronicled in the same way, had certainly been evolving alongside sacred music: the twelfth century saw a fully formed tradition emerge in France. The

Miniature with Notre Dame, Paris, by Jean Fouquet, mid–15th century

The cathedral dominates the town around it, emphasizing the extent to which religion dominated the medieval mind.

43

church was a wealthy patron, but the aristocracy was even wealthier; the difference lay in the fact that the aristocracy placed less emphasis on learning. The standards and beliefs of secular culture were seldom set down in writing until the twelfth century, when vernacular (native language) literature began to increase, and members of the upper classes became more typically able to read. This was the era of the Crusades, of chivalric ideals, of courtly life. In the world of chivalry, knightly valor, gallantry, loyalty, and courtesy were of the utmost importance. The new royal and princely courts of the age required noblemen to show as much prowess on the dance floor as on the hunting field, in courtly love as in battle; to express themselves as ably through poetry, languages, and music as through the arts of war and sport.

It was against this background that the secular music of medieval France developed. The early performers were minstrels (*jongleurs* or *ménestrels*) who went from village to village eking out a living by providing very basic entertainment. From these emerged troubadours (*trouvères* in northern France), poet-composers who belonged to the nobility and performed songs about courtly love and the political and moral issues of the day. In Germany, musicians known as *Minnesinger* flourished, performing a similar function (these were superseded by the more widely known *Meistersinger*). Doubtless there were corresponding movements in England, Spain, and Italy, but little documentation survives. The music of the troubadours was MONOPHONIC (as opposed to the more sophisticated polyphony of the new religious music) and relatively limited in scope, but innovations included the evolution of many formal, structured patterns. Such forms included the BALLADE and RONDEAU; both influenced composers of sacred polyphony.

Social and musical developments

Towns now developed rapidly across Europe, with a corresponding growth in agriculture. Fine buildings housed universities at centers of learning such as Bologna, Oxford, Cambridge, and Paris in the early thirteenth century, and Prague and Heidelberg in the fourteenth. While papal power

Illustration from a French Bible, c.1250

Medieval musicians at a feast playing (left to right) a fiddle, a hurdy-gurdy, a harp, and a psaltery.

remained strong, the power of the monasteries was being steadily usurped by the new city centerpieces — the cathedrals — which were in turn creating their own schools of learning, such as at Lyons and Chartres.

Musically, by about 1250 the importance of organum and its related forms was declining, and for the next 50 years the medieval motet dominated both secular and liturgical worlds. From 1150 until as late as 1300, new and old liturgical music stood side by side, and historians have christened the period Ars Antiqua (old art) — as distinct from the important Ars Nova (new art) movement that followed. A remarkably rich anthology of music covering this period survives to this day in a manuscript of the satirical poem *Le Roman de Fauvel* (The Story of Fauvel). The collection contains some of the earliest known examples of Ars Nova, five songs by the French composer Philippe de Vitry on courtly love.

The Ars Nova movement, which exerted an influence on music over several centuries to come, derived its name from a tract written by Vitry in the early fourteenth century. His treatise set out the theories of music notation and harmony that were the innovative developments of his day. It was Guillaume de Machaut, however, who was the most important Ars Nova

MUSICAL DEFINITIONS

MONOPHONY Greek, 'single-sounded.' The use of a single melody in a piece of music, a style dominant before, but not totally supplanted by, the development of polyphony.

BALLADE and RONDEAU Forms of medieval polyphonic song (poetry set to music), the rondeau using sections of words and music that recurred. (These are not the same as the later piano ballade or the 17th-century rondo.)

composer. He dominated both in sheer volume of work and in the further development of the motet and polyphonic songs that characterized the movement, replacing the restrictive plainchant and organum of Ars Antiqua with greater freedom of rhythm and a new complexity in multi-part songs.

Religious and political upheaval

Following a period of feuding with the Italian nobility and cardinals, in 1309 the papal court moved from Rome to the Provençal city of Avignon. There it remained until 1377, increasingly subject to French influences. On the court's return to Rome, such unrest was generated that in 1378 dissenting cardinals established a rival pope. For the next 30 years, in a period of church history known as the Great Schism, two popes contested the leadership of Christendom, and the papal reputation suffered severe damage. In England, early religious discontent was sown by the reformer John Wycliffe, who a century ahead of his time — rejected papal power and circulated extracts of the Bible translated from Latin into English so ordinary people could understand.

In northern Europe, a series of conflicts known as the Hundred Years War raged between France and England from

Page from *Le Roman de Fauvel*, 14th century
The donkey Fauvel is about to go to bed with the daughter of Fortune (top panel), until disturbed by a carnival procession.

about 1337 to 1453. On top of continual warring and religious unrest, fourteenth-century Europe also suffered a crisis brought on by famine and disease. Populations, weakened by a succession of bad harvests, were decimated by waves of plagues like the Black Death, which recurred throughout the century and, indeed, the centuries to come. Survivors were gripped by a deep-seated fear of having in some way offended God: this led to witch-hunts against any suspect groups. The specter of heresy became a dark and lasting undercurrent of the age. Artistically, although this was a period of revival, a strong stream of pessimism persisted, shown in such specific themes as the Dance of Death.

However, such dramatic depopulation did have some positive results, eventually including better wages, improved diets, and, not least, a rapid end to serfdom.

Humanism and the Renaissance

In Italy, where the musical center of the time was Florence, the poet Petrarch was developing his Humanist ideals. These he based on an enthusiasm for the classical civilization of ancient Rome, which he considered the high point of human creativity. It was Petrarch who first suggested that the entire thousand-year period preceding his own was an age of darkness. His own time, he believed, was barbarous; a revival of classical learning was essential to produce any improvement in society. His views corresponded with a tremendous surge of energy in the creative arts. The Humanist convictions, together with the rise of a new style of painting and sculpture, marked the start of the powerful Renaissance movement that predominated in Italy. This movement

Left: Part of the *Good and Bad Government* cycle by A. Lorenzetti, 1338–39
Lorenzetti's frescoes reflected society around him and illustrated the importance of the bustling new towns.

Below: Fresco of the Triumph of Death, Pisa, c.1350
Paintings of death were commonplace in the Middle Ages, particularly after the devastation caused by the Plague.

exerted a dramatic influence across Europe in the fourteenth, fifteenth, and sixteenth centuries and beyond. Renaissance art looked back to the classical age for its inspiration, enbracing both secular and religious themes. It celebrated individual human potential, and used innovative techniques like perspective in painting. Many of the great Renaissance artists, such as Leonardo da Vinci and Michelangelo, were also skilled scientists, architects, engineers, and poets.

From 1384 to 1477 the state of Burgundy was dominated by four powerful and politically astute dukes, and became the most prosperous area of northern Europe, assuming a position of great prominence. It is generally accepted that the Renaissance in music began here. The Burgundian dynasty was the focus of northern Europe's intellectual, artistic, and musical activity throughout the first half of the fifteenth century. The court provided patronage for the cream of Europe's creative talent, including artists like Jan van Eyck and composers such as Guillaume Dufay, who, though French, had strong links to Italy. John Dunstable and others brought new musical techniques from England that strongly influenced the Burgundian style. The Mass became increasingly important as a sacred musical form in its own right. Meanwhile secular music saw the evolution of CHANSONS (three-part songs) and freer forms than had been usual in Ars Nova. These songs — typically secular but also religious — were often accompanied by instruments such as the medieval harp, the lute, the flute, and the organ.

Influences from the court of Burgundy extended much wider afield in the second half of the fifteenth century. Musical emphasis became concentrated on what is known as the Franco-Flemish school. The name reflects the dominance of musicians from the affluent and relatively stable Low

Above: *An Ideal City* by Piero della Francesca, c.1475
This utopian image reflects the search for order and harmony that was central to Renaissance thinking.

Below: Study for the Sistine Ceiling by Michelangelo, 16th century
With the rise of Humanism, the nude began to assume a fundamental role in western art.

MUSICAL DEFINITIONS
CHANSON Generally a secular song in three parts, one sung, the others instrumental. Flourished in the 15th and 16th centuries.

Countries, rather than the geographical position of the school, which was not tied to one location. These musicians traveled through Europe, both absorbing and spreading stylistic innovations, and were greatly in demand at aristocratic courts. Three composers stand out particularly: Ockeghem, Obrecht, and Josquin Desprez. They and their peers developed the techniques that formed the basis for much sixteenth-century music and continued to influence later developments. The Franco-Flemish were not restricted by the three-voice writing common in Burgundian music: they wrote for four voices (what we would now call soprano, alto, tenor, and bass), allowing for more variety of rhythm and a wide range of expression.

Religious dissent and the Reformation

The new musical techniques spread swiftly, not only as a result of the peripatetic nature of the Netherlands musicians, but also of the invention of printing in the mid-fifteenth century. It is almost impossible now to conceive of the power of this invention; its impact must have been akin to the sudden advent of television in the twentieth century. The first printing press appeared in the German town of Mainz in 1450, and printing spread rapidly across Europe; in 1501 publication of printed music commenced. For the first time, information could be easily, cheaply, and widely dispersed among a public increasingly hungry for knowledge.

The newfound power to inform catered well to the upper classes as they absorbed themselves in the classical concepts of the Renaissance. It also fed the rising discontent within the Catholic Church, and ultimately influenced the start of the Protestant Reformation. In 1517 the German Augustinian monk and theologian Martin Luther published his dissatisfaction with many of the church's ways. This dramatic move led three years later to his excommunication, after which he rejected the authority of the pope altogether. Luther's protest was spread by preachers and also, significantly, by the newly powerful printed word. In a similar movement in Geneva,

John Calvin succeeded in his attempts at reforming both the church and the government. Calvinists went on to lead the reform movement later in the sixteenth century (although being against the Catholic Church did not necessarily mean being in sympathy with other reformers).

In 1534, the Tudor monarch Henry VIII broke with the Church of Rome, thus heralding the start of the English Reformation. In 1558, following the brief reigns of Edward and Mary, Elizabeth I came to the throne, and a year later she formally established the Church of England, with the monarch at its head. Under her reign the arts flourished. Many European artists and musicians were attracted to the English court by its religious tolerance and independence from Rome. In this way important cultural influences arrived from the continent, adding to the glories of the Elizabethan golden age.

Italy: the High Renaissance

The Renaissance was now at its peak. Italy, the preeminent cultural center of Europe at this time, consisted of separate city-states. Of these, Mantua and Ferrara maintained independent, flourishing princely courts; Naples and Milan fell into invaders' hands. Venice flourished spectacularly, and developed a reputation for the splendor of its ceremonies. Florence was held in the grip of the powerful Medici family, who exerted considerable influence in Italy and were patrons

Detail from *The Hunt of Philip the Good,* 16th-century copy of a lost painting

A hunt on the eve of the marriage of this powerful Burgundian duke to Isabella of Portugal in 1430.

of such extraordinary talents as Michelangelo, Botticelli, and Leonardo da Vinci. Feast days and celebrations were great events, often based on classical myth, with music incorporated to complement the visual presentations and pageants.

Italy was especially important in musical terms during the sixteenth century. Music was an indispensable social art, and composers relished the freedom of the secular forms in which they could experiment. New techniques developed with almost astonishing swiftness, aided by the ease (via printing) with which they could now be dispersed, as well as by the general

mood of excitement and adventure across all the arts. A new harmonic system began to evolve in secular music, which would supplant the system used until then. The madrigal (a refined expression of poetry set to music) flowered in this period — especially at the end of the century, when the form grew more complex with five or six voice parts. It was enthusiastically embraced in Elizabethan England, which also saw the emergence of the ayre, a solo-voice song with an instrumental (often lute) accompaniment. Madrigals caught on less in France: in their place emerged the polyphonic chanson, a form

48

A painting of a village kermis by David Vinckboons, 16th century

This picture of a kermis (a Dutch festival) shows how developed towns had become by the 16th century. At the market stall in the center, musical instruments can be seen for sale.

The Counter-Reformation

As the Reformation gained influence over religious thought, the Catholic Church reacted by convening the Council of Trent with the intention of reforming from within. The council met in three sessions between 1541 and 1563, but the results merely further polarized the factions and enshrined the differences between Catholic and Protestant doctrines. An era of artistic repression ensued, when the council condemned what it saw as creeping corruption within the arts, music included. It banned the depiction of sensuality and anything that could be considered blasphemous. Under its decree, music was expected to be pious and to celebrate religion: the purity of works such as those by Palestrina was encouraged.

Discoveries and changes

Sixteenth-century Europe had seen kings establishing themselves firmly as absolute sovereigns over their lands, commanding vast armies and resources. Nations embarked on ambitious expeditions, fueled by a lust for conquest that was epitomized by the Spanish discovery of the New World and the riches that poured from it. King Charles I of Spain ruled over an immense empire, but much of the wealth he gained from the Americas was lost in continual wars against France, Germany, the Turks, and Barbary pirates in the Mediterranean. Despite the various wars, this was a century of unprecedented growth in Europe, as populations increased and cities flourished. Maritime expansion had encouraged trade, and new methods of production were starting to transform agriculture. Access to printing accelerated cultural and political changes, and fostered the great rise in strength of social groups other than the traditionally powerful hereditary aristocracy — the middle classes.

By the end of the sixteenth century, the divisions within organized religion were accentuated by a combination of the strong secular movement linked to Humanism and the Renaissance, and the rapid social changes that were taking place across Europe and beyond. Through the efforts of its Counter-Reformation, the Catholic Church was recovering some of the power and impetus that had been drained away by the spread of Protestantism; yet several forms of Protestant religion had by now firmly established themselves, particularly the Calvinists, Lutherans, and the Church of England. In common with all aspects of cultural life, music continued to evolve. The preceding centuries had seen the dramatic developments of the Ars Nova movement and the almost incredibly rapid evolution of new musical techniques. The turn of the century would prove to be another remarkable turning point in the history of music.

in which the music was essentially fitted to the rhythm of the poetic text. Religious music experienced fewer radical developments, but was nonetheless affected by the changes taking place in secular music. The Mass and the motet remained the principal forms of sacred vocal music, but variants evolved with the influence of the new secular techniques. Sacred polyphony reached its height with the great composers Palestrina and Lassus. The Reformation also had an effect on church music, leading to new forms of music for Protestant worship, including the anthem in England and psalm tunes in Calvinist areas.

Featured Composers

Hildegard

Hildegard of Bingen 1098 – 1179

RECOMMENDED WORKS
Sequences and Hymns
Disc: 'A feather on the breath of God'
Hyperion CDA66039
Gothic Voices/Christopher Page
A compelling recording of devotional verses dedicated to the Virgin Mary, both with and without instrumental accompaniment: ecstatic and melodious emotions projected with a rare clarity.

REPRESENTATIVE WORK
Ordo virtutum

Hildegard was one of ten children born to noble parents in the village of Bemersheim in what is now western Germany. At the age of eight she was placed in the care of Jutta of Spenheim, the abbess of a group of nuns attached to the Benedictine monastery near Bingen. After Jutta's death Hildegard became abbess, and shortly after, in 1141, she saw tongues of flame descend upon her from the sky. From this time on she devoted her life to trying to express her mystical visions through composition, poetry, and playwriting.

By virtue of her visionary experiences Hildegard was able to exercise a strength and authority unusual for women at the time. Combining religious and diplomatic activities, she made several missionary journeys through Germany over a period of ten years. She was a prolific writer as well as an accomplished physician, and her works reflected a close and creative alliance between science and the arts. As well as writing on natural history and medicine, she composed much lyrical poetry, and she recorded her prophetic

Portrait miniature from the illustrated manuscript
*Liber divinorum operum simplicis hominis, c.*1230

and symbolic visions in her manuscript *Scivias*. Her morality play, *Ordo virtutum*, consists of a discourse on the virtues; 16 of these were represented in performance by

Hildegard's nuns; the only male part — the Devil — was taken by her secretary.

Merging her passions for poetry and music, Hildegard collected her compositions together under the title *Symphonia armonie celestium revelationum* (Symphony of the Harmony of Celestial Revelations). She added to this work constantly over the years, and from this collection come the sequences (a chant form) and hymns found on the recommended recording.

Hildegard thought of herself as 'a feather on the breath of God,' a mystic rather than a composer; most of her works involve deeply devotional religious texts set to long, flowing melodies, mainly for solo voices. In the composition entitled *O Jerusalem* she likens Jerusalem to the nunnery that she founded at Rupertsberg, near Bingen, on the site of a monastery that had been previously razed to the ground by Normans. Hildegard died at Rupertsberg in the autumn of 1179.

Hildegard's vision, from the illustrated manuscript
*Liber divinorum operum simplicis hominis, c.*1230

Known as 'the Sibyl of the Rhine,' Hildegard successfully combined the roles of composer, diplomat, and mystic.

Key to Recommended Works

arr. arrangement (by)	**contr** contralto	**hpd** harpsichord	**Op., Opp.** Opus(es)	**pno** piano	**ten** tenor	**vcl** violoncello ('cello)
bar baritone	**gtr** guitar	**mez** mezzo-soprano	**org** organ	**sop** soprano	**treb** treble	**vln** violin

Pérotin

Pérotin c.1160–1225

RECOMMENDED WORKS
Conducti and Organa
Disc: 'Sacred Choral Works'
ECM New Series 837 751-2
Hilliard Ensemble/Paul Hillier
Seven male voices skillfully weave the complex patterns of Pérotin's music; the recording location (Boxgrove Priory, Sussex, England) provides a persuasive feeling of echo and reverberation, evoking a vivid sense of the great Gothic cathedrals where these works would originally have been performed.

REPRESENTATIVE WORKS
Exiit sermo V. Sed sic
Sancte Germane V. O sancte Germane

The details of Pérotin's life are shrouded in mystery. What is certain is that he was one of the two great masters of the Notre Dame school, an important group of composers and singers working under the patronage of the Notre Dame cathedral in Paris during the twelfth century. He may also have been a canon there. One of the activities of this school was the development of musical pieces using harmony — that is, very early polyphony. Pérotin's music far surpassed in beauty and complexity the basic, unadventurous polyphonic styles that were usual for his day.

A slightly earlier composer of Notre Dame, named Léonin, compiled a vast cycle of polyphonic music celebrating all the major feast days of the church year, known as the *Magnus liber organi* (Great Book of Organum). Pérotin expanded and developed the collection as well as improving music notation. He did not, as far as we know, create original compositions himself; rather, he developed what was at his disposal, such as the works of Léonin and others. Léonin wrote mainly for two vocal parts, as was the custom. Pérotin's compositions included three, even four, voices. His ability to weave together multipart vocals to create works

of extraordinary beauty earned him a high reputation. The vast, resonant interior of the mighty new Gothic cathedral of Notre Dame must have greatly amplified these impressive plainchants.

Two of the pieces on the recommended recording, *Sederunt principes* and *Viderunt omnes* (the latter may have been written for Christmas celebrations in 1198), are written for four voices. Pérotin's melodic lines, ornate and rich, extended the known capabilities of the human voice. The long, sustained notes of the basic plainchant (called the tenor) that formed part of these works may have been carried by a singer or played on a simple

Amiens Cathedral nave by architect Robert de Luzarches, 1218–36

The magnificent vaulted choir of the church illustrates the superb acoustics that Gothic architecture provided for sacred music.

organ; the upper voices sang shorter notes in a number of inventive rhythms. Both pieces last as long as an individual movement in a classical symphony or concerto. As such, they are astonishing feats of composition for their time and true representatives of Pérotin's achievement — the crafting of new ways of expressing the language of music.

Machaut

Guillaume de Machaut c.1160–1225

RECOMMENDED WORK

Messe de Nostre Dame
Angel CDC7 47492-2
Taverner Consort and Choir/Andrew Parrott
Machaut's four-part polyphony is augmented by plainchant, the ringing of churchbells and the clanking of holy incense carriers, creating a stirring sense of occasion that is enhanced by the male-voice choir.

REPRESENTATIVE WORKS
Hoquetus David
Foy porter, honneur garder
Je ne caisse de prier, 'Le lai de la fonteinne'
Ma fin est mon commencement

French miniature, 14th century
An allegorical scene in which Nature offers Machaut three of her children — Sense, Rhetoric, and Music.

Probably born in Rheims, Machaut was the leading exponent of the Ars Nova movement that flourished in France during the fourteenth century. In 1323 he joined the royal household of John of Luxembourg, King of Bohemia, and served as a clerk for about 20 years, widely respected as a poet as well as a composer. He traveled with the court, but increasingly spent his time composing rather than in administration. His first verified composition was a motet written in 1324 for the election of the Archbishop of Rheims. Through the efforts of King John, Machaut was granted several benefices, in particular the canonry of the new Gothic cathedral in Rheims, which was granted in 1337. He took up residency there in 1340, leaving his formal work with the king though remaining in service until the monarch's death at the battle of Crécy in 1346.

Machaut was one of the earliest known users of syncopated rhythm, and was at the forefront of rhythmic experimentation in both his religious and his secular music. His *Hoquetus David* is one of the first pieces of purely instrumental music in modern Western times. In addition, he composed for voices in a wider vocal range than was previously thought possible. In all, he wrote more than 140 (mainly polyphonic) compositions, although fewer than two dozen have been found outside his own collections, suggesting that he protected his work fiercely. After the outbreak of the Black Death in France at the end of the 1340's, Machaut prepared elaborate collections of his compositions for his patrons, who included John, Duke of Berry and the future King Charles V of France. These unique, beautifully illuminated manuscript editions combined motets, ballades, and many other forms with a wide selection of his poetry.

Machaut's *Messe de Nostre Dame* is, deservedly, the best-known composition of the entire age. He wrote the principal components of the Mass (Kyrie, Gloria, Credo, Sanctus/Benedictus, and Agnus Dei) polyphonically rather than in the customary plainchant. It is also one of the first Masses to have been written as a whole by a single composer; previously the different components of the Mass were assembled from different composers. This, together with its innovative rhythmical techniques, makes it a milestone in the evolution of the Mass as a musical form in its own right.

Manuscript illumination, 14th century
Singers performing one of Machaut's works from a rotulus (music roll).

Dufay

Guillaume Dufay c. 1400 – 1474

RECOMMENDED WORKS

Sacred and Secular Vocal Works

Disc: 'The Garden of Zephirus'
Hyperion CDA66144
Gothic Voices/Christopher Page
The noble art of courtly love is portrayed evocatively in these polyphonic songs, with the spirit of the music captured perfectly by the singers. Listening with the translations in front of you will bring the Renaissance world to life.

REPRESENTATIVE WORKS
Missa Ecce ancilla Domini
Missa Ave regina celorum
Missa Se la face ay pale
Missa L'homme armé
Nuper rosarum flores/Terribilis est locus iste

Dufay was the foremost Franco-Flemish composer of the fifteenth century. Born near Cambrai in northern France, he began his musical career as a choirboy in the city's cathedral. There his musical gifts came to the attention of the bishop, who encouraged his development. He spent a large part of his adult years living and traveling in Europe, including a period between 1428 and 1436 as a singer in the Papal choir in Rome. Dufay became the leading composer of the culturally important Burgundian court, and his patrons extended to the highest levels of Church and State, including the powerful courts of France, the Netherlands, and Italy.

Dufay's development was, therefore, subject to several influences. His musical style grew out of a synthesis of the late medieval French traditions (such as Ars Nova) and the early Renaissance styles that he absorbed from his travels in Italy. A further element derived from the influence of John Dunstable, an Englishman who was present with Dufay at Burgundy. Dunstable emphasized a more natural, expressive sound in polyphony; this fresh approach coincided with the Humanist

Miniature from *Le Champion des Dames*, French, 15th century

Dufay, on the left, with a portative organ, and his fellow composer Gilles de Binchois (c. 1400–1460) with a harp, representing sacred and secular music.

and Renaissance tendency toward the exploration of personal emotion.

Essentially, Dufay's good fortune was to be in the right places at the right time and to possess the talent to make the best of the situation; his position at the Burgundian court allowed him to use the best singers and instrumentalists available. Without being particularly innovative, his compositions were technically sophisticated as well as notably melodic. He wrote many of his works for the noble families of Europe, for whom he undertook commissions; these works often commemorated public or social events, or accompanied religious occasions.

Utilizing ideas promoted by other composers, Dufay established himself at the forefront of the changes taking place in church music. During his lifetime, the Mass assumed an increasing importance as the main form of sacred musical expression, and Dufay composed a number of complete polyphonic settings of the Mass, often merging secular with liturgical themes, as was becoming common in the fifteenth century.

He also wrote a substantial amount of purely secular music, particularly rondeaux, which were smaller-scale, more intimate chansons than the ballades favored by fourteenth-century tastes. Many of his rondeaux give clear indications of Dufay's ability to embrace new

technical ideas — he uses dissonant sounds, for example, in *Mon cuer me fait* on the recommended recording. His chansons also showed a new flexibility: this was due to the increased use of higher voices (pioneered in part by Machaut), which meant that composers could write for a wider vocal range. Often his music is suffused with emotions of love and tenderness, and would possibly have been accompanied by an instrument such as the medieval harp.

In 1436, Pope Eugene IV granted Dufay the canonicate to his home-town cathedral of Cambrai. He finally settled there around the year 1458, and remained until his death in 1474.

Painting by the Master of the St. Lucy Legend, c. 1485
Detail from Mary Queen of Heaven showing three medieval recorders, a harp, a dulcimer, and a lute.

Ockeghem

Johannes Ockeghem c.1410 – 1497

RECOMMENDED WORKS

Chansons
L'Oiseau-Lyre 436 194-2
Medieval Ensemble of London/Peter Davies,
Timothy Davies
Performances that capture the composer's blending of three or four voice parts to achieve a masterly form of early polyphony. Dip in and select a small group from these 30 songs to get a flavor of the secular aspect of Ockeghem's art.

REPRESENTATIVE WORKS

Missa Pro defunctis
Missa prolationum
Missa Mi-mi
Missa Ecce ancilla Domini

Records of Ockeghem's life are scarce. Franco-Flemish, he was probably born in Hainaut. In 1443 he was noted as a singer at the cathedral in Antwerp, and within a year or two he gained employment in the court of Charles I, Duke of Bourbon, based in Moulins.

Blessed with a fine voice and considerable diplomatic skills, Ockeghem spent the rest of his life in the service of three successive kings of France. In about 1452

The *Chansonnier de Tournai*, 15th century
This celebrated early manuscript of love songs and ballads includes examples by Ockeghem, as well as his contemporary Josquin Desprez.

he became a singer at the royal chapel of Charles VII in Paris, where he enjoyed a favored position. He progressed to the status of Master of the Royal Chapel, and his service at the royal court continued uninterrupted through the reigns of Louis XI and Charles VIII. At various points he was treasurer of the Abbey of St. Martin at Tours and a canon of Notre Dame in Paris. Although most of his life was spent in France, Ockeghem traveled to Spain and to Bruges, and there are hints that these might have been, at least in part, diplomatic trips for the King. The last surviving court record relating to him is from 1488, when he was present at a Maundy Thursday service where Charles VIII tended the feet of the poor.

During the fifteenth century many new compositional techniques were emerging. While Ockeghem was not a revolutionary, neither was he a rigid traditionalist; he would certainly have been aware of the new developments and was able to use them in his own compositions. A particular quality found in his sacred music is the broad sweep of the melodies that he employs: long, floating lines, often for all the voices in a piece (rather than just one voice singled out from several, as in fourteenth-century motets). This required not only musical imagination but also ingenuity to ensure that the piece 'worked.' To facilitate these ornate, flowing lines, Ockeghem increasingly used four voices instead of three. Whereas the Dufay generation had extended the vocal range upward, using higher voices, Ockeghem and his peers explored downward, including the bass register more and more.

In his secular songs he reflected the Burgundian tradition, composing mainly

Detail from Ghent Altarpiece by Jan Van Eyck, 1432
An angelic choir. Van Eyck worked at the Burgundian court and would have been well acquainted with its choral tradition.

in the rondeau form. As with his sacred music he used long, graceful lines, employing various new techniques to create an expressive aural picture, with all the beauty of multiple voice parts seamlessly blending together. Despite the complexity, the effect is effortlessly melodious.

In addition to benefiting from royal favor, Ockeghem enjoyed high esteem throughout his life from fellow musicans; among his friends were the composers Binchois, Dufay, and Josquin Desprez. Numerous tributes testify to his standing, and on his death Josquin wrote a substantial requiem in his honor.

Josquin Desprez

Josquin Desprez c.1440–1521

RECOMMENDED WORKS
Missa Pange lingua
Missa La sol fa re mi
Disc: 'Two Masses'
Gimell CDGIM009
Tallis Scholars/Peter Phillips
Two different settings of the Mass, in which the performers sing with great purity of sound, bringing out the way Josquin made the musical lines deeply expressive of the emotions behind the words.

REPRESENTATIVE WORKS
Nymphes des bois/Requiem, La déploration sur la mort de Johannes Ockeghem
Missa L'homme armé super voces musicales
Missa De beata vergine
Missa Hercules Dux Ferriarae
Miserere mei, Deus
Stabat mater dolorosa/Comme femme desconforté

Relief of singing angels by Luca della Robbia, c.1435

Josquin Desprez — often known simply as Josquin — is the centerpiece of this period, the greatest composer of the Franco-Flemish School and of the early Renaissance. Regarded highly within the music world, as much during his lifetime as after his death, he is considered the equal in his own era of Bach or Beethoven in theirs. More than any other composer before him, Josquin made the available compositional techniques his own, at the same time adding a great breadth of imagination to the craft of writing music.

Born in Burgundian territories in northern France, Josquin followed in the footsteps of many of his illustrious Franco-Flemish predecessors and traveled south to Italy. From 1459 to 1472 he was a singer at Milan Cathedral, and following that, at the ducal court of the Sforza family in Milan. Moving to Rome, he became a member of the Papal choir in 1486, where he remained for more than ten years. He spent some time as court composer to King Louis XII of France, and then moved back to Italy, where he became director of music at the court of Duke Hercules of Ferrara — and the highest-paid court member ever. He returned to France in 1504 and finally became provost of Notre Dame in Condé-sur-l'Escaut; there he remained for the rest of his life.

Josquin may have been a pupil of Ockeghem's. He certainly built on Ockeghem's mastery of the complex harmonies and sophisticated techniques that

were typical of the Netherlands composers; a flexibility and fluency in his style are evidence of Italian influence. He wrote in the customary forms of the time — the Mass, motets, and chansons — yet he achieved a freer expression of emotion, employing the technique of 'word-painting' to convey feelings. Word-painting matches the sound of the music to the meaning of the text; for example, Latin words such as *descendit* or *ascendit* might be supplied with music that descended or ascended (as in the *Miserere* motet), emphasizing the emotional qualities of the work. The music of the late medieval composers had been concerned with intellectual ingenuity and almost mathematical complexity. With Josquin, music became harnessed to the emotional needs of the text, so that for the first time a listener could gain an idea simply from the sound of the music (rather than the words) what it was about.

Though his output was prolific and wide-ranging, one of the highest peaks of Josquin's career was his *Missa Pange lingua*, with its rich harmonies, inventiveness, and melodic subtleties. A favored form of composition of the time was the 'Missa Parodia' (parody Mass), in which the parts from an existing work — secular or sacred — were used as the basis for a new piece. Josquin used this technique in Masses such as *Malheur me bat*, based on a chanson by Ockeghem, and *L'homme armé*, probably based on an old crusader song.

Josquin was one of the first composers to use passages from the Old Testament as a basis for motets, where his individuality came to the fore. In his motets and chansons he frequently composed for four parts, achieving great depth and a wide vocal range, as well as a variety of moods. The spirituality and compassion that he managed to portray took music out of the Middle Ages, and made Josquin the first composer truly to fulfill the criteria of the Renaissance movement.

Manuscript of 'Nymphes des Bois,' 1497
The song 'Nymphes des Bois' is a lament for the death of Ockeghem, and Josquin used heavy black notation to underline its melancholy purpose.

Tallis

Thomas Tallis *c.*1505–1585

RECOMMENDED WORKS

Spem in alium
Lamentations of Jeremiah
Disc: 'Sacred Choral Works'
Hyperion CDA66400
Winchester Cathedral Choir/David Hill
A representative survey of Tallis's music, recorded at Winchester Cathedral, which gives an awesome, resonant perspective, particularly conveying the monumental nature of the extraordinary 40-part motet Spem in alium.

REPRESENTATIVE WORKS

O nata lux de lumine
In ieiunio et fletu
Salvator mundi
Salve intemerata virgo

Portrait engraving by an unknown Italian artist

Little is known about the life of Thomas Tallis, although he was one of the most important English composers of sacred music of his time. In 1532 he was employed as an organist for the Benedictine Priory of Dover, and in 1537 he worked for the church of St. Mary-at-Hill in London, again probably playing the organ. He may have moved to Waltham Abbey about a year later, attracted by its three organs and its choir; certainly, he was the organist there at the time of the Abbey's closure in 1540 as part of King Henry VIII's Dissolution of the Monasteries. For the next two years he worked as a lay clerk for Canterbury Cathedral, before joining the court as a Gentleman of the Chapel Royal — where from 1572 he was joint organist with fellow composer William Byrd. During his decades of service to the court his compositional skills earned him a considerable reputation.

Tallis's career spanned the reigns of four very different monarchs (Henry VIII, Edward VI, Mary Tudor and Elizabeth I), and throughout the frequent religious turnarounds of the era he retained the musical skill and diplomacy to serve each. He composed mainly sacred music, initially in Latin for the Catholic Church and later in English after the Protestant Reformation. In 1575, Tallis and William Byrd were granted an exclusive patent by Queen Elizabeth to print and market music, but this venture was not entirely successful until after Tallis's death in Greenwich in 1585. The first music they

Detail from the *Seven Planets* series by Hans Sebald Beham, 1539

The woodcut illustrates a small positive organ, operated with bellows and pedals.

published was a collection of 34 Latin motets by himself and Byrd, titled *Cantiones sacrae* (Sacred Songs).

Reflecting the currents of change brought by the Reformation, Tallis in the main avoided the florid, ornate writing that was much used by his English predecessors and contemporaries; yet he was capable of brilliant technical feats. *Spem in alium* is an extraordinary 40-part motet using eight choirs of five voices. Possibly written for the fortieth birthday of Elizabeth I, it would be remembered only as a curiosity were it not for the power of its message stemming from its treatment of the words, 'I have never put my hope in any other but you, O God of Israel . . .' Starting with two voices introducing the cry of hope, it builds to a climax, when all the voices join together to enunciate this fervent cry.

Palestrina

Giovanni Pierluigi da Palestrina c.1525–1594

RECOMMENDED WORK

Missa Papae Marcelli
Disc: 'Italian Sacred Choral Works'
Archiv Produktion 415 517-2
Westminster Abbey Choir/Simon Preston
Eloquently sung using boys' voices from an Anglican choir, recorded in the warm and sympathetic acoustics of All Saints' Church, Tooting, in south London. A fervent performance.

REPRESENTATIVE WORKS

Missa Aeterna Christi munera
Missa Assumpta est Maria
Hodie Christus natus est
Tu es Petrus

Probably born in, and taking his name from, a small town near Rome, Palestrina gained his musical education in Rome itself. He was a choirboy there, and lived most of his life in the city, with years of service to three important basilicas: St. Peter's, St. John Lateran, and Santa Maria Maggiore. First an organist and choirmaster for the cathedral in Palestrina, he became choirmaster of the Cappella Giulia (Julian Chapel) in St. Peter's in 1551. While there he published his first book of Masses, in 1554, citing Pope Julius III as his patron. Within a year of this he became a member of the Papal choir in the Sistine Chapel, although, having been married since 1547, he had to leave when a new pope introduced a celibacy ruling. He went on to be choirmaster at St. John Lateran (succeeding Lassus), and then at the more important Santa Maria Maggiore.

During the 1570's Rome was hit by plague, which claimed the lives of Palestrina's wife, two of their children, and a brother — tragedies that led him to start training for the priesthood. However, within eight months of his wife's death he had married a wealthy widow, and he went on to excel himself at managing her fur business. In 1571, he was reappointed

Portrait by an unknown Italian artist, c.1590

to the Julian Chapel, where he remained as choirmaster until his death. Offers from Duke Guglielmo Gonzaga in Mantua and the Emperor Maximilian II in Vienna could not entice him away from Rome.

Palestrina was a prolific composer, writing mainly sacred music such as Masses, motets, and Magnificats, in the *a cappella* style (no instrumental accompaniment), as well as both secular and sacred madrigals. The pinnacle of his achievement is in his Masses, of which he wrote more than one hundred.

He spent his working life under the influence of the Counter-Reformation. The Council of Trent in particular savagely censored the arts, condemning, among other things, the inclusion of secular material in sacred work, and the overuse of instruments. It was claimed that the polyphonic style of composition was too ornate, and that the complexity of such music obscured rather than enhanced the words of the religious service. Some reformers urged a return to the simpler, monophonic plainchant as the permissible form of celebrating the Liturgy. With his famous *Missa Papae Marcelli* (dedicated to Pope Marcellus II), Palestrina proved that polyphonic music could project its sacred message with sufficient clarity to comply with the Council's dictates. Legend has it that he wrote the Mass expressly for the Council; whether this is true, it is for this composition that he is deemed by some to have the 'savior of Church music.'

Title page of Palestrina's *First Book of Masses*, 1594
The engraving shows the composer offering his work to Pope Julius III.

Lassus

Orlande de Lassus c.1532–1594

RECOMMENDED WORK
Lamentations of Jeremiah
Disc: 'Lamentationes Hieremiae a 5'
Harmonia Mundi HMC90 1299
La Chapelle Royale Orchestra/Philippe
Herreweghe
*An appropriate continental style comes from this
13-voice Parisian choir: full of vibrant tones and
careful attention to the dissonant sounds in the
music, which is a deeply contemplative reflection of
the Holy Week text.*

REPRESENTATIVE WORKS
Psalmi Davidis poenitentiales
Lagrime di San Pietro
La nuict froid et sombre
Matona mia cara

Orlande de Lassus was one of the greatest exponents of sacred music during the second half of the sixteenth century. Perhaps the last Franco-Flemish champion, he was an incredibly prolific composer, and by the time he died in his sixties he had written more than two thousand sacred and secular works.

Portrait of Lassus aged 39 by J. Meysens

Born in the Franco-Flemish province of Hainaut, Lassus was blessed with such a beautiful voice that he was abducted two or three times by talent hunters in search of singers for the courts of Europe. At the age of 12 he entered the service of Ferrante Gonzaga, a general to the Emperor Charles V. Traveling with Gonzaga in Italy, Lassus experienced the Renaissance glories of the Mantuan court as well as those of Sicily and Milan.

Lassus spent the early part of his life traveling from one court or chapel in Europe to another, working for princes or the church. In about 1550 he entered service with an academic household in Naples. He next spent a short period in Rome, initially working for the Archbishop of Florence (who was based in Rome at that time) and then as the Maestro di Cappella at the church of St. John Lateran. In 1554, hearing that his parents were gravely ill, he returned to his home town of Mons. After their deaths he lived briefly in Antwerp, where he supervised the publication of several of his early motets and chansons. Shortly afterward he moved to Munich as a singer in the chapel of Duke Albrecht V of Bavaria. He remained in Munich for the rest of his life, in 1558 marrying Regina Wächinger, the daughter of a lady-in-waiting.

Lassus eventually rose to become Kapellmeister to the court. His duties included recruiting musicians, and he continued to make frequent journeys in Europe for this purpose. His fame as a composer spread, yet he resisted every offer to move from his family's home — even when asked by the King of France.

Lassus dominated the sacred music of his day not only because of the vastness of his output but also because of its extraordinary quality. He assimilated a wide range of styles, combining his own inventiveness with important Italian, French, German, and Flemish influences. His technically sophisticated madrigals and chansons show an amazing variety of moods, ranging from melancholy to comic, from sensual to jaunty — even boisterous drinking songs — and an equal mastery is evident in his religious compositions (more than 1,500). Many of his Masses and Magnificats are parody treatments (using original secular or sacred works as their theme) and convey a deep spirituality. His musical genius reached its peak in his motets, composed for the many devotional, reflective, and penitential texts acceptable under the dictates of the Counter-Reformation, and are especially notable for the expressiveness with which Lassus portrays the imagery of the sacred words.

Detail from the title page of the composer's *Masses for Five Voices*

The engraving shows Lassus seated at the keyboard, directing musicians at the Bavarian court in Munich.

Victoria

Tomás Luis de Victoria 1548–1611

RECOMMENDED WORKS
Missa O quam gloriosum
Missa Ave maris stella
Disc: 'Sacred Choral Works'
Hyperion CDA66114
Westminster Cathedral Choir/David Hill
Although Victoria's music is often thought severe, the music on this disc — especially the Missa Ave maris stella *— is often joyful, sometimes beautifully so, with the recording capturing all its fervor and passion.*

REPRESENTATIVE WORKS
Missa Pro victoria
Officium defunctorum
Tenebrae Responsoriesa

Victoria was the greatest Spanish composer of the sixteenth century. A profoundly religious man, he wrote only sacred music. More than anywhere else in Europe, Spain was gripped at this time by a strident, zealous Catholicism, most clearly evident in the purges of the Inquisition, in Ignatius Loyola's foundation of the Jesuit order in 1534 and in the creation of several new monastic orders. Such deep-seated religious fervor permeated all aspects of life, including the composition of church music. Victoria's music is a reflection of this highly charged and passionate attitude.

Born in Ávila, the seventh of 11 children, Victoria grew up with religion an integral part of his life. Two of his uncles were priests, one of whom took care of the young Victoria after the death of his father when he was nine. He went to study at a local Jesuit school, sang in the choir of Ávila Cathedral, and built up a strong reputation locally.

When his voice changed he was encouraged by both the Cathedral and King Philip II of Spain to further his studies in Rome. There he joined the Jesuit Collegio Germanico, where he trained for the priesthood as well as practicing music. Palestrina was at that time the Maestro di Cappella at the nearby Seminario Romano, and it is likely that he taught Victoria. Undoubtedly some sort of exchange of musical ideas took place between the two composers.

Victoria remained in Rome for over 20 years. He became a priest in 1575, and held several appointments at churches and religious institutions. Equally valuable to his musical development was the fertile contact with other composers living in or visiting Rome. He published a number of particularly beautiful books of his music, and in a dedication of *Missarum libri duo* to Philip II in 1583 he expressed a desire to return to his beloved Spain. In 1587 his wishes were granted when the King appointed him chaplain to the Dowager Empress Maria, widow of Maximilian II, who lived in retirement in Madrid. Victoria served at her convent for the rest of his life. In 1603 the Dowager Empress died and Victoria composed her Requiem, the mighty *Officium defunctorum*. Little more was heard from him before his own death in 1611.

Victoria's Masses are for four to 12 voices, often divided up into two or three choirs — an innovative arrangement. The rest of his work includes motets, Magnificats and a variety of other sacred works. His music expresses the ardent, fatalistic Catholicism peculiar to his country and time. While the *Officium defunctorum* is deeply reflective, Masses such as *O quam gloriosum* and *Ave maris stella* are more joyful, holding out more hope for this life, as opposed to the next; all demonstrate his passionate faith.

Above: *The Resurrection* by El Greco, c.1596/1610
Spain was the most fervently Catholic country in Europe, and Victoria's music echoed the religious intensity of El Greco's paintings.

Below: Polychrome monument of Victoria's royal patron, Philip II, with his third wife, Elizabeth, 1632

Portrait engraving by Vandergucht after Haym

Byrd

William Byrd 1543–1623

RECOMMENDED WORKS

Masses for three, four, and five voices
Gimell CDGIM345
Tallis Scholars/Peter Phillips
Using female as well as male voices, this recording manages to avoid being overpious. The singers give a purity of sound and security of intonation that bring out Byrd's characteristic 'word-painting' effects, whereby the music conjures up and underlines the emotion behind individual words.

REPRESENTATIVE WORKS
Ave verum corpus
Great Service
Come to me grief for ever
Pavans
Galliards

William Byrd was known as 'the father of English musick': he was the last great English composer of Catholic church music, as well as the first in the Elizabethan 'golden' age of secular music. Under the Protestant reign of Elizabeth I, many Catholics feared that they would be persecuted for their faith; Byrd's devout Catholic beliefs, however, seem to have been largely tolerated by the Queen, despite his close association with many Catholic recusants (those who refused to submit to Church of England dictates).

Little is known about Byrd's early years. He may have been a pupil of Thomas Tallis in London; the first authenticated records reveal him as organist and choirmaster at Lincoln Cathedral in 1563. In 1570 he was invited to join the Chapel Royal as a singer, although he did not actually leave Lincoln to take up his post until two years later. Even in London he continued to receive partial pay from the cathedral in return for further compositions — of Anglican church music. In 1572 he was appointed organist of the Chapel Royal, a position he initially shared with Thomas Tallis, and for the next 20 years or so Byrd remained in service at the court. In 1575 he and Tallis were granted a royal monopoly on the printing and selling of music.

During a period of general persecution of Catholics in the late 1570's, Byrd moved out of London with his family and settled in Harlington, Middlesex. His wife, Juliana, was listed for refusing to attend Church of England services, which at that time was compulsory. In 1581 several Jesuits were executed. Byrd's house was searched and he was fined for his beliefs, but he remained free. In the 1590's, after Juliana's death and his second marriage, he moved to Essex, where he lived for the rest of his life.

Byrd's music was as often dedicated to prominent Catholics as to Anglican patrons. His music encompassed both instrumental and vocal works, secular and sacred, Anglican and Catholic. He usually wrote his secular vocal music for solo voice accompanied by viol consort (ensemble), rather than the lute preferred by his contemporaries. His greatest instrumental music was for the viol, and he also wrote about 150 pieces — often dance movements — for keyboards.

Byrd wrote many Anglican Church music settings, including anthems, but his most sublime music was composed to Latin texts (for the Catholic Church), such as the motet for four voices, *Ave verum corpus*. His three Masses, for three, four, and five voices, use the typical English technique of imitation — melodic phrases repeated by different voices at various points in a composition. This technique allowed a great deal of emotion to be expressed, and in the case of Byrd's Masses — written for the private use of his fellow Catholics, and relatively compressed — the emotion was that of a deeply felt religious belief, a belief under attack. The music is powerful and austere, yet essentially positive.

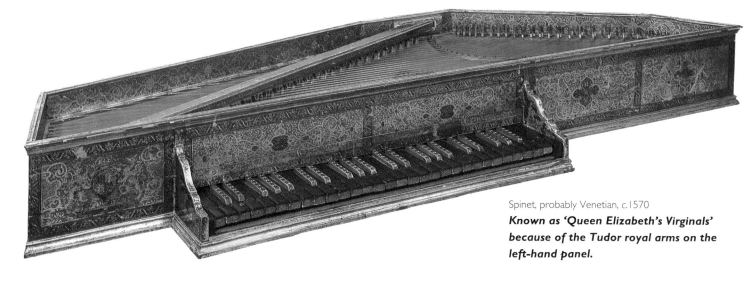

Spinet, probably Venetian, c.1570
Known as 'Queen Elizabeth's Virginals' because of the Tudor royal arms on the left-hand panel.

Dowland

John Dowland c.1563–1626

RECOMMENDED WORKS

Works with Lute and Voice
Disc: 'The English Orpheus'
Virgin Classics Veritas VC7 59521-2
Emma Kirkby (sop); Anthony Rooley (lute)
A selection of songs combining Dowland's famous melancholy with a more cheerful aspect, lute songs neatly balancing instrumental solos, and singer and accompanist showing a true empathy.

REPRESENTATIVE WORKS
Lachrimae
Fortune my foe
Selections from Songs, Books 1–4

John Dowland was the greatest English lutenist and song composer. The late sixteenth century saw the development of the lute as an instrument to accompany consort songs, and in England a distinctive song type evolved: the ayre. This form, for solo voice with lute or viols, supplanted the madrigal in popularity. It was as a composer of ayres that Dowland excelled.

Dowland traveled extensively in Europe, partly because he had failed to

gain a position as royal lutenist to Elizabeth I. At the age of 17 he had spent a period in Paris, in service to Sir Henry Cobham, the Ambassador to the King of France, during which time he converted to Catholicism; and it is probably as a result of this that he may have felt more comfortable on the Continent. He himself was convinced that his Catholic sympathies led to prejudice against him at the English court. In the 1590's he was received at various courts in Germany, including that of the Duke of Brunswick and the Landgrave of Hesse at Kassel, and in Italy. In Florence he met up with other disenchanted English Catholics, only to discover that they were plotting to assassinate Queen Elizabeth. He immediately moved on to Nuremberg. From there, in November 1595, he wrote to Sir Robert Cecil in England exposing the Catholics' plot. After that he probably returned to Hesse.

In 1598, Dowland was employed as a lutenist — for a very high salary — at the court of King Christian of Denmark. Five years later, after receiving funds for his latest book of music, he returned to London, where he met with Queen Anne. In 1605 he went back to Denmark, but the pressure of his accruing debts forced him home again, and in 1609 he entered the service of Lord Walden, a man well connected with royal circles. In October 1612 he eventually gained a position as lutenist to King James I. Despite the royal appoint-

Lute by Marx Unverdorben, 1580

ment, he never enjoyed as great a renown in England as he did abroad.

Dowland wrote a great number of pieces for solo lute, many of them in dance forms; sacred music such as psalms; and four books of ayres (1597–1612), which were widely published and achieved immense popularity. Descriptions of the composer indicate a certain duality of character; he is variously described as 'a cheerful person . . . passing his days in lawful merriment' and as a man 'filled with melancholy.' This ambivalence is reflected in his music: his light and tuneful English ayres contrast sharply with other, more somber pieces, such as 'In darkness let mee dwell.' With his ability to give intense musical expression to the emotion of the poetry, using rhythmic devices and techniques such as word-painting, it is in his gentler, elegiac songs that Dowland's talent is without rival.

Detail of *A Festival in a Palace Garden* by Sebastian Vrancx
Music-making for pleasure. The singers are accompanied by a lute and early bowed and woodwind instruments.

Gesualdo

Carlo Gesualdo 1561–1613

RECOMMENDED WORKS

Madrigals
Disc: 'Quinto Libro dei Madrigali'
L'Oiseau-Lyre 410 128-2
Consort of Musicke/Anthony Rooley
Superbly clear rendition of some of Gesualdo's finest secular music, madrigals whose music reflects the mood of the poems.

REPRESENTATIVE WORKS
Responsoria

Detail of an Italian altarpiece showing Gesualdo, early 17th century

A man of violent temperament and ferocious passions, Carlo Gesualdo was as notorious for having murdered his first wife and her lover as he was famous for his music. One of classical music's great experimenters, he displayed an individual approach seen clearly in his madrigals.

Don Carlo Gesualdo was an Italian nobleman, Prince of Venosa. He lived most of his life in Naples, where his uncle was archbishop (later a cardinal). Although he initially used a pseudonym to disguise his real love of writing music, discretion was not his best trait. His controversial marriage to his own cousin, Maria d'Avalos, came to an abrupt end in 1590 when he discovered that she was engaged in an affair with another nobleman: Gesualdo murdered them both. After this incident he continued his musical career under his own name.

In 1594 he entered a rather more conventionally acceptable marriage with Leonora d'Este, the niece of Duke Alfonso of Ferrara. The couple led largely separate lives, but the Ferrara court, a thriving center of musical and artistic activity, was ideal for Gesualdo, and he published his first four books of madrigals there between 1593 and 1596. He returned to Naples in 1597, and as he grew older became distinctly world-weary, turning more and more to his music. Rumors circulated of possible divorce, and there was speculation concerning his sanity. He became preoccupied by morbid reverence toward his late uncle; he was also deeply concerned about the end of the family line. His and Leonora's only son, Alfonsino, died in 1600, a tragedy that prompted him to commission the famous altarpiece in the church of the Capuchins at Gesualdo, which portrays himself, Leonora, his revered uncle, and the purified soul of the child.

Writing during the transitional period when the controlled style of the Renaissance was giving way to the more dramatic expressiveness of the Baroque, Gesualdo brought an extreme, ardent individuality to his music. Nowhere is this more evident than in his madrigals, and especially in his fifth and sixth books, published in 1611. To express changes in mood — doubtless a reflection of his unstable emotional state — he used a violent chromaticism. (Chromaticism is the use of chords containing notes not included in the basic scale.) Although he was writing within the strong madrigal tradition, and like his peers producing works for three to five unaccompanied voices, his unorthodox techniques were far in advance of his time and can border on the eccentric. As such Gesualdo's style did not influence future generations (although Stravinsky was intrigued by the chromatic explorations of his madrigals). Nevertheless his compositions display a truly original voice made comprehensible by his mastery of the technical requirements of writing music and by an undeniably compelling emotional power.

Gabrieli

Andrea Gabrieli c.1510–1586
Giovanni Gabrieli c.1553/6–1612

RECOMMENDED WORKS

Sacred Choral and Instrumental Works
Disc: 'A Venetian Coronation, 1595'
Virgin Classics Veritas VC7 91110-2
Gabrieli Consort and Players/Paul McCreesh
The splendor, pomp, and ceremony of Venetian polyphonic music — both of voices and of brass instruments — is displayed here in this hypothetical reconstruction of the ceremonial music, by both Andrea and Giovanni, for the coronation of a Venetian Doge.

REPRESENTATIVE WORKS (Giovanni)
Hodie Christus natus est
In ecclesiis
Quem vidisitis pastores
Sonata a 15

Although these two related Venetian composers (uncle and nephew) are usually coupled together, each earned his own place in the development of music. Toward the end of the sixteenth century, Venice was at the height of its prosperity, with the cathedral of St. Mark's at the hub

of its ceremonial and sacred occasions. The Gabrielis were among the first Italians to hold important positions there, following the eminent Franco-Flemish composer Adrian Willaert, who was Maestro di Capella there from 1527.

The young Andrea Gabrieli was probably one of Willaert's pupils. Certainly he sang in St. Mark's, was organist at the church of San Geremia and traveled as part of Duke Albrecht's retinue, meeting Lassus in Germany. He became Maestro di Capella at St. Mark's in 1555, gaining a reputation as a composer, organist and teacher. He remained there until his death.

His madrigals were lighter and more pastoral than those of his peers, and he decorated his themes with rhythmic patterns. He was also responsible for evolving a style of sacred music appropriate to the performing requirements of St. Mark's, as well as suited to the Venetian love of pomp. He used several choirs (*cori spezzati*, or 'spaced choirs') placed around the galleries of the church, which were often accompanied by groups of instruments such as violins and violas, cornets, trumpets, trombones and bassoons, and the organ. Such polychoral or 'antiphonal' works are typical of, although not exclusive to, Venetian music of the time.

Giovanni came to be regarded as Italy's greatest exponent of High Renaissance music. Taught by his uncle, he followed very much in Andrea's footsteps, including

service in Duke Albrecht's court and a post at St. Mark's as organist from 1585 until his death in 1612.

Giovanni was the earliest known composer to use the word 'concerto,' in a volume he published in 1587 titled *Concerti* that contained a variety of works by himself and Andrea. Although he was primarily an organist, many of his most important instrumental compositions were ensemble works. His motet *In ecclesiis* for 14 voices plus instruments is one of the greatest polychoral works of the time, even using the Baroque-oriented concept of soloists. Giovanni also used the 'dialogue' technique — an aspect of the Venetian tradition — in which an independent instrumental accompaniment was set in contrast to the vocal lines.

Giovanni's work, and in particular his teaching of composers such as the German Heinrich Schütz, had considerable impact across the Alps in Austria and Germany. Both Andrea and Giovanni were important to the music of the Italian High Renaissance; Giovanni especially, with his more expressive style of composition and foward-looking techniques, provides a link between the Renaissance and Baroque eras.

Bird's eye view of Venice by J. Heintz, 17th century

In the Gabrielis' time, Venice was a proud and independent republic with powerful maritime interests.

Additional Composers

Although the church was the chief sponsor of music in ancient times, the *Carmina Burana* — a thirteenth-century collection of songs about gambling and drinking — shows that other concerns were given voice. Carl Orff's famous updated version of the songs was first performed in 1937.

Also outside the direct influence of the church in the twelfth and thirteenth centuries was the work of the troubadours, a scattered company of singers and poets ranging from serfs and tradesmen to royalty (including Richard the Lionheart), who sang of courtly love, chivalry, and adventure. Prolific composers such as southern French **Bernart de Ventadorn** (*c.*1130–*c.*1190) and **Jaufré Rudel** (mid-twelfth century) provided a somewhat more sophisticated entertainment than the minstrels who frequented sumptuous medieval banquets and jousts.

Germany, too, had its courtly singers in the shape of the *Minnesinger*, a tradition that Wagner later drew on in *Die Meistersinger von Nürnberg*. In Italy the first flowering of secular music came in the fourteenth century when composers such as **Francesco Landini** (*c.*1325–1397) and the Belgian **Johannes Ciconia** (*c.*1335–1411) composed madrigals, chansons, and dancing-songs, often to texts by great writers such as Dante Alighieri, Petrarch, and Boccaccio.

Medieval music from the British Isles abounds in splendors, among them the *Worcester Fragments* and carols such as *Sumer is icumen in*. At the end of the fifteenth century, British music reached a peak with the collection of sacred works called the *Eton Choirbook*, containing music in which soaring musical lines are the aural equivalent of the Perpendicular style of architecture in cathedrals such as Canterbury and Winchester.

Although Victoria would sum up the robustness, richness, and earthiness of Spanish Catholicism later in the sixteenth century, the country's earlier musical heritage — both sacred and theatrical — was boldly painted by the composers **Juan del Encina** (1468–1529), with songs such as *Mas vale que trocar* and *Fata la parte*, and **Francisco de Peñalosa** (*c.*1470–1528), with liturgical music, including the Mass *Nunca fué pena mayor*. In addition a host of songs developed around the time of Christopher Columbus concerning his much-discussed voyages at the end of the fifteenth century.

Throughout western Europe, music-making was always at the forefront of society's concerns: only today are we learning of similar achievements in Latin America, Scandinavia, and eastern Europe.

The Baroque Era
17th to mid-18th century

The conflict between Catholic and Protestant climaxed in the Thirty Years' War, devastating central Europe. While King Louis XIV enforced his absolute rule in France, England's Civil War led the island nation to found a new constitutional government. In the rush for empire, Europe's rulers focused on the New World, opening a new stage of world history. By the end of the seventeenth century, the decline of Turkey, the growth of Prussia, and Russia's victories over Sweden had changed the map of eastern Europe.

With these political changes came a vast outpouring of literature. Shakespeare, Molière, and Racine contributed masterpieces of drama; Donne and Milton produced poetry of unprecedented power; and the first novels appeared, including Cervantes' *Don Quixote*. The exuberant self-confidence of the Baroque style showed in the sculpture of Bernini, the paintings of Caravaggio and Rubens, Louis XIV's château at Versailles, and Wren's St. Paul's Cathedral in London. From the Netherlands came the glorious art of Rembrandt and Vermeer.

It was an age of technological advance and discovery. The telescope and microscope revealed astounding new worlds. Kepler and Galileo laid the foundations for Newton's great works on motion and gravitation. These and other developments in the understanding of anatomy and physiology encouraged people to believe that they could win control over nature. The way was paved for the rationalism of the following century.

In music, opera, the cantata, and the oratorio made their first appearance, as did the sonata and the concerto. In Italy, the birthplace of most of the age's new musical ideas, Scarlatti and Vivaldi predominated, and Monteverdi's genius promoted opera. It was in Germany, however, with Bach and Handel, that Baroque music reached its greatest heights.

Featured Composers

Albinoni 87	**Charpentier** 81	**Monteverdi** 76	**Schütz** 78
Allegri 77	**Corelli** 84	**Pachelbel** 82	**Telemann** 92
Arne 95	**Couperin** 85	**Purcell** 82	**Vivaldi** 86
Bach 88	**Handel** 90	**Rameau** 93	
Carissimi 79	**Lully** 80	**Scarlatti** 94	

The Family of Louis XIV by Jean Nocret, 1670

'The Sun King' as Zeus, king of the gods, portrayed in a splendor typical of the Baroque — an era when the monarchy was central to society.

The Baroque era witnessed a triumphant revival in the fortunes of Catholicism, reversing some of the setbacks that had occurred in the sixteenth century. During that turbulent period, the Reformation had torn the church in two, dividing Europe into competing Protestant and Catholic factions; the Turks had continued to threaten the eastern fringes of the Holy Roman Empire; and Rome itself, the Holy See, had been sacked in 1527.

The papacy did not respond to these disasters in a spirit of compromise, but with a determination to reassert its authority. In contrast to the Protestant values of austerity and simplicity, it encouraged the creation of grandiose architecture and works of art. Elaborate new churches and altarpieces were intended to evoke the same sense of awe and majesty that the great cathedrals of the Middle Ages had inspired.

Ecstasy of St. Theresa by Bernini, 1645–52

During the Counter-Reformation, artists injected a new sense of drama and passion into religious themes.

Baroque style: drama and complexity

The Baroque style developed to meet the needs of this Catholic revival. The term probably derived from *barroco*, Portuguese for an irregularly shaped pearl. The emphasis is on 'irregular,' as the Baroque implied a departure from the symmetry and harmony of the Renaissance. In architecture, this resulted in buildings conceived on a grand scale, featuring willfully complex designs and using the richest materials. The style was pioneered in Rome by the seventeenth-century painter, sculptor, and architect Gianlorenzo Bernini — who designed the colonnade in front of St. Peter's and the magnificent canopy over the High Altar — together with Francesco Borromini and Pietro da Cortona.

Baroque painters made similar attempts to appeal powerfully to the emotions and the senses. Artists like Caravaggio in Italy and Rembrandt in Protestant Holland sought to achieve this end through dramatic lighting effects, while others, such as Rubens, imbued the figures in their compositions with vigorous, sometimes contorted movements.

The renovated interior of St. Peter's, Rome, by Giovanni Paolo

The decision to rebuild St. Peter's, the most important church in the Catholic world, underlined the papacy's determination to increase its prestige.

Baroque music and the emergence of opera

In a musical context, 'Baroque' is a much less precise term, often used to suggest little more than an ornate and rather theatrical style. Composers of the time, however, were conscious of a break with the past. In 1605, Monteverdi made a firm distinction between a PRIMA PRATTICA and a SECONDA PRATTICA (first and second practice), the former referring to the intricate

Renaissance style of composition, the latter to a new emphasis on the clarity of the text. At the heart of the new style was the development of the BASSO CONTINUO (thorough bass), a system of notation for the secondary instruments.

Such innovations bore fruit almost immediately, helping to stimulate the emergence of opera. Since the 1570's, an informal academy in Florence known as the Camerata (Companionship) had met to discuss a variety of cultural topics. One of the subjects under consideration was ancient Greek drama, in which, it was believed, music had played a vital role. Several members attempted to revive the form, using 'recitative' (a method of solo singing reflecting the patterns of normal speech) as the means of conveying the dramatic dialogue to the audience. In so doing, they were effectively echoing Monteverdi's stricture that music should be subordinate to its text.

The oldest surviving opera is Jacopo Peri's *Euridice*, commissioned in 1600 for the festivities celebrating the marriage of Henri IV of France to the Florentine Maria de' Medici. However, the first masterpiece in the new genre was Monteverdi's 1607 opera *Orfeo*, which was composed for the Gonzaga family at Mantua. This was produced on an entirely different scale from the earlier experiments. While Peri had made use of just a few lutes and a harpsichord in his operas, keeping them discreetly hidden behind the scenery, Monteverdi employed a full orchestra consisting of some 40 instruments.

Engraving of an *intermedio* at the Uffizi Palace, Florence, 1617

Intermedi (interludes) were a blend of music and drama. This one was performed at the wedding celebrations of Ferdinando Gonzaga, Duke of Mantua.

The taste for opera spread; Rome and Venice became the new centers of musical excellence. Rome took the lead in the 1620's, largely because of patronage from high-ranking clergymen. Cardinal Barberini had a well-appointed opera house constructed in his palace in 1623, while one of the most talented librettists of the period, Giulio Rospigliosi, became pope in 1667. Venice was to all appearances a wealthy city, although the façades of its buildings often concealed the decay behind. Despite not having Rome's exalted operatic connections, it played a crucial role in bringing the genre to a wider audience.

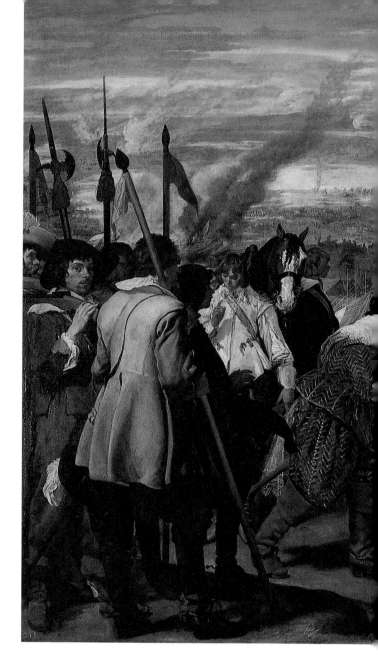

The first public opera house opened there in 1637, and at least 15 more were built before the end of the century. Each neighborhood had its local theater, similar to movie theaters today.

Italian divisions

Opera was the most exciting new art form of the age, consolidating the reputation of the Italian regions as the cultural focus of Europe. This fact belies the conception that political and artistic success go hand in hand, for the Italian peninsula then contained little more than a motley assortment of independent princedoms and satellite states. The glories of the regions might prove a draw to artists and connoisseurs. They also attracted invaders. Throughout the era, most of Italy was ruled by either Spain or Austria. Rome, the seat of the papacy, exerted influence among the Catholic nations, while Venice and Genoa were independent mercantile cities of some standing. Many of the remaining territories, however, were merely bargaining chips — petty possessions that were passed around between the greater European powers as they jostled for supremacy within the continent. This state of affairs persisted in some measure until the unification of Italy in the nineteenth century.

The Surrender at Breda by Velásquez, 1634–35

The Dutch town at Breda was a key stronghold in the war against Spain; it fell in June 1625 following a ten-month siege.

The Thirty Years' War

Italy's problems paled beside the destruction in central Europe caused by the Thirty Years' War, which plowed a bloody furrow across the continent between 1618 and 1648. The conflict had begun as a seemingly minor internal dispute within the Austrian Hapsburg Empire. In 1619, the Protestant citizens of Bohemia (now the Czech Republic) rejected the Catholic emperor Ferdinand II and chose Frederick the Elector Palatine as monarch. The next year, the Imperial forces reacted by defeating Frederick's army at the Battle of the White Mountain, and it appeared the rebellion had been quashed.

Instead, the religious overtones of the conflict soon triggered further violence. Fearing that the Catholic influence would spread farther north, two other Protestant powers, Denmark and Sweden, joined the fray. The Danish army proved no real threat and sued for peace at the Treaty of Lübeck in 1629. However, the Swedish forces, led by Gustavus

Adolphus, the so-called 'Lion of the North,' cut a swathe through the German provinces. Mainz and Munich both fell, and even Vienna came under threat. Only the death of Gustavus at the Battle of Lützen in 1632 threw the outcome of the war back into the balance.

A new twist was added in 1635, when the French became involved in the final phase of the conflict. Although a Catholic power, France sided with the Protestants of Holland and Sweden in a bid to undermine the powerful Hapsburg Empire. By and large, it was successful, and when the Peace of Westphalia finally brought an end to hostilities in 1648, France was established as the leading force in European affairs.

Civil war in England

While the last act of this protracted struggle was being played out, an equally destructive war raged on the other side of the Channel. There, too, religious and political differences intermingled with disastrous effect. On the surface, the reign of Charles I (1625–49) was blighted by a long-running constitutional dispute between the king and his parliament. Charles attempted to govern like an absolute monarch, but lacked the political flair to carry it off. For 11 years, he ruled without Parliament, until the outbreak of war in Scotland forced him to

The beheading of Charles I: detail from a contemporary Flemish painting

The trial and execution of a monarch by his subjects were unprecedented events that horrified courts across Europe.

recall the governing body in 1640. Behind the inevitable resentment that had simmered during these years of 'tyranny' there lay a growing suspicion about the king's commitment to the Church of England. Charles's Catholic queen was deeply unpopular and, when the Archbishop of Canterbury revamped the Anglican liturgy, critics condemned it as an imitation of the Roman Mass. So, when the Civil War finally erupted in 1642, it was not surprising that the Puritan factions should ally themselves with Parliament against the king.

The struggle between the Royalists and the Parliamentarians — one of whose leaders was Oliver Cromwell, a committed Puritan — was to last for seven years. Following catastrophic defeats at the battles of Marston Moor in 1644 and Naseby in 1645, the initiative drifted away from the king. He surrendered at Newark in 1646. Supporters of the parliamentary cause agonized for some time over what should be done with their regal captive, but in the end, compromise proved impossible. Charles was put on trial and was beheaded at Whitehall in 1649.

England was declared a Republic and named the 'Commonwealth.' This state of affairs continued for just 11 years; for much of that time the reality of power was vested not in parliament but in Cromwell, who assumed the title of Lord Protector in 1653. Under his leadership, Britain regained much of its authority abroad — winning victories in Ireland, gaining possession of Dunkirk and Jamaica, and successfully concluding the Anglo–Dutch War. None of this counted for

anything, though, when the monarchy was restored in 1660 two years after Cromwell's death and Charles II ascended the throne. Cromwell's body was exhumed from its resting place in Westminster Abbey and hanged on the gallows at Tyburn, near London, the place of execution for criminals. His head was impaled on a pole and displayed outside parliament.

The New World: trade and colonization

While the countries of Europe were occupied with such turbulent events, they were also increasingly concerned with affairs in the New World across the Atlantic, as well as with their better-established trading concerns in the Indies (southern Asia). In the sixteenth century, colonial expansion had been largely limited to Portugal and, especially, Spain, whose conquistadors established a large empire in Central and South America, destroying the Aztec civilization in the process. In the early years of the seventeenth century the eastern seaboard of North America was settled by France, Britain, and Holland,

Dutch trading post at Hugly, painted in 1665

The Dutch East India Company was the cornerstone of Holland's maritime success. Hugly, situated on the banks of the Ganges, was its headquarters in Bengal.

Engraving of English colonists in Virginia by de Bry, 1590

One of the earliest English ventures in the New World was the settlement founded by Sir Walter Raleigh in Virginia. He named it after Elizabeth I, 'the Virgin Queen.'

Initially, therefore, the newly discovered parts of the world were viewed as an unlimited opportunity for commercial exploitation and profit. Increasingly, however, these areas, particularly the Americas, were settled, often by people seeking to escape religious persecution. In 1605, French settlers established Quebec; in 1612, New Amsterdam (now New York) was founded by the Dutch on Manhattan Island; and in 1620, the Pilgrim Fathers — Puritan Separatists who had fled England — established Plymouth as the first permanent colony in New England. As the first successful bases in the colonization of the continent by the rival European powers, such settlements marked a significant phase in the great European expansion that had begun in the 1490's with Columbus and da Gama. The New World was viewed by many as offering real hope for new ways of life.

English opera

In England, in the mid-sixteenth century, the influence of the Puritans ushered in an era of austerity. The theaters were closed down for the duration of the Commonwealth, soldiers were quartered in Westminster Abbey, and a large portion of King Charles I's splendid art collection was sold off. Ironically, the same period also witnessed the first stirrings of English opera. Plays set to music qualified as 'concerts' and thus escaped the ban that affected the stage. Hence *The Siege of Rhodes*, which was first performed in 1656 and was described by its authors as 'a story sung in recitative musick,' has been tentatively acknowledged as the earliest English opera. In truth, this and most of its immediate successors might be defined more accurately as 'semi-operas.' Henry Purcell, whose father had been one of the performers in *The Siege of Rhodes*, wrote several semi-operas, among them *The Fairy Queen* and *King Arthur*,

and competition for the seemingly endless possibilities of overseas wealth was fierce. Overseas trading companies were set up by governments to exploit the production of valuable commodities, each having a trading monopoly in a given area and often wielding considerable political influence. The most famous of these were the British, Dutch, and French East India Companies. In the Americas, the growth of valuable export products such as coffee, sugar, and tobacco came to depend on slave labor. A trading triangle developed in which slaves were taken from Africa and traded for goods in the Americas, where they were set to work in the plantations — the ships that had brought them meanwhile returned with their cargoes to Europe, where their owners amassed fabulous wealth.

and also produced the first English opera of genuine merit with his *Dido and Aeneas* in 1689.

The expanding role of music

Although the church and the court remained the principal sources of patronage, it gradually became accepted that music might also serve a useful purpose outside these relatively limited circles, in Britain and elsewhere. Vivaldi, for example, was employed for much of his career as a violin teacher at the Pio Ospedale della Pietà in Venice, an orphanage for girls. The regular performances given by the girls under Vivaldi's direction were not commercial undertakings — public concerts of this sort did not really take root until the Classical era — but rather emblems of civic pride.

The broadening appeal of music had several important consequences. First, it led to an extraordinary increase in the volume of music that was required. The concept of playing the 'classics' or of having a stock repertoire did not exist. New pieces of music were composed and then discarded at an alarming rate, Vivaldi's notoriously prodigious output being an example of this. Sometimes, they would be played only once — perhaps for a particular occasion — before being set aside and forgotten. This, in turn, meant that the ability to write quickly was essential. A hastily produced piece of music was not seen as the telltale sign of a casual attitude but rather as proof of the composer's professional skill.

Detail of *A Musical Celebration* by Giovanni Panini, c.1729

This sumptuous event was organized by the French ambassador in Rome to mark the birth of the Dauphin in 1729.

Closely allied to this was the growing importance of the individual performer. The Baroque era was the age of the showman — the virtuoso. For the first time, both singers and instrumentalists were really encouraged to stretch their talents to the limit. In the realm of opera, this made stars of the castrati — male singers whose beautiful, youthful voices were artificially maintained through castration. This practice was at its peak during the heyday of the Baroque Italian opera. These virtuosos did, however, help to undermine the sort of dramatic tension that had been achieved in the type of opera developed by Monteverdi. Increasingly the recitative, which carried the storyline of the play, was interrupted by more and more arias — often complex, beautiful, set-piece melodies in which the singers could show off their skills.

Exhibitionist tendencies were not confined simply to vocalists. Composers, equally, were eager to put their talents in the spotlight. One of the most popular ways of doing this was to create music that mimicked natural sounds. *The Four Seasons* by Vivaldi, with its birdsong and weather effects, is probably the best-known example, but the practice became commonplace. Johann Kuhnau's *Biblical Sonatas* contained a clever imitation of the sound of David unleashing his sling

Detail of a painting of Versailles by Pierre Martin, 1722

Louis XIV transformed Versailles into the most splendid court in Europe, making it a potent symbol of his personal authority.

against Goliath — played on a harpsichord, of all things. J. S. Bach used the same instrument to convey the noise of coach horns in his *Capriccio on the Departure of a Beloved Brother*. But the supreme keyboard virtuoso was Domenico Scarlatti: hidden within the compositions that he produced for the Spanish court were ingenious imitations of street cries, strumming guitars, and hoofbeats.

This kind of showmanship surfaced partly because musical entertainments were growing longer — a full-scale opera, for example, gave composers far greater scope for elaboration — and partly because instruments were becoming more sophisticated. The main development here was in the field of violin manufacture. The violin had appeared in the early years of the sixteenth century, but it was in the Baroque era that the town of Cremona in Italy produced the three giants of violin-making — Nicolò Amati, Giuseppe Guarneri, and, most famous of all, Antonio Stradivari.

The fact that a provincial Italian city should have become the center for such an important craft is no coincidence, for Italy remained the dominant musical force in Europe throughout most of this period. Composers as diverse as Bach and Handel both had their roots in Italian styles, while Jean-

Baptiste Lully, the musician who did most to devise a distinctive national school in France, was actually born Giovanni Battista Lulli, an Italian.

Louis XIV: the Sun King

The emergence of an independent style of music in France was hardly surprising, given the political strength of the country during the long reign of Louis XIV (1643–1715). The king was less than five years old when he acceded to the throne, his early years clouded by a series of civil disturbances called the *Frondes* (after the slings used by the rioters). At times, the violence grew so bad that the child had to be hustled away from Paris to St. Germain, where he slept on straw. The memory of these terrifying episodes left Louis with a permanent dislike of Paris and a pathological loathing of disorder.

Accordingly, when he was old enough to manage his affairs, the king determined to leave his hated capital and move the seat of government to his newly enlarged château at Versailles. Believing literally in the divine right of kings, he was anxious to reduce the influence of the old nobility and the *parlement* (the powerful Paris law court), concentrating all power in his own hands. He kept the nobles in check by encouraging them to lose themselves in the excesses of his court at Versailles, corrupting them with a dazzlingly extravagant life-style and thus weakening their capacity to act against him. However, there was much more to Louis's reign than superficial display: under his rule, France acquired new road systems, ports and canals, a modern police force, navy and merchant marine, a manufacturing industry, and a flourishing export business. '*L'État c'est Moi*' ('I am the State') was Louis's motto, an eloquent description of absolutism.

In cultural matters as much as in politics, Louis exercised complete control, presiding over a golden age in the arts. France became the epitome of civilization, envied and emulated by the rest of Europe. French classical drama was at its peak, exemplified in the tragedies of Corneille and Racine, as well as in the satirical comedies of Molière. The same period also witnessed the creation of the Royal Academy of Painting and Sculpture in 1648 and the reorganization of the Gobelins, the celebrated tapestry factory, in 1662. Louis became known as *le Roi Soleil* (the Sun King), a reflection of the splendor and brilliance of his regime.

Music, too, had the king's stamp on it. Louis surrounded himself with music, in his personal life and on ceremonial occasions; his military victories would be celebrated with specially composed Te Deums. A musician and enthusiastic dancer himself, Louis actively encouraged the development of the *comédie-ballet*, a new operatic form that grew out of a collaboration between Lully and Molière. This extravagant mixture of song, dance, comedy, and spectacle was supremely elegant and formal, yet also much lighter than the prevailing strains of Italian opera, having been adapted to suit French tastes.

The splendor of the court at Versailles eclipsed all others and spawned countless imitations. Critics later argued that it isolated the monarch from his subjects and, in so doing, sowed the seeds of the French Revolution. There may be some truth in this, but there was, nevertheless, a logic behind Louis's actions. Like the papacy at the start of the century, he was seeking to project an aura of grandeur that would make the monarchy an institution worthy of reverence, inspiring both loyalty and obedience.

During the first half of Louis's reign, this grandiose image was reinforced by victories on the battlefield. In 1667, he invaded the Spanish-controlled southern Netherlands. His initial advance was checked, but a second invasion in 1672 was more successful, and the Dutch only managed to hold him back by opening their dikes and flooding the country. Louis's triumphs were recognized in the Treaty of Nijmegen (1678), when Hainaut and the Franche-Comté were ceded to France.

The golden age of Holland

Despite setbacks such as these, the United Provinces of Holland (the northern part of the Netherlands, which had won independence from Spain in the previous century) enjoyed a golden age of their own at this time. The Republic's extensive trade with the Baltic region and the Indies had helped to turn Amsterdam into the financial capital of the world, and the city's banking, insurance, and share-dealing services had boosted its reputation still further. This prosperity, and the sense of security it generated, served to stimulate a flowering of the arts and

sciences. Christiaan Huyghens invented the pendulum clock, while Anton van Leeuwenhoek and Jan Swammerdam made important discoveries in the field of microscopy. In the art world Holland produced geniuses of the stature of Rembrandt, Vermeer, and Frans Hals. Musically, the most significant figure was Jan Sweelinck, sometimes known as 'the Father of the Fugue,' who was the city organist in Amsterdam from 1577 until 1621. His teachings made him a household name as far afield as Poland, although he is probably best remembered today for his influence on J. S. Bach.

A Woman and her Maid by Pieter de Hooch, mid-17th century

In contrast to the grandeur of much Baroque art, Dutch painters liked to depict simple, everyday scenes. Their pictures were intended for the affluent middle classes.

Music and the Protestant Church

In Germany, as in Holland, organ music played a crucial role in Protestant worship. It is necessary to distinguish between the Lutherans and the more extreme followers of Calvin. Martin Luther had been an enthusiastic musician — he possessed a fine tenor voice and composed music himself — and he actively encouraged the continuing tradition of church music. This was in sharp contrast to the Calvinists, who, in keeping with their precepts of religious asceticism, prohibited organ music and tore out the instruments from their places of worship.

These acts of ideological vandalism were particularly disturbing to many communities, as the organ was seen as a tangible symbol of municipal pride. Indeed, individual cities vied to sign up the most prestigious performers on the organ with a rivalry often as intense as the competition between present-day football teams. At Leipzig in 1723, for example, the city council were disappointed when they only managed to secure the services of Bach as their Director of Music. He had been their third choice after Telemann, who had used the situation to demand a raise in salary at his post in Hamburg, and Graupner,

An organ from Freiburg Cathedral, Germany, 1710–14

Protestants tended to make their services as plain as possible. Music was often exempted from this stricture, as many communities regarded their organ as an emblem of civic pride.

who was still under contract to another employer. Perhaps because he was not a technical innovator, Bach enjoyed a comparatively modest reputation in his own lifetime.

The career of Handel could hardly have been more different, although he was born in the same year as Bach. Where the latter was content to continue working in provincial seclusion, Handel sought and found the limelight, enjoying a roller-coaster career in London as both composer and impresario. His methods could be unconventional — there is a story that he once dangled one of his divas out of a window and threatened to drop her if her singing did not improve — but they soon brought him international acclaim. When the fashion for Italian opera began to wane, Handel switched his attentions to its religious equivalent, the ORATORIO.

The end of an era

The fact that Handel chose to settle in London, which had hitherto been something of a backwater in operatic terms, may well reflect the shift that had taken place in the European balance of power.

After 1680, the supremacy of the French began to look less secure. In the East, the threat of a Turkish invasion receded when Jan Sobieski and his Polish forces relieved the siege of Vienna in 1683. This, however, left the Austrian emperor free to turn his attention toward the West. Five years later, Louis XIV suffered the even greater blow of England's 'Glorious Revolution,' when the Catholic James II was ousted from the English throne, to be replaced by his old adversaries, William and Mary (respectively Stadholder of the Netherlands and James's daughter). The presence of Protestant monarchs across the Channel was all the more disastrous in the wake of the Revocation of the Edict of Nantes in 1685. With this act, Louis had canceled the rights to freedom of worship that had been granted in 1598, provoking the hostility of the entire Protestant cause.

The scale of the problem became apparent during the War of the Spanish Succession (1701–14), when French troops were committed on four separate fronts — in Germany, the Netherlands, Italy, and Spain. Resounding defeats at Blenheim in 1704 and Malplaquet in 1709 threatened to undo all Louis's achievements, although the unexpected victory at Denain in 1712 partly retrieved the situation. The Treaty of Utrecht in 1713 left France territorially intact, but brought great benefits to the growing British Empire, including the acquisition of Gibraltar, Minorca, and Nova Scotia.

The death of Louis XIV in 1715 after a 72-year reign marked the passing of an era. Jeers and catcalls could be heard at his funeral procession, signifying the death knell of absolutism. In France, the theologian and writer François Fénelon argued that the divine right claimed by the monarchy contravened Christian teachings; in England, philosopher John Locke asserted that it was incompatible with the inalienable rights of the individual. People were beginning to challenge the notion that the authority of a pope or a king should be accepted without reservation. The Baroque, with all its emphasis on grandeur and obedience, was giving way to the rational values of the Enlightenment.

MUSICAL DEFINITIONS

ORATORIO Extended musical setting of a (usually) religious text with solo voices, chorus, and orchestra. Developed in Rome in the mid-17th century, it had a similar structure to an opera but was presented in concert rather than acted out on stage.

Featured Composers

Monteverdi

Claudio Monteverdi 1567–1643

RECOMMENDED WORK
Vespro della Beata Vergine (Vespers)
L'Oiseau-Lyre 425 823-2
New London Consort/Philip Pickett
Monteverdi's Vespers service — a collection principally of choral concertos, psalms, and plainchant — is given a breathtaking performance by this British ensemble. Although a small number of performers is used, there is no lack of splendor or power — try especially the duet between the two sopranos in 'Pulchra es.'

REPRESENTATIVE WORKS
La favola d'Orfeo
L'incoronazione di Poppea
Madrigals — Hor ch'el ciel e la terra; Non havea Febo ancora, 'Lamento di Ninfa'; Zefiro torna
Beatus vir

Portrait of a musician, believed to be Monteverdi, possibly by the Italian artist Cremonesi, *c.*1600

Monteverdi had a somewhat disrupted childhood. The son of a chemist who actually practiced medicine (at that time an illegal act usually undertaken surreptitiously from small shops or stalls), he was born in Cremona, Italy, and had a brother and sister. Their mother, Maddalena, died when he was nine; their father's second wife when he was 16. The following year their father married a third time and finally became recognized by the Milanese authorities for his medical work. Despite these disruptions, Monteverdi received a good musical education under the cathedral's Maestro di Cappella. By the age of 15 he had already published a three-part motet, at 16 the first of his eight books of madrigals appeared, and the next year a book of his canzonettas.

At the age of 17, Monteverdi entered the service of the powerful Gonzaga family in Mantua as a string player. This rich and ornate court was then under the musical guidance of Flemish composer Giaches de Wert. Gradually Monteverdi's status grew and he eventually became part of the Duke of Mantua's traveling court on his military expeditions in Europe, particularly to Danube in 1595 and Flanders in 1599. De Wert died in 1596 and Monteverdi entertained hopes of taking his place as Maestro di Cappella, but this did not happen until 1601. Around this time he married a court singer named Claudia, who bore him three children, two of whom survived.

In 1607, Monteverdi's opera *La favola d'Orfeo* (The Legend of Orpheus) was premiered at Mantua. Although Jacopo Peri had composed the first-ever opera some years before, Monteverdi's was the first to use an array of instruments and to employ music as an integral feature of the work, rather than mere decoration. Unlike previous settings of the Orpheus legend, including one by Peri that Monteverdi would have studied, Monteverdi's work retained the original tragic ending — Orpheus losing Euridice when he looked behind him upon leaving the underworld. Also novel was Monteverdi's use of stringed instruments to represent the character of Orpheus, who is traditionally associated with the lyre.

Also in 1607, Monteverdi's wife died, a blow compounded by poverty, overwork, and illness. With an eye on a lucrative church appointment in Rome or Venice, Monteverdi attempted his first foray into sacred music with the famous *Vespro della Beata Vergine*, or *Vespers*, of 1610, a collection of movements notable for combining polyphonic vocal writing typical of the late Renaissance with newer Baroque techniques. These emphasized one melodic line combined with a well-defined bass, and increased the use of instruments.

Interior of Teatro Olimpico, Vicenza, built *c.*1580
Palladio's magnificent stage captured the spirit of the classical world.

Monteverdi's long-cherished ambition to leave the service of the Duke of Mantua was finally realized in 1612 when the Duke died. The following year Monteverdi was appointed Maestro di Cappella of St. Mark's in Venice. There he gradually built up the standards of the choir, commissioned some important new repertoire from leading composers, and himself composed a stream of sacred works for which he became renowned throughout Europe.

As Monteverdi grew older, his pace of work slowed, although he wrote the music for a Mass of Thanksgiving in 1631, celebrating the end of the plague that had ravaged Venice the previous year. In 1632 he was admitted to holy orders, and he would probably have drifted from public attention had it not been for the opening in Venice of the first public opera house in 1637. This renewed his interest in opera, and toward the end of his life he composed *Il ritorno d'Ulisse* (The Return of Ulysses) and *L'incoronazione di Poppea* (The Coronation of Poppea). These operas further developed the techniques used in *La favola d'Orfeo,* and featured characters that were recognizably human, rather than symbolic.

Monteverdi made one final visit to Cremona in 1643, and died in November of the same year, having just returned to Venice. He was buried in Venice in the vast Gothic basilica, the Frari, in a tomb at the very center of the church, near that of the great Venetian artist Titian, whose masterpiece, the *Assumption,* towers above the high altar.

Monteverdi lived and worked in a period of change, as the late Renaissance was giving way to the Baroque. Although he eschewed revolutionary means, he encouraged this transition, and used his genius to develop and transform every aspect of music he came into contact with. The eight books of madrigals published in his lifetime, in which he introduced instrumental accompaniments and exploited to the full the dramatic possibilities of the medium, taken together with the *Vespers* and his ground-breaking operas, confirm Monteverdi's crucial position in the history of music.

Allegri

Gregorio Allegri 1582–1652

RECOMMENDED WORK

Miserere
Disc: 'Italian Sacred Choral Works'
Archiv Produktion 415 517-2
Westminster Abbey Choir/Simon Preston
Boys' voices from a Church of England choir sing the Miserere, with its justly famous soaring treble or soprano line, in a recording that has stood the test of time. The disc includes other examples of Italian late Renaissance and early Baroque sacred music.

REPRESENTATIVE WORKS
Missa Vidi turbam magnam
Dilectus meus
Sinfonia in G major

Portrait of Allegri from an engraving dated 1619

Little is known of Allegri's parents or home life. From the age of nine he was a choirboy in Rome, going on to become a tenor at San Luigi dei Francesi in Rome, where he remained between the ages of 14 and 22. He then studied under the composer Giovanni Nanini until he was nearly 30, an intensive period of learning during which he was strongly influenced by Palestrina. From 1607 to 1621 he was a singer and composer at Fermo, then at

Tivoli; finally he progressed to the rank of Maestro di Cappella at the church of Santo Spirito in Sassia (Rome), by which time he was 46 and had had 37 years of musical training and practice.

Toward the end of 1630, at the age of 48, Allegri joined Urban VIII's papal choir. In this inspiring environment, not only did his singing develop but he was able to evolve new compositional ideas. The legacy of Palestrina's teaching, together with his own experience in the papal choir, led Allegri to write a number of works for the choir's use. Among these was his setting of the Penitential Psalm 51, the famous *Miserere*.

In essence, this is a simple chant on one chord sung by an unaccompanied five-part choir with a second four-part choir adding further elements, including passages for solo treble which climb to a high C — a rarity at that time. The effect was to give a supreme, ethereal quality to the music that enhanced its celebration of the glory of God.

The *Miserere* was written to be part of the important Holy Week celebrations at St. Peter's in Rome, and it proved so powerful that it became a traditional part of the Holy Week service sung in the Sistine Chapel every year. The musical score of the work was kept under guard; only three copies are known to have existed. To copy it was an offense punishable by excommunication. Wide-scale performance of the *Miserere* became possible only after Mozart, at the age of 14, wrote out the complete score from memory after listening to only one or two performances.

Allegri's music was sung for more than 100 years in the Sistine Chapel, especially his six- and eight-part Masses. In these, like Palestrina, he used the *a cappella* technique of writing for unaccompanied voices, featuring instruments only when they doubled the vocal parts. He also published a number of compositions that were influenced by the musical fashions of northern Italy and not suited to the religious needs of Rome. Allegri's music subtly explored new musical ground, combining his decades of discipline and experience in church music with elements of madrigals and dance rhythms.

Key to Recommended Works

arr. arrangement (by)	**contr** contralto	**hpd** harpsichord	**Op., Opp.** Opus(es)	**pno** piano	**ten** tenor	**vcl** violoncello ('cello)
bar baritone	**gtr** guitar	**mez** mezzo-soprano	**org** organ	**sop** soprano	**treb** treble	**vln** violin

Schütz

Heinrich Schütz 1585–1672

RECOMMENDED WORK

Musicalische Exequien
Disc: 'Sacred Choral Works'
Archiv Produktion 423 405-2
Monteverdi Choir; English Baroque Soloists/John
Eliot Gardiner
*The Musicalische Exequien, called a 'concerto in the
form of a Burial Mass,' is given an assertive reading
— listen for the atmospheric concluding section, the
'Nunc dimittis.' The recording also includes four richly
characterful motets.*

REPRESENTATIVE WORKS
Christmas Story
Fili mi, Absalon
St. John Passion
Latin Magnificat

Contemporary portrait of the composer

Schütz was born in Köstritz in modern-day Germany and received a musical education. First a choirboy, he went in 1609 to study with Giovanni Gabrieli in Venice, where he was exposed to Italian musical influences. He moved to Dresden in spring 1617, married the daughter of a court official, and rose in influence as the

Engraving from the *Geistreiches Gesangbuch* (1676)
Schütz directing the court choir in Dresden. The building is shown after the restorations of 1662, by which time Schütz was no longer Kapellmeister.

director of the leading musical center of Protestant Germany, under the patronage of Johann Georg I, Elector of Saxony.

April 1627 was spent at the elector's castle at Hartenfels celebrating the marriage of the elector's daughter. On April 12, Schütz premiered his pastoral tragicomedy *Daphne*. The score has not survived, but *Daphne* is considered the first German opera and initiated a great tradition in Germany. After the marriage, Schütz visited Italy and spent time with Monteverdi in Venice.

In 1635, Prince Heinrich of Reuss, Schütz's patron and friend, died. The prince left precise details of the music he wanted for his funeral, and Schütz responded by writing his largest and most important funeral work, the *Musicalische Exequien*. The work is in several sections and calls for various combinations of soloists and choirs with a cello and harpsichord accompaniment.

The financial pressures caused by the Thirty Years' War led to a depletion of the Dresden court's resources. Schütz was therefore pleased to travel to Copenhagen when asked by the Crown Prince of Denmark to arrange the music for his wedding in 1634. Schütz rose to become Kapellmeister, and after a similar post in Hanover returned to Dresden in 1645.

Now approaching 60, Schütz sought retirement. This was denied, but he was allowed to work only six months of each year for the following decade. He sought full retirement on three further occasions, complaining of the shameful state of the court musicians, which failed to inspire him. Eventually, Elector Georg died (in 1656) and his replacement granted the release Schütz so richly deserved. Schütz continued to compose during retirement, concentrating as he had throughout his life on sacred music. *Christmas Story*, based on Gospel texts, was first performed in 1660; and around 1665 he wrote the *St. John Passion*, one of three Passions from late in Schütz's life, which in line with liturgical practice in Dresden feature unaccompanied voices. It is considered one of the pinnacles of the composer's work and influenced Bach when he came to write his great Passion settings. At the end of his life Schütz suffered from failing eyesight and hearing, and in his eighty-fourth year he died following a stroke. His compositions managed to amalgamate the ornateness of the Italian Baroque with the more sober musical traditions of Germany, a grafting of styles that was a vital part of Schütz's great contribution to German music.

Carissimi

Giacomo Carissimi 1605–1674

RECOMMENDED WORKS

Jephte
Jonas
Judicium Extremum
Erato 2292-45466-2
Ruth Holton (sop); Susan Hemington Jones (sop);
Nigel Robson (ten); Mark Tucker (ten); Stephen
Varcoe (bar); Monteverdi Choir; His Majesties
Sagbutts and Cornetts; English Baroque
Soloists/John Eliot Gardiner
*This recording testifies to Carissimi's ability to bring
changing moods and characterization to a score.
Jephte and Jonas are the stronger of the three early
Baroque oratorios on the disc. The Monteverdi Choir
delivers the biblical texts with great sensitivity — listen
particularly for two of its soloists, Ruth Holton and
Susan Hemington Jones.*

REPRESENTATIVE WORKS

Baltazar
Historia divitis
A piè d'un verdee alloro
Vittoria, mio core
Lucifer caelistis olim

Giacomo Carissimi, born in Marini, near
Rome, was the youngest child of an artisan
and grew up against the background of
religious reform in Europe. A member of
the Tivoli cathedral choir and an organist
there until 1627, he found his real niche at

Portrait engraving of Carissimi by L. Visscher after
W. Vaillant

the Collegio Germanico in Rome. This
was a leading center of Jesuit teaching.
The Jesuits at that time had a particular
influence in strengthening the Catholic
Church through a program of education
and missionary work. Carissimi became
Maestro di Cappella in 1629; during his
service, the talent of the young composer
fused with the energies and objectives of
the Jesuit order. Despite invitations to
serve the Governor of the Netherlands in
Brussels, and the chance to follow in
Monteverdi's footsteps at St. Mark's,
Venice, in 1643, Carissimi elected to continue his work with the Jesuits. He
remained in Rome all his life, dedicating
himself to the development of the boys'
choir, to the general students, and to the
musical output of the college and its associated church Sant' Apollinare.

Carissimi became the teacher of many
other composers and gained a reputation
throughout Europe. His main areas of
musical interest as a composer were the
cantata and the oratorio. His cantatas, such
as *A piè d'un verdee alloro*, written around
1650, were strongly influenced by Luigi
Rossi's work earlier in the century, and in
many of these works he experimented
with varying approaches to arias. His work
with oratorios was seminal and can be said
to have helped to create this musical form
— even if its actual name emerged only
later. In works such as *Jephte*, *Jonas*, and
Baltazar, Carissimi drew on Old Testament
texts and used a narrative voice, divided
among several singers, to tell the story. He
also used choruses, whether for dramatic,
narrative, or meditative purposes, as an
integral part of the works.

Regrettably, much of Carissimi's work
exists only in copied form — most of his
original manuscripts were lost after the
dissolution of the Jesuit order in 1773.
However, his influence notably pervaded
the thinking of several other composers.
The works of Charpentier, who studied
under Carissimi in the 1650's, and Handel,
whose oratorios *Samson* and *Alexander's
Feast* bear certain similarities to Carissimi's
Jephte, confirm Carissimi's status as one
of Italy's most influential seventeenth-
century composers.

Engraving of a Baroque choral group by Corvinus
**A notable feature of Baroque church
music was the use of two contrasting
choirs, a practice originating in Venice.**

Lully

Jean-Baptiste Lully 1632–1687

RECOMMENDED WORK

Armide
Harmonia Mundi HMC90 1456/7
Guillemette Laurens (mez) Armide; Howard
Crook (ten) Renaud; Véronique Gens (sop);
Noémi Rime (sop); Collegium Vocale; La Chapelle
Royale Orchestra/Philippe Herreweghe
*A striking display of the sophisticated beauties of
French Baroque secular music. The mainly French
performers deliver the mythic tale of the sorceress
warrior Armide, involved in a love battle with the
knight Renaud, with clarity and skill. Laurens and
Crook sing with beauty and precision.*

REPRESENTATIVE WORKS
Miserere
Salve regina
Alceste
Atys

Portrait engraving of the composer

Louis XIV as 'the Sun King', 1651

***Louis XIV took an enthusiastic interest in
the musical life of his court, frequently
performing in costume.***

Born Giovanni Battista Lulli, a miller's son
from Florence, Lully grew up with no significant connections with music. At the
age of 14 he was hired by Roger de
Loraine (Chevalier de Guise) to go to Paris
and help his niece, Mlle. de Montpensier,
practice Italian. In her employ at the
Tuileries Court for six years, Lully gained
access to balls and court entertainments,
building up a knowledge of the dances and
themes of the time that became the models
for his early works. He also studied various
musical instruments, developed his dancing, and was coached in composition.

Mlle. de Montpensier was exiled when
Lully was 20, but the composer retained
his circle of contacts in Paris, to the extent
that early in 1653 he danced with the 14-
year-old King Louis XIV in a ballet. They
were clearly dancing in step; by March,
Lully had been appointed 'Compositeur
de la Musique Instrumentale du Roi,'
responsible for music in court ballets. He
became known for his dancing, compositions, conducting, and comic abilities.

In 1661 he started describing himself as
'Jean-Baptiste de Lully, esquire, son of
Laurent de Lully, Florentine gentleman.'
Once granted naturalization, he married
Madeleine Lambert, daughter of the king's
master of chamber music. The marriage
contract was signed by Louis XIV.

From 1664, Lully collaborated with the
great comic dramatist Molière. Together
they created a series of comedy-ballets,
including *Le Bourgeois Gentilhomme*, in
which Lully turned to good account his
years of observing dance and theater at the
court. Lully and Molière parted company
after *Le Bourgeois Gentilhomme*, and in 1673
Lully wrote the first of his *tragédies lyriques*.
These featured continuous music, arias,
recitative, and choruses, and dominated
French opera until the mid-eighteenth
century. The librettist for this first venture, *Cadmus et Hermione*, was Philippe
Quinault, who became Lully's regular collaborator and author of the text of their
most famous work, *Armide*. Particularly
significant in the latter opera is its attention
to development of character and the
attempt to form a psychological portrait of
the main character, Armide. Other collaborations between Quinault and Lully
included *Alceste* (1674) and *Atys* (1676).

Lully had already obtained, through
royal decree, a monopoly on music performance in Paris. After Molière's death the
king granted him the playwright's old theater, the Palais Royal, free of charge. He
was also granted a number of patents giving him yet more control over French
stage performances — any non-Lully production had to limit its musicians to a max-
imum of just eight players, including the
singers. Lully's position of power was the
cause of much ill will against him, but this
did not prevent his promotion to the noble
rank of Secrétaire du Roi.

By the time he died, Lully owned five
big houses, his humble beginnings long
forgotten. Ironically for so exalted a figure,
he suffered a somewhat ignominious end.
He stubbed his big toe while conducting a
celebration for Louis XIV's recovery from
illness, causing an abscess followed by gan-
grene, from which he died.

The celebration of love and courtly
behavior in Lully's works ensured that he
pleased the right people, but he was also
responsible for some substantial musical
achievements. Lully absorbed elements of
both Italian and French styles, and through
his annual productions with Quinault
became the leading French theatrical composer of the seventeenth century.

Charpentier

Marc-Antoine Charpentier c.1645–1704

RECOMMENDED WORKS
Te Deum
Missa Assumpta est Maria
Disc: 'Sacred Choral Works'
Harmonia Mundi HMC90 1298
Les Arts Florissants/William Christie
William Christie, the American director of this French vocal and instrumental ensemble, has done much to rehabilitate the music of Charpentier. Here he combines the Missa Assumpta est Maria (surely the culmination of Charpentier's writing of sacred choral music) with the ceremonial Te Deum, which fairly oozes a sense of grandeur, not least in the famous opening Prelude.

REPRESENTATIVE WORKS
Messe de minuit pour Noël
Miserere mei
Te Deum
Actéon
Médée
Pastorale sur la Naissance de Notre Seigneur Jésus Christ

La Comédie Française by Watteau, after 1716
This, the national theater company of France, was founded in 1680, when Louis XIV amalgamated several rival troupes of actors.

Virtually nothing is known about Charpentier's early life — even his date of birth is uncertain. What is generally agreed is that he studied counterpoint and choral writing under Giacomo Carissimi in Rome for a time, and readily embraced the Italian music of the mid-seventeenth century. As a result, his initial compositions did not find a ready place in his native France; they were performed away from fashionable circles. Some of his first commissions were from the Duchess of Guise, and he remained in her service until her death in 1688, writing motets, dramatic works and sacred material for the convents in which she had interests. These were all pieces with the unusual feature of being composed specifically for performance by female voices.

When Lully moved on from his work with the French dramatists, leaving Molière without a collaborator, Molière approached Charpentier. Together they developed productions for his theatrical company, which in time would be known as the Comédie Française. Charpentier created new overtures and *intermèdes* to replace Lully's, and even after Molière's death in 1673 continued to work with this famed troupe.

In the early 1680's he was employed by the dauphin, the king's eldest son. He wrote a grand motet to mark the death of Queen Marie-Thérèse, as well as a number of well-received sacred works and two large-scale dramatic works. He later became music teacher to both the Regent of France and to the Duke of Chartres.

Charpentier's love for music and his ability to progress without courtly favors made him a perfect candidate for the position of Maître de Musique and composer to the church of St. Louis, the main Jesuit church in Paris. At this time the Jesuits were an influential force; Charpentier wrote Latin dramas for their colleges as well as a great deal of music for their services. So illustrious a position in French musical life allowed the composer to combine his early Italian influences with his interest in drama. In 1693, *Médée*, Charpentier's only *tragédie lyrique*, modeled on Lully's work, was performed, but with little success.

Early in the summer of 1698, Charpentier was appointed Maître de Musique at Ste.-Chapelle, the second most prestigious musical position in all France (the first being the directorship of the Royal Chapel at Versailles). He occupied the post until his death in 1704 and there wrote some of his most impressive music, including the *Missa Assumpta est Maria*. This Mass displays a vast range of expression and shows Charpentier's skill at contrasting chorus and orchestra. The *Te Deum*, also written at Ste.-Chapelle, features a four-part choir with eight soloists, and shows Charpentier's total command of religious music, combined with a rare gift for melodic writing.

Pachelbel

Johann Pachelbel 1653–1706

RECOMMENDED WORK
Canon and Gigue in D
Disc: 'Baroque Classics'
Angel CDM7 69853-2
Taverner Players/Andrew Parrott
Many listeners may be put off Baroque instrumental music, either by its remoteness from our own times or by the hard, strident sounds that some 'authentic performances' might produce. Here, however, is a recital of the crème de la crème of Baroque fare — a thoroughly pleasurable collection of 'hits,' including Pachelbel's inventive Canon and Gigue, performed with joy and relish.

REPRESENTATIVE WORKS
Magnificat in D
Christ lag in Todesbanden
Chaconnes

Organ from monastery church at Bamberg, c.1730
Pachelbel's skill both as a player and as a composer would have been perfected on an instrument such as this.

Like Allegri, whose famed *Miserere* eclipsed everything else he achieved in his career, Johann Pachelbel's name is automatically linked to the ever-popular three-part *Canon in D*. Born in Nuremberg in the autumn of 1653, Pachelbel showed an early appetite for learning. In addition to school, he had two music teachers, one who introduced him to the fundamentals of music while the other taught him to play and compose. He was briefly at the University of Altdorf before taking a position in 1673 as assistant organist at the cathedral of St. Stephen in Vienna. Four years later he became the court organist to the Duke of Saxe-Eisenach. He became restless there, and requesting a letter of reference from his employers, left after a year. His reference described him as a 'rare and perfect virtuoso.'

Subsequently Pachelbel became the organist at the Erfurt Predigerkirche, where he spent 12 happy years. His first wife succumbed to the plague, but within a year he had remarried and subsequently had seven children. This period was a time of increasing contentment and creative growth. In 1690, he became organist in Stuttgart at the Wurttemberg Court. The threat of a French invasion curtailed this position two years later, and Pachelbel returned to his hometown of Nuremberg to take up the post of organist at St. Sebald. There he lived out his final decade, writing ever more imposing works.

It is not known when Pachelbel composed his famous *Canon*. The work is scored for three violins and continuo, each violin entering in turn and elaborating on a simple theme as the piece gathers in strength and builds to a climax. But Pachelbel's importance is, in fact, perhaps greater as a composer for the organ; his chorale preludes, based on hymn tunes, strongly influenced J. S. Bach. He was also the author of a great many motets, arias, Masses, and 13 Magnificats that feature solo singers and a choir as well as an orchestra often including wind and brass. His body of work reflects the cultural contrasts between his own Protestant ways and those of the higher church, and certainly deserves to be known at least as well as his celebrated *Canon*.

Purcell

Henry Purcell 1659–1695

RECOMMENDED WORK
Dido and Aeneas
Chandos CHAN0521
Emma Kirkby (sop) Dido; David Thomas (bass) Aeneas; Judith Nelson (sop) Belinda; Jantina Noorman (mez) Sorceress; Taverner Choir and Players/Andrew Parrott
One of the earliest English operas, Dido and Aeneas is given a bright, stylish perfomance, with springing rhythms bringing Purcell's Restoration tragedy to life. Emma Kirkby is a youthful and appealing queen (a less tragic interpretation than that of many sopranos), a characterization amply balanced by David Thomas's burly Aeneas.

REPRESENTATIVE WORKS
Come ye sons of art, away
Hail, Bright Cecilia
Rejoice in the Lord Alway, 'The Bell Anthem'
Chacony in G minor
Funeral Music for Queen Mary

One of four sons, Henry Purcell revealed his musical skills at a very early age and joined the Chapel Royal in London as a boy chorister. Choristers were encouraged to develop their talents, and the eight-year-old Purcell duly obliged by composing a three-part song, 'Sweet Tyranness,' which became a part of leading publisher Playford's 'Can That Catch Can.'

After his voice changed, Purcell left the choir and was engaged as assistant to the Keeper of the King's Instruments. He progressed to supervision and tuning of the organ at Westminster Abbey (1674–78) and in 1677 replaced Matthew Locke as Composer-in-Ordinary (for violins). Two years later he succeeded John Blow as the Abbey's organist and shortly after married Frances Peters, with whom he settled in a house provided with the employment.

From this stable domestic setting his compositions flowed. He wrote Latin anthems for the royal chapels, a book of trio sonatas, and other occasional pieces for the court; in all he catered with great

Contemporary portrait in chalk by the English artist Sir Godfrey Kneller

Engraving of the Coronation of James II in 1685

The choir can be seen in the gallery to the right; trumpeters and kettledrums are in the center.

versatility to the distinct musical differences between the royal court, public ceremonies at Westminster Abbey, and the theater — the last an increasing interest with Purcell. In 1685 he composed the anthem *Rejoice in the Lord Alway*, known as the *Bell Anthem* because of the 'pealing' effect of its instrumental introduction.

He had become the official organist to the Chapel Royal in 1682 and a year later was made Organ Maker and Keeper of the King's Instruments. Purcell was evidently well able to fulfill an administrative role while remaining a creative musician, for his court positions were reconfirmed by James II, and again in 1689 when William III and Mary took the throne. For the coronations of each, Purcell composed anthems and played on the Abbey organ.

Purcell's affinity for the theater led him to explore the medium of opera. In his thirties his efforts bore fruit with the 1689 premiere of his famous *Dido and Aeneas*, the first English opera of lasting significance. Although less than an hour long, it contains dances and choruses in many styles and spans a wide variety of human emotions, from elation to despair. Its most famous aria is Dido's Lament, 'When I am laid in earth,' sung over a repeated bass line of falling semitones (the smallest interval between two notes used at that time), representing Dido's descent into the grave after her desertion by Aeneas.

After *Dido*, Purcell wrote largely for the theater. Between 1690 and 1695 he composed music for no fewer than 37 productions, including *King Arthur* in 1691 and *The Fairy Queen* in 1692. He continued to write pieces for royal occasions, and in 1694 composed an ode, *Come ye sons of art, away*, for the birthday of Queen Mary, wife of William III. The piece includes the aria 'Sound the trumpet,' usually sung by a pair of dueling countertenors.

When Queen Mary died of smallpox late in 1694, Purcell wrote a series of pieces for her funeral, held in Westminster Abbey in March 1695. The *Funeral Music for Queen Mary* comprises an anthem, four profoundly bleak pieces for trumpets and trombones, and two elegies. The same year, some of the music was used at Purcell's own funeral. His death at the early age of 36 was an immense loss to England and the musical world. His funeral, like Queen Mary's, was held at Westminster Abbey, with both the Chapel Royal choir and the Abbey choir in attendance, and he was laid to rest close to the organ at Westminster Abbey that he had spent years maintaining.

Autograph manuscript by the composer, c.1690
A page from Purcell's handwritten score for A Book of Solo Songs and Duos.

Corelli

Arcangelo Corelli 1653–1713

RECOMMENDED WORK
Concerti grossi, Op. 6
Archiv Produktion 423 626-2
The English Concert/Trevor Pinnock
A rich vein of Baroque sophistication and discernment runs through this group of concertos. Pinnock stylishly balances the two orchestral forces — the concertino and the orchestral ensemble. A just winner of a Gramophone Award.

REPRESENTATIVE WORKS
Violin Sonata, Op. 5 No. 12 in D minor, 'La follia'
Trio Sonatas, Opp. 1–4

Portrait of Corelli by Jan Frans van Douven

The youngest of five children, Corelli is thought to have received his first musical education from a priest in Faenza; but his formative period was to come later, at the age of 13, when he went to Bologna to study the violin. Not only did the city possess one of the largest churches, San Petronio, but it was also a leading center of the Italian school of chamber music. Young Corelli's appetite for the violin together with Bologna's musical importance would prove an important combination.

At 17 he was admitted to the city's Accademia Filarmonica. Over the next few years he became one of Italy's leading violinists, performing in churches and theaters all over Rome. This led him to enter the service of Queen Christina of Sweden, who had a home in the city and created her own academy of chamber musicians. Corelli began composing pieces for Christina and dedicated to her his Opus 1 collection of trio sonatas for two violins, cello, and harpsichord. He also worked as the leader of ten violinists in San Luigi in 1682 and went on to make annual visits there for over a quarter of a century.

In 1684, Corelli became a member of the Congregazione dei Virtuosi di Santa Cecilia. His increasing renown led him to play for Cardinal Pamphili, to whom he dedicated his Opus 2 chamber works. Corelli became music master to Cardinal Pamphili in 1687, and took up residence in the Cardinal's palace, where he performed trios with his fellow violinist Matteo Fornari and Spanish-born cellist Giovanni Lorenzo Lulier.

Eventually the Cardinal moved away from Rome, and in 1690 Corelli was adopted by Cardinal Ottoboni. He now directed regular Monday concerts as well as operatic performances and in 1694 dedicated a set of chamber trios to the Cardinal. After ten years he was appointed leader of the instrumental section of the Congregazione dei Virtuosi di Santa Cecilia, and was eventually elected to the Arcadian Academy, an institution for the promotion of music.

His distinguished work brought Corelli into contact with most of the leading musical figures of the day. He played in Handel's *Il trionfo del tempo* in 1707 and led performances of that composer's *La resurrezione* the following spring. A year later he withdrew from public life to concentrate on revisions to his own work. As old age and worsening health intruded, he moved in 1712 from the Cardinal's palace into his own home, where he died a year later. He was buried in the Pantheon in Rome, close to the artist Raphael.

Corelli declared that the purpose of his music was to display the violin, and this is shown to best effect in his *Concerti grossi*, Opus 6. These 12 pieces were written over a period of many years and collected into a set published the year after Corelli's death. Mainly in three movements, each contrasts a group of solo instruments — two violins and harpsichord — against the rest of the orchestra. Eight of the works are *da chiesa*, in the church style, and have a serious character. The remaining four are *da camera*, of a lighter nature. Number 8, the 'Christmas concerto,' which is intended for performance on Christmas night, has enjoyed particular popularity. The pieces were a milestone in the development of the solo concerto as we know it today.

Violin by Antonio Stradivari, 1703

A native of Cremona, Italy, Stradivari has remained unsurpassed as a violin maker.

Couperin

François Couperin 1668 – 1733

RECOMMENDED WORKS

Harpsichord works
Harmonia Mundi HMA190 354/6
Kenneth Gilbert (hpd)
*A highlight of the Baroque keyboard repertory,
Couperin's four-volume anthology is full of subtle,
evocative music and a sense of the good life. Kenneth
Gilbert, playing a Hemsch harpsichord, has recorded
all 27 Ordres with authority and poetry. Especially
recommended are Ordres Nos. 6–10, particularly
Les baricades mistérieuses and the Passacaille in B
minor, from Ordre No. 8.*

REPRESENTATIVE WORKS
Concerts royaux
L'Apothéose de Lully
Organ Masses
Leçons de ténèbres

Harpsichord by Jean-Antoine Vaudry, 1681
**A superb instrument, with japanned
decoration based on engravings of
peasant scenes.**

Musically, François Couperin bridged two eras, the Baroque and the Classical, to which many of his ideas look forward. He was born in Paris into a family with a musical tradition stretching back 200 years. Their church, St. Gervais, employed a member of the Couperin family as organist for an unbroken period of 173 years.

Portrait engraving of the composer by Flipart, 1735

The ten-year-old Couperin's musical abilities were already evident when, upon his father's death, the position of organist to St. Gervais was formally offered to him, postponed until his eighteenth birthday. In the meantime a temporary appointment was made, although accounts suggest that in fact Couperin frequently played at services and was given a wage before he was 18. He married Marie-Anne Ansault when he was 21, and the following year secured a royal license to publish his only two organ Masses.

Couperin was an admirer of Corelli and around 1692 composed a set of four sonatas; this marked the beginning of his lifelong affection for the Italian Baroque. At this time it was principally as a keyboard player that Couperin's reputation grew. He became one of four organists to Louis XIV in 1693 and gained an increasing reputation as a harpsichord teacher, his pupils including the king's children, the Duke of Burgundy, the Count of Toulouse, the daughters of the Duke of Bourbon, the Dowager Princess of Conti, and numerous others. Performing also made great demands on his time, and there are accounts of his playing at Versailles, Sceaux, and Fontainebleau.

In 1696 he was presented with his own coat of arms, and six years later had the distinction of receiving the Order of Chevalier de Latran. He became the king's harpsichordist, and when in 1715 the king died, the composer's position remained secure as the new court surrounding Louis XV brought a fresh influx of distinguished pupils. Around this time Couperin composed one of his most impressive pieces of religious music, *Leçons de ténèbres*, a setting of sacred texts for solo voices with sparse accompaniment, to be performed during Holy Week.

Couperin's most important achievements, however, are the four books of harpsichord works that he wrote between 1713 and 1730. The individual pieces are known as *Ordres*, consisting, like suites, of a succession of dance movements. Each *Ordre* has a title that might be the name of a person or object, or might be intended to evoke a particular scene or mood. Examples are *Les Ombres Errantes* (The Roving Shadows), *La Visionaire* (The Dreamer), and *Papillons* (Butterflies). The works display a great variety of techniques and clearly demonstrate Couperin's success at fusing elements of French and Italian music.

Vivaldi

Antonio Vivaldi *c.*1678 – 1741

RECOMMENDED WORKS

The Four Seasons
Angel CDC7 49557-2
Nigel Kennedy (vln); English Chamber Orchestra
One of the most recorded of classical pieces, its sheer vitality has inspired soloists to dazzling displays of virtuosity. Kennedy's overtly modern performance seeks not period perfection but raw energy.

Gloria in D, RV589
Chandos CHAN0518
Emma Kirkby (sop); Tessa Bonner (sop); Michael Chance (alt); Collegium Musicum 90/Richard Hickox
A thoughtful reading of this magical choral work that is both charming and moving; dominated by the pure soprano of Emma Kirkby.

REPRESENTATIVE WORKS
Concerto in E, 'L'amoroso'
L'estro armonico
Magnificat in G minor
Stabat mater
Juditha triumphans
Orlando

Portrait of Vivaldi by an unknown artist

The son of a baker, Antonio Vivaldi grew up in a simple Venetian home. His father, Giovanni Battista, broke with the family tradition and gave up baking to become a musician, and from 1685 was employed at St. Mark's as a violinist.

A career in the church was an attractive escape from poverty, and Antonio began training for the priesthood at the age of 15. He simultaneously developed his own skills on the violin and occasionally deputized for his father at St. Mark's. In 1703 he took holy orders, but after 1705, supposedly because of a chest complaint, he no longer said Mass. (This was to cause him problems later on when, in 1737, a production of one of his operas was banned by the papal authorities, describing the composer as a nonpracticing priest who had an alleged relationship with a female singer.) Also, in 1703 Vivaldi became the Maestro

di Violino at the Pio Ospedale della Pietà, an orphanage for girls in Venice, where music played an integral part in the curriculum. At the hospice he raised musical standards to a high level; the regular concerts given by the hospice's orchestra, performed behind a 'modesty' screen, were extremely popular and, according to a contemporary account, the equal of anything in Paris. Writing in 1740, the traveler Charles de Brosses described the orphanage girls: 'They are reared at public expense and trained solely to excel in music. And so they sing like angels . . . .'

For Vivaldi the appointment was a golden opportunity to develop the concerto form, and he produced a large number of works for unusual combinations of instruments as aids to his teaching. Having established himself as a teacher and composer with the publication in 1711 of *L'estro armonico* (Harmonic inspiration), a collection of concertos for one, two, and four solo violins, Vivaldi also garnered a reputation as a virtuoso violinist of great energy and daring. He became interested in having his works published and arranged for editions to be printed in Amsterdam to give him a professional advantage in northern Europe. Vivaldi was quick to capitalize on his newfound fame with a string of performances and compositions, sometimes altering the dedication of works to flatter illustrious persons passing through Venice. He stopped publishing music when he found it more lucrative to sell direct to visitors.

In 1713, Vivaldi's first opera, *Ottone in villa*, was performed in Vicenza. This was

followed by *Orlando*, which opened the 1714–15 season at Sant' Angelo, Venice, and subsequently by at least another 40 operas during his career. Around the same time Vivaldi is believed to have composed his *Gloria in D*, one of a number of sacred works by this prolific composer. Cast in nine movements, the *Gloria* features solo voices and is full of contrasts in scoring, style, mood, and key.

Vivaldi's one period of work away from Venice was between 1718 and 1720 in the employ of Prince Philip of Hesse-Darmstadt at Mantua. In the heartland of northern Italy he worked in the extraordinary splendor of the court, with its vast rooms painted with murals, its elaborate Zodiac Hall, and Hall of Rivers. Undoubtedly this environment, rather than the mudflats of the Venetian basin, was the inspiration for *Le quattro stagioni* (*The Four Seasons*). This famous work is part of Vivaldi's Opus 8, which appeared in 1725. Of Vivaldi's 500 concertos, more than 230 are for solo violin, and *The Four*

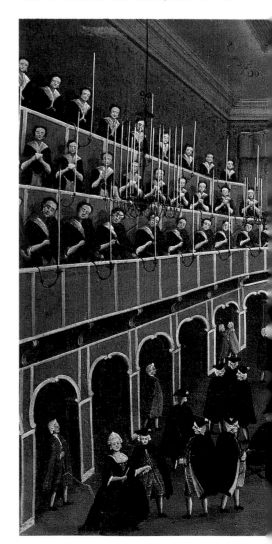

Seasons consists of four of them. As in the *Gloria*, Vivaldi's variety of technique is given free rein. The piece is an early example of program music (where the music tells a story or depicts a scene). In it Vivaldi employed various instruments to represent, for example, birdsong, a sleeping shepherd, and a barking sheepdog.

After Vivaldi's death his work suffered a rapid decline in popularity, and for a long time he was remembered only as a virtuoso musician. In the nineteenth century, however, German research into J. S. Bach revealed that he had transcribed a number of Vivaldi's works for keyboard. Interest in Vivaldi's work was reawakened, and its rich variety and inventiveness became appreciated; in the late twentieth century his music is even more popular than when he was alive.

Painting of a concert by Gabriele Bella, c.1700–50
A concert given by a combined orchestra from several Venetian orphanages in honor of the Russian Grand Duke Paul.

Albinoni

Tomaso Albinoni 1671–1751

RECOMMENDED WORK
Adagio in G minor (arr. Giazotto)
Disc: 'Baroque Favourites'
Collins Classics 1017-2
Consort of London/Robert Haydon Clark
This characterful performance by a British group of Albinoni's most famous work uses modern instruments. The addition of a contrasting work, Domenico Zipoli's Elevazione, helps bring to life the musical charms of the Baroque.

REPRESENTATIVE WORKS
12 Concerti, Op. 5
Concerti a cinque, Opp. 7 & 9
Cleomene

Tomaso Albinoni was born into a family of Venetian paper merchants in 1671. His father, Antonio, owned a number of shops as well as other properties around Venice. Being the eldest child, Tomaso was given a solid musical education, but appears to have enjoyed his personal freedom too much to consider taking employment within the church.

By the age of 23, however, he had begun to find his way. He composed an opera, *Zenobia Regina de Palmireni*, which was staged, and followed this with a set of 12 trio sonatas. These two genres, secular vocal music and instrumental works, were Albinoni's two main concerns throughout his composing life, although his reputation rests largely on the latter, as little survives of his output of over 50 operas.

There are suggestions that Albinoni might have been briefly employed by the Duke of Mantua, but most likely he merely dedicated a work to him following a meeting at the opera in Venice. His operas began to enjoy success in Italy, and in 1705 he married the soprano Margherita Rimondi. Despite rearing six children, she managed to continue her performing career, but died in her thirties.

View of an 18th-century concert
An orchestra featuring the many types of instrument at Albinoni's disposal.

Albinoni's difficulties continued when he was the victim of a legal action by one of his father's creditors, which resulted in the family's losing its shops.

Albinoni continued to write instrumental compositions and in 1707 published a set of 12 concertos for strings, followed in 1715 by two sets of oboe concertos that show his gift for fluid, melodic lines. His fortunes improved after he dedicated 12 concertos to Maximilian Emanuel II, Elector of Bavaria, in 1722, when he was invited to Munich to supervise the staging of one of his operas at Prince-Elector Karl Albert's marriage celebrations.

Ironically, the piece for which Albinoni is best known in fact owes little to him. The *Adagio* for strings and organ was elaborated from a fragmented manuscript by the twentieth-century Italian musicologist, Remo Giazotto. The piece owes its romantic character to some particularly lush string writing.

Albinoni associated little with his fellow composers, and although the influence of Corelli and Vivaldi can be traced, his musical ideas were relatively undiluted by others. This individuality, particularly in his instrumental works, along with the popular success of his apocryphal *Adagio*, makes Albinoni well worth discovering.

Bach

Johann Sebastian Bach 1685–1750

RECOMMENDED WORKS

Brandenburg Concertos
Archiv Produktion 423 492-2
The English Concert/Trevor Pinnock
These concertos are characterized by a kaleidoscope of musical forms and an innovative combination of instruments. This period instrument group has the soloists to match Bach's taxing demands, particularly Simon Standage's extraordinary violin in the Presto of Concerto No. 4, *oboist David Reichenberg, and Pinnock himself, especially in* Concerto No. 5. *The disc also features* Orchestral Suites.

St. Matthew Passion
Deutsche Harmonia Mundi/BMG RD77848
Christoph Prégardien (ten); Max van Egmond (bass); Christian Fliegner (treb); Maximilian Kiener (treb); René Jacobs (alt); David Cordier (alt); Markus Schäfer (ten); Tölz Boys' Choir; La Petite Bande/Gustav Leonhardt
Leonhardt's reading is infused with singing and playing that match what we know of Bach's intentions. Sterling solo readings, notably from Prégardien as the Evangelist, accompanied by a forceful male German/Dutch choir and Dutch period instrument orchestra.

REPRESENTATIVE WORKS
Violin Concertos in E & A minor
Double Violin Concerto in D minor
The Well-Tempered Clavier
Goldberg Variations
Art of Fugue
Mass in B minor
St. John Passion
Magnificat

Born in Eisenach in eastern Germany, Johann Sebastian Bach was the most significant member of a vast musical family. Both his parents died by the time he was ten, whereupon he moved into his elder brother's Ohrdruf home and spent the next five years attending the Lyceum. His brother, Johann Christoph, was an organist and taught Bach both to play and to build the instrument. At 15 he was sent to the Michaelisschule at Lüneburg, where he sang in the choir until his voice changed. At 17 he applied for and received

Above: Bach and three sons, by B. Dennis, c.1730
Bach fathered 20 children, several of whom shared his musical gifts.

the post of organist in Sangerhausen, but the Duke of Weissenfels overruled the decision in favor of an older organist.

Instead, Bach spent a few months as a court musician at Weimar before visiting Arnstadt in 1703 to see the new organ at the Neuekirche. He so impressed the authorities that he was offered the job of organist, already promised to Andreas Borner. His playing was clearly astonishing, but he was too young to be an effective teacher; conflicts arose between Bach and the authorities over the teaching of choristers. Matters deteriorated further in 1705 when Bach took an extended leave of absence to walk to Lübeck to hear the composer Buxtehude play the organ.

Two years after this episode, Bach resigned and took another post in Mühlhausen. That year he married; he was settling into his post when, in 1708, he was required to play before the Duke of Weimar, who promptly offered him better

Below: Autograph manuscript by the composer
The manuscript of Bach's Cantata No. 180, Schmücke dich, o liebe Seele.

Above: Engraving of music in a German church
The motto on the organ — 'The Lord loves everything that has breath' — was particularly appropriate.

employment as organist and chamber musician and later as Konzertmeister.

At Weimar, Bach developed his composing. He studied and made arrangements for organ or harpsichord of a number of Vivaldi's concertos, experience that was later to influence his own two *Violin Concertos in E* and *A minor* and the *Double Violin Concerto in D minor*.

During 1716, Bach heard rumors that the Duke of Weimar intended to hire Telemann as his Kapellmeister, a position he had expected himself. Bach responded by finding a rival Kapellmeister's position in the court at Cöthen. In order to prevent his taking up the post, the Duke had Bach imprisoned in November 1717. A month later he was discharged, and he and his family left the court in disgrace.

Prince Leopold at Cöthen was a far more congenial patron; it was under his patronage that Bach composed the six

Brandenburg Concertos, named after their dedication to Christian Ludwig, Margrave of Brandenburg, in 1721. The pieces were described as 'concertos for several instruments' and feature a group of soloists contrasted against the bulk of the orchestra. Unlike the *Concerti grossi* of Corelli, the *Brandenburg Concertos* call for unusual combinations of instruments: the fifth concerto, for example, has a solo group consisting of flute, violin, and harpsichord; the second combines trumpet, flute, violin, and oboe. While at Cöthen, Bach also wrote prolifically for the keyboard, including his *Italian Concerto* and Book 1 of the *Well-Tempered Clavier*, consisting of preludes and fugues in every key.

Bach's wife died in 1720, and the next year he married Anna Magdalena Wilcke. His position at Cöthen soured late in 1721 when Prince Leopold himself married. The prince's wife did not enjoy music and disliked Bach's involvement at court. Fortunately, in 1722 the position of Cantor at the Thomasschule in Leipzig fell vacant. It was initially offered to Telemann and then to Johann Graupner, but neither was released by his current employer. Bach was eventually invited to accept the position and in 1723 moved to Leipzig, where he was to remain the rest of his life.

Bach approached the new task with enthusiasm. His duties at the school included teaching music and other subjects to the 50 or 60 pupils, and writing a cantata for Sunday services and church feasts. The wealth of singers and instrumentalists at the school allowed Bach to compose works on a grand scale: one such piece was the *St. Matthew Passion*. This huge work is a setting of the Gospel text for soloists, a double choir, and 40 players and was first performed in the Thomaskirche in Leipzig on Good Friday 1727 or 1729. It combines chorales (hymn settings) with choruses and arias, all woven together by a narrator, the Evangelist, who sings the Gospel text to a simple organ accompaniment. Together with the *St. John Passion*, first heard in 1724, the work represents the pinnacle of devotional music up to that time.

In a letter to the diplomat Georg Erdmann in 1730, however, Bach voiced his great dissatisfaction with the remuneration and irksome duties of his employment and expressed the desire for another opportunity elsewhere. He tried for a post at Dresden, submitting the Gloria and Kyrie from his then unfinished *B Minor Mass*, but was not successful. His teaching workload grew enormously, and council records register his frequent absence from some duties — presumably because he was teaching or composing at home.

Bach entered on a new phase of composition with the *Goldberg Variations*, published in 1741, which was commissioned by the insomniac Count Heyserling for his harpsichordist, Johann Gottlieb Goldberg, to play to him during his sleepless nights. Bach followed this with two works that reflected his increasing preoccupation with the fugue — the *Musical Offering* and the *Art of Fugue*, the latter of which remained unfinished at his death.

Toward the end of his life Bach was troubled with cataracts, which made work increasingly difficult. Two operations failed to cure the problem, and in the last few months of his life Bach was practically blind. In the summer of 1750, weakened by the operations, he died of a stroke, leaving his fellow musicians to mourn one of the world's greatest composers.

Portrait of Gottfried Reiche by E. Haussman
Reiche was a leading musician and solo trumpeter in Bach's orchestra.

Handel

George Frideric Handel 1685–1759

RECOMMENDED WORKS

Messiah

L'Oiseau-Lyre 430 488-2
Judith Nelson, Emma Kirkby (sop); Carolyn
Watkinson (contr); Paul Elliott (ten); David
Thomas (bass); Christ Church Cathedral Choir,
Oxford; Academy of Ancient Music/Christopher
Hogwood
Hogwood is faithful to Handel's original intentions —
a boys' choir and an orchestra whose size and
instruments Handel would have recognized.

Water Music

Archiv Produktion 410 525-2
The English Concert/Trevor Pinnock
Perhaps the most enchanting of Handel's orchestral
scores. Pinnock's period instrument ensemble brings to
life the verve and regal pomp that one can believe
were present at the river journey premiere.

REPRESENTATIVE WORKS
Music for the Royal Fireworks
Concerti grossi, Opp. 3 & 6
Organ Concertos, Opp. 4 & 7
Air and Variations, 'The Harmonious
Blacksmith'
Giulio Cesare
Acis and Galatea
Judas Maccabeus

Handel was born in Halle in Saxony (now
Germany), the son of a 63-year-old bar-
ber-surgeon. His father intended that he
should study law, but Handel longed to
explore music — so much so that he
smuggled a small clavichord into their
attic. On a visit to the court of Saxe-
Weissenfels, where his father was the court
barber, Handel was overheard playing the
organ by the Duke, who managed to con-
vince the reluctant parent of the boy's
musical potential. Handel subsequently
studied both law and music, mastering the
organ, violin, and harpsichord, composing
in different musical forms, and spending
hours copying scores from the manuscript
collection of his teacher, the organist and
composer Friedrich Zachau.

Portrait by Philippe Mercier, probably post-1720
Handel's wit and elegance shine through
in this fine portrait.

Handel entered Halle University in
1702 and within a month was engaged as
the probationary organist at the Calvinist
cathedral in Halle. He enjoyed a year of
free lodgings before moving on to Hamburg, the only German city, excluding the
courts, with an opera house. He was
employed as a violinist at the opera house,
then harpsichordist, and within three years
his first two operas were staged. In 1706 he
met the heir to the Grand Duke of Tus-
cany, who invited him to Florence — the
start of three formative and creative years
in Italy. There he met many leading composers, including Corelli, the Scarlattis,
and Vivaldi, all of whose influences can be
heard in his music. He was inspired to
write operas — notably *Agrippina,* which
was performed 27 times — as well as oratorios and more than 150 cantatas. He created quite a name for himself, particularly
in Venice, before traveling to Innsbruck to
meet the Governor of the Tyrol. From
there he journeyed to Hanover to work as
the Kappellmeister to the Elector, the man
destined to accede to the English throne.

In 1710, Handel visited London to produce his opera *Rinaldo,* and was inspired by
its success to settle there permanently.
Queen Anne awarded him a pension of
£200 per annum, but Handel's position
became difficult when she died and the
Elector of Hanover, from whom he had
played truant, became King of England.
One story relates that a reconciliation was
effected when King George made a sailing
excursion on the Thames: a second barge
carrying 50 musicians under Handel's
direction shadowed the royal boat, performing the now famous *Water Music.*
The king was so captivated that he
requested three renditions of the hour-
long concert, forgiving the composer and
raising his pension to £600.

Consisting of three suites divided into
20 short movements, the *Water Music* is
scored for trumpets, horns, oboes, bassoons, recorders, flutes, and strings. It

notably displays Handel's gifts for orchestration, the sound of trumpets and horns across water being especially effective.

From 1718 to 1720, Handel served as music director to the Duke of Chandos, and during this period he wrote the *Chandos Anthems* and the dramatic oratorio *Acis and Galatea*. He generally found patrons easily; in the winter of 1718–19 the nobility combined forces to create and fund the Royal Academy of Music to promote Italian opera in London, with Handel as music director. For eight years the focus for operatic activity in Europe was London, and Handel enjoyed many triumphs, including *Giulio Cesare* in 1724. He was appointed composer to the Royal Chapel, moved to a house in Grosvenor Square, and sought English naturalization.

The Academy faltered as a result of the costs of its opera productions, but Handel's career seemed blessed. A modest first performance of his *Esther*, the first oratorio to be heard in London, took place at a tavern in the Strand during the winter of 1732. It was a triumph, and at Princess Anne's request was transferred to the King's Theatre. Handel expanded it, and the six performances were a great success.

In 1740, Handel composed his 12 *Concerti grossi*, Opus 6, for strings and optional woodwind, which with Bach's *Brandenburg Concertos* represent the peak of instrumental writing during this period. The next year he went to Dublin, where he began a series of 'musical entertainments' that were an instant success. On April 13, 1742, he premiered his oratorio the *Messiah* to an enraptured Dublin audience. The *Messiah* was written in just one month in 1741. It is based on texts from the Bible and falls into three parts: the anticipation of the Messiah and Christ's birth, Christ's Passion, and Christ as the Redeemer. Handel altered the work's orchestration to suit the demands of various performances: during his lifetime there was no one definitive edition. Of the famous 'Hallelujah Chorus,' Handel was moved to say, 'I thought I saw all Heaven before me, and the great God himself.'

The following year, Handel took the work back to England, where it was initially less well received but gradually found

Above: Firework display at Whitehall in 1749
Part of the celebrations for the Treaty of Aix-la-Chapelle, for which Handel wrote his Music for the Royal Fireworks.

Below: Detail of an engraving by Hogarth, 1725
The exceptionally tall figure of a castrato in Handel's opera Flavio.

favor. At Covent Garden he initiated a series of concerts and in 1744 staged the oratorios *Belshazzar* and *Hercules*. For the 1744–45 season he returned to the King's Theatre, but his earlier success was not repeated and the series closed early.

Handel continued composing unabated and in 1746 produced the hugely popular oratorio *Judas Maccabeus*. The king subsequently commissioned music to accompany a spectacular fireworks display to celebrate the Treaty of Aix-la-Chapelle. Even the rehearsal, in London's Vauxhall Gardens, caused an impromptu audience of 12,000 to stop traffic for three hours.

After the *Fireworks*, Handel wrote relatively little. He was unsuccessfully operated on for eye cataracts, which left him blind for the last seven years of his life. He died in London at the age of 74 and was buried in Westminster Abbey.

Telemann

Georg Philipp Telemann 1681–1767

RECOMMENDED WORK

Tafelmusik

Teldec 2292-44688-2
Vienna Concentus Musicus/Nikolaus Harnoncourt
In their massive three-part anthology of Telemann's German 'table music' this Viennese ensemble has succeeded in bringing out the composer's eclecticism. There is something for everybody in this late Baroque confection, including dance suites, quartets, concertos, trios, and solo sonatas. For those daunted by over four hours of music, excerpts are available.

REPRESENTATIVE WORKS
Violin Concertos
Overture: Suite in G
Burlesque de Don Quichotte
Essercizii Musici
Paris Quartets
Der Tag des Gerichts

Portrait engraving by Georg Lichtensteger, 1744

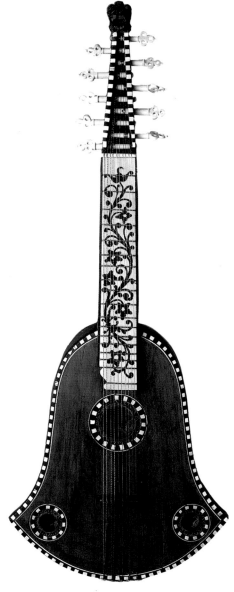

A zither made in Hamburg
An ancient plucked instrument, this was especially popular in Bavaria and Austria.

Telemann was born in the German town of Magdeburg into a family with strong links to the clergy. He received no specific musical education, yet by the age of ten had learned to play the keyboard, flute, violin, and zither; by the time he was 12 he had even written an opera. Unimpressed, his mother confiscated his instruments and sent him away to school. There, fortunately, the superintendent was a music theorist, and during the next four years Telemann outwardly continued to please his family with formal studies while developing his understanding of musical composition.

His education progressed to the Gymnasium Andreanum in Hildesheim, where he was again lucky in finding a teacher who encouraged him to compose music for school dramas and for the local Catholic church. After a spell at Leipzig University studying law, Telemann settled in Leipzig and wrote a psalm setting, which was performed at the Thomaskirche and led to an invitation from the mayor to compose a cantata for every second Sunday. This annoyed the new cantor at the church. He tried to curb Telemann's increasing influence, but it was not long before the commissions were requested for every Sunday.

In 1702 the young composer founded the Collegium Musicum, with which he staged regular concerts. The same year he was appointed music director of the Leipzig Opera and started to compose operas, giving roles to some of his students. When a new organ was installed in the University church, he offered his Collegium Musicum to provide sacred music on feast days.

Telemann left Leipzig in 1705 and briefly held the position of Kapellmeister to Count Erdmann II of Promnitz in Sorau (now Poland), composing courtly music in the style of Lully at the Count's request. In 1708 he became Konzertmeister to the Eisenach Court, leading the court orchestra and writing cantatas and instrumental music. He took up a post in Frankfurt in 1712 and two years later married the daughter of a Frankfurt council clerk, with whom he raised ten children.

In 1721, Telemann was appointed Cantor of the Hamburg Johanneum, and eventually became Music Director of the Hamburg Opera. He increased the city's musical activity by mounting a series of concerts and operas, including works by Handel. During this period he composed his three collections of *Tafelmusik* (Table Music). As the name suggests, these pieces were to be played as accompaniment to banquets in noble and middle-class circles. Each set begins with a French-style overture, followed by a sequence of melodic pieces that could be played in any order.

Over the years, Telemann's energy declined; but toward the end of his life, encouraged by Handel — a friend of some 50 years' standing — he turned to writing oratorios, a genre in which he had previously shown little interest. In the course of seven years, from 1755 to 1762, he wrote six oratorios, including in 1762 *Der Tag des Gerichts* (The Day of Judgment). These, together with his vast output of 600 Italian overtures, as well as 47 concertos for solo instruments (21 for violin) and 40 operas, ensure his enduring reputation.

Rameau

Jean-Philippe Rameau 1683 – 1764

RECOMMENDED WORK

Platée
Erato 2292-45028-2
Gilles Ragon (ten) Platée; Jennifer Smith (sop) La Folie, Thalie; Guy de Mey (ten) Thespis, Mercure; Vincent le Texier (bass-bar) Jupiter; Guillemette Laurens (mez) Junon; Bernard Deletré (bass) Cithéron; Véronique Gens (sop) L'Amour, Clarine; Michel Verschaeve (bass) Momus; Françoise Herr Vocal Ensemble; Musiciens de Louvre/Marc Minkowski
Rameau's Platée serves as a trustworthy introduction to late Baroque French opera, and Minkowski's direction of this performance is second to none. The curious tale of a marsh nymph who is the butt of cruel jokes played on her by the gods, this comédie-lyrique is imbued with the best in Rameau's vocal scorings and instrumental music (try the Marché pour la danse). Suitable fare for its premiere, at the marriage in 1745 of the French Dauphin to the Infanta Maria Theresa of Spain.

REPRESENTATIVE WORKS
Pièces de clavecin en concert
In convertendo
Les Indes galantes
Castor et Pollux
Dardanus
Zoroastre

Contemporary portrait by Louis Carmontelle

Engraving of Madeleine Sophie Arnould, Paris, 1761
Arnould singing the role of Thelaïre in Castor et Pollux.

Jean-Philippe Rameau was born in Dijon, one of 11 children, and studied at a Jesuit College — his father's initial intention being that he should become a lawyer — before being allowed to go to study music in Milan at the age of 18. After a number of appointments as organist, he settled in Clermont in 1715, where he was organist at the cathedral for eight years.

During this period Rameau wrote his first collection of harpsichord pieces and in 1722 published his book on music theory, *Treatise on Harmony*. He tried to move to Paris, the center of creative activity, but encountered resistance from his employers in Clermont. It is said that on a particular feast day he simply refused to play, and when pressed, performed with so many discordant notes that he was released from duty. He moved to Paris, but for a decade he failed to secure a formal position, though he continued to compose and published his second and third books of harpsichord works. He made a living by teaching music, in 1732 becoming organist at Ste. Croix-de-la-Bretonnerie and the following year at the Jesuit novitiate.

Rameau's desire to write an opera received help from an admirer — the wife of a financier, Le Riche de la Pouplinière, who funded a private orchestra. Through this circle the composer met the writer Abbé Simon-Joseph Pellegrin, and together they created his first opera, *Hippolyte et Aricie*, based on Racine's tragedy *Phèdre*. It was performed in 1733 at Pouplinière's residence, and then at the Opéra in Paris three months later.

Rameau was 50 when his *Hippolyte et Aricie* was performed, and he spent the rest of his working life producing operas. In these he stressed musical elements more than Lully had done, stating, 'Lully needs actors but I need singers.' *Les Indes galantes* in 1735 and *Castor et Pollux* in 1737 were great successes, showing Rameau's bold harmonies and establishing him as Lully's successor as the leading light of French opera. A comic opera, *Platée*, was also successful when performed at the Paris Opéra in 1745, in part because it parodied the set language and conventions of serious opera. Some of its jests were sentimental words set to inappropriate music, incorrect stress of words or syllables, and the use of 'unoperatic' phrases and expressions.

Rameau died just before his eighty-first birthday, shortly after Louis XV, in recognition of his long service and lifetime of creative effort, had made him 'Compositeur du Cabinet du Roy.' His death was marked by a number of memorial services, the passion and vibrance of his music ensuring a great sense of loss at his passing.

Scene from *Le Temple de la Gloire*, 1745
The libretto for this opera-ballet was written by Rameau's friend, the satirist and philosopher Voltaire.

Scarlatti

Domenico Scarlatti 1685–1757

RECOMMENDED WORKS
Keyboard Sonatas
Deutsche Harmonia Mundi/BMG RD77224
Andreas Staier (hpd)
From Scarlatti's collection of 555 keyboard sonatas, Staier has selected 17 to play on a modern replica of a contemporary harpsichord. His choice emphasizes the influences of Scarlatti's many years on the Iberian Peninsula; the inexhaustible diversity of rhythms, melodies, and harmonies reflects the sounds the composer heard — from castanets to folk music.

REPRESENTATIVE WORKS
Stabat mater
Salve regina
Tetide in Sciro

Domenico Scarlatti was one of the ten children of Alessandro Scarlatti, himself a notable opera composer. Domenico grew up in Naples and by the age of 16 had become organist and composer at the Neapolitan Royal chapel. Accompanied by his father, he sought work in Florence

Portrait engraving by Weger, late 18th century

before returning to Naples and composing two Neapolitan operas in 1703 and performing a substantial rewrite of Pollarolo's *Irene* the following year.

Scarlatti spent the next four years in Venice, and in 1709 went directly into the service of Maria Casimira, the exiled Polish queen then living in Rome. He composed intensively, producing seven operas for the court, including in 1712 *Tetide in Sciro*, one of his 70 surviving operas. In 1713 he was appointed Maestro di Cappella to the Basilica Giulia in the Vatican, followed the next year by an appointment to the Portuguese ambassador to the Vatican, the Marquis de

Harpsichord by Jacob Kirckman, c.1766
A harpsichord with two keyboards offered the composer far greater scope.

Fontes. This succession of posts allowed him to expand his interests in both sacred and secular music. Regular weekly recitals under the auspices of Cardinal Ottoboni, who had already taken Corelli under his wing, gave him the opportunity to meet Corelli and Thomas Roseingrave, an Irishman who later helped spread his fame in England. The Cardinal also introduced Scarlatti to Handel, and arranged a harpsichord-playing contest between the two.

In 1719, Scarlatti resigned his position; he spent the next two years as harpsichordist at the Italian Opera in London. He then went to Lisbon in Portugal, where he became the Mestre to the Patriarchal chapel. He made only a handful of return visits to his native country, one in 1725 to visit his dying father and another to Rome in 1728 to marry Maria Gentili, aged 16 and some 27 years his junior.

Scarlatti finally settled in the employ of the musically gifted daughter of King John V, the Infanta María Barbara, and entered an extraordinary period of writing. His two 15-volume collections of sonatas for unaccompanied keyboard, mostly written for the Infanta, contain more than 500 works and established Scarlatti as one of the leading composers for the harpsichord. The Iberian influence is at times evident in these works, revealed in a guitarlike strumming effect achieved by rapid repetition of notes, and the sudden shifts from major to minor. These notoriously difficult pieces require the player to cross hands and produce very rapid scales and arpeggios.

When the Infanta moved to Madrid, Scarlatti, with his wife and five children, moved as part of her court, and he eventually became Maestro de Camara in 1746. Such loyalty to his daughter impressed King John, who sponsored Scarlatti in his application to become a Knight of the Order of Santiago.

Scarlatti's move to the Iberian Peninsula was a significant event for the development of keyboard music. The Neapolitan style at that time, based around opera, was very limiting. Scarlatti, by moving away from this tendency, allowed himself a greater degree of experimentation and freedom to develop a wholly new form and style of keyboard composition.

Arne

Thomas Arne 1710–1778

RECOMMENDED WORKS

Songs

Disc: 'Emma Kirkby sings Mr. Arne'
L'Oiseau-Lyre 436 132-2
Emma Kirkby (sop); Academy of Ancient Music/
Christopher Hogwood
*Emma Kirkby, a veteran of the early music revival in
Britain, relishes the beauty in tracks such as 'Ariel's
Song' and 'Rise, glory, rise,' from the stage work
Rosamond. The disc includes some pieces by Handel.*

REPRESENTATIVE WORKS
Six 'Favorite Concertos'
Under the Greenwood Tree
Artaxerxes
Judith

Thomas Arne was born into a family of London upholsterers and educated at Eton College. A quick grasp of music enabled him to teach his brother and sister to sing; when he was 23, they appeared in his first opera, *Rosamond*, styled 'after the Italian manner.' Its success led to commissions to write music for Drury Lane Theatre.

Arne composed many songs for productions of Shakespeare's plays, including *As You Like It* and *The Tempest*. 'Under the Greenwood Tree' and 'Where the Bee Sucks,' for example, reveal his unique talent for lyrical, melodic writing. Of his other songs, the most famous is 'Rule Britannia,' from the masque *Alfred*, which was requested by the Prince of Wales and performed at Cliveden House on the Thames in 1740. Arne published annual collections of his vast output of songs, which in the main celebrate the rhythms of life and nature. In 1745, during the threat to the English Crown posed by the Young Pretender, Bonnie Prince Charlie, Arne's setting of 'God Save the King' was sung every night by the gentlemen in the audience until the dangers had receded.

He had married the singer Cecilia Young in 1737, but after a trip to Ireland in 1755 — during which, together with Arne's sister, they gave musical performances in Dublin, including Handel's *Messiah* — the marriage broke up.

Arne also turned his hand to the oratorio, writing *Judith* for Lent in 1761. In 1762 he premiered *Artaxerxes*, introducing the grander Italian style to many English concertgoers; it was the only English opera to be regularly performed until the nineteenth century.

For 20 years Arne gave concerts at London's pleasure gardens, such as Marylebone, Ranelagh, and Vauxhall. In his last decade he wrote *Shakespeare Ode* and the masque *The Fairy Prince*. Rheumatism finally affected his ability to play, and he died in March 1778, comforted by a reconciliation with his wife Cecilia.

Engraving of a riot at Covent Garden in 1763
Artaxerxes *was so popular that the management withdrew cut-price tickets, sparking off a riot.*

Additional Composers

One of the most notable features of the Baroque era was the development of opera. The Roman composer **Emilio de' Cavalieri** (1550–1602) is credited with the composition of the first play set completely to music, the *Rappresentazione de Anima e di Corpo* (1600). Even during Cavalieri's lifetime there was dispute between him and the Florentine opera composers **Giulio Caccini** (c.1545–1618) and **Jacopo Peri** (1561–1633) as to who had invented the new style of speech-like singing of parts of the text (recitative). Caccini and Peri both wrote settings of *Euridice* in 1600. The most important opera composer in the period following Monteverdi was the Venetian **Francesco Cavalli** (1602–1676). The revival of *Ormindo, Calisto,* and *Egisto* in the 1960's and 1970's by the British musicologist and conductor Raymond Leppard revealed in these works a sense of theater that has survived the 300 years since their composition. **Alessandro Scarlatti** (1660–1725), the father of Domenico, was known as the founder of the Neapolitan school of eighteenth-century opera. The variety and sensitivity of his characterization in such operas as *Il Mitridate Eupatore, Telemaco,* and *Griselda* make him a worthy predecessor of Mozart himself.

In instrumental genres, the organ music of the Danish **Dietrich Buxtehude** (c.1637–1707) had such a reputation that J. S. Bach traveled to Lübeck to hear the venerable organist play. Two violin virtuosos who composed notable works were the Bohemian **Heinrich Biber** (1644–1704) and the Italian **Francesco Geminiani** (1687–1762). Biber wrote operas, choral works, and chamber music, but his fame rests mainly on such spectacular violin works as the *Mystery* or *Rosary* sonatas, which employ all sorts of special tunings to achieve unique effects. Geminiani settled in London eventually, composing fine, sonorous violin sonatas and *concerti grossi* that draw on the example of Corelli.

Alongside Purcell in England, the music of **John Blow** (1649–1708) had a deservedly high reputation. Anthems such as 'I beheld, and lo!...' and works such as the *Ode on the death of Mr. Henry Purcell* have considerable interest and distinction, though they lack the blazing genius of his younger contemporary.

In France, **Michel-Richard de Lalande** (1657–1726) composed *Grands Motets* and instrumental works such as the *Sinfonies pour les soupers du Roi* for the royal court at Versailles, while **Marin Marais** (1656–1728) wrote sets of pieces for the bass viol.

The Classical Era
mid-18th to mid-19th century

During the Classical era, new ideas took shape and swept through Western culture, leaving it dramatically changed. Ordinary people questioned how society should be organized and the basic rights of the individual. In North America, British colonists staged their famous Boston Tea Party in a protest against taxes. The Declaration of Independence and the war it inflamed gave republican ideals a focus. These resurfaced as France's population rose against King Louis XVI and his queen, Marie-Antoinette, and ushered in the age of Napoleon.

This was the age of reason, in which the arts and architecture underwent dramatic change. Artists looked to the ancient civilizations of Greece and Rome, which seemed emblematic of their own ideals. While Goya, Piranesi, and Constable abandoned the flourishes of the Rococo artists who preceded them, Goethe and Schiller transformed German drama and poetry, and Samuel Richardson and Henry Fielding pushed the English novel into the forefront. Classical architecture that reflected the ancient civilizations was raised in one major city after another — the White House in Washington, London's British Museum, the Winter Palace of St. Petersburg, and others.

The pace of technological change and innovation accelerated. With the development of steam power and the invention of the first mass-production spinning machine, the Industrial Revolution gave western nations unprecedented wealth, and set in motion the forces that would lead to another era of social upheaval.

It was in this unsettling and exhilarating time that composers, among them Haydn, Mozart, and Gluck, set their unique marks, with the relative simplicity and restraint of their music. The symphony, the concerto, and the sonata all underwent a significant evolution.

Featured Composers

The surrender of General John Burgoyne at Saratoga in 1777, painted by John Trumbull

This was a significant victory for the republican forces in the American War of Independence, leaving the British monarch, George III, and his government with little hope of retaining their lucrative American colonies.

The eighteenth century is often described as the Age of Reason. As philosophers and scientists began to challenge traditional assumptions about the nature of belief and authority, they called into question the unfettered power of the church and the monarchy. Their spirit of inquiry was rooted in a critical approach, which did much to spawn the turbulent events that were soon to engulf the Western world.

The Rococo

In the middle of the century, however, these upheavals were distant clouds on the horizon. The prevailing style in the arts was the Rococo, a style that epitomized the elegance and sophistication of courtly life. The term came from the *rocaille,* or decorative shellwork, which French architects had introduced in order to soften the severe grandeur of High Baroque design. Its hallmarks were grace, frivolity, and sensual pleasure.

In painting, the Rococo found its prime exponents in the French artists Jean-Antoine Watteau and François Boucher, while its finest architecture was produced in southern Germany and Austria. The sheer abundance of decoration inside the Bavarian church of Die Wies (1745–54) and at the abbey church of Ottobeuren (1748) demonstrate Rococo's potential for hedonism and overindulgence.

The musical equivalent of the Rococo was the *Style galant,* which laid a similar emphasis on lightness and elegance by replacing the complex schemes of Baroque music with free-flowing melodies. In Germany the style, described as '*empfindsam*' (sensitive), assumed a more sentimental character. It flourished in the 1750's and 1760's, finding its fullest expression in the music of C. P. E. Bach.

The emotional side of the style heralded the appearance of the *Sturm und Drang* (Storm and Stress) movement that dominated German cultural life in the 1770's and 1780's. Particularly associated with this influential literary tendency is Johann Wolfgang von Goethe, who, together with his friend Friedrich Schiller, created some of Germany's greatest drama and poetry. Goethe's masterpiece, *Faust,* provided enduring inspiration for artists and composers. In England the literary scene was dominated by Samuel Johnson. Johnson single-handedly composed a *Dictionary of the English Language,* but is remembered as much for his witty, acerbic conversation, recorded by his biographer, James Boswell. The novel also developed during this period, after early models by Samuel Richardson and Henry Fielding.

Interior of 18th-century Minorite church in Linz, Austria

The interior of this long, single-nave church is decorated in the typically elaborate Rococo style.

The Age of Enlightenment

As the eighteenth century wore on, reaction set in against both the stylistic extremes of the Rococo and the type of society that had generated it. Critics could look at the canvases of a painter like Watteau, where figures in masquerade disport themselves in dreamy, parkland settings, and argue that they were the product of a regime far too absorbed in its own artificial pleasures and utterly cut off from the all too evident sufferings of its people.

These grumblings were most evident in France, where a group of writers known as the 'Philosophes' (philosophers) laid the groundwork for the French Revolution in a movement known as the Enlightenment. At their head, the brilliant but scathing essayist Voltaire attacked religion as mere superstition and promoted instead the human virtues of reason, tolerance, and justice.

Engraving of Thomas Paine, 1791

Paine was the author of, among other works, Common Sense, a political tract in support of the American Revolution. In 1792 he fled America for France, to escape charges of treason.

Voltaire himself believed in the value of enlightened despotism, but in his wake there followed writers who were more eager to uphold the cause of democracy and the rights of the individual. Thomas Paine, the radical English-born political theorist who defended the American colonists against Britain, was one of the leading lights of this crusade. In France, the philosopher and writer Jean-Jacques Rousseau in particular captured the revolutionary spirit of the age in his most famous work, *The Social Contract*, with its fusion of morality and politics.

The American Revolution

The Philosophes advocated change and progress, and their hopes were fulfilled in the most dramatic fashion possible. Trouble had been brewing in the North American colonies since the early 1760's, as the English government unwisely sought to impose a series of punitive taxes on its distant colonies. 'No Taxation without Representation' was the rallying cry, as the colonists fiercely resisted such measures as the Sugar Act (1764), the Stamp Act (1765), and the Tea Act (1773). The last precipitated the 'Boston Tea Party' of December 1773, when three shiploads of imported tea were unceremoniously dumped into the harbor by citizens of Boston as a protest against taxes on tea and the trading monopoly given to the East India Company.

The English parliament responded bullishly to the situation, and the crisis rapidly turned into open rebellion. The first

Marie Antoinette at Versailles by J. F. Gautier d'Agoty

A fashionable 'ruelle' — a social gathering normally held in a lady's bedchamber. The extravagant ways of the Austrian-born French queen made her deeply unpopular with the people.

Execution of Louis XVI by an unknown Danish painter, 1793

Named after its inventor, Joseph Ignace Guillotin, the guillotine was first used in April 1792; Louis was executed the next year, and over the following weeks thousands were beheaded.

shots were fired in 1775, and a year later the Declaration of Independence, drafted by Thomas Jefferson, was signed. It took the colonial revolutionaries a further seven years to turn this resolution into hard reality, but geography and dogged determination finally tipped the scale. For the British government, waging a war 3,000 miles away, while also contending with hostile European neighbors, posed too stern a task. In 1783, the English forces finally capitulated. Peace was sealed by the Treaty of Paris in the same year, and in 1789 George Washington became the first president of the United States of America.

The French Revolution

France had sided with the American rebels during the conflict, largely as a means of discomfiting its old adversary across the Channel. Less than a decade after the end of that war, however, the French monarchy found itself struggling to suppress the same unquenchable fervor for democracy and republicanism. In 1789, France stood on the brink of economic collapse. It was a measure of the gravity of the situation that the national assembly, the States General, was summoned to consider the crisis.

The last such meeting had been called in 1614. The States General was composed of three sections: the Nobility and the Clergy — both of whom were anxious to defer much-needed reforms in order to maintain their privileges — and the Third Estate, representing the remainder of the community. When the different parties could not agree, the Third Estate broke away, declaring its exclusive right to be seen as the true National Assembly. Louis XVI opposed this, but his hand was weakened by rioting in Paris and, in particular, by the storming of the Bastille, the city's prison-fortress, on July 14, 1789.

From this point on, the revolutionary tide was unstoppable. The Parisian disturbances were repeated in the provinces, and the King's authority gradually ebbed away. In 1791, he tried to flee with his queen, Marie Antoinette, but the couple were intercepted at Varennes and taken back to the capital in disgrace. This encouraged the radical elements in the National Assembly. The following year Louis XVI was removed from office and imprisoned, and in 1793 both he and Marie Antoinette were executed. In a decisive break with the past, the newly elected Convention announced that 1792 was to be Year 1 of the new Republic.

Classicism

Significant developments in the art world echoed these momentous events. Here, the vehicle for change was Classicism — an influence made more confusing by the different contexts in which the term itself is used.

On one level, 'Classicism' relates to the influence of the ancient cultures of Greece and Rome. This is most evident in areas such as architecture, where there are obvious models to imitate. In a field such as music, the allusion is far less clear. Here, 'Classical' can refer to those qualities that were most prized by the artists of the ancient world — clarity, simplicity, moderation, and balance. In practical terms, this meant a departure from the complex polyphony of Baroque music and a greater reliance on unadorned melody and harmony.

'Classicism' can also be used as a contrast to the term 'Romanticism.' While a Romantic artist might be described as one who gave free rein to the emotions in his work, a Classical artist would take a more detached, intellectual approach. Used in this sense, 'Classical' is a stylistic rather than a historical term. Thus Mozart, whose music is passionate but also highly controlled, can be seen as the quintessential Classical composer. Beethoven, on the other hand, is not so easily categorized and

Below: *The Palace of Minerva* by David Roberts, 1859
Roberts' paintings, recording his extensive travels around the Mediterranean Basin and in the Near East, raised public awareness of the cultural heritage of the ancient world.

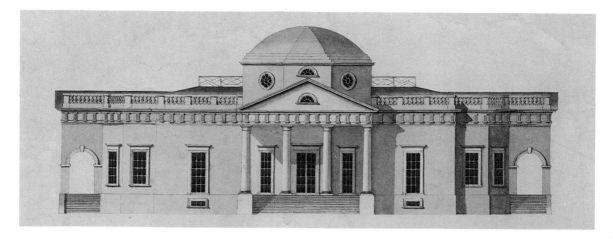

Southwest elevation of Monticello, near Charlottesville, Virginia

Monticello, designed by Thomas Jefferson as a country house for himself, was a successful blend of the English Palladian style with the elegance of a Parisian mansion.

is often seen as representing a bridge between the Classical and Romantic eras. Although he lived during the Classical period, many of his works anticipate Romanticism, and he is taken by many to exemplify the Romantic artist.

The stimulus for the Classical revival of the late eighteenth century came from two main sources. On the one hand, it developed as a natural reaction against the fussiness and apparent superficiality of the Rococo style. At the same time, it stemmed from some exciting new archeological discoveries. The marvels of the ancient world had retained their appeal ever since the Renaissance, and throughout the eighteenth century, a visit to the antique ruins in Rome remained a highlight of the Grand Tour, that essential element in the education of every wealthy young man. This interest greatly increased following

Designs for curtain cornices, girandoles, and folding doors by Adam, 1774

Robert Adam drew on a rich repertoire of Greek, Etruscan, and Pompeian motifs in creating his influential Neoclassical style.

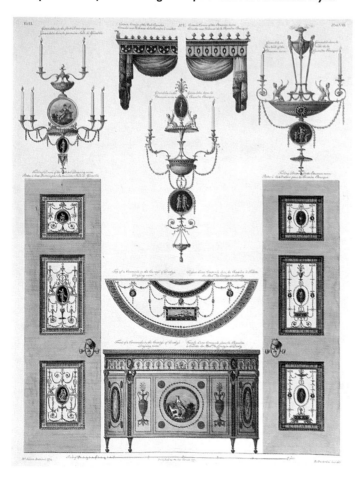

the excavations at Herculaneum in 1737 and at Pompeii in 1748. It was further enhanced by the writings of Edward Gibbon, who began his monumental *Decline and Fall of the Roman Empire* in 1773 and finally completed it in 1788, and by the work of Johann Winckelmann, a German antiquarian and scholar who helped to establish the superior qualities of ancient Greek culture and to spread enthusiasm for Classicism to all branches of the arts.

In architecture, Englishmen such as William Chambers and Robert Adam led the way. The latter's remodeling of Syon House (1762–69), near London, for example, featured an opulent Roman anteroom; his work at nearby Osterley Park included a highly decorative Etruscan Room. In the emerging United States, too, the Classical style was clearly in favor. A particularly fine example can be found at Monticello (built between 1770 and 1775, with later alterations), the elegant country house near Charlottesville, Virginia, which Thomas Jefferson designed for himself.

Music in the Classical era

In the musical sphere, these trends were most evident in the growing taste for simplicity and restraint. In Vienna, for example, Christoph Gluck introduced his 'reform' operas during the 1760's. He declared that the function of music was to serve the text and the demands of the plot, and sought to eliminate COLORATURA singing (the florid elaboration of vocal lines, usually by sopranos). He boosted the roles of both the chorus and the orchestra to compensate for this omission.

The blossoming role of the orchestra was not confined exclusively to the realm of opera. For the first time in the history of music, instrumental forms took precedence over vocal ones. The orchestra itself developed into a comparatively stable performing unit, a recognizable precursor of the ensemble that we know today. The harpsichord gradually disappeared from its ranks, and the main emphasis started to fall upon the strings. The principal difference from today's orchestras was size. Whereas a modern orchestra contains approximately 100 instrumentalists, its eighteenth-century equivalent rarely

The Oath of the Horatii by Jacques-Louis David, 1785

A truly revolutionary painter, David became a Deputy under the new regime and voted for the execution of the king.

exceeded 35. Even the Mannheim orchestra in Germany — the most prestigious outfit of its day, whose discipline and controlled sound were renowned throughout Europe — boasted fewer than 50 musicians. In 1756, its makeup consisted of 20 violins; four each of violoncellos, violas, and double basses; a pair each of oboes, flutes, horns, and bassoons; and a harpsichord. Occasionally, trumpets or kettledrums might be added.

The rise of orchestral music fostered the popular success of both the SYMPHONY and the CONCERTO. The former originated as an operatic overture, but was greatly expanded during the eighteenth century, gaining acceptance as an independent piece, with its traditional core being the four-movement pattern of the SONATA. Haydn, who composed more than 100 symphonies, was the first acknowledged master of the form and is sometimes called 'the father of the symphony.' The concerto, which had already become popular in the Baroque period, continued to develop as it gained prominence. Essentially, the format consisted of a musical exchange between a solo instrument and the orchestra. Normally, this solo instrument was the violin, but the Classical period witnessed the growing sophistication of the pianoforte — so called because its action enabled

it to be played softly (*piano*) or loudly (*forte*) — and this offered scope for wider variation.

In some ways, the restrained and disciplined character of the music of this period scarcely seems to reflect the turbulent, frequently violent events that were taking place on the political stage. However, in certain areas, particularly painting, the revival of Classicism produced art that clearly responded to its historical moment.

The paintings of David

Nowhere was this more evident than in the paintings of Jacques-Louis David, who worked under the shadow of the French Revolution. Ostensibly his pictures illustrated scenes from Roman history, but David's contemporaries understood their true meaning. They were in fact thinly disguised comments on the current state of France, brilliantly catching the mood of the time. *The Oath of the Horatii* (1785), for example,

---

MUSICAL DEFINITIONS

COLORATURA An elaborate, highly ornamented style of singing particularly suited to a light, high, and agile soprano voice.

SYMPHONY An instrumental composition in three or four movements, having the structure of a sonata but played by a full orchestra. The symphony traditionally consisted of three or four movements: a lively opening movement (allegro); a slower, lyrical passage (andante or adagio); a lighter dance sequence (often a minuet); and a vivacious finale. The Classical symphony was perfected by Haydn and Mozart, but the form was greatly expanded by Beethoven and later composers, including Brahms and Mahler.

CONCERTO A composition for one or more solo instruments and orchestra, usually in three movements, established in its modern

form by Mozart. In each movement the soloist may play a cadenza — initially an opportunity to display his or her virtuosity by improvising on some of the themes from the movement. During the Classical period it became usual for the cadenza to be written down.

SONATA Originally a piece of music for instruments as opposed to a cantata, which was sung. It evolved into an extended composition in several contrasting but related movements, written for one or more instruments, usually including a keyboard instrument. The sonata reached its greatest expression during the Classical era in works by Haydn, Mozart, and Beethoven. Haydn and Mozart generally wrote sonatas of three movements (fast-slow-fast), but Beethoven introduced a fourth into many of his works.

which showed a father proffering a cluster of swords to his three sons, was a provocative battle cry, urging the use of force as the only answer to the country's problems. Four years later, David expanded on this theme when he produced *The Lictors Bringing Brutus the Bodies of His Sons*. Brutus had allowed his children to be executed for taking up arms against the Republic, and the warm reaction to David's picture, a stern metaphorical lecture on patriotism and sacrifice, has a piquant relevance when one considers the long list of French men and women who were soon to perish on the guillotine.

Napoleon Bonaparte

The initial euphoria generated by the Revolution turned to disenchantment after 1793, when the executions of Louis XVI and Marie Antoinette unleashed an orgy of killing. During the height of 'the Terror,' more than 1,300 victims were beheaded within the space of six weeks. Even the revolutionary leaders did not escape: Marat was stabbed to death in his bath, while

The Coronation of Napoleon by Jacques-Louis David, 1804

By adopting the imperial title, Napoleon conferred respectability on his military conquests. His decision to crown himself underlined his independence from the church.

Danton, Desmoulins, and Robespierre all went to the guillotine. Amid such mayhem, it seemed cruelly ironic that in a wave of Enlightenment zeal the cathedral of Notre Dame had just been renamed the 'Temple of Reason.'

Out of the vacuum, Napoleon Bonaparte emerged to take control. His successful Italian campaign of 1796–97 brought him to prominence, and within a decade, France was in his grip. On December 2, 1804, in a move calculated to evoke memories of Charlemagne, he crowned himself emperor, while the pope stood in attendance. Through a succession of

stunning military victories, Bonaparte then transformed the map of Europe; for a time, much of present-day Germany, Italy, Holland, Switzerland, and Spain lay at his disposal. Ultimately, only his own excessive ambition defeated him. His disastrous Retreat from Moscow in 1812, which saw the elimination of all but 50,000 of his 600,000 troops, set him on the road to ruin. The Duke of Wellington, in command of the British forces, delivered the *coup de grâce* at Waterloo in 1815.

From 1789 to 1815, France had been the dominant force in European politics. But following Napoleon's decline, as the four 'Great Powers' — Britain, Austria, Russia, and Prussia — met at the Congress of Vienna in 1814, a sense of relief prevailed. The flames of revolution, which had spread throughout North America and France and threatened to unseat the other European monarchies, appeared to have been extinguished. With the restoration of the Bourbons in France (Louis XVIII became king in 1814, Louis XVII having died in prison in 1795), it seemed that the old order had been preserved.

Vienna and the growth of the bourgeoisie

In fact, this was not the case. Dynamic changes continued in Europe, but they advanced through social rather than political developments. Some indication of their strength can be gleaned from the situation in Austria. For most of the Classical period, and certainly between 1780 and 1828, Vienna was the musical capital of Europe. The four greatest composers of the age — Haydn, Mozart, Beethoven, and Schubert — all had strong connections with the city.

For all its attractions, however, the Austrian court was not the power center that Burgundy had been in the fifteenth century, or that Versailles had been under Louis XIV. Quite apart from the Napoleonic invasion, Austria had recently lost territories in Italy and the Netherlands, while in 1806, Francis II (Austria's king) had lost his imperial title when the Holy Roman Empire ceased to exist. As a result, both the crown and the nobility were leading far less ostentatious life-styles and spending less on the arts. The Hungarian Esterházy dynasty was alone in maintaining the grandiose cultural standards that had once been expected of the aristocracy, and this was only possible because the Hungarian provinces had not yet felt the full effect of the Austrian economic reforms.

Despite these setbacks, Vienna managed to retain its cultural ascendancy because an important new source of patronage was emerging from the ranks of the bourgeoisie. This expanding, upwardly mobile class owed its increasing prosperity to a series of economic reforms and to the early effects of the

Facing page, top: Painting by Meytens, 1760
A theater performance in celebration of the marriage of Joseph II, showing the glittering opulence of Viennese society.

Facing page, bottom: Painting of a view of Vienna by Bernardo Bellotto, 1759–61
Vienna was the seat of the Holy Roman Empire and, in musical terms, the cultural heart of Europe.

Industrial Revolution, which during the nineteenth century spread throughout northern Europe from its origins in Britain. A series of labor-saving inventions had ushered in an age of mechanized mass production. Archaic guild restrictions and the vestiges of feudalism were swept away, to be replaced by more efficient working practices. Large factories, able to accommodate a thousand specialized workers under a single roof, overshadowed both the smaller undertakings on manorial estates — which had only survived because of their monopolies and privileges — and the erratic output from the inmates of poorhouses. In Lower Austria the number of people employed in manufacture almost doubled between 1783 and 1790. The key to commercial success shifted from privilege to enterprise.

The rise of the bourgeoisie had significant consequences for musicians. Hitherto, it had been vital for any aspiring composer to seek out a royal appointment or attach himself to a noble household. By the end of the eighteenth century, this was no longer the case. A popular artist might also work on a freelance basis, attempting to earn a living through public performances. In Vienna, for example, two of the mainstays of cultural life were the subscription concert and the salon. For the former, groups of individuals, both aristocratic and middle-class, banded together to fund a concert. The salons, meanwhile, were more intimate musical gatherings held in private households. Once again, the patrons of these soirées might just as easily be bourgeois as noble. Both represented potential sources of income for composers.

Development of the music industry

The rapid pace of change is readily discernible in the contrasting fortunes of Haydn, Mozart, and Beethoven. Haydn had the most traditional career pattern of the three, holding the post of Kapellmeister (director of court music) at the Hungarian court of Prince Esterházy for some 30 years. Mozart tried in vain to obtain a similar court appointment, but was ultimately obliged to earn the bulk of his income from giving subscription concerts. By contrast, Beethoven (whose career bridged the Classical and Romantic traditions) was far less dependent on royal patronage and could afford to have informal relations with those of the aristocracy who did sponsor him. Possibly the first successful 'freelance' composer, he earned a living through commissions, sales of his music, and public concerts.

The diversity of Beethoven's sources of income illustrates just how far the music business had evolved by this stage. Most major cities could now boast at least one public concert venue. A Music Hall had opened in Dublin as early as 1741. Seven years later, it was followed by the Holywell Music Room at Oxford, the first establishment of its kind in England. Popular concerts could also be heard at the Vauxhall Gardens, on the south bank of the River Thames in London. James Boswell reported that the music there was 'vocal and instrumental, not too refined for the general ear,' although the Gardens did play host to a public rehearsal of Handel's *Music for the Royal Fireworks* in 1749. This attracted an audience of more than

Above: Vauxhall Gardens by Rowlandson, 1784
Pleasure gardens such as Vauxhall provided music to suit all tastes.

Above: Engraving by Holzhalb, after Schellenberg
Performance of a harpsichord concerto at a subscription concert in Zurich, 1777.

Above: Painting by Barthelemy, 1766

The boy Mozart playing the clavichord at an English tea party hosted by the Princesse de Conti.

12,000 people, rendering London Bridge impassable to traffic for more than three hours.

By the end of the century, music publishing had become a significant industry, complemented by a fast-developing music press. Even the professional music critic had made an appearance. The new journals that sprang up contained reviews of the latest concerts, along with helpful advice for the growing number of amateur musicians who wished to play at home. Refined manufacturing techniques had brought down the prices of most musical instruments, and it was becoming fashionable to regard a modicum of musical ability as a necessary social accomplishment.

Beethoven, forward-looking in this respect as in many others, was anxious that his music should not be reserved for privileged minorities, but should appeal to the broad spectrum of humanity. This attitude in itself reveals how far the democratic ideals of the Enlightenment were fulfilled. Before 1750, music was created mainly for the benefit of the church, the nobility, and the crown; during the Classical era, its enjoyment was made available to many other levels of society; the following Romantic age would provide music for the individual.

Textile factory near Preston, engraved by Tingle after Allom, c.1840–50

The textile industry was revolutionized by technical advances, leading to the building of huge factories that dominated their surroundings and employed hundreds of workers.

Featured Composers

Gluck

Christoph Willibald Gluck 1714–1787

RECOMMENDED WORK
Orfeo ed Euridice
Sony S2K48040
Michael Chance (alto) Orfeo; Nancy Argenta
(sop) Euridice; Stefan Beckerbauer (treb) Amore;
Stuttgart Chamber Choir; Tafelmusik/Frieder
Bernius
*An invigorating experience, with alto Michael Chance
reveling in the original castrato role of Orfeo. The
period-instrument playing is sensitive, the conducting
perceptive, the sound excellent.*

REPRESENTATIVE WORKS
Alceste
Iphigénie en Aulide
Iphigénie en Tauride

Above: Engraving by Saint-Aubin, 1777
A performance of Gluck's Armide, a powerful and dramatic interpretation of a poem by Quinault.

Portrait of Gluck by an unknown contemporary artist

Born in Bohemia, Gluck was one of nine children of a forester. The family's itinerant existence was not to Gluck's liking, and at the age of 13, denied parental support for his musical ambitions, he ran away to Prague, earning his keep by playing at rural dances and singing in churches. In time his father recognized Gluck's love of music and gave him some support. At the age of 21, he was employed as a musician to Prince Melzi in Vienna. Following the Prince's marriage in 1737, the household, including Gluck, moved to Milan.

This was a wonderful opportunity for the young composer, who had been spellbound by Italian opera in Prague. He became a pupil of the composer Giovanni Battista Sammartini, and after four years of study wrote his first opera, *Artaserse*, to a libretto by Pietro Metastasio. It opened the season at the Teatro Regio Ducal in Milan and was an instant success. Commissions for operas flooded in.

After three hectic years, Gluck left Italy for England in 1745. The second of the Jacobite revolts had left London subdued, but Gluck was nonetheless commissioned by the Italian Opera of London to create two operas — in direct competition with projects by Handel. Gluck's operas were relatively successful, though Handel commented that Gluck knew no more about counterpoint than his cook. Before Gluck left London, he took part in two concerts playing the glass harmonica, a popular fairground instrument. Tapping 20 or more partly filled water glasses, he captivated his audience with the delicacy of sound.

In 1746 he took up an appointment to conduct Pietro Mingotti's Italian opera company, and traveled with them in Austria and Denmark over the next few years. He settled in Vienna in 1750 and married a successful merchant's daughter, Maria Anna Bergin. In 1754 the Empress Maria Theresa appointed him Kapellmeister, a post he held for more than 15 years. During this time Gluck developed his ideas for the reform of opera. *Orfeo ed Euridice* (first performed, in Italian, in 1762) exemplifies these ideas, chief among them that music should be subjugated to the demands of the text. In addition, Gluck gave a more central role to the chorus. In the introduction to *Alceste*, another 'reform' opera, Gluck made explicit his revolutionary theories. First performed in an Italian version in Vienna in 1767, *Alceste*, like *Orfeo*, has a classical theme. The chorus plays a particularly significant part and is given a character of its own, representing the people of Thessaly. Greatly revised, the opera was presented in Paris in a French version in 1776. Both versions were highly successful.

Gluck moved to Paris in 1773. It was there that he composed *Iphigénie en Aulide* in 1774, *Armide* in 1777, and *Iphigénie en Tauride* in 1778, all of which show his increasing mastery of dramatic form. He eventually retired to Vienna, where he lived in luxury until his death in 1787.

Haydn

Franz Joseph Haydn 1732–1809

RECOMMENDED WORKS

Symphony No. 94 in G, 'Surprise'
Symphony No. 104 in D, 'London'
Philips 434 153-2
Concertgebouw Orchestra/Colin Davis
With engagingly characterful conducting, imaginative playing, and full-bodied ambient sound, this proves among the most delightful of Haydn symphony CDs.

Die Schöpfung (The Creation)
Deutsche Grammophon 425 077-2
Gundula Janowitz (sop); Christa Ludwig (contr); Fritz Wunderlich, Werner Krenn (ten); Walter Berry (bass); Vienna Singverein; Berlin Philharmonic Orchestra/Herbert von Karajan
One of Karajan's most joyful recorded performances, beautifully sung (especially by Fritz Wunderlich) and well transferred to CD.

REPRESENTATIVE WORKS

Symphonies Nos. 6–8, 49, 100, 101, & 103
Trumpet Concerto
Cello Concertos
The Seasons
String Quartets
Seven Last Words of Our Saviour on the Cross
Nelsonmesse

Portrait of the composer by Johann Zitterer, c.1795

Haydn was born in March 1732 into a Europe still dominated by powerful dynasties — the Hanovers in England, Bourbons in France, and Hapsburgs in Austria. The family lived on the borders of Austria and Hungary. Influenced from an early age by his father's love of folk music, Haydn was spotted by the choirmaster of Vienna's St. Stephen's Cathedral at the age of eight. He was taken to Vienna and sang in the choir until his voice changed.

With borrowed money, Haydn bought a secondhand clavier; he then started to teach as well as to refine his playing and composition techniques. Along the way, he also met useful contacts, such as the fashionable poet Pietro Metastasio and the singing teacher Nicola Porpora, who taught Haydn composition.

In 1759 an aristocratic patron, Count Morzin, employed Haydn to supervise his private orchestra and Haydn wrote his first symphony. This attracted the attention of Prince Paul Esterházy, who in 1761 appointed him vice-Kapellmeister. Haydn moved to the Eisenstadt court of this powerful and wealthy Hungarian family. The prince, who himself played the violin and cello, wanted to enhance the court's image by encouraging orchestral and operatic music; this duly became the vice-Kapellmeister's duties.

The prince died within a year and was replaced by his brother, who had even more expansive ideas, calling for a continuous stream of compositions, both operatic and instrumental, from Haydn. This prince, Nikolaus the Magnificent, played the baryton (a six-stringed, bowed instrument). Haydn discreetly mastered it himself and over the years composed over 150 pieces for the prince to play.

In 1764, Prince Nikolaus visited the Palace of Versailles, an experience that prompted him to build the glorious Esterháza palace. With its 126 guest rooms and expansive gardens, built on what had been an inhospitable area of marshland by Lake Neusiedler, the palace became Haydn's home. The Esterházys' increased status required yet more music — 14 stage works in as many years, quite apart from daily needs and special occasions. In 1768 the prince built a 400-seat theater in which he expected some kind of performance every day; five years later he added a separate puppet theater which also performed Haydn's operas. By then Haydn was in sole charge, the Kapellmeister having died in 1766, and in one year alone there were 125 performances of 17 operas.

Those in service could not escape the sense of isolation on the stretch of damp

Haydn's orchestra at Esterháza
Haydn, at the keyboard, oversees an opera performance for his patrons.

109

After the watercolor by Balthasar Wigand

A gala performance of The Creation, given in Haydn's honor at Vienna University in March 1808.

marshland, estranged from their families. From 1766 to 1772, Haydn responded to this environment with a series of dark compositions, provoked also by the stirrings of the German literary movement later called *Sturm und Drang* (Storm and Stress). The intense string quartets that form Haydn's Opus 20 were composed at this time; with these pieces Haydn's reputation as founder of the classical string quartet was established. His next pieces in this form (Opus 33) so impressed Mozart that the younger composer dedicated six of his own quartets to Haydn.

In 1784, Haydn was invited to compose six symphonies by the Parisian Masonic Lodge. These became known as the *Paris Symphonies* (Nos. 82–87) and were later followed by three more (Nos. 90–92). His fame spread to Spain, and he was invited by Cádiz Cathedral to write for Good Friday the seven haunting movements of the oratorio *Seven Last Words of Our Savior from the Cross* — for which he was apparently paid with a large chocolate cake stuffed with gold coins. He returned to this piece later, arranging it for string quartet and as a cantata with soloists.

In 1790, Prince Nikolaus died at the age of 77. In the wake of the French Revolution, his son Anton curbed many of the court's excesses and dismissed the orchestra but offered a substantial pension to Haydn in recognition of his long and distinguished service. In January 1791, Haydn went to London, where he was immediately treated as a celebrity. Oxford University conferred an honorary degree on him, and Haydn repaid the compliment by composing his *Oxford Symphony* (No. 92). During the two seasons of 1791–92 and 1794–95 he composed the 12 symphonies now known as the *London Symphonies*. Various of these bear nicknames intended to attract audiences: *The Surprise* (No. 94) includes a sudden loud chord at the start of the slow movement, and *The Clock* (No. 101) has a 'tick-tock' running throughout the slow movement.

After his acclaimed second season, various attempts were made to persuade him

to remain in England. But after Prince Anton Esterházy's death, the new prince, Nikolaus II, wanted Haydn as his Kapellmeister. At the age of 59, Haydn returned to Eisenstadt and began shaping the musical life of the new court. In 1796 he wrote a *Trumpet Concerto* for his friend Anton Weidinger, a trumpeter in the Vienna Court Orchestra. Three years previously, Weidinger had invented a type of trumpet with keys, and Haydn's concerto explored the possibilities of the new instrument.

The new prince, however, was not fond of instrumental music, so Haydn began to write a series of Masses. These incorporated all his knowledge of opera and symphonies. Each had a theme and a name: the *Missa in Tempore Belli* (Mass in time of war, 1796); *Heiligmesse* (Holy Mass, 1796); *Missa in angustiis* (Nelson Mass, 1798); *Theresienmesse* (Theresia Mass, 1799); *Schöpfungsmesse* (Creation Mass, 1801); and *Harmoniemesse* (Wind-Band Mass, 1802).

Haydn's great oratorio *The Creation* was performed in 1798. Like the Masses, *The Creation* was an outlet for Haydn's devout religious feelings. Starting with a slow, mysterious depiction of chaos, the work falls into three parts — 'Creation of the Earth'; 'Creation of the Living Creatures'; 'Creation of Adam and Eve' — and is a loving portrait of nature, using music to mimic the flight of birds and the motion of the sea, and even employing a contrabassoon (a rare instrument at the time) to represent the equally rare hippopotamus. *The Creation* was followed by *The Seasons*, a secular oratorio based on a poem by James Thomson, first performed in Vienna's Schwarzenberg Palace in 1801.

Haydn was released from the Esterházy family in 1804 after 40 years' service. He attended a gala performance of *The Creation* to honor his seventy-sixth birthday and was so moved by his reception that he had to be taken home before the end. Never again would he make a public appearance. As Napoleon's invading troops bombarded Vienna, the 77-year-old Haydn lay dying in his home on the outskirts of the city, and as a final mark of respect Napoleon placed a guard of honor outside his Gumpendorf house.

Boccherini

Luigi Boccherini 1743–1805

RECOMMENDED WORKS
Cello Concertos in G & B flat
Virgin Classics VC7 59015-2
Steven Isserlis (vcl); Ostrobothnian Chamber
Orchestra/Juha Kangas
*Elegantly phrased and with vital accompaniments,
these beautifully graded (and recorded) performances
reveal the measure of Boccherini's graceful style.*

REPRESENTATIVE WORKS
**Symphonies in D minor, G506, 'La casa del
Diavolo'; in A, G511; in E flat, G513**
**String Quartets in A, G170; in G, G223, 'La
Tiranna'**
**Guitar Quintet in C, G453, 'La ritrata di
Madrid'**
Octet in G, G470

Portrait of Boccherini, c.1765–68

Boccherini was born in the Italian town of
Lucca into a family of talented artists and
musicians. His father, a double-bass player,
was impressed with his young son's abilities as a cellist. He sent him at the age of 13
to study in Rome with the Maestro di
Cappella at St. Peter's, and later accompanied him to the Royal Court in Vienna —
the first of three visits before Boccherini
was 21. In 1764, Boccherini visited the
composer and organist Giovanni Battista
Sammartini in Milan, and the same year
returned to Lucca to play in the Theater
Orchestra. He composed intensively and
formed a string quartet, one of whose
members was his friend Filippo Manfredi.
In 1766 he set off on a concert tour with
Manfredi, and visited northern Italy before
arriving in Paris in 1767. There an outstandingly favorable reception at the
Concert Spirituel gave Boccherini the
opportunity to publish quartets, trios, and
sonatas for keyboard and violin.

The eighteenth century was the era of
technical virtuosity; what Corelli and his
followers had done for the violin,
Boccherini proceeded to do for the cello,
with a series of ten cello concertos that
stretched players' abilities to the full. Most
of these are thought to have been written
before he settled in Madrid in 1769 to concentrate on chamber music. The invitation to visit Spain came from the Spanish
ambassador to Paris; Boccherini soon
became a composer at the Spanish court.
There he wrote a large amount of music
suitable for court performance, mostly
quartets and quintets.

This post was followed by a spell at the
court of Prince Wilhelm of Prussia, but
after Wilhelm's death Boccherini returned
to Spain, and from 1800 he organized concerts and composed for Lucien Buona-
parte, Napoleon's brother. Boccherini's
popularity was such at one stage that his
publisher in Paris issued quartets by other
composers under Boccherini's name.
Nevertheless, Boccherini died in poverty
in Madrid in 1805.

Boccherini wrote 18 symphonies, but
his lyrical gifts show themselves most
strongly in his 300 chamber works. He
composed 93 string quintets, with two
cellos in place of the customary cello and

Guitar made by Rafael Vallego in Granada, c.1785
**Boccherini exploited the growing
popularity of the Spanish guitar,
sometimes even mimicking its sound on
other instruments.**

double-bass contributing a vibrant and
sensuous bass line. Nine guitar quintets
also form a part of his chamber output, in
which darting accents lend a bright and
nervous freshness to music of exceptional
clarity. Already endowed with plenty of
Italian elegance and brio, the young man
discovered in Vienna the beginnings of
Romantic passion, the spirit of *Sturm und
Drang* that adds so much drama to middle-
period Haydn. His discovery of Spanish
dance rhythms and the elaborate guitar
music of Andalusia resulted in a distinctive
and individual style that won the admiration of Gluck, as well as influencing
Mozart and Haydn.

Mozart

Wolfgang Amadeus Mozart 1756–1791

RECOMMENDED WORKS

Symphony No. 41 in C, K551, 'Jupiter'
Philips 434 149-2
Orchestra of the 18th Century/Frans Brüggen
A riveting account of Mozart's most affirmative symphonic masterpiece, played on authentic 18th-century instruments (or accurate modern replicas), superbly conducted and beautifully recorded.

Don Giovanni, K527
Angel CDS7 47260-8
Eberhard Wächter (bar) Don Giovanni; Joan Sutherland (sop) Donna Anna; Elisabeth Schwarzkopf (sop) Donna Elvira; Graziella Sciutti (sop) Zerlina; Luigi Alva (ten) Don Ottavio; Guiseppe Taddei (bar) Leporello; Piero Cappuccilli (bar) Masetto; Gottlob Frick (bass) Commendatore; Philharmonia Chorus and Orchestra/Carlo Maria Giulini
Vintage stereo recording that outclasses most modern rivals and features some of the finest singers of the time. Giulini conducts with a strong sense of theater.

REPRESENTATIVE WORKS

Symphonies Nos. 25, 29, 38, 39, & 40
Piano Concertos Nos. 19, 20, & 27
Sinfonia concertante for violin and viola
String Quartets: the 'Hunt,' the 'Dissonance'
String Quintet No. 4 in G minor, K516
Le nozze di Figaro
Così fan tutte
Die Zauberflöte
Requiem in D minor, K626

Wolfgang Amadeus Mozart was born in Salzburg in Austria, the son of Leopold, Kapellmeister to the Prince-Archbishop of Salzburg. By the age of three he could play the piano, and he was composing by the time he was five; minuets from this period show a remarkable understanding of form. Mozart's elder sister Maria Anna (known as Nannerl) was also a gifted keyboard player, and in 1762 their father took the two prodigies on a short performing tour, of the courts at Vienna and Munich. Encouraged by their reception, they embarked the next year on a longer tour, including

Posthumous portrait by Barbara Krafft, 1814

two weeks at Versailles, where the children enchanted Louis XV. In 1764 they arrived in London. There Mozart wrote his first three symphonies, influenced by Johann Christian Bach, youngest son of Johann Sebastian, who lived in the city.

After their return to Salzburg, there followed three trips to Italy between 1769 and 1773. In Rome, Mozart heard a performance of Allegri's *Miserere*. The score of this work was closely guarded, but Mozart managed to transcribe the music almost perfectly from memory. On Mozart's first visit to Milan, his opera *Mitridate, rè di Ponto* was successfully produced, followed on a subsequent visit by *Lucia Silla*. The latter showed signs of the rich, full orchestration that characterizes his later operas.

A trip to Vienna in 1773 failed to produce the court appointment that both Mozart and his father wished for him, but did introduce Mozart to the influence of Haydn, whose *Sturm und Drang* string quartets (Opus 20) had recently been published. The influence is clear in Mozart's six string quartets, K168–173, and in his *Symphony in G minor*, K183. Another trip in search of patronage ended less happily. Accompanied by his mother, Mozart left Salzburg in 1777, traveling through Mannheim to Paris. But in July 1778 his mother died. Nor was the trip a professional success: since he no longer passed for a prodigy, Mozart's reception there was muted and hopes of a job came to nothing.

Back in Salzburg, Mozart worked for two years as a church organist for the new archbishop. His employer was less kindly disposed to the Mozart family than his predecessor had been, but the composer

Interior of the Teatro Regio by Domenico Oliviero
A performance of a typical Italian opera seria at the Turin theater.

Detail of a painting of Joseph II's wedding in 1760
The child Mozart sits in the musician's box at the wedding of his future patron.

nonetheless produced some of his earliest masterpieces. The famous *Sinfonia concertante* for violin, viola, and orchestra was written in 1780, and the following year Mozart's first great stage work, the opera *Idomeneo*, was produced in Munich, where Mozart also wrote his *Serenade for 13 wind instruments*, K361. On his return from Munich, however, the hostility brewing between him and the archbishop came to a head, and Mozart resigned. On delivering his resignation, he was verbally abused and eventually physically ejected from the archbishop's residence.

Without patronage, Mozart was forced to confront the perils of a freelance existence. Initially his efforts met with some success. He took up residence in Vienna, and in 1782 his opera *Die Entführung aus dem Serail* (The Abduction from the Seraglio) was produced in the city and rapturously received. The same year in Vienna's St. Stephen's Cathedral, Mozart married Constanze Weber. Soon afterward he initiated a series of subscription concerts at which he performed his piano concertos and improvised at the keyboard. Most of Mozart's great piano concertos were written for these concerts, including those in C, K467; A, K488; and C minor, K491. In these concertos Mozart brought to the genre a unity and diversity it had not

had before, combining bold symphonic richness with passages of subtle delicacy.

In 1785, Mozart dedicated to Haydn the six string quartets that now bear Haydn's name. Included in this group are those known as the *Hunt*, which makes use of hunting calls, and the *Dissonance*, which opens with an eerie succession of dissonant chords. Overwhelmed by their quality, Haydn confessed to Leopold Mozart, 'Before God and as an honest man I tell you that your son is the greatest composer known to me either in person or by name.' The pieces are matched in excellence in Mozart's chamber music output only by his *String Quintets*, outstanding among which are those in C, K515; G minor, K516; and D, K593.

Also in 1785, Mozart and Lorenzo da Ponte collaborated on the first of a series of operatic masterpieces. *Le nozze di Figaro* (The Marriage of Figaro) was begun that year and performed in 1786 to an enthusiastic audience in Vienna and even greater acclaim later in Prague. In 1787, Prague's National Theater saw the premiere of *Don Giovanni*, a moralizing version of the Don Juan legend in which the licentious

nobleman receives his comeuppance and descends into the fiery regions of hell. The third and last da Ponte opera was *Così fan tutte* (Women are all the same), commissioned by Emperor Joseph II and produced at Vienna's Burgtheater in 1790. Its cynical treatment of the theme of sexual infidelity may have been responsible for its relative lack of success with the Viennese, who responded with such enthusiasm to the comedy of *Figaro*.

Mozart wrote two more operas: the *opera seria La clemenza di Tito* (The Mercy of Tito) and *Die Zauberflöte* (The Magic Flute). The latter was commissioned by actor-manager Emanuel Schikaneder to his own libretto. Its plot, a fairy tale combined with strong Masonic elements (Mozart was a devoted Freemason), is bizarre, but drew from Mozart some of his greatest music. When produced in 1791, two months before Mozart's death, the opera survived an initially cool reception and gradually won audiences over.

The year 1788 saw the composition of Mozart's two finest symphonies. *Symphony No. 40*, in the tragic key of G minor, contrasts strikingly with the affirmatory *Symphony No. 41* (*Jupiter*). Neither helped alleviate his financial plight, however, which after 1789 became critical. An extensive concert tour of Europe failed to earn significant sums. A new emperor came to the Austrian throne, but Mozart was unsuccessful in his bid to become Kapellmeister. He was deeply in debt when, in July 1791, he received an anonymous commission to write a Requiem. (The author of the commission was Count Franz von Walsegg, who wished to pass off the work as his own.) Mozart did not live to finish the *Requiem*. He became ill in autumn 1791 and died on December 5; his burial the next day was attended only by a gravedigger. Rumors that Mozart had been poisoned abounded in Vienna after his death, many suggesting that rival composer Antonio Salieri was responsible. Many now believe a heart weakened by bouts of rheumatic fever caused his death.

Mozart's legacy is inestimable. A master of every form in which he worked, he set standards of excellence that have inspired generations of composers.

Clementi

Muzio Clementi 1752–1832

RECOMMENDED WORKS
Keyboard Sonatas
RCA GD87753
Vladimir Horowitz (pno)
A highly dramatic rendition of music that is in many ways prophetic of Beethoven. The recording is quite old, but Horowitz's dynamism transcends the mono sound barrier.

REPRESENTATIVE WORK
Symphony No. 3, 'Great National'

Portrait engraving after Thomas Hardy, 18th century

Clementi was the eldest son of a Roman silversmith who was also a keen amateur musician. By the age of seven he was receiving organ lessons, and in open competition with adults was appointed the local church organist. At the age of 14 he went to study in England, after the Englishman Peter Beckford heard him play and was impressed enough to become his patron. Clementi made his first London appearance in 1775. In 1779 he published his six *Piano Sonatas* Opus 2; these established the piano sonata as distinct from the harpsichord sonata and made Clementi's reputation.

In 1781 he visited Europe and was astonished in France by the excitement his work generated. He engaged in public competition with other pianists, including the famous 'piano duel' with Mozart, in which each player improvised upon his own compositions. Neither was declared outright winner: Mozart considered Clementi 'a Charlatan — like all Italians,' while Clementi was more gracious about Mozart's gifts.

Clementi continued his travels in Europe and wrote more sonatas (his final tally was over 100). By adding a third movement to the two that were typical of the Italian style, Clementi brought the sonata to a new level of development. He settled in London in spring 1785 and remained there for the next 20 years, re-establishing old links with the Hanover Concert series and enjoying rising status as a soloist and conductor. He turned his attentions to composing symphonies, but his works suffered from comparison with those of the greatly revered Haydn, who visited London in 1791 and probably contributed to Clementi's lack of success. None of his own efforts was published during his lifetime.

In 1802, by now a partner in a successful piano-manufacturing business, Clementi took his ex-pupil, John Field, on a tour of Europe to promote pianos. Field remained in St. Petersburg while Clementi continued traveling. In 1810 he returned to London, continuing to prove himself a shrewd businessman. Approaching 60, he married Emma Gisborne, with whom he had four children. He continued to compose and in 1813 joined the board of the Philharmonic Society. He made visits abroad in pursuit of a wider audience for his symphonies, but by now the Continent was enraptured by Beethoven — some of whose works Clementi published.

In 1817, Clementi began *Gradus ad Parnassum*, a volume of studies and five-finger exercises still in use today as a piano lesson, responsible for Clementi's influence on generations of pianists (although Debussy parodied him in his piano piece *Dr. Gradus ad Parnassum*). He retired to Evesham in Worcestershire and died after a short illness at the age of 80.

Grand piano made by Clementi, 1821
Clementi was a renowned piano player and wrote more than 100 sonatas for the instrument.

Cherubini

Luigi Cherubini 1760–1842

Portrait by Jean-Auguste Ingres, §842
***It was a mark of the composer's
reputation in France that he was painted
by the foremost portraitist of the day.***

Born in Florence, Cherubini revealed his musical gifts early; by the age of 18 he had written 35 compositions, including a cantata performed in the cathedral of Florence to honor the future emperor Leopold II. Suitably impressed, Leopold granted funds for the young composer to study in Milan under the leading opera composer, Giuseppe Sarti.

Cherubini's first opera, *Quinto Fabio*, was performed in 1780 but met with little response. He set his sights on London, and wrote *La finta principessa* in 1785 and *Giulio Sabino* in 1786 for the King's Theatre, earning the respect of both the intelligentsia and the English royal circle. While the theater was in summer recess, he visited Paris, where he was presented to the French queen, Marie Antoinette. He settled in the city and with the librettist Marmontel created his first French opera, *Demophon*, performed in December 1788 without great success.

Over the next few years Cherubini conducted several operas for an Italian opera company in Paris started by the queen's hairdresser. He introduced changes to the orchestra and intensified the dramatic action, mirroring the temperament of a society in the throes of revolution. The theater group broke up in 1792, and Cherubini spent the next year in the Normandy countryside working on *Eliza*.

Returning to an ever more turbulent Paris, Cherubini was eventually offered a post at the newly established Institut National de Musique, which two years later became the Conservatoire. He wrote several more operas, including in 1797 *Médée*, based on the myth of Medea, who after rejection by Jason murdered her own children. The main focus of the opera is the psychological torment of Medea, who dominates the stage in a display notable for the huge range, in both pitch and dynamics, of her vocal part.

In 1805, Cherubini moved to Vienna, where he received the praise of both Haydn and Beethoven. When Napoleon marched into the city in 1809, to Cherubini's surprise the Emperor requested his return to Paris: Cherubini complied. His *Requiem in C minor* was later composed at the request of the government to commemorate the anniversary of the execution of Louis XVI. The work was first performed in 1816 and was much admired by Beethoven, who preferred it to the more famous *Requiem* by Mozart. It has no soloists, but its bare choral writing is lifted by colorful orchestration.

Relations with Napoleon soured, however, when the Emperor found fault with one of Cherubini's compositions. Cherubini's retort — 'Your Majesty knows no more about it than I about a battle' — resulted in his losing his official post. Temporarily abandoning music, he retired to the chateau of the Prince of Chimay, where he studied painting and botany. However, the local church's need for a new Mass tempted him to begin composing again, and the resultant Mass was a resounding success. In 1822 he became director of the revitalized Conservatoire, a post he held for almost 20 years. After 1835, when he composed another *Requiem*, Cherubini concentrated on teaching, his pupils including Halévy and Auber. He died in 1842.

Field

John Field 1782–1837

RECOMMENDED WORKS
Nocturnes Nos. 1, 2, 4–6, 8–16, 18
Telarc CD80199z
John O'Conor (pno)
Few pianists have balanced Field's Romanticism and Classicism as effectively as John O'Conor and Telarc; the artists do both sides of his nature proud with an extremely lifelike piano sound.

REPRESENTATIVE WORKS
Piano Concertos
Piano Sonata in B
Variations in B flat on a Russian Air, 'Kamarinskaya'

Contemporary portrait engraving of the composer by C. Mayer

Born into a musical Dublin family, John Field showed an early interest in music. By the age of nine he had begun lessons with Tomaso Giordani, and in the spring of 1792 gave his first public performances on the piano to an ecstatic reception. In 1793 the family moved to London, where his father, a violinist, joined the orchestra at the Haymarket Theatre while Field took employment in the showrooms of Muzio Clementi's piano warehouse. He undertook a seven-year apprenticeship to Clementi and in 1793 made his first London appearance in a benefit concert playing a piece described as 'a lesson on the new grand piano forte.'

In his final year of apprenticeship, Field took the bold step of presenting his *First Piano Concerto* at a concert held at the

Engraving of St. Petersburg, c.1835
Following his concert at the Philharmonic Hall, Field became the darling of fashionable society in St. Petersburg.

King's Theatre early in 1799. He basked in two seasons of great popularity, in the second year publishing his important *Piano Sonatas*, Opus 1, dedicated to Clementi in recognition of his guidance over the years. In 1802, Clementi reciprocated by taking Field on a continental tour starting in Paris and ending in St. Petersburg.

Field decided to remain in Russia, and lived under the patronage of an important Russian general, Marklovsky. Within a year he made his concert debut at the Philharmonic Hall in St. Petersburg. He became much in demand for teaching, concerts and for private performances in fashionable homes. He toured Russia, making his Moscow debut in 1806, and eventually divided his existence between St. Petersburg and Moscow. From Field's early days in Russia date *The Bear Dance* and *Variations on a Russian Air*, both piano duets. The latter is based on a Russian folk tune and is a forerunner of the nationalistic works of Glinka and Balakirev.

Field flourished as a piano virtuoso of rare talent. He wrote seven piano concertos, but his most important compositions are his *Nocturnes*, a form he developed to illustrate the expressive side of his playing, which countered his sheer technical brilliance. The interpretive style he forged influenced Romantic piano composers such as Chopin and Liszt. He published 19 *Nocturnes* between 1812 and 1836, all characterized by a mood of melancholy and the use of widely spaced broken chords in the left hand while the right hand carries the melody.

While living in St. Petersburg, Field married one of his pupils, Adelaide, but he also kept a French mistress; both women bore him sons. Adelaide left him, however, and Field's creative work seriously diminished as alcoholism gripped him. In 1831 he returned to London for cancer treatment. He gave concert performances in England, France, Switzerland, Belgium, and Italy, but these were poor shadows of his performances in Russia. In Naples his health deteriorated, and for most of 1834 he lay in the hospital until rescued by a Russian benefactor. He returned to Moscow, where he worked intermittently until his death in 1837.

Auber

Daniel-François-Esprit Auber 1782–1871

RECOMMENDED WORK

Fra Diavolo: overture
Mercury 434 309-2
Detroit Symphony Orchestra/Paul Paray
Parisian gaiety and color combined with formidable orchestral discipline; a recording that virtually brings the orchestra into your living room. The disc includes other overtures by Auber and Suppé.

REPRESENTATIVE WORKS
La Muette de Portici
Le Domino noir
Le Cheval de bronze
Le Maçon

Colored etching after Johann Schoeller, c.1835
A scene from **Le Serment ou les Faux-monnayeurs,** *Auber's comic opera about a scurrilous counterfeiter.*

Portrait photograph by Nadar, c.1860

Auber was one of the leading nineteenth-century exponents of *opéra comique*. The son of a huntsman turned art dealer, he was born in Normandy and at an early age revealed his gift for playing the piano. By the time he was a teenager, he had written Italianate concert arias, a piano sonata, and a string quartet.

In 1802, England and France signed the Peace of Amiens. Auber's father sent him to England to acquire skills in commerce, but the following year England again declared war on France, and Auber returned home to concentrate on music. His single-act *pasticcio* (a composition formed by combining the music of two or more composers), *L'Erreur d'un Moment*, was performed in Paris in 1805 and was seen by Cherubini, who agreed to give him further instruction. He began to compose prolifically in many forms, and with Cherubini's guidance achieved his first successful *opéras comiques* with *La Bergère châtelaine* in 1820 and *Emma* in 1821. This led to his meeting the important librettist Eugène Scribe, with whom he struck up a working friendship that would last 40 years.

Auber deviated from the French style of opera for the next three productions, drawing on Rossini's work, which he much admired. He reverted to the French idiom in 1824 with *Léocadie* and in 1825 with *Le Maçon*, which epitomized the best of French *opéra comique*. Other successes followed, Auber and Scribe achieving a musical cocktail of French opera with the flair of Rossini's ideas and alternately funny and sad reflections upon life from the pen of Scribe. The partnership grew in strength, and they were invited to compose the opera *La Muette de Portici* for the Académie Royale, which was successfully performed in 1828. An opera on a grand scale based on the French Revolution, its impact was such that its premiere in Brussels is said to have sparked off a revolt to free Belgium from Dutch rule. Typically of Grand Opera, it features dramatic stage effects and huge crowd scenes.

In all, more than 45 operas by Auber were presented in Paris, 37 in collaboration with Scribe. A good example of Auber's comic opera style is *Fra Diavolo*, in which the story of the pursuit and capture of a Robin Hood–like criminal is accompanied by simple, well-orchestrated melodies, punctuated by decorative figures that allow the singers to show off.

In 1825, Auber was awarded the Légion d'Honneur by Charles X, and in 1852 Napoleon III appointed him music director of his Imperial Chapel. Following in the footsteps of Cherubini, in 1842 he became director of the Paris Conservatoire, a post he occupied until a year before his death in 1871.

Meyerbeer

Giacomo Meyerbeer 1791–1864

RECOMMENDED WORK
Les Patineurs
Sony CD46341
Philadelphia Orchestra/Eugene Ormandy
With his key operas being grand in length as well as conception, the ballet music from various operas brought together in this suite serves as a splendid introduction to Meyerbeer's world. An engaging performance by an orchestra of virtuosos. Disc includes highlights from Swan Lake *and* Giselle.

REPRESENTATIVE WORKS
Robert le Diable
Le Prophète
Dinorah
L'Africaine

Above: The ballet scene in *Le Prophète*, 1849
This is one of the earliest known photographs of an opera performance.

Meyerbeer enjoyed a privileged upbringing as the son of a rich and influential Jewish merchant who was an official contractor to the army in Germany and owner of sugar factories. His mother's family were well-regarded bankers, and their home near Berlin was something of a focal point for gatherings of the cultural elite, including nobility — Meyerbeer's music teacher also coached the royal princes. The composer made his first public appearance as a pianist at the age of seven.

By the age of 19 he had collaborated with the head ballet-master of the Royal Opera and created a 'ballet pantomime' called *Der Fischer und das Milchmädchen* (The Fisher and the Milkmaid). In the same year, 1810, he moved to Darmstadt to continue his musical education. There he met other students and under the loose leadership of Carl von Weber formed a circle who wrote reviews of each other's work under pen names. During this period he wrote two operas, *Der Admiral* (The Admiral) and *Jephtas Gelübde* (Jephta's Vow). He traveled to Munich and managed to have *Jephtas Gelübde* staged at the end of 1812, to a rather indifferent audience; the following year, a comic opera,

Portrait engraving based on a photograph, c.1860

Wirth und Gast (Host and Guest), met the same fate in Stuttgart. In 1814, Meyerbeer became court composer to the Grand Duke of Hesse.

Meyerbeer's compositions continued to receive mixed receptions, while his playing generated much admiration. His friend Salieri suggested he lighten the rather heavy Germanic construction of his operas, and in 1816 Meyerbeer traveled to Italy to absorb the freer approaches of the Italian style. With interruptions to oversee foreign productions, he remained in Italy for nine years. During this time he was greatly influenced by the works of Rossini and wrote six increasingly successful operas. Of these, *Il Crociato in Egitto* (The Crusader in Egypt) in 1824 was a particular triumph and led to productions in London and Paris, where Meyerbeer met the well-known librettist Eugène Scribe.

In 1827 he and Scribe began their first collaboration, the Grand Opera *Robert le*

Diable (Robert the Devil), performed to huge acclaim in 1831. Initially conceived as an *opéra comique*, it was revised so that its theme of good versus evil would create a greater impression. The *Revue Musicale* of 1831 shows its impact: '. . . the score of *Robert le Diable* is not just M. Meyerbeer's masterpiece; it is a work remarkable in the history of art. . . . It incontestably places M. Meyerbeer at the head of the present German school.' Seventy-seven theaters in a dozen countries staged the opera, later described by Wagner as having a sinister 'deathless' atmosphere. Meyerbeer was awarded the Légion d'Honneur three years later, and finally settled in Paris.

Within a year of this success, Meyerbeer and Scribe were again at work on Meyerbeer's greatest accomplishment, *Les Huguenots*, premiered at the Paris Opéra in 1836. The opera drew on the conflicts between Catholics and Huguenots in sixteenth-century France, and, typically of Grand Opera, included as many ballets, choruses, and crowd scenes as possible. It was an overwhelming success and was the first opera to be performed more than one hundred times at the Paris Opéra.

Scribe and Meyerbeer followed up with *Le Prophète*, performed successfully in 1849. Meyerbeer's last opera, *L'Africaine*, was based on the travels of the explorer Vasco da Gama. Begun in 1837, it was laid aside for work on *Le Prophète* and was not completed until 1863, receiving its first performance in 1865, the year after Meyerbeer's death.

In all Meyerbeer's Grand Operas he gave preference to singers over the orchestra, and showed himself a composer who loved experimentation and considered music to be entertainment rather than high art. His operas made him a rich man, and although praise for his works turned to criticism in later years, his influence can be felt throughout nineteenth-century opera, especially in Verdi's *Don Carlos* and *Aida* and in Wagner's early opera *Rienzi*. The recommended work, *Les Patineurs*, is a ballet score by English composer Constant Lambert, written for the Sadler's Wells Ballet, London, in 1937. It draws on music from two Meyerbeer operas, *Le Prophète* and *L'Étoile du Nord*.

Berwald

Franz Berwald 1796–1868

RECOMMENDED WORK

Symphony No. 3 in C, 'Sinfonie singulière'
Deutsche Grammophon 415 502-2
Gothenburg Symphony Orchestra/Neeme Järvi
Järvi fully understands Berwald's quirky but endearing musical language, and his Gothenburg orchestra responds to him with evident enthusiasm.

REPRESENTATIVE WORKS
Symphony No. 1, 'Sinfonie sérieuse'
Symphony No. 2, 'Sinfonie capricieuse'
String Quartet No. 2
Grand Septet

Contemporary portrait engraving

Franz Berwald was born in Stockholm, the son of a German violinist in the royal orchestra. He was largely self-taught, although he did study music with his father and composition with J. B. E. De Puy. He joined the orchestra as a violinist at the age of 16 and apart from one brief period remained there until 1828, when he composed a *Grand Septet* for clarinet, bassoon, horn, and string quartet.

However, the lack of enthusiasm in his home country for his highly original style provoked Berwald to leave Sweden to try

and make a career abroad. Following a tour of Norway he spent time studying in Berlin, and then lived for a period in Vienna, where his opera *Estrella di Soria* was performed.

He married in Vienna in 1841, and his works were staged to increasingly supportive audiences. In 1842 he wrote a symphony, *La Sérieuse* — the only one of his symphonies that he saw performed in his lifetime. On his return to Sweden in that year, however, his reception was cool, and the Royal Opera's production of his operetta *Modehandlerskan* in 1845 was a failure. Nonetheless Berwald persevered and produced three more symphonies, including *La Capricieuse* and *La Singulière*. The latter in particular, which has only three movements instead of the usual four, reveals his skill as an orchestrator, and is perhaps his finest work.

Berwald spent a further three years traveling in Europe, where he met with varying degrees of success. In Paris neither the Conservatoire nor the Opéra-Comique showed interest, but in Vienna he did see a performance of his opera *Ein Landliches Verlobungsfest in Schweden* (A Swedish Country Betrothal). Back in Sweden, however, he was thwarted in his efforts to become musical director at Uppsala University, and was also denied the position of court conductor.

Forced by his lack of musical success into a series of jobs to earn his living, Berwald was manager of a Swedish glass factory in Angermanland from 1849 to 1859. Despite the demands made on his time by work, he continued to teach and compose, his output including piano trios, piano quartets, and symphonic poems. In the early 1860's he published some of his chamber works to encouraging reviews, and the Stockholm Royal Opera eventually performed *Estrella di Soria* in 1862.

He completed one last opera in 1864, *Drottningen av Golconda* (The Queen of Golconda), and was finally accepted as a Fellow of the Swedish Academy, rising to the post of professor of composition in 1867. This was the pinnacle of his career, but his success was shortlived: within only a year of his appointment Berwald died of pneumonia.

Schubert

Franz Schubert 1797–1828

RECOMMENDED WORKS

Symphony No. 9 in C, 'The Great'
London 400 082-2
Vienna Philharmonic Orchestra/Georg Solti
A clear-headed, bracing version of Schubert's symphonic epic, played in inimitable style by an orchestra that has the music in its blood.

Die Winterreise, D911
Deutsche Grammophon 437 235-2
Dietrich Fischer-Dieskau (bar); Gerald Moore (pno)
No other singer has brought more pathos or perception to these wonderful songs. An indisputable classic and probably the most wholly satisfying of Fischer-Dieskau's many Winterreise recordings.

REPRESENTATIVE WORKS
Symphonies Nos. 5 & 8
'Trout' Quintet, D667
String Quartet No. 14, 'Death and the Maiden'
String Quintet in C, D956
Impromptus, D899 & D935
Piano Sonatas in A, D959 & B flat, D960
Die schöne Müllerin

Portrait by Gabor Melegh, 1825

This lyrical painting captures the wistful side of the composer.

Of the great composers associated with Vienna — the others being Haydn, Mozart, and Beethoven — Schubert was the only one born in the city, and the only one who failed to achieve international fame in his lifetime. His shyness and lack of instrumental virtuosity contributed to the hardships he endured, but he was responsible for a magnificent body of work that is still appraised and appreciated today.

Born in the suburb of Lichtental, he was the fourth son of a schoolmaster. From his family he learned the piano and violin, soon outstripping everyone else in the household. At 11 his serious musical education began when he won a choral scholarship to the Konvikt, Vienna's Imperial College. Under Salieri's tutelage he wrote an opera and a series of quartets by the age of 15. He left the college in 1813 to train as a teacher before returning home to work in his father's school. Over the next five years alone, in an inexhaustible surge of creativity, he wrote five symphonies, six operas, and 300 songs (*Lieder*).

It was through song that Schubert's genius was first recognized. In 1814 he discovered Goethe's *Faust*, which led to his first masterpiece, *Gretchen am Spinnrade* (Gretchen at the Spinning Wheel). *Erlkönig*, depicting a terrorized child whose soul is swept away during a ride through a stormy night, followed the next year. The sensibility Goethe had awakened swiftly led Schubert to explore all the great poets of his time and unleashed what has been called 'a Shakespearean canvas of characters.' His sense of melody and movement, his unique awareness of changing key and the interplay possible between singer and pianist, his master storyteller's sense of timing and shifting nuance — all these gave the *Lied* a power that nobody had imagined. 'There's not one of Schubert's songs,' wrote Brahms, 'from which you cannot learn something.'

Schubert was fortunate to be born into a Vienna alive with cultural activity and debate. His music seized upon the image of the Romantic hero promulgated in literature and painting. Schubert's artistic world was the land of night and dreams — of *Sehnsucht*, a longing for the mystic world of the spirit, with the visible everyday world as a mere mirage. The hero, discovering incandescent love before bitter rejection, wanders alone through nature and there finds his solace and strength. These Romantic ideals underlie much of Schubert's work — such as the song *Auf dem Wasser zu singen*, whose fluttering juxtaposition of major and minor captures a mood of fervor and serenity — or the poetry Schubert prefaced to his symphonies, sonatas, and chamber music.

By 1816 the drudgery of the schoolroom had become unbearable. Schubert abandoned teaching to live in Vienna with Franz von Schober, a friend who worked to spread the composer's reputation and open his eyes to cultural trends. A meeting with leading baritone J. M. Vogl was crucial. He championed many of Schubert's

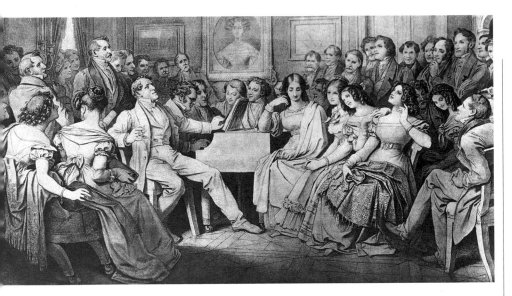

Sepia drawing of a 'Schubertiad' by von Schwind

Schubert at the piano, performing at the house of his friend Joseph von Spaun.

songs, and a visit in 1819 to Vogl's birthplace in the mountains at Steyr liberated in the composer a powerful, happy impulse. There he began the *Trout Quintet*, marking his coming of age in instrumental music. Scored for violin, viola, cello, double-bass, and piano, the quintet takes its name from his earlier song *Die Forelle* (The Trout), which is the basis of a set of variations in the fourth movement of the quintet.

This is the radiant Schubert everybody thinks they know. Yet our notion of a fat, jolly amateur, leaving his coffeehouse only to dash off another carefree masterpiece, is a myth. In reality Schubert died prematurely of a disfiguring disease, his mind poisoned by the idea of the fate that inevitably awaited him.

Schubert contracted syphilis in 1823. It transformed his entire outlook, and while many reasons are put forward for his failure to complete his *Eighth Symphony*, begun the year before his illness, it may be that it marked a period in his life that came to repel him. Nevertheless, he returned to the symphonic form soon afterward to compose the *Symphony No. 9 in C* (The Great), a work grander and more profound than any of Schubert's other symphonies.

Some of the songs for his first song-cycle, *Die schöne Müllerin* (The Fair Maid of the Mill), were written in the hospital in 1823. The cycle depicts the ill-fated love of a young man for a miller's daughter. Although it contains much joyful music, its sad ending anticipates the tone of his tragic second cycle, *Winterreise* (Winter Journey), written in 1827 after four years of illness. In the latter cycle, where the hero has lost his love before the cycle's

beginning, the songs create an unrelenting portrait of gloom set in the frozen landscape of death. Yet Schubert was still able to put his morbidity aside, albeit temporarily; 1827 is also the date of several lighter pieces for piano — the *Impromptus* and the *Moments Musicaux* — which form the ideal introduction to his instrumental music and anticipate the *Ballades* of Chopin and Brahms, while revealing a greater emotional range than either.

Some of Schubert's finest compositions were written during the last year of his life, including his masterly trio of *Piano Sonatas* in C minor, A major, and B flat. But the fullest portrait of Schubert's musical personality is the remarkable *String Quintet* in C. Its opening movement is one of the great masterpieces of classical organization; the slow movement alternates between a theme of sublime calmness in E major and a furiously anguished section in F minor; the scherzo (a generally jaunty movement that may take the place of the minuet in a sonata or symphony) has little in common with those of Haydn or Beethoven, but pits a boisterous hunting theme against an apparition as chillingly remote as anything from *Winterreise*; and the finale ends ambiguously in neither major nor minor. As always in mature Schubert, the sunshine is more intense for being inseparable from an awareness of the dark. Soon after completing the *Quintet*, Schubert entered the final phase of his illness, and died at the age of 31 in 1828.

Additional Composers

Although the achievements of Haydn, Mozart, and Schubert have naturally tended to dwarf those of their contemporaries, many of these produced far from negligible music. **Carl Philipp Emanuel Bach** (1714–1788), for example, was not only the most famous of J. S. Bach's sons but also an innovative and often visionary composer in his own right. The influence of his father is heard strongly in the splendidly jubilant *Magnificat* (1749), but his most personal and imaginative music is found in his *Symphonies* and, above all, in the keyboard collections of Sonatas, Rondos, and Fantasias '. . . für Kenner und Liebhaber' ('for connoisseurs and amateurs').

Johann Christian Bach (1735–1782) spent much of his busy career in London, where in 1764 he befriended eight-year-old Mozart, who was greatly influenced by the Italianate elegance and stylish craftsmanship of Bach's music. These qualities are shown in such operas as *Orione* and *La clemenza di Scipione*, in the *Six Grand Overtures*, Opus 18, and in such charming chamber works as the sets of *Quintets*, Opus 11 and Opus 22.

Giovanni Pergolesi (1710–1736) in *La serva padrona* and **Domenico Cimarosa** (1749–1783) in *Il matrimonio segreto* made significant contributions to Italian comic opera, while the Catalan **Antonio Soler** (1749–1801) followed the lead of Domenico Scarlatti with his 120 keyboard sonatas.

Johann Stamitz (1717–1757) developed his orchestra at Mannheim into the most famous of its time, celebrated for its precision and range of dynamics; his 58 extant symphonies exploit its virtuosity and brilliance, as well as exploiting predominantly a four- rather than the three-movement structure. His son, **Carl Stamitz** (1745–1801), the Viennese **Carl Ditters von Dittersdorf** (1739–1799), and, in Paris, **François-Joseph Gossec** (1734–1829) all wrote expert, characterful symphonies.

Two prolific composer-pianists on the border between Classicism and Romanticism are the Bohemian **Jan Ladislav Dussek** (1760–1812) and the Austrian **Johann Nepomuk Hummel** (1778–1837). As well as some works of rather tawdry brilliance, Dussek wrote a number of piano sonatas of a most imaginative sensitivity and passionate virtuosity — those in A flat, Opus 64 (*Le retour à Paris*), and in F sharp minor, Opus 61. Hummel was still more highly renowned in his time, writing opera and sacred music, as well as piano works: in his large output, works such as the *Piano Concertos* in A minor and D minor stand out, anticipating so much in Weber, Mendelssohn, and Chopin.

The Romantic Era
19th century

With Napoleon's defeat, hopes for a return to the old European order died. The impact of democratic ideals and the Industrial Revolution were changing the nature of society. Subject nations wanted independence, and popular uprisings occurred throughout Europe in the first half of the century. Britain and France made war on Russia to support the declining Ottoman empire. Italy achieved unity in 1870, as did Germany in 1871, after conflicts with Austria and France. The United States grew from a cluster of 13 rural settlements into one of the most powerful nations on earth, its future sealed in a bloody civil war.

A wave of Romanticism swept through Europe, gripping the imagination of a whole generation. The power of nature and of human emotion became central themes in the novels of Sir Walter Scott and Victor Hugo and in the poetry of Wordsworth. Architects turned to the Middle Ages for inspiration — as in London's Gothic Houses of Parliament — while painters made nature's beauty their primary subject.

Western civilization was propelled into industrial urbanization by steam power. With railroads and the telegraph, people gained an unheard-of ability to move and communicate quickly over vast distances. Spectacular advances were achieved in science, particularly in medicine and biology, with the invention of anesthetics and the work of Mendel and Darwin.

In music the Romantic standard-bearer was Beethoven, who expanded traditional musical forms to convey great depth and intensity of feeling. While nature's grandeur inspired Mendelssohn, Schumann, and Liszt, the operas of Wagner and Verdi and the work of Russian composers reflected the era's growing nationalism. The virtuoso performances of Chopin and Paganini held the interest of popular audiences.

Featured Composers

The Wanderer by Caspar David Friedrich, 1818
**Individualism came to the fore in the Romantic era, and the influence of
nature — cruel as much as beautiful — played an important part.**

After Napoleon's final defeat at Waterloo in 1815, every effort was made by the victorious powers to restore the old order in Europe, which had been undermined by 20 years of war and revolution. Yet the apparent triumph of conservatism was to prove a delusion. The forces of liberalism and nationalism unleashed by the French Revolution had been only temporarily subdued and, although war between the nations of Europe was successfully avoided for the next 40 years, they remained potent disruptive elements.

The origins of Romanticism

As an adjective the word 'romantic' had a long pedigree. It derived from the old 'romances' — the tales of chivalry popularized by troubadours in the Middle Ages — and was used to convey the evocative, imaginative qualities typical of these works. As early as 1666, the diarist Samuel Pepys could describe a castle as 'the most romantic in the world.' The word retained this fairly loose meaning until the late eighteenth century, when it was adapted by a group of German writers that included Schiller, Goethe, and Novalis. They drew a clear division between 'Romantic' and 'Classical' literature, a distinction soon applied to all other branches of the arts.

The Romantics opposed Classicism by proclaiming the superiority of emotion over reason. They demanded the right to free expression in place of the old emphasis on restraint, and elevated the power of the imagination to near-divine status. Artists could make such claims largely because patronage had shifted away from aristocratic courts to the middle classes. Painters and composers had more control over their careers. In many ways the Romantic movement provided them with the artistic equivalent of a declaration of independence.

These changes were not immediate. During the early nineteenth century the line dividing Classicism and Romanticism was often blurred. Beethoven, Schiller, and Goya all had a foot in each camp. The Spaniard Goya illustrated this ambivalence by his reaction to the French occupation of his country in 1808. He was court painter to Charles IV, the king deposed by Napoleon, and was later employed by Ferdinand VII when the monarchy was restored in 1814. Despite his official position, Goya's *Disasters of War* series (1810–14) is an unflinching record of the atrocities, both French and Spanish, perpetrated during the bitter guerrilla war. This notion of the artist as spokesman of his times was a feature of the Romantic movement.

Detail from *Arthur in Avalon* by Sir Edward Burne-Jones, 1881–98
Burne-Jones was associated with the Pre-Raphaelite group of painters, and shared their taste for medieval subjects.

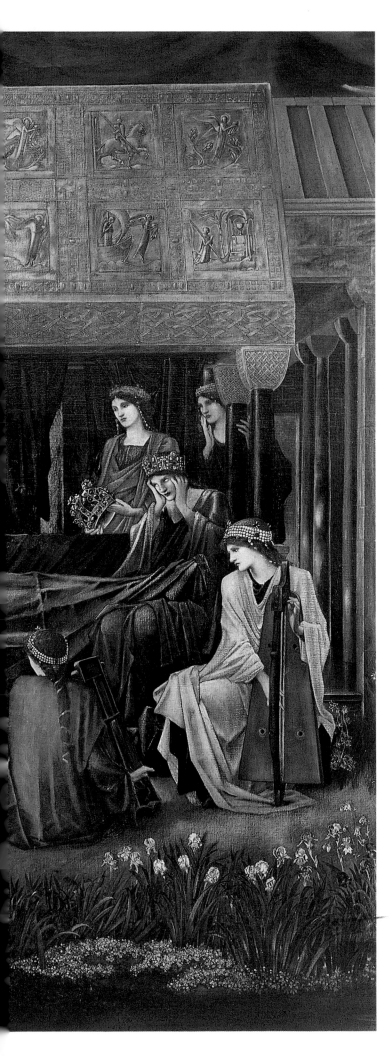

The New World

Napoleon's involvement in Spain demonstrated his willingness to wage war on all fronts in Europe. Outside the continent, however, it was a different matter. In 1803, Bonaparte agreed to sell the Louisiana Territory to the United States, following a discreet hint by President Jefferson that the territory might otherwise be taken by force. Britain's disastrous experience of waging a long-distance war against its American colonies in the previous century no doubt informed his decision.

The British government learned more slowly. In 1812, Britain engaged the United States in a second war, largely over the question of maritime rights. British forces occupied Washington, burning the Capitol to the ground. However, their success was short-lived and peace was concluded at Ghent in December 1814, with the United States once more victorious.

Surprisingly, the war hastened industrial growth in the former colonies, since the conflict made it difficult to import goods from Europe. At the same time the United States itself expanded, admitting six new states to the Union by 1821. Two years later the country's independence was reaffirmed with the so-called Monroe Doctrine, President James Monroe's warning to the European powers that the United States would brook no further interference in the affairs of the New World.

This parting of ways between Europe and the United States did not yet extend to the musical sphere. Inevitably, the earliest American composers of note were immigrants — Moravians such as Johann Friedrich Peter and David Moritz Michael, and the Bohemian musician Anthony Philip Heinrich. Native-born American composers often wanted to travel to Europe to learn their craft, though Europe did not always welcome them. Louis Gottschalk, for example, went to Paris where, reportedly, the Conservatoire refused to admit him purely on the grounds that he was an American. Undeterred, the young man gained instruction from Berlioz and made a name for himself with Romantic piano pieces such as *The Dying Poet* and *The Last Hope*.

The sources of Romanticism

The Romantics looked back on the Middle Ages with the enthusiasm their predecessors had reserved for ancient Greece and Rome. This taste for medievalism permeated all the arts. In architecture it produced the Gothic Revival style, pioneered by figures such as A. W. N. Pugin and Viollet-le-Duc. In literature it was represented by Sir Walter Scott, whose *Waverley* novels were popular throughout Europe. It also inspired groups of painters such as the Nazarenes and the Pre-Raphaelite Brotherhood to emulate the medieval artists.

The Nightmare by Henry Fuseli, 1782
This scene reflects the Romantics' love of horror. The crouched demon is an incubus, said to prey on women while they sleep.

Opera in Germany, France, and Italy had a distinct character during this period. Romantic German opera, given impetus by Beethoven's *Fidelio*, was firmly established by Carl Maria von Weber. Weber's operas *Der Freischütz, Euryanthe,* and *Oberon* incorporated themes from fantasy and folklore. Together with operas by Heinrich Marschner, they paved the way for the monumental music dramas of Richard Wagner, whose greatest works drew on Arthurian legend (*Parsifal* and *Tristan und Isolde*) or on the folk tales contained in the thirteenth-century *Nibelungenlied*. In France, Auber and later Gounod popularized the *opéra comique* (generally light works, though not necessarily comic, that included spoken dialogue). Meyerbeer, a leading figure of Grand Opera, composed epic five-act operas featuring a host of spectacular effects that impressed the young Wagner when he saw them in Paris. In Italy, Rossini's sparkling comic operas developed the *bel canto* (beautiful singing) technique, which stressed the lyrical qualities of the voice over raw power, and paved the way for Bellini and Donizetti. Heir to the legacy of all three Italian composers was Verdi, who like Meyerbeer treated historical subjects, but with a decidedly political slant.

The Romantics distanced themselves from the values that had prevailed during the Age of Reason. It naturally followed that they should take an interest in the irrational. Accordingly, a taste for the macabre figured prominently in their aesthetic, with madness, horror, and the supernatural as common themes. Artists like Géricault and Goya produced penetrating studies of lunatics, while Mary Shelley's *Frankenstein* (1818) led the craze

for the 'gothick' horror novel. In music this influence can be seen, for example, in Berlioz's *Symphonie fantastique* (1830), in which the composer sought to evoke a series of opium-induced hallucinations. These visions became increasingly disturbed, culminating in an orgiastic witches' sabbath, during which the heroine danced on her former lover's grave and a section of the Catholic Mass was burlesqued.

Given such dark subject matter, it may seem surprising that the other great preoccupation of the Romantics was nature. Schumann's *Rhenish Symphony* (1850), for example, was intended as a tribute to the beauties of the German Rhineland district where he lived. Similarly, Mendelssohn's *Italian* and *Scotch* symphonies (1833 and 1842 respectively) were inspired by his travels in those countries. In his *Fingal's Cave* overture (1832), Mendelssohn responded to the rock formations on the island of Staffa, confirming his genius for composing musical landscapes.

Once again, other branches of the arts produced parallels. Wordsworth and Coleridge wrote emotionally charged poetry about the imposing beauty of the Lake District, while painters such as Constable, Turner, and Corot brought to their canvases lyrical visions of the world they saw around them.

Of course, an appreciation of nature was not new, but the Romantic version developed in direct response to various factors of the time. The spread of the Industrial Revolution and the increasing urbanization of society made the countryside seem idyllic. At the same time there was a fierce reaction against the perceived artificiality of courtly life in the preceding era. Where Classical artists had sought to arrange natural elements in order to create a harmonious effect, the Romantics did not try to modify nature but only to record their personal impressions of it. They felt themselves to be at the mercy of the elements, rather than in control of them.

Liberty Leading the People by Eugène Delacroix, 1830
This stirring picture celebrates the July Revolution of 1830, when Charles X was ousted from the French throne.

The value the Romantics attached to their personal feelings, and to individualism in general, extended to all other aspects of society. These rebellious tendencies often brought them into conflict with authority as the subversive champions of liberty and change.

Uprisings and revolutions

The first half of the nineteenth century was no more violent than other ages, but it was marked by a different type of struggle. Alongside the usual territorial aggression and dynastic jealousies, a spate of internal revolts erupted, characterized by the same democratic impulses that had spawned the French Revolution.

In 1831 the Polish army joined the populace in mounting a challenge to their Russian rulers. However, a lack of planning and unity doomed the attempt; by the end of the year Russian troops were back in control, and many dissident Poles were expelled. Most of them took refuge in France, where the campaign for a 'Free Poland' enjoyed warm support. One of the expatriates who found a new home in Paris was Frédéric Chopin. Although Chopin was never to return to Poland, his music bristles with the typical rhythms and melodic strains of his native land. His polonaises and mazurkas were lively dance forms that evoked among his fellow exiles the pride and grandeur of Poland's noble past.

French support for the Polish cause was probably boosted by its own domestic upheavals. Since 1824 the country had been ruled by Charles X, who harbored bitter memories of the Revolution and did his utmost to restore some of the monarchy's lost power. Accordingly, when the elections of 1830 went against him, Charles dismissed his Chamber of Deputies and tried to rule by decree. A popular uprising in Paris soon forced him to abdicate, and after frenzied negotiations, the crown was offered to Louis Philippe, the Duke of Orléans.

Louis Philippe's moderation guaranteed him a certain measure of support, although there were dangerous enemies waiting in the wings. These included the Republicans, who were seeking a return to revolutionary principles; the Legitimists, who argued for the restoration of the monarchy to the Bourbon dynasty; and the Bonapartists, who regretted the loss of power and prestige that France had suffered since the defeat of the emperor Napoleon.

The Greek War of Independence

These turbulent events attracted some attention from contemporary artists — Delacroix's painting *Liberty Leading the People*, for example, is one of the most familiar icons of the period. But it was a distant war, fought on the fringes of Europe, that truly stirred the Romantic imagination. In 1821, encouraged by the waning influence of the Ottoman Empire, Greek insurgents made a bid for independence. Their struggle struck a chord with educated Europeans, and Greek societies were set up in London, Paris, and Berlin. This fund of goodwill greatly increased after 1822, when Turkish forces butchered 20,000 inhabitants on the small island of Chios. The atrocity prompted the poet Lord Byron to offer his services, and in 1823, he sailed out to Missolonghi, the center of Greek resistance. There, Byron agreed to finance and train a small private army, but was struck down by a fever before he could put this plan into operation.

The Romantics' interest in Greece differed sharply from that of the previous generation. Where the exponents of Classicism had revered the ancient civilization as a superior culture and had sought, in some degree, to re-create it, Byron's contemporaries were more moved by the sense of decay; the Romantics cared less for the bygone splendor of the culture than for the picturesque qualities of its ruins.

The war in Greece fired the imaginations of intellectuals, as the Spanish Civil War was to do in the twentieth century. Independence was achieved in 1830, and these middle-class revolutionaries turned their attention increasingly toward the question of social reform.

Social reform

A growing concern over social issues came naturally in the wake of the Industrial Revolution. In Britain its technical advances brought prosperity to the national economy and to individual entrepreneurs, but often at the expense of the work force. Mass migration to the cities produced overcrowded, disease-ridden living conditions, and dangerous and exploitative working conditions — the poet William Blake described the new factories as 'dark satanic mills.'

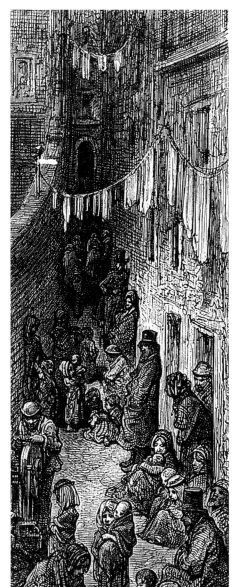

The Slums of Drury Lane by Gustave Doré, 1870
Poverty and overcrowding were the price of the Industrial Revolution; the slums of London's Drury Lane were notorious.

Individually, workers may have been no more exploited than in previous times, but the fact that they were now brought together in large numbers gave them the courage to do something about it. In 1811–12, Luddite rioters in the Midlands smashed the machinery that they felt had robbed them of their jobs. Seven years later came the shock of the 'Peterloo Massacre' in Manchester, when a group of peaceable demonstrators demanding parliamentary reform were brutally dispersed by an inexperienced yeomanry and professional soldiers, leaving 11 people dead and hundreds injured. In 1834, a scandal arose over the 'Tolpuddle Martyrs,' six agricultural laborers who were sentenced to transportation following their attempts to form a trade union.

Gradually this pressure produced results. In 1832, the Great Reform Act gave a broader spectrum of British society a political voice, and in the following year, a Factory Act placed restrictions on the use of child labor. The same year also witnessed the abolition of slavery in the British Empire, thanks to a determined campaign by William Wilberforce.

Developments in music

The economic benefits that flowed from the Industrial Revolution had considerable advantages for musicians. The spread of education and the growth of the professional classes provided a new audience, enabling some players to achieve great fame. The virtuoso performers were the real beneficiaries. The greatest, Niccolò Paganini, wove such magic on his violin that he was rumored to have made a pact with the devil. The maestro undoubtedly encouraged this sort of sensationalist publicity, though some took it seriously. In fact, for five years after his death his body was denied burial in consecrated ground.

Paganini's showmanship inspired Liszt, who transcribed some of Paganini's compositions for the piano. With his exaggerated mannerisms and his histrionic playing style, Liszt also managed to ape much of the violinist's success. The concert circuit also included a growing number of lesser-known pianists, such as Sigismond Thalberg, Alexander Dreyschock, and J. B. Cramer, whose dexterity caused one commentator to suggest that he had two right hands.

This sort of virtuosity was stimulated by technical advances in the manufacture of instruments, in particular that of the piano. The gradual introduction of the metal frame enabled it to withstand greater stress and allowed for the addition of more

Liszt at the Piano, a contemporary painting by Josef Danhauser

Liszt gazes at a bust of Beethoven as he plays, watched with admiration by Alexandre Dumas, Paganini, Rossini, and others.

strings. The expanded range of the piano in turn encouraged musicians to become ever more daring in their compositions.

One side effect of this trend was the creation of a widening gulf between 'light' and 'serious' music. The technical difficulty of many pieces made them the preserve of only the most expert players. Conscious of this, some Romantic composers began to make a distinction between the different levels of their listening public and, in so doing, created a certain elitism. This was itself something of an irony, as within what was essentially a middle-class movement, it became fashionable to mock bourgeois taste as 'philistine.'

A similar split developed in the scale of musical production. On the one hand, shorter, small-scale works were performed to select audiences in the intimate surroundings of salons. On the other hand, the size of the orchestra was gradually increasing to accommodate the rich effects of the full-blown Romantic symphony. This, in turn, helped to establish the role of the conductor. Just a generation earlier Haydn had been able to direct performances of his work while seated at his harpsichord among the players. Now, as the music assumed greater complexity, a more disciplined approach was required. The baton became a standard piece of equipment after 1850, and the

---

MUSICAL DEFINITIONS

SYMPHONIC POEM or TONE POEM A large-scale orchestral work, usually in one movement, that is based on a nonmusical subject. Structurally it is often similar to the sonata form of the first movements of symphonies. Taking its inspiration from a wide variety of literary and artistic sources, or from the natural world, the symphonic poem was designed to conjure up the idea of a person, a place, a picture, or some other object.

ÉTUDE or STUDY A short composition, usually for solo instrument, designed primarily to improve or to demonstrate technical ability. A number of composers, notably Chopin, Debussy, and Scriabin, wrote études intended for concert performance.

PRELUDE A piece of music originally intended as an introduction to another, such as a fugue or suite. In the 19th century it came to be applied to a short, independent composition, usually for piano.

IMPROMPTU An instrumental piece that is designed to convey an impression of improvisation or in which the composer gives some scope to the imagination. Schubert and Chopin, in particular, wrote notable examples.

conductor's influence grew as the century wore on. Indeed, some musicians felt that they took too many liberties with their arrangements; Verdi was once heard to complain that the conductor had replaced the singer as a composer's worst enemy.

The dominant trend after Beethoven moved toward grander works. Brahms, Bruckner, and Wagner all expanded the sonata form to suit their large-scale designs, and Liszt coined the term SYMPHONIC POEM for his single-movement works, which described subjects from mythology or literature. Chopin had earlier suggested the possibility of shorter, more intimate pieces, his preferred compositional forms being ÉTUDES, PRELUDES, and IMPROMPTUS.

1848: the year of revolutions

In 1848 a wave of political unrest swept across Europe. Once again French instability provided the tinder for the flames of revolution. In February of that year rioting in Paris persuaded a weary Louis Philippe to abdicate in favor of his grandson. Radical insurgents refused to accept this nomination, however, and pressed for a return to republicanism. Their demands were met, and a new constitution was approved in November. Louis Napoleon Bonaparte, nephew of Napoleon Bonaparte, was sworn in as the first president, and it appeared that the Republic would survive. But in December 1851 he staged a coup and declared himself Emperor Napoleon III.

News of the 1848 riots in Paris had meanwhile brought discontent to the surface in one city after another. Rebels took to the streets in Vienna, and Klemens Metternich, the autocratic Austrian Chancellor and self-appointed 'policeman of Europe,' fled to England. Taking advantage of the confusion, nationalists in other parts of the Austrian Empire — Bohemia, Hungary, Serbia, and Italy — all rose up against their Hapsburg overlords.

Revolutionary activities in Europe, 1848
Widespread rioting throughout the continent made this the most turbulent year since 1789. Here we see the barricades in the Michaelerplatz in Vienna (above), Ana Ipatescu leading the first group of Transylvanian anti-Russian insurgents (left), and rebels storming the Château d'Eau at the Palais Royal in Paris (below).

After the initial shock the Austrian authorities fought back. Prague was occupied in June 1848, and the collapse of Czech resistance soon followed. In Italy the rebels were sought out, and the defeat of Charles Albert of Piedmont at Novara in March 1849 brought a temporary halt to hostilities. Hungary mounted the stiffest resistance. Under the leadership of Kossuth it repelled a Croat invasion in September 1848 and regained control of Buda and Pest in the following spring. It was only when Tsar Nicholas I sent in Russian troops to help stem the revolt that the cause proved hopeless. Kossuth acknowledged defeat and went into exile.

When the dust had settled, it seemed that order had been restored. The flurry of nationalism appeared to have dispersed as the Austrian leadership resumed its grip on its vast domains. In fact, the problem had simply been deferred. Nationalism was a time bomb, and the fuse had only just been lit.

Crystal Palace, the British Machinery Department, a print by Charles Buxton, 1851

London's Crystal Palace was the site of the 1851 Great Exhibition, which celebrated the scientific and economic achievements of the Industrial Revolution.

Europe at mid-century

While Romanticism held sway in the music world, it was gradually supplanted in literature and the visual arts after the middle of the century, with the Realist movement producing writers such as Flaubert and Zola. In 1850 the painter Courbet exhibited his masterpiece of realism, *Burial at Ornans*, and in 1866 Manet's *Olympia* foreshadowed the Impressionist movement.

The sense of disillusionment that followed the failure of the 1848 revolutions contributed to this change of attitude. At the same time, the spectacular achievements of science gave the age great confidence and a firm belief in progress. In 1851 the Great Exhibition at Hyde Park in London demonstrated the extent of recent scientific and technological advance: the development of electricity; the isolation of new chemical substances that were to have important industrial uses; and the discovery of anesthetics. Geologists were beginning to examine the fundamental nature of the earth itself, and Darwin's publication of *On the Origin of Species* in 1859 would soon revolutionize humankind's conception of its place in nature. The power of the steam engine had upset all previous ideas about distance, and by 1840 the electric telegraph was already in use in England and France. In 1861 experiments began in the United States with a new source of energy: petroleum.

Russia: nationalism and music

In 1848, the very year in which the continent of Europe was rocked by a series of popular uprisings, Karl Marx declared nationalism a movement without a future. The proletariat — 'a class without a country' — he believed would be at the core of new developments. Marx's analysis of social evolution proved prophetic in many ways but, in this instance, he could not have been more wrong. In the latter part of the century nationalism would become a powerful instrument for change, with music playing a vital role at the heart of the movement.

A Religious Procession in the Province of Kursk by Ilya Repin, 1880–83

Repin belonged to a group of painters, the 'Wanderers,' who illustrated the pressing need for social reform in Russia.

The failed 1830 uprising in Poland was followed by a second, equally disastrous Polish revolt in January 1863. After its suppression, Tsar Alexander II sought to eliminate the problem by expelling patriots and by Russianizing the culture of his troublesome Polish domains. But Alexander's subjugation of Poland could not mask the fact that Russia, too, had yet to assert its cultural independence. By Western standards the country was industrially backward, with illiterate serfs constituting 80 percent of the population. Alexander began the long process of freeing these peasants in 1858, but widespread emancipation did not take place until the 1880's.

Russian art mirrored this situation. Music, for example, was still the preserve of the nobility, who expected it to follow Italian, French, or German models. Serf orchestras were common, but the most talented musicians received their training abroad. Catherine the Great had initiated some changes, encouraging her Italian court composers to use Russian librettos. The real breakthrough, however, came with Mikhail Glinka.

After learning his craft in Italy and Germany, Glinka returned home to produce *A Life for the Tsar* (1836), which with its patriotic theme can be classed as the first genuine

Austria had added their weight to the Allied cause. Given the strength of the opposition, Russia sued for peace, bringing the Crimean War to a close in early 1856.

The American Civil War

Like Russia, the United States was a nation still coming to terms with its own identity. Here the tension focused on slavery. The songs of Stephen Foster — 'Camptown Races,' 'My Old Kentucky Home' — may have conjured up a rosy picture of life on the Southern plantations, but the Northern outcry against the institution and spread of slavery grew.

The immediate catalyst for war was the election of Abraham Lincoln to the presidency in 1860. South Carolina seceded from the Union in December of that year, to be followed by six more states at the start of 1861. The Southern Confederates' attack on Fort Sumter in April marked the official outbreak of hostilities.

The North should have won easily, with its advantage of greater numbers (23 states against the South's 11) and superior economic resources, but the issue remained in doubt for a full two years. Only with the decisive Northern victory at Gettysburg in July 1863 did conflict end; an armistice was eventually signed in April 1865. The widespread euphoria in the North that accompanied this achievement was rapidly cut short, however, when Lincoln was assassinated at Ford's Theater in Washington shortly afterward.

The true sense of nationhood that eventually resulted from the War Between the States did not bring with it an immediate appreciation of homegrown culture. The most acclaimed composers were those who had received their training in Germany and who worked in distinctly European styles. The first truly successful integration of American elements into the European mainstream came in fact from the Czech Dvořák, in his symphony of 1893, *From the New World*.

Russian opera. He followed this with *Ruslan and Lyudmila* (1842), in which the musical roots of his native land were still more apparent. In his footsteps came Alexander Dargomyzhsky. Both men were profoundly influenced by the writings of Pushkin, the Romantic poet and dramatist credited as the founder and creator of the modern Russian language.

The nationalist trend initiated by Glinka continued through the group of Russian composers known collectively as 'The Mighty Handful' or 'The Five' (Balakirev, Borodin, Cui, Mussorgsky, and Rimsky-Korsakov). They were anxious to avoid the Germanic playing style taught in the official academies such as the St. Petersburg Conservatory and determined to take responsibilty for their own tuition. The results were unconventional and, in the opinion of some critics, amateurish. The St. Petersburg Opera twice refused Mussorgsky's *Boris Godunov* as being too unsophisticated for public taste.

In the political sphere, however, national pride took a dent when Russia became embroiled in a war with Britain and France. The crisis was precipitated by the gradual collapse of the Ottoman Empire in the east. Fearing that Nicholas I would attempt to absorb these Turkish territories, Britain and France sent a fleet to the Black Sea in January 1854. In the ensuing war, the Allied armies laid siege to Sebastopol, Russia's great naval fortress in the Crimea, a lengthy operation that was not concluded until September 1855. By this time Piedmont and

The Taking of Fort Wagner by Courrier and Ives, 1863

The isolation of the Southern states, due to their reluctance to abandon slavery, was the root cause of the American Civil War.

On the Thames by James Tissot, 1876

Britain's maritime power was the key to its imperial success, and the Thames became a thoroughfare for commercial traffic, here seen as a backdrop to the pleasure boat.

The Paris Opera House, designed by Garnier and completed in 1874

Dubbed the 'Palais Garnier,' this architectural masterpiece was the inspiration for Gaston Leroux's Phantom of the Opera.

France and Britain

After a shaky start Napoleon III's administration in France, which lasted from 1852 to 1870, ushered in a period of great prosperity and artistic exuberance. Nothing could have symbolized this better than the wholesale transformation of Paris under the supervision of the Emperor's Prefect, Baron Georges Haussmann. In place of the congested, filthy slums of the medieval city, Haussmann designed and created a modern Paris, with wide boulevards, leafy parks, and handsome public buildings, the crowning example of which was Charles Garnier's Opera House, commissioned in 1858. Although compared by some to 'an overloaded sideboard,' the sumptuous decoration of Garnier's creation fitted the mood of the age to perfection. Though Grand Opera might seem a likely musical counterpart to this new Paris, it was in fact the *opéra bouffe* (comic opera) or operetta, popularized by Jacques Offenbach, that came into vogue. Offenbach's witty, gently satirical productions were the rage of Paris in the 1860's, and proved a fertile source of inspiration for the English 'Savoy Operas' of Gilbert and Sullivan.

The Savoy Operas, like their French counterparts, were celebratory in tone, reflecting the zenith of Britain's imperial power. During the reign of Queen Victoria (1837–1901) the country reaped the benefits of its long-term political stability and its commitment to the Industrial Revolution. The growing railway and shipbuilding enterprises found obvious outlets in the expanding Empire, while the success of banking and insurance operations turned the City of London into the financial capital of the world.

Il Risorgimento

The nationalist trend evident in Russia and the United States was also visible in Europe. In Italy the growing clamor for unification, also known as Il Risorgimento (Resurrection), had been an active force since the early years of the century. It began with republican revolutionaries like the Carbonari and Giuseppe Mazzini, who founded the Young Italy movement in 1831. Toward the middle of the century, however, a new vision emerged. Count Camillo Cavour, the Prime Minister of Piedmont and Sardinia, began to argue the case for a monarchy, with his master, Victor Emmanuel II, as the leading candidate. This ambition lay behind Cavour's willingness to commit troops to the Crimean War. He hoped that this involvement would raise his country's international standing, and, indeed, Piedmont was rewarded with a place at the peace negotiations, alongside the major powers.

In the long term, though, the dream of Italian independence could be achieved only if a wedge were driven between France and Austria, which had effectively divided Italy between them. Cavour drove the wedge in 1859, when he persuaded Napoleon III to support his call for Austrian withdrawal. The French Emperor envisaged the creation of a confederation of Italian states dependent on France and had been promised Savoy and Nice as the price of his assistance.

But Napoleon had underestimated the strength of nationalist feeling in Italy. He was alarmed at the number of states that voluntarily joined with Piedmont, and when Garibaldi and his 'Red Shirts' invaded Sicily in May 1860, he proposed Anglo-French intervention. The British government refused, openly supporting Italian unification. Napoleon's hands were tied. Sicily and Naples fell, and in March 1861 the independent Kingdom of Italy was established. Venice and Rome were added to the union in 1866 and 1870 respectively.

Progress toward independence was echoed in the music of Giuseppe Verdi. Indeed, his very name represented freedom, reflecting as it did the initials of *Vittorio Emmanuele Re D'Italia* (Victor Emmanuel, King of Italy), and 'Viva Verdi!' became a rallying cry for revolutionaries. On the strength of his popularity, Verdi was eventually elected to serve in the first national Parliament, holding office until 1865.

Toward German unification

Verdi's career is often compared to that of Richard Wagner. Exact contemporaries, the two men were linked to the nationalist movements in their respective countries. In Wagner's case this proved almost fatal. Following his participation in a local rebellion at Dresden in 1849, a warrant was put out for his arrest and he was forced to flee. He stayed in exile, living mostly in Switzerland, until he was allowed to return in 1861.

Wagner's banishment coincided with a long cat-and-mouse game between the Prussian and Austrian governments as they wrestled for control of the disparate German states. (Prussia consisted of northern and central Germany, extending from France to Poland.) In September 1850, Prussian troops entered Hesse, a show of aggression that resulted in an emergency meeting of the German states. Prussia was forced to withdraw, leaving Austria supreme under its powerful Emperor, Franz Josef.

Despite the political defeat, however, Prussian fortunes were in the ascendant. An economic boom was under way in northern Germany, the railway system was expanding, and Berlin's stature as a banking center had increased dramatically. All Prussia required was a statesman with the vision to transform this wealth into power.

Prussia's salvation arrived with Otto von Bismarck, who was appointed prime minister in 1862. Certain that Austrian domination would never be removed by diplomacy or democratic means, but only by 'blood and iron,' Bismarck channeled Prussia's resources into military reform, creating an engine of war that would be a match for any army in Europe.

Bismarck soon saw an opportunity to deploy these forces. The death of the Danish king, Frederick VII, in November

Photograph of the Austrian princely family, taken in 1860

A family portrait of the powerful Hapsburgs; the Emperor is on the left of the picture; to his left is his brother Maximilian.

1863, provided a pretext for the annexation of the German-speaking duchies of Schleswig and Holstein. Prussia took control of the former and Austria the latter but, in 1866, Bismarck complained that Vienna was abusing its power in the province and ordered his troops into Holstein. At the same time, as part of a prearranged agreement with Bismarck, Italian nationalists invaded the Austrian territories around Venice. Fighting on two fronts, the divided Austrian army was rapidly overwhelmed. Its defeat at Sadowa in July 1866 effectively removed Austria's influence from German affairs. Bismarck's decisive campaign had lasted just one month.

Wagner's conversion to the Prussian cause was symptomatic of the patriotic sentiments that Bismarck managed to inspire. In his early days the composer had been a committed democrat, sharing the liberal ideals of the 'Young Germany' group and the left-wing poet Heinrich Heine. However, as unification turned from a dream into reality, Wagner was swept up in the excitement, dedicating verses to Bismarck and writing the *Kaisermarsch* in celebration of his victory in the Franco-Prussian War.

Austria's troubled empire

The Austrian government, as it represented such a variety of cultures, feared exclusion from German affairs and so redoubled its efforts to Germanize its domains. This naturally caused resentment among the Austrian people and stoked the fires of nationalism. The events of 1866 led some Austrian subjects to renew their claims for independence. These were rejected, but the recent reverses had shown the Emperor, Franz Josef, the value of moderation. Thus, when dealing with Hungary in 1867, his government negotiated the *Ausgleich* (Compromise). This left the Hapsburg territories intact, but also established the Dual Monarchy, which granted the Hungarians internal autonomy and a share in the running of the Empire.

Other ethnic groups were offered less generous terms. The *Ausgleich* gave the Poles of Galicia and the Serbo-Croats limited rights of self-government, but for most the situation remained unchanged. The Czechs, for example, would have to wait until after World War I for the creation of their nation state. However, their nationalist aspirations were to find expression in their rich output of music in the second half of the century.

Portrait of Bismarck by Franz von Lenbach

Bismarck's shrewd statesmanship was vital in creating the German nation.

German supremacy in Europe

The Prussian victory at Sadowa enabled Bismarck to bring northern Germany under his control. His opportunity to complete the unification process arose in 1870, when the vacant Spanish throne was offered to Prince Leopold, a member of the Hohenzollern family. The French, horrified at the prospect of a German monarch in Spain and demanding the withdrawal of Leopold's candidature, were cunningly maneuvered by Bismarck into declaring war.

The ensuing struggle was a virtual repeat of the Austro-Prussian conflict. Less than two months after declaring war, Napoleon was defeated at Sedan. Paris fell after a bitter four-month siege, and France was forced to surrender Alsace and Lorraine. With peace negotiations under way, Bismarck managed to persuade the southern German states to join with Prussia in a new union. Accordingly, on January 18, 1871, the Prussian king, Wilhelm, was crowned Kaiser (Emperor) of Germany at Versailles.

The French had still further indignity to suffer. In Paris radical Republicans took control of the city and established a revolutionary commune that rejected the authority of the French government after the surrender to Prussia. The Paris Commune survived for just two months before being violently suppressed. Meanwhile, outside the capital, German troops remained on French soil until the autumn of 1873.

By the 1870's, Russia had become once again the focal point of European concern. After the Franco-Prussian War the German Empire was the dominant force on the mainland, preserving a fragile balance of power between its neighbors. It was in the east, where the Ottoman Empire continued to crumble, that the greatest danger lay. Trouble erupted in 1875 when Bosnia rebelled against its Turkish rulers. Serbia, Montenegro, and Bulgaria soon joined the fray, hoping to enlist the support of Russia. Western leaders were torn between sympathy for the predominantly Christian rebels, and suspicion that the crisis had been provoked by Pan-Slav agitators in Russia. Their fears increased as the Tsar's army invaded Turkey and marched on Constantinople. Western pressure halted its progress ten miles short of the capital, and a European summit was called at Berlin. At the Congress of Berlin in 1878, segments of the Ottoman Empire were shuffled like cards and dealt out to the major powers, and Serbia, Romania, and Bulgaria all achieved a measure of independence. Serious hostilities had been averted for the time being, but the tangled web of nationalist jealousies in the Balkans remained unresolved.

Romanticism had played its part in arousing the revolutionary and nationalistic fervor of the nineteenth century, and its extolling of personal feelings and the individual acting as a potent force for both political and artistic change. Beginning with Beethoven, a rich seam of musical innovation was mined throughout the era. As time went on, the Romantic movement would become generally less significant, although in the musical world its influence was to remain powerful for many years.

Above right: The Proclamation of the German Kaiser by Anton von Werner, 1885

The coronation, in January 1871, of Wilhelm I as Kaiser (Emperor) of Germany at the Palace of Versailles, outside Paris, was humiliating for the defeated French nation.

Below right: Photograph showing the destruction of the Vendôme Column, 1871

The artist, Courbet (seen to the right of the back row), was imprisoned for his part in the defiant destruction of this statue of Napoleon during the Paris Commune.

Featured Composers

Beethoven

Ludwig van Beethoven 1770–1827

RECOMMENDED WORKS

Symphony No. 9 in D minor, Op. 125, 'Choral'
Philips 432 995-2
Sylvia McNair (sop); Jard van Nes (contr); Uwe Heilmann (ten); Bernd Weikl (bar); Leipzig Radio Chorus; Leipzig Gewandhausorchester/Kurt Masur
A big-hearted performance, warmly recorded and played with genuine devotion. The singing, too, is first-rate and the recording one of Philips's best.

Piano Sonata No. 23 in F minor, Op. 57, 'Appassionata'
Deutsche Grammophon 413 435-2
Wilhelm Kempff (pno)
A master Beethovenian in full cry, yet Kempff never stints on detail or lets his emotions blur the music's outlines. The recording is bright and well focused.

Piano Concerto No. 5 in E flat major, Op. 73, 'Emperor'
Deutsche Grammophon 435 098-2
Maurizio Pollini (pno); Vienna Philharmonic Orchestra/Karl Böhm
An Olympian reading of this grandest of piano concertos. Excellent sound and a generous coupling in the superb Fourth Concerto.

REPRESENTATIVE WORKS

Symphonies Nos. 3 (Eroica), 5, 6 (Pastoral), & 7
Piano Concertos Nos. 3 & 4
Violin Concerto
Violin Sonata No. 9 (Kreutzer)
String Quartets Nos. 7 & 14
Piano Sonatas Nos. 14 (Moonlight) & 32
Mass in D (Missa Solemnis)

Portrait of Beethoven by Christian Horneman, 1803

Beethoven was born in Bonn in Germany, the son of a singer in the service of the Elector of Cologne. His father was weak-spirited and drank excessively, but he recognized his son's talent and was disappointed when he failed to emulate Mozart as a child prodigy. However, Beethoven soon held positions as harpsichordist in the court theater and assistant organist in the Electoral chapel, where he obtained composition lessons from the court organist.

During his first visit to Vienna in 1787, Beethoven impressed Mozart with his improvisations at the keyboard. Before any formal tuition could take place, however, news that Beethoven's mother was dying took him back to Bonn. By the time he returned to Vienna in 1792, Mozart too was dead. He went instead to Haydn for composition lessons, but the two men were temperamental opposites, and the instruction he received from Johann Albrechtsberger proved more valuable.

Meanwhile, Beethoven's career as a pianist made a promising start. His passion and dynamism at the keyboard more than compensated for a lack of polish. He made his first appearance in Vienna in 1795 playing his *Piano Concerto No. 2* in B flat, and was soon established as the city's leading pianist. Other compositions from the 1790's include piano sonatas, cello sonatas, and violin sonatas. The two forms that were to have special significance for

Beethoven were still to come: he completed his first symphony in 1800 and his first set of string quartets in 1801.

Beethoven was Vienna's first successful freelance musician: he never again held a court position after leaving Bonn. Instead he had wealthy aristocratic friends, patrons, and perhaps lovers, to whom he dedicated his early compositions in return for payment. His success in such circles, despite notoriously awkward manners, an unpredictable temper, and a refusal to defer to superior social rank, can be attributed to his genius and personal magnetism.

Beginning in 1798, Beethoven experienced a continual humming and whistling in his ears that gradually grew stronger, eventually prompting the agonizing realization that he was going deaf. In 1802, in a state of desperation in which he contemplated suicide, Beethoven retired to the secluded village of Heiligenstadt and addressed to his brothers a statement

Key to Recommended Works

arr. arrangement (by)	**contr** contralto	**hpd** harpsichord	**Op., Opp.** Opus(es)	**pno** piano	**ten** tenor	**vcl** violoncello ('cello)
bar baritone	**gtr** guitar	**mez** mezzo-soprano	**org** organ	**sop** soprano	**treb** treble	**vln** violin

Concert in the Malfatti household, artist unknown

Therese von Malfatti (seen here at the piano) rejected Beethoven's proposal of marriage in 1809 — a bitter blow.

expressing his anguish. The 'Heiligenstadt Testament,' as it is known, marks the start of a new period in Beethoven's output; the next ten years saw one of the most prodigious outpourings of masterpieces in the history of music. By 1812 he had completed *Symphonies 2–8*, *Piano Concertos 4 and 5*, the *Violin Concerto*, his opera *Fidelio*, the three *Rasumovsky String Quartets*, and a wealth of piano sonatas and other works.

Haydn and Mozart had demonstrated that melody alone, no matter how beautiful, could not hold an audience's attention for more than a minute or two. They had in consequence mastered the use of harmonic tension to sustain large-scale structures. But Beethoven went further; with the first movement of the *Eroica Symphony* (1803) he created a single span of uninterrupted music of unprecedented length. He also widened the scope of the piano sonata to symphonic proportions with his *Waldstein Sonata* (1803) — dedicated to his

Two of Beethoven's ear trumpets

The realization in 1802 that he was going deaf profoundly affected Beethoven.

old friend Count Waldstein — and even more with the *Appassionata* (1804–5). In this he introduces new dynamic extremes, shattering the thoughtful calm of the opening with sudden fortissimo chords.

This music was revolutionary, and not only in technique. Beethoven's expanded forms broadened the scope for emotional expression, giving voice to the revolutionary spirit of the age. He was a passionate democrat and greatly admired the young Napoleon, whose name in fact originally appeared on the title page of the *Eroica Symphony*. When Beethoven heard that Napoleon had declared himself Emperor, however, he tore the page out and substituted 'In Memory of a Great Man.'

What raises Beethoven's genius in music to the level of Shakespeare's in literature is his supreme mastery of musical form. He was able to create vast and complex musical structures stemming from the fundamental building blocks of music itself. For him a simple musical figure had manifold implications that could generate an entire symphony. So, for example, the opening four notes of his *Fifth Symphony* (1807), supposedly depicting Fate knocking at the door, are especially portentous, since some derivation of them is heard in nearly every bar of the first movement.

After 1812, Beethoven's output dropped drastically. He became involved in a number of lawsuits, including one over royalties for his only truly programmatic and probably his worst published work — *Wellington's Victory*. In 1820 he won custody of his nephew Karl, following the death in 1815 of Beethoven's brother. Although there is no doubting his good intentions and love for the boy the arrangement was not a success. Beethoven had never married and wanted to treat Karl as his own son, but deepening poverty and a frenetic resumption of composition meant that his nephew was neglected. The year before Beethoven's death, the boy attempted suicide.

Beethoven began composing intensively again in 1817. Most of 1818 was taken up with his colossal *Hammerklavier Sonata*, and the years until 1824 were divided between the last three *Piano Sonatas*, the *Diabelli Variations*, the *Missa Solemnis* — a Mass commissioned by Beethoven's patron Archduke Rudolph, delivered three years late owing to the complexities of its composition — and the *Ninth Symphony*. This work, whose final movement is a triumphant setting of Schiller's *Ode to Joy*, again broke new ground in terms of scale and introduced choral forces into the symphony for the first time. After the first performance Beethoven stood stone deaf on the stage, oblivious of everything, until one of the soloists turned him around to see the thunderous applause.

In his final years Beethoven turned once again to the string quartet. In 1825 and 1826 he produced five works, at once profoundly complex and serene, for this intimate medium. He had become preoccupied with fugal techniques, just as in later life Bach had done, and the *Grosse Fuge* — originally the finale to his *Quartet in B flat* — is one of the most extended and elaborate examples of the form.

These last works were far ahead of their time and still challenge scholars and listeners. Beethoven did not live to complete sketches he had made for further works. At his funeral in 1827 he was mourned by a huge crowd, including fellow artists and aristocratic friends. His tombstone bore a single word: 'Beethoven.'

Paganini

Niccolò Paganini 1782–1840

RECOMMENDED WORK
24 Caprices, Op. 1
Angel CD7 47171-2
Itzhak Perlman (vln)
A dazzling catalogue of violinistic effects, brilliantly exploited by one of the great virtuosos of the age, and cleanly recorded.

REPRESENTATIVE WORKS
Violin Concertos Nos. 1 & 2
Le streghe (Witches' Dance)

Paganini was born in Genoa in Italy. He was given a violin by his parents, who cherished hopes he would become a great virtuoso — something his father sought to encourage by locking the boy in a room to practice for hours at a time. At the age of 11 he made his first public appearance, performing a set of his own variations to a rapt audience; at 13 he made his first tour.

In 1801, Paganini moved to Lucca and soon became leader of the new national orchestra. There he was persuaded by his lover to take up the guitar and wrote several delightful compositions, including 12 sonatas for violin and guitar. In 1805, Napoleon Bonaparte's sister, Princess Elisa, was installed in Lucca. Paganini improvised for her a piece on two strings of his violin, intending to represent a pair of lovers; he commemorated Napoleon's birthday with his *Sonata Napoleone* for performance entirely on one string.

Paganini left Lucca in 1809 and toured Italy, mesmerizing audiences with his brilliant musicianship, performing any piece of music at sight. In order to show off his abilities, he composed pieces of exceptional difficulty, one such being the 24 *Caprices* for solo violin, whose technical demands are so great that for a long time they were thought of as unperformable except by their composer. He turned his hand to orchestral works as well, writing

Portrait of Paganini playing while walking a tightrope, by Mantour, 1831

numerous violin concertos and the *Le streghe* (Witches' Dance) variations for violin and orchestra. An aura of mystery began to surround Paganini. With his unkempt appearance and wild stare, he was thought by many to derive his uncanny gifts from a pact with the devil, and was dubbed 'the devil's son.'

In 1824, Paganini started a liaison with Antonia Bianchi. When the relationship later faltered, he gained custody of their son, Achille. Paganini gave triumphant performances in Vienna, Berlin, and Paris from 1828 to 1831, but his experiences in London were less happy. Exorbitant ticket pricing gave rise to a furor of protest conducted through the pages of *The Times*. The admission prices were reduced, and *The Times* was forced to acknowledge Paganini's genius, although a reputation for meanness was less easily dispelled. From 1834 increasing illness put an end to Paganini's playing career. He developed an interest in gambling and even bought a stake in a Parisian casino, before succumbing in 1840 to cancer of the larynx.

Paganini's influence was twofold. For other performers he provided a model of technical brilliance and advanced the cult of the virtuoso; for composers he pointed to the possibilities of including virtuoso elements in their music. Chopin's dazzling *Études* owe a debt to Paganini, as do various works by Brahms and Schumann. A final indication of his appeal is the range of composers who have composed variations based on his *Caprice No. 24* in A minor, including Brahms, Rachmaninov, Lutoslawski, and Andrew Lloyd Webber.

The Witches' Tree, a scene from Paganini's ballet *Il Noce di Benevento, c.1780*

Paganini also used the theme of witches in his Witches' Dance variations.

Rossini

Gioacchino Rossini 1792–1868

RECOMMENDED WORK

Il barbiere di Siviglia
Philips 411 058-2
Thomas Allen (bar) Figaro; Agnes Baltsa (mez)
Rosina; Domenico Trimarchi (bar) Bartolo; Robert
Lloyd (bass) Don Basilio; Francisco Araiza (ten)
Almaviva; Ambrosian Opera Chorus; Academy of
St. Martin in the Fields/Neville Marriner
*With vocal contributions that combine great character
and irresistible verve, this Il barbiere has the added
advantage of buoyant conducting, chipper orchestra
executions, and excellent sound.*

REPRESENTATIVE WORKS

**Overtures: Tancredi; La scala di seta; La gazza
ladra; Il Signor Bruschino**
Guillaume Tell
L'Italiana in Algeri
Stabat mater

Caricature of Rossini by H. Mailly on the occasion
of his seventy-fifth birthday in 1867

Born in Pesaro in Italy, Rossini was the
only child of the town trumpeter. His
mother was a singer, providing a useful
source of income when his father was
imprisoned for insubordination — which
happened more than once.

The family moved to Bologna when
Rossini was 12, and the young boy contributed to the family finances by singing
in churches until his voice changed, and
then by playing the keyboard in the opera
house. Even at this tender age Rossini
could write down an aria after only two
hearings, and in 1806 he went to study at
the Bologna Academy. There he learned a
great deal from studying scores by Mozart
and Haydn, and wrote his first opera while
still a student. Rossini was an amazingly
prolific composer and had already composed nine operas before his reputation
was established with performances in
Venice in 1813 of *Tancredi* and *L'Italiana in
Algeri*. The first is a setting of a play by
Voltaire, and the second a comedy; both
brimmed with spice and vitality, appealing
enormously to the audience of the day.

Costume designs for Rossini operas, 1820s–1830s
*The two left-hand pictures are characters
from* La donna del lago. *The others are
Figaro in* Il barbiere di Siviglia *(right)
and Isabella in* L'Italiana in Algeri
(extreme right).

In 1815, Rossini became music director of the opera house at Naples and there
met his first wife, at that time the mistress
of the impresario Domenico Barbaia. His
employment required him to provide two
operas a year. Not a man to be daunted by
a challenge, Rossini fulfilled his obliga-
tions, in some cases by borrowing material
from his own earlier operas.

Now in full swing, in 1816 he composed music for *Il barbiere di Siviglia* (The
Barber of Seville), whose famous overture
he had twice used before. The legend of
the barber had already been successfully
set by Paisiello, and Rossini's misgivings
about repeating the feat appeared to be

borne out when his own version met with
a muted reception. Since then, however,
the delightful comic plot and brilliantly
fashioned music have won almost universal approval and made it one of the best
loved of all operas. *La Cenerentola* from the
following year is based on the Cinderella
fairy tale and shares with *Il barbiere* the
Rossini trademarks of a large-scale finale
with elaborate build-up and the use of
'patter-songs' — in which words are sung
very fast for comic effect.

In his later operas, such as *Semiramide*
and *Mose in Egitto*, Rossini turned to more
dramatic subjects and forms. Despite their
huge success, he was only 37 when in 1829
he composed his last opera, *Guillaume Tell*
(William Tell), the story of a Swiss hero
who rebels against Austrian rule. After its
premiere, Rossini worked at the Bologna
Conservatory before settling in Paris to
indulge his second love in life, food;
indeed he became famous for his gastro-
nomical gifts, bequeathing to the world
the fillet steak dish Tournedos Rossini.

Rossini was widowed in 1843 and married his long-standing mistress, Olympe
Pélissier. His days of prolific composition
for the theater were over, but he did not
entirely renounce music. In 1864 his *Petite
messe solennelle* (Little Solemn Mass) was
performed, followed by what would be his
final work, *Péchés de vieillesse* (Sins of Old
Age), a collection of songs and piano
pieces written over a period of ten years.
He completed them in 1868 — the year of
his death — the same year that saw con-
firmation of his greatness as an opera
composer with the five-hundredth performance of *Guillaume Tell*.

Donizetti

Gaetano Donizetti 1797–1848

RECOMMENDED WORK

Lucia di Lammermoor
London Grand Opera 411 622-2
Joan Sutherland (sop) Lucia; Renato Cioni (ten)
Edgardo; Robert Merrill (bar) Enrico; Cesare Siepi
(bass) Raimondo; Ana Raquel Satre (mez) Alisa;
Kenneth Macdonald (ten) Arturo; Rinaldo
Pellizoni (ten) Normanno; Santa Cecilia Academy
Chorus and Orchestra/John Pritchard
*Spectacular coloratura singing from the young Joan
Sutherland and a strong supporting cast. With
authoritative conducting and excellent sound, this
is a real must for opera buffs.*

REPRESENTATIVE WORKS

Don Pasquale
L'elisir d'amore
Anna Bolena
Lucrezia Borgia
Maria Stuarda

Scene from the 1843 production of *Don Pasquale* at
Her Majesty's Theatre, London

**Don Pasquale *was Donizetti's last major
success before his descent into illness.***

Portrait of Donizetti by Induno Girolamo

The opera composer and conductor
Johann Mayr recognized the talent in the
spirited young Donizetti. He took him
from an impoverished and unmusical
background in the streets of his birthplace, Bergamo, in northern Italy, to give
him a thorough musical education. As he
neared adulthood, Donizetti studied for
two years in Bologna with Padre Mattei,
the renowned counterpoint teacher. Although benefiting musically, Donizetti
found the old priest somewhat dour, and
he reserved his lifelong affection exclusively for his original teacher.

Donizetti returned to Bergamo in 1817
and worked swiftly on a variety of compositions, often completing one in a single
day. The string quartets of this period
show him as a prodigiously gifted apprentice. It was in his eventual output of some
70 operas, however, that he showed his
true mastery.

In 1818 he evaded conscription with an
exemption bought by a wealthy admirer
and took employment in Venice, where
his first opera was produced that same year.
His first significant success came with
Zoraida di Granata in Rome in 1822, the
commission having been passed on to him
by his old teacher Mayr. This secured a
series of commissions from Naples, including, in 1826, a contract for four operas a
year. With poor librettos, however, no
masterpieces resulted.

The year 1830 was a good one for
Donizetti. His *Anna Bolena* brought him
international fame for the first time, and
Rossini's retirement from opera composition gave him supremacy in the field for
the next decade. From Rossini he inherited the characteristic *bel canto* (melodic
singing) style — often featuring coloratura
passages — and his own rapid craftsmanship enabled him to complete the enduring comedy *L'elisir d'amore* in 1832 in less
than a month. The price of this facility,
however, was a lack of consistent dramatic
power. This was true even in the more
serious *Lucia di Lammermoor* of 1835, based
on a novel by Sir Walter Scott and containing the well-known 'Mad Scene.'
Nevertheless, its sextet provides a moving
and masterful climax to what is probably
his greatest work.

Relations between Donizetti and his
Neapolitan patrons became strained in the
1830's. Donizetti broke his contract in
1832, and although a new one was drawn
up in 1834, the authorities in Naples
objected to his next opera, *Maria Stuarda*,
and the consequent rapid revision ruined
the first production. Then, in 1837,
Virginia, his beloved wife since 1828, died
of cholera. His new work, *Poliuto*, was
banned for depicting the martyrdom of a
saint, and so a grieving, dispirited Donizetti finally left Naples for Paris.

The Parisians greeted him warmly,
mounting productions of his works in four
of the city's theaters, much to the disgust of
Berlioz and other French composers.
Donizetti responded with the composition of a number of his best operas, culminating in his last great work, the three-act
comic masterpiece *Don Pasquale*, first produced in Milan in 1843.

By then he had secured the position of
Kapellmeister to the Hapsburg Court in
Vienna, but had also begun to suffer worsening symptoms of a syphilitic illness that
attacked his nervous system. By the end of
1843 he was incapable of further composition, and Parisian doctors declared him
insane the following year. Through the
persistent efforts of his nephew he was
eventually taken back to his native
Bergamo, where friends cared for him
until his death.

Bellini

Vincenzo Bellini 1801–1835

RECOMMENDED WORK

Norma
Angel CDS7 47304-8
Maria Callas (sop) Norma; Ebe Stignani (mez)
Adalgisa; Mario Filippeschi (ten) Pollione; Nicola
Rossi-Lemeni (bass) Orovesco; Paolo Caroli (ten)
Flavio; Rina Cavallari (sop) Clotilde; Chorus and
Orchestra of La Scala, Milan/Tullio Serafin
*Maria Callas in a classic realization (the better of two
that she recorded) of what was perhaps her most
famous role; an unforgettable production, beautifully
transferred to CD.*

REPRESENTATIVE WORKS

Il pirata
I puritani
La sonnambula

Vincenzo Bellini is today honored by a museum that stands in his birthplace of Catania in Sicily. He seemed destined to become a composer, and guided by his grandfather, also a composer, wrote his first piece at the age of six.

In 1819 he went to the San Sebastiano Conservatory in Naples, but for a boy of such promise he was slow to develop. Various minor pieces date from these student days, but it was only when he turned to opera and wrote *Adelson e Salvini* that he discovered the form that was most congenial to him.

The work had a tremendous impact on the impresario Barbaia, who in 1827 commissioned *Il pirata* for La Scala, Milan. *Il pirata* demonstrates well Bellini's style, which favors a pure, simple vocal line. This delighted his teacher Zingarelli, who had always warned his pupils against Rossini's music, claiming that the very florid vocal lines were physically dangerous! Bellini also expected the librettos for his operas to have simple plots with fast-moving action, and the brilliant dramatist Felice Romani was an ideal partner. Their next collaboration was in 1830 on the

Portrait of Bellini by Giuseppe Cammarano

opera *I Capuleti ed i Montecchi*. This version of *Romeo and Juliet* was made exaggeratedly melodramatic by Romani to suit the popular tastes of the day.

The partnership was again fruitful with *La sonnambula* (The Sleepwalker). This time the inclusion of just a hint of contemporaneous popular song made the opera an instant hit. *Norma*, premiered later the same year of 1831, was again very well received, largely for the clearly rebellious sentiments it contained, particularly in the final-act chorus 'Guerra, Guerra' (War, War). Today its best-known aria is 'Casta Diva,' in which the pure soprano solo line soars above the chorus.

Opera composition did not keep Bellini from affairs of the heart, and after he failed to win his first love due to opposition from her parents, he turned his attentions to Giuditta Turina. The relationship lasted five years, although for all that time the young woman was married to someone else.

After *Norma*, Bellini and Romani argued and Bellini wrote his final opera, *I puritani* (The Puritans) with Carlo Pepoli. Although the libretto was poor, the weaknesses were more than compensated for by the beauty of the melodies, the development of Bellini's style, and the magnificence of the premiere production: the opera was another triumph. After the exhausting task of composing and staging *I puritani*, Bellini was suddenly struck down with a fatal illness, and died in 1835 aged just 34. His place in the history of opera is assured, not only for the beauty of his own operas but also as a forerunner to the genius of Giuseppe Verdi.

A climactic scene from Bellini's *Il pirata*, 1827
A tragedy in which the heroine's lover kills her husband, Il pirata *was first produced in Milan in 1827.*

Glinka

Mikhail Glinka 1804–1857

RECOMMENDED WORK

A Life for the Tsar
Sony Classical S3K 46487
Boris Mantinovich (bass) Ivan Susanin; Alexandrina Pendachanska (sop) Antonida; Chris Merritt (ten) Sobinin; Stefania Toczyska (mez) Vanya; Sofia National Opera Chorus and Festival Orchestra/ Emil Tchakarov
At long last a recording that matches the original Russian intensity of Glinka's seminal masterpiece. Using a restored score, Tchakarov blends a capable cast with rich, characterful chorus.

REPRESENTATIVE WORKS
Ruslan and Lyudmila: overture
Jota aragonesa
Kamarinskaya

Glinka was the father of the nationalist tradition in music. He was born in Smolensk, and his first musical influences were Russian folk songs and church bells. He went to school in St. Petersburg until 1822 and remained there until 1830, earning a meager living as a pianist and singer. His early compositions were crude, but showed an instinctive feeling for folk melody.

In Italy from 1830 to 1833 he encountered Bellini and Donizetti, but ultimately felt uncomfortable with the Italian operatic style and moved on to Berlin for his first formal composition instruction, from Siegfried Dehn. He returned to Russia on hearing news of his father's death, and married shortly afterward.

In 1835 and 1836, Glinka worked on his first opera, *A Life for the Tsar*. Based on a story by Zhukovsky, it tells how Ivan Susanin, at the cost of his own life, saved the first Romanov Tsar from a band of Poles. It was an instant success, not least with the Tsar, and Glinka was appointed Imperial Kapellmeister the following year.

Glinka immediately set to work on his next opera, but the distractions of marital break-up delayed its completion until 1842. The result, *Ruslan and Lyudmila*, was not a great success. Pushkin's fairy tale was unsuitable as an operatic plot and the work suffered from dramatic limpness, despite containing some of Glinka's best music. Somewhat discouraged, in 1844 he left for Paris, where he got along well with Berlioz, and also visited Spain; but on his return to Russia in 1847 he brought little new music. Regardless, during a stay in Warsaw in 1848 he composed the orchestral piece *Kamarinskaya*, which profoundly influenced Tchaikovsky and the composers known as 'The Five.' *Kamarinskaya* uses a 'changing background' technique to present some 70 variations of a folk tune. As the term suggests, the melody remains unaltered while the accompaniment evolves continually, and the work as a whole shows Glinka at his most inventive.

In his final years, Glinka returned to Paris before visiting Dehn again in Berlin, where he died early in 1857.

Portrait of Glinka at work on *Ruslan and Lyudmila* by Ilya Repin, 1842

Mendelssohn

Felix Mendelssohn 1809–1847

RECOMMENDED WORKS

Symphony No. 4 in A, Op. 90, 'Italian'
London 433 811-2
San Francisco Symphony Orchestra/Herbert Blomstedt
An alert, buoyant reading, with delightful instrumental solos and full-bodied orchestral sound.

Elijah
Philips 438 368-2
Elly Ameling (sop); Annelies Burmeister (contr); Peter Schreier (ten); Theo Adam (bass); Leipzig Radio Chorus; Leipzig Gewandhausorchester/ Wolfgang Sawallisch
A performance that liberates Mendelssohn's inspired vision from all the usual interpretive stodginess. An exultant reading, magnificently sung by the Leipzig Radio Chorus, and beautifully recorded.

REPRESENTATIVE WORKS
Hebrides
Violin Concerto
A Midsummer Night's Dream
Octet
Songs without words

The musical development of the young Mendelssohn was not troubled, as it was for so many others, by struggle and financial hardship. Born in Hamburg, he was the son of rich and cultured parents, whose resources and encouragement were always at his disposal. The family soon moved to Berlin, where he studied the piano with his mother and took lessons in theory with Carl Zelter. From the age of 12 he composed prolifically, and his works were performed in the musical salon at the family home that became famous in Berlin. Weber visited in 1821 and made a lasting impression on the young composer.

Mendelssohn was very close to his sister Fanny, also prodigiously talented but lacking the support her brother received. In 1826 they read Shakespeare together, resulting in Mendelssohn's overture *A Midsummer Night's Dream*. The assured

Portrait of Mendelssohn by Wilhelm Hensel

mastery of this work and the radiant *Octet* of the previous year were astonishing achievements for a boy in his late teens, and it is no surprise that he was compared with Mozart. *A Midsummer Night's Dream* bears the Mendelssohn hallmark of elegant melodic invention, effortlessly interweaving one or two programmatic effects, such as a musical donkey's 'hee-haw,' without interrupting the musical flow. Later he added other movements to complete the incidental music for the play.

A keen advocate of the music of J. S. Bach, in 1829 Mendelssohn conducted the first performance of the *St. Matthew Passion* since its composer's death, giving a boost to the revival of Bach's works then under way and leading to a performance of sections of the *Passion* in London in 1837.

About this time he decided to establish himself independently as a professional musician. The Berlin musical scene was not ideal: his only opera had been a failure there in 1827. Other musicians resented his privilege and found him egotistical — complaints that were made more acute because they were mixed with a strain of anti-Semitism against his Jewish family background. It made no difference that Mendelssohn's parents were converted Christians and he himself was baptized.

He then embarked upon a number of tours in search of employment and late in 1829 arrived in London on the first of ten visits to England. He also toured Scotland, where stunning rock formations on the island of Staffa inspired the *Hebrides* overture. Mendelssohn's melodic genius was never better displayed than in the main theme of this beautifully lyrical work.

His travels to Scotland and a visit to Italy the following year also provided an impression of the national musical character of the two countries, later translated into the *Scotch* and *Italian* symphonies. Although his melodies are undoubtedly Romantic, these symphonies still keep to the basic Classical forms. Mendelssohn's habit was to compose first for piano and orchestrate later, indicating a Classical concern for structure before color.

After further travels — including a visit to Paris, where he met Chopin and Liszt — Mendelssohn finally secured a directorial position in Düsseldorf in 1833. But his somewhat despotic approach encountered resistance, and in 1835 he moved to Leipzig as conductor at the famous Gewandhaus. This post was more congenial and lasted until 1846. The orchestra's leader was the accomplished violinist Ferdinand David, who became a good friend and inspired the *Violin Concerto* of 1844. Mendelssohn also found happiness in love and in 1837 he married Cécile Jeanrenaud.

He continued to travel, especially to England, where he conducted his oratorio *St. Paul* and, during a later visit in 1842, played for Queen Victoria and Prince Albert, to the screeching accompaniment of the royal parrot.

In 1840 he had proposed the establishment of a conservatory in Leipzig but was interrupted in his negotiations by an invitation, then virtually a royal command, to go to Berlin as Kapellmeister to the King of Prussia. Again he was greeted rather sourly by musicians and public alike, and soon tendered his resignation. With the compromise of a reduction in his responsibilities, he was able to return to Leipzig, and the Conservatory opened in 1843.

Mendelssohn continued to conduct at the Gewandhaus and to direct and teach at the Conservatory. He put heart and soul into his great oratorio *Elijah*, which he conducted at its premiere in Birmingham in 1846, when it showed Mendelssohn at his most dramatic and romantic. He was already exhausted by travel and overwork when the shattering news of his sister Fanny's death brought on a severe depression. Fits of shivering and head pains followed, leading to a fatal stroke. When he died at just 38, he was mourned especially by Schumann, who felt that Europe had lost a potential successor to Beethoven.

A page from Mendelssohn's diary kept during a visit to Scotland in 1829

The Hebrides overture resulted from Mendelssohn's impressions of Scotland.

Berlioz

Hector Berlioz 1803–1869

RECOMMENDED WORK
Symphonie fantastique, Op. 14
Philips 432 151-2
Vienna Philharmonic Orchestra/Colin Davis
A combination of Classical poise and Romantic fever, warmly played and superbly recorded. Surely the best of Davis's three recordings of the work.

REPRESENTATIVE WORKS
Harold in Italy
Les Nuits d'Été
Benvenuto Cellini
Les Troyens

Hector Berlioz was born near Grenoble in the French Alps. As a child he was a voracious reader, particularly of Virgil, Shakespeare, and Goethe. He never learned to play the piano, and lessons on the flute lasted just a year. Only on the guitar, a gift from his father, did he attain a degree of proficiency.

Despite young Berlioz's musical aspirations, parental expectations of a career in

Photograph of Berlioz, around 1850

Caricature from an 1846 issue of the Vienna Theater Newspaper

Berlioz's use of huge orchestras made him the frequent subject of satire.

medicine led first to studies at a medical college in Paris. But the desire to be a composer was too strong, and to his parents' chagrin he abandoned medicine and went to the Paris Conservatoire to study composition. Berlioz proved to be a troublesome student. His ideas were conceived on a grand scale and were difficult to perform because of the large forces required. Nevertheless he was awarded the Prix de Rome in 1830, and his father finally accepted that his son was a composer.

Berlioz's first major piece was the *Symphonie fantastique*, one of the most original and revolutionary concepts ever penned. Like many works from the Romantic period the *Symphonie* is 'program music': the second movement describes a ball; the third, a successor to Beethoven's *Pastoral Symphony*, is a depiction of nature; and the fourth is a gruesome 'March to the Scaffold.' The inspiration for this monumental work was unrequited love; the main musical idea throughout the work represents the woman in question, actress Harriet Smithson. Berlioz had seen the performances of Shakespeare that had made her the darling of the French

capital, but she refused to let him woo her. When she heard the symphony she had inspired, however, she fell in love with its author and the two were married.

In 1834, Berlioz was commissioned by Paganini to write *Harold in Italy*, another massive work that has a major solo part for the viola. Paganini was disappointed that the solo role did not give him more to play and never performed the work, but he remained friendly with Berlioz and in 1838 his gift of 20,000 francs enabled the Frenchman to give up music criticism, which he loathed, to concentrate on composing. More large-scale works followed, including a *Requiem* commissioned by the French government in 1837 that required a monumental 220 players and 200 voices.

After all his efforts, Berlioz's first marriage was a failure and he separated from Harriet in 1844. Undeterred, he married again, this time Marie Recio, whom he had met in 1841. This was also the year he completed the charming song cycle *Les Nuits d'Été* (Summer Nights) for mezzo-soprano and piano. In 1856, Berlioz orchestrated the work, in which form it is better known today. A master of orchestration, Berlioz wrote a pioneering essay on the subject in 1844. It remains an important reference for composers today.

In 1856, Berlioz embarked on his grandest work, the opera *Les Troyens* (The Trojans), regarded by many as his masterpiece. He used the operas of Gluck as models, perhaps because of the Classical rather than Romantic subject matter, and took three years to complete it. Because of its length, *Les Troyens* was divided into two parts to facilitate staging, Acts 1 and 2 becoming *La Prise de Troie* (The Capture of Troy) and Acts 3 to 5 *Les Troyens à Carthage* (The Trojans in Carthage).

Berlioz died in 1869 and was buried in Montmartre in Paris. Curiously, the French did not automatically take him to their hearts, and for many years his works were more popular in Germany, England, and Russia — the countries he regularly visited on conducting tours — than in his native land.

Portrait of Harriet Smithson by George Clint, 1822

Berlioz's infatuation with the actress inspired the composition of his Symphonie fantastique.

Gounod

Charles Gounod 1818–1893

RECOMMENDED WORK

Faust
Angel CDS7 54228-2
Richard Leech (ten) Faust; Cheryl Studer (sop) Marguérite; José van Dam (bass-bar) Méphistophélès; Thomas Hampson (bass) Valentin; French Army Chorus; Toulouse Capitole Choir and Orchestra/Michel Plasson
Plasson presides over a consistently painstaking, faithful, and perceptive account of Gounod's masterwork. The set also includes four previously unrecorded numbers and the complete ballet music.

REPRESENTATIVE WORKS
Mireille
Funeral March of a Marionette
Petite Symphonie

The French composer Charles Gounod composed a work which for more than half a century was the staple of every opera house in the world. Although *Faust* is no longer fashionable, and Gounod's reputation has dwindled to that of a relatively minor figure, his influence during his lifetime was considerable and his craftsmanship and elegance give enduring pleasure.

Born in Paris in 1818, Gounod studied at the Paris Conservatoire. In 1839 he won the coveted Prix de Rome and during the resulting three-year stay in Rome steeped himself in the sixteenth-century choral music sung in the Sistine Chapel. Palestrina was a particular revelation to him, and sacred music was to constitute a large, though now largely forgotten part of Gounod's output. Between 1846 and 1849 Gounod actually studied for the priesthood and throughout his life he vacillated between the spiritual and the carnal.

In 1842 he visited Vienna, Berlin, and Leipzig, where he met Mendelssohn — a composer he resembles in many ways. Back in Paris he became the organist at the Missions Etrangères. He married in 1852 and started to compose operas, initially

Detail of scenes from Goethe's *Faust*, painted by Carl Vogel von Vogelstein, c.1845

Gounod's opera, inspired by Goethe's work, was his greatest triumph.

unsuccessful works in the style of Meyerbeer and then lighter and happier works such as *Le médecin malgré lui* in 1858.

But it was with *Faust* in 1859 that Gounod struck gold. The enduring popularity of the work is due above all to the extraordinary richness of melodic invention: from Marguérite's sparkling 'Jewel Song' to Faust's fervent '*Salut, demeure chaste et pure*' there is scarcely an unmemorable tune in the whole opera.

The operas *Mireille* (1864) and *Roméo et Juliette* (1867) were also successful, but his stay in England between 1871 and 1874 was a mixed blessing. He was favored by Queen Victoria and found an audience for his oratorios *La rédemption* and *Mors et vita*, but he also came under the sway of the eccentric and notorious singer Georgina Weldon. Gounod's infatuation drew him into a turbulent, hysterical world. She was often involved in lawsuits, even attempting to blackmail Queen Victoria to obtain funds for her singing academy. Gounod returned to Paris in 1874, but although he lived on for two decades, his rich period of creativity was over. Only the *Petite Symphonie* (Little Symphony) for wind instruments has a youthful freshness that reminds the listener of his happier years.

Chopin

Frédéric Chopin 1810–1849

RECOMMENDED WORK
Piano Sonata No. 3 in B minor
Deutsche Grammophon 415 346-2
Maurizio Pollini (pno)
A strong, wonderfully cogent interpretation of Chopin's masterpiece, realistically recorded and coupled with an equally compelling performance of the famous Second Sonata ('Funeral March').

REPRESENTATIVE WORKS
Piano Concertos in E minor & F minor
Solo piano works: Preludes, Scherzos, Ballades, Waltzes, Mazurkas, Barcarolle

Portrait of Chopin by Eugène Delacroix, 1838

The Polish composer Frédéric Chopin was born in Zelasowa Wola and studied music from the age of six. By the time he was seven, he had begun his career as a concert pianist and had his first piece published. He entered the Warsaw Conservatory and after diligent study emerged with honors in 1829.

His first trip abroad was to Vienna, where he gave two successful concerts. Life outside Poland was seductive, and after a brief visit home Chopin left his native land for good, eventually settling in France, his father's homeland. Although only 20, he was already an accomplished pianist noted for his sensitive playing and imaginative improvisations. He had also composed two of his largest works, both piano concertos. In each work the orchestra's role is secondary to that of the soloist, whose part demands virtuoso playing of the highest standard.

Arriving in Paris in 1831, Chopin quickly made influential friends, but success was slower to come his way. Although a gifted musician, he was not a natural performer: his introverted nature did not appeal in the concert hall and his first appearance was coolly received. Chopin's response was to perform only in the Parisian Salon, which earned him the reputation of a snob. However, it was there that his intimate music was heard to best effect and he soon became one of the most popular and well-paid performers in the French capital.

The vast majority of Chopin's 170 compositions are for the piano. Bach

Chopin in the salon of Prince Anton Radziwill by Henryk Siemiradzki, 1887

Chopin's music was perfectly matched to the intimate atmosphere of the salon.

exerted an influence, but even more so the operas of Bellini. Chopin adored soaring melodies and long sustained lines and incorporated them into his works with a generous splash of ornamentation. But paramount as an influence were the folk songs and dances of his native country. Chopin borrowed their idiosyncratic rhythms and unusual melodies for his *Ballades* and *Mazurkas* and from this rich source developed his characteristic harmonies and daring use of discords. His love of dance music can be heard in his numerous *Waltzes*, which are in fact impossible to dance to because of their frequent changes of tempo.

In 1837, Chopin met the novelist George Sand, with whom he lived for ten years. It was she who inspired him during his most prolific times and cared for him during the long periods when he was incapacitated with tuberculosis. After a break with Sand, Chopin gave concerts in England and Scotland in 1848, but died the next year in Paris. He left behind a rich legacy of music that has influenced composers as diverse as Brahms, Fauré, and Debussy and remains as popular as ever today.

Portrait of George Sand by Eugène Delacroix

Sand encouraged the composition of some of Chopin's greatest works.

Schumann

Robert Schumann 1810–1856

RECOMMENDED WORK
Piano Concerto in A minor, Op 54
Philips 412 923-2
Stephen Kovacevich (pno); BBC Symphony Orchestra/Colin Davis
A highly communicative interpretation, poetic and assertive by turns, and sympathetically conducted by Colin Davis. The sound is excellent.

REPRESENTATIVE WORKS
Symphonies Nos. 1–4
Manfred
Cello Concerto
Violin Concerto
Piano Quartet
Piano Quintet
Carnaval
Fantasy in C
Davidsbündlertänze
Kreisleriana

Born at Zwickau in Germany, Schumann grew up in a literary environment. His father was a writer and publisher and encouraged his son's enthusiasm for the Romantic authors of the time. His interest in music was nurtured by performances given locally, but was discouraged by his mother. After his father died when he was 16, it was decided that he should go to Leipzig University to study law.

He did not take studies seriously, preferring to indulge in the excesses of student life and, of course, music. He attended concerts at the Gewandhaus, took piano lessons with the fiercely idealistic Friedrich Wieck, and, during further 'study' in Heidelberg, began to perform and compose. He gave up law and returned to Leipzig for further lessons with Wieck, but ruined any chance of a career as a pianist by dislocating a finger with a stretching machine he had invented.

In 1833, Schumann became ill with a depressive disorder that would recur for the rest of his life. He composed almost entirely during happier periods of intense

Zwickau, seen from the Brückenberg, 1840, painted by G. Täubert

A contemporary painting of Schumann's birthplace in eastern Germany.

creativity that alternated with these bouts of illness. Schumann also devoted his energy to music criticism through his journal *Die Neue Zeitschrift für Musik* (New Musical Journal), which he founded in 1834 and edited for ten years. Its aim was to sift out genius from mere talent and thus combat mediocrity in German music. He proved to be a discerning critic, recognizing the burgeoning mastery in very early works by Chopin and Brahms, enthusing over Mendelssohn, and generously acknowledging Berlioz, Wagner, and Liszt, although they did not conform to his own ideal — 'Liszt's world is not mine.'

Schumann often wrote under two pseudonyms — Florestan and Eusebius, who led an imaginary *Davidsbund* (League of David) in the fight against musical philistinism and represented the 'ecstatic' and 'sensitive' sides of his personality. The two characters appear in the piano works that dominate his output from the 1830's. 'F' and 'E' are credited with authorship of the various *Davidsbündlertänze* (Dances for the League of David), and their respective musical portraits form two of the movements of *Carnaval*, probably Schumann's finest solo piano work. The League of David appears once more in the final 'March against the Philistines.'

Schumann, with Clara seated at the piano; an engraving from a daguerrotype, 1847

In *Kreisleriana* — another important piano work of the 1830's — he paints a musical portrait of E. T. A. Hoffmann's Romantic hero Kreisler, but the work is also a tribute to Clara, the virtuoso pianist and daughter of Wieck, to whom Schumann was engaged. Wieck strongly opposed the relationship at first, fearing a threat to Clara's career (and hence his own vicarious success), but eventually consented and the two were married in 1840. Clara became a regular performer and lifelong champion of Schumann's works, and much of his fame is due to her efforts.

Schumann's work diversified in the 1840's. An initial creative period resulted in the *Dichterliebe* (Poet's Love) song cycle of 1840, the first two symphonies of 1841, the *Piano Quintet,* and the *Piano Quartet* of 1842. But in 1843 he suffered an attack of nervous exhaustion, and depression struck

again the following year. The Schumanns moved to Dresden, and Robert gradually emerged from his morbid state in 1845 for another highly creative phase of six years. He completed his *Piano Concerto* and as a result of a preoccupation with Goethe's *Faust* composed *Scenes from Faust* in 1848 — 'the most fruitful year of my life' — which also saw the composition of his outstanding overture to Byron's *Manfred*. The *Rhenish Symphony* (1850), his third, was his most successful, and although it suffers from overdense orchestration, it demonstrates a true grasp of symphonic form for the first (and only) time.

In 1850, Schumann was appointed conductor of the choir and orchestra in Düsseldorf, which should have provided performance opportunities and inspiration for new works. But he was too introspective and absentminded a person to carry out his duties effectively and quickly became unpopular. When he fell ill yet again in 1852, the authorities suggested that he retire on grounds of health, but he took it badly and considered himself to be the victim of a 'Philistine' conspiracy.

A brief light in the darkness of these final years was provided by the arrival of the young Brahms in the Schumann household, where he was hailed by Robert as the future savior of German music. But Schumann's mental condition deteriorated soon afterward, and, following an attempt to drown himself, he spent the last two years of his life in an asylum.

Autograph of the song 'Du bist wie eine Blume'
Schumann wrote this setting of a Heine poem for his wife, Clara, on June 8, 1830.

Liszt

Franz (Ferencz) Liszt 1811–1886

RECOMMENDED WORK
Piano Sonata in B minor
Philips 423 048-2
Alfred Brendel (pno)
Intelligence, poetic insight, and a rare but commanding sense of structure inform this performance.

REPRESENTATIVE WORKS
A Faust Symphony
Piano Concertos Nos. 1 & 2
Années de pèlerinage
Etudes d'exécution transcendante
Mephisto Waltzes
Hungarian Rhapsodies
Prelude and Fugue on the name B-A-C-H

Liszt was born in Raiding, Hungary, and grew up in a musical environment — his father was an official at the Esterházy court where Haydn had worked. The family soon moved to Vienna, where Liszt studied the piano with Carl Czerny and composition with Mozart's rival, Antonio Salieri. At a concert given in the presence of Beethoven, Liszt is said to have been rewarded with a kiss on the forehead from the aging master.

In 1823 Liszt arrived in Paris, where he soon became a celebrated performer and toured France. In 1824, he also played in England, where he was received by King George IV, before illness and the death of his father from typhoid prompted his return. In 1826, he went back to Paris, where he befriended Berlioz and Chopin and began his career as a progressive and visionary composer. He also considered becoming a priest and in addition to everything else fell in love — these three sides to his character competed for ascendancy during the rest of his life.

As a composer Liszt was influenced by leading Romantics, such as the author Victor Hugo and the painter Eugène Delacroix; while Chopin brought out his poetic nature, Berlioz encouraged the

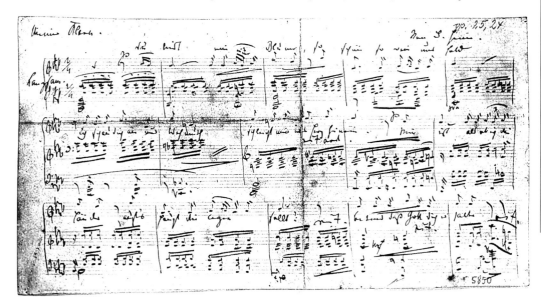

The young Liszt, by Karl Ernest Lehmann, 1839

latent Mephistophelian character in his music. On hearing Paganini's playing in 1831, Liszt set out to match the violinist's astonishing virtuosity in his own work, and wrote a piano transcription of Paganini's *La Campanella*. These diabolical and fiendishly virtuoso elements would later find expression in the swirling *Mephisto Waltzes* for piano.

In 1834, Liszt began a long affair with the Countess Marie d'Agoult, and the couple moved to Geneva the following year. He continued to perform widely, and won a famous piano duel against his rival Sigismond Thalberg in 1837. In 1839 he began touring extensively as he sought to raise funds for a Beethoven memorial in Bonn. His piano playing created a sensation wherever he went. He was honored

in his native Hungary, where he rediscovered the interest in gypsy music that would later inspire his *Hungarian Rhapsodies*. He also proposed the establishment of a national conservatory in Budapest. But his long absences from home cost him his relationship with the countess, and they separated in 1844.

Liszt had a succession of mistresses during these touring years until, in 1847, the Princess Carolyne Sayn-Wittgenstein of Kiev persuaded him to give up traveling and settle as a full-time conductor and composer in Weimar, Germany. In the course of the next 12 years he conducted music by Wagner (including the first performance of *Lohengrin* in 1850), Schumann, Berlioz, Verdi, and others, in addition to performances of his own works. Weimar became the shrine of the 'New German School,' and pianists and composers flocked there for lessons or consultations with Liszt, for which he refused payment. However, his cohabitation with the married princess was becoming a court scandal, and his enthusiastic support of Wagner (then a political exile) was highly controversial. He resigned his post in 1858 and eventually left Weimar in 1861.

Liszt is credited with the invention of the symphonic poem, and he completed all but one of the works employing this quintessentially Romantic form during his Weimar years. The main technique was 'thematic transformation,' in which one or more musical themes, representing heroic people or ideas, evolved throughout the work, providing both musical structure and Romantic narrative. The technique reached its zenith in his *Piano Sonata in B Minor* (1853) and in the *Faust Symphony* (1854).

Liszt eventually joined Princess Carolyne in Rome, where she had tried, in the end unsuccessfully, to persuade the Pope to grant a divorce. He remained there for eight years, occupying himself mainly with music inspired by religion, including the reflective *Années de pèlerinage* (Years of Pilgrimage) for piano. These pieces are in three volumes: the first deals with Swiss subjects, the second with Italian, and the third is an unauthorized

volume published after Liszt's death. In 1865 he took the four minor orders of the Catholic Church.

Invitations to Weimar in 1869 and to Budapest in 1871 marked the beginning of a new phase in his life, and he subsequently traveled continually between these two cities and Rome. The three centers symbolized the visionary artist, the passionate gypsy, and the pious Catholic that lived within the same man.

Liszt's final tour in 1886 took him once again to Paris and London, but he soon became weak with dropsy and spent his last days in the Wagner festival town of Bayreuth. There he was looked after by Cosima, his second daughter by the Countess d'Agoult and by then Wagner's widow, and was able to attend a production of *Parsifal* before dying from pneumonia. Liszt left behind more than 400 original works in addition to many transcriptions and arrangements, and he made an impact during his life as the most phenomenal pianist of his time.

Autograph manuscript of Liszt's *Etude d'exécution transcendante No. 2*

This transcription for piano of one of Paganini's Caprices for violin was dedicated to Clara Schumann.

Strauss

Johann Strauss II 1825–1899

RECOMMENDED WORKS

Waltzes and Other Dances
Disc: 'New Year's Day Concert in Vienna, 1987'
Deutsche Grammophon 419 616-2
Kathleen Battle (sop); Vienna Philharmonic
Orchestra/Herbert von Karajan
A winning memento of a memorable occasion.
Karajan's selection contains many favorites from the
whole Strauss family, and the great conductor's
affection for this repertoire is evident in every bar.

REPRESENTATIVE WORKS
Waltzes, polkas, marches, and dances
Die Fledermaus
Der Zigeunerbaron

Photographic portrait of Johann Strauss II, 1894

Franz Josef at the Vienna State Ball, 1900 by Gause
Strauss's waltzes would have been
essential fare at a ball such as this one.

Johann Strauss the Younger was the most famous and accomplished member of the musical dynasty that began with his father, Johann Strauss the Elder (1804–49), a noted violinist, conductor, and composer. Together with his brothers Josef and Eduard, who both wrote waltzes and polkas, the younger Strauss effectively ruled the dance music world of Vienna, the city of his birth, for most of the nineteeth century.

He wrote his first waltz at the age of six; but it was not until his father, who had wanted him to go into banking, deserted the family in 1842 that he began his formal musical education. He soon formed his own small orchestra, and their debut in 1844 was such a success that he became his father's leading rival overnight. When his father died five years later, the two orchestras were merged under his direction.

In the 1850's, Strauss introduced some of the compositional techniques of Wagner and Liszt into his waltzes, receiving a rebuke from the fiercely anti-Wagnerian critic Eduard Hanslick. The public was in favor, however, and in the 1860's he became increasingly busy both composing and conducting, particularly during the ball season of Vienna's high society. Most of his finest waltzes date from this decade — *Morning Papers* (1864), the ever popular *Blue Danube* (1867), *Tales from the Vienna Woods* (1868), and *Wine, Women and Song* (1869) among them.

Strauss's waltzes all fit a basic pattern, consisting of a slow, scene-setting introduction, followed usually by five waltz sections. They finished with a coda (end section) that reintroduced the main waltz tunes in a continuous sequence, creating a sense of quickening musical pace. It was a format that any competent composer could use to good effect; but Strauss's best waltzes were more poised and better orchestrated, his rhythmic combinations more finely balanced, and his melodies simply more graceful than those of anyone else. They captured the particular mood of nineteenth-century Vienna — its sophistication and its hedonism.

The 'Waltz King' was naturally expected to tour. During the 30 years beginning in 1856, Strauss made appearances all over Europe, from England to Russia, and was hailed as Austria's most successful ambassador. He was invited to Boston, Massachusetts, in 1872 for an 'Inter-national Peace Jubilee' marking the end of the Franco-Prussian War. It was a huge gala affair, in which he was forced to endure numerous performances of *The Blue Danube* and *Wine, Women and Song*, but it brought him worldwide popularity. In 1876 he dedicated his Centennial Waltzes to the American people in honor

A scene from Strauss's operetta *A Night in Venice*
The singers are Skiza (left) and Collin in an 1883 production.

of the one hundredth anniversary of the Declaration of Independence.

Comic opera and operetta had become popular in Vienna, particularly the works of the Parisian composer Jacques Offenbach. In the 1870's, theater directors and librettists turned to Strauss for a distinctly Viennese contribution to the genre. He had never had to fit his free-flowing melodies to a text before, and he was no discerning judge of librettos suitable for the task. Of his 18 published stage works only two operettas passed into the repertory, largely due to their excellent librettos. *Die Fledermaus* (The Bat) from 1874 does, however, sparkle with all the wit and elegance of his best waltzes, while *Der Zigeunerbaron* (The Gypsy Baron), dating from 1885, uses gypsy melodies and exotic harmonies to capture the Hungarian flavor of its subject.

In 1885, Strauss converted to the Protestant faith in order to divorce his second wife Angelika (his first, Henriette, had died) and marry the young widow Adele Strauss (no relation). This cost him his Austrian citizenship. He assumed that of Saxe-Coburg-Gotha for the rest of his life, but Vienna was always his home. When he died there in 1899, a part of the Austrian Empire died with him.

Sullivan

Arthur Sullivan 1842–1900

RECOMMENDED WORK

The Pirates of Penzance
Telarc CD80353
Soloists; Chorus and Orchestra of the Welsh National Opera/Charles Mackerras
Quality light music sung, played, and conducted with great flair and treated in spectacular, state-of-the-art digital sound.

REPRESENTATIVE WORKS
The Mikado
The Gondoliers
H. M. S. Pinafore
The Yeomen of the Guard

A waltz by Bucalossi inspired by *The Mikado*
Sullivan's enormously popular melodies spawned numerous offshoots.

Arthur Sullivan was born in south London, the son of a clarinetist whose post as Sergeant Bandmaster at the Sandhurst Military Academy allowed the young Sullivan to explore a variety of wind instruments. Sullivan was given a formal musical education as a Chapel Royal chorister before entering the Royal Academy of Music in London and then the Leipzig Conservatory. Throughout, his mother supported his ambitions to become a composer, and in later years acted as his secretary. From the late 1860's on, Sullivan also had a relationship with a married American woman, Mary Francis Ronalds, an attachment that remained secret until his death in 1900.

Initially he aimed at 'serious' composition and wrote symphonies and oratorios, but early audience enthusiasm soon waned. The turning point in Sullivan's career came in 1871, when he met the playwright William Schwenk Gilbert. Together they collaborated on the string of operettas for which the names Gilbert and Sullivan are now renowned. Their first success, *Trial by Jury*, came in 1875. Sullivan composed the music for the operetta in just three weeks. The work's success resulted in the impresario Richard D'Oyly Carte's leasing London's Opéra-Comique Theatre specifically for Gilbert and Sullivan productions.

With *H. M. S. Pinafore* in 1878 the duo became firmly established and economically successful. *The Pirates of Penzance* swiftly followed; then, in 1881, *Patience*, which made fun of Oscar Wilde and the aesthetic movement, received its premiere in London. During the run of *Patience*, D'Oyly Carte opened the Savoy Theatre. The many operas produced there — known as the Savoy operas — included *Iolanthe*, *Princess Ida*, *Ruddigore*, *The Mikado*, and *The Gondoliers*. Sullivan was knighted in 1883.

During the run of *The Gondoliers*, Gilbert and Sullivan quarreled, which led to a temporary parting of the ways. At this time Sullivan composed his Grand Opera *Ivanhoe*, but it did not achieve the popularity of his lighter works.

The musical style of Sullivan's operettas derived in part from Offenbach, whose music was popular in nineteenth-century London. Sullivan showed his surest talent in his catchy melodies, simple orchestration, and ingenious parodies: Wagner, Verdi, Handel, and Donizetti are all cleverly imitated in his works. It was the crisp and witty librettos of Gilbert, however, that made them distinctive.

Photograph of the composer taken toward the end of his life

Borodin

Alexander Borodin 1833–1887

RECOMMENDED WORK
Symphony No. 2
Deutsche Grammophon 435 757-2
Gothenburg Symphony Orchestra/Neeme Järvi
Järvi gives us a sympathetic, full-blooded reading, with an expansively romantic account of the slow movement. Part of a thoroughly desirable two-CD set containing all three Borodin symphonies.

REPRESENTATIVE WORKS
In the Steppes of Central Asia
String Quartet No. 2
Prince Igor

Borodin was the illegitimate son of Prince Luka Gedianov but was registered as the legal son of Porfiry Borodin — one of the Prince's serfs — a practice typical of the time. His mother, a cultured woman, educated him at home in St. Petersburg, where he showed an aptitude for chemistry and languages while also learning the flute, piano, cello, and composition.

From 1850, he studied at the Medico-Surgical Academy in St. Petersburg and graduated in 1856 with high honors, completing his doctorate two years later. His academic work involved a number of trips abroad, particularly to Germany, where he became friends with the chemist Mendeleyev. He also met Ekaterina Protopopova, herself an accomplished pianist, who was being treated for tuberculosis. They fell in love and married in 1863 after returning to St. Petersburg, where Borodin was appointed chemistry professor at the Medico-Surgical Academy in 1864.

Throughout this time he remained interested in music, playing string quintets with friends and piano duets with Ekaterina. He met Mussorgsky and Balakirev in 1862 and became part of the group of Russian nationalist composers known as 'The Five.' They encouraged him in the composition of his *First Symphony*, which took five years to complete. The first public performance in 1869 was a success, and the same year he began his second.

Borodin also began work on an opera, *Prince Igor*, whose Russian theme appealed to his nationalist sentiments. It did not progress well, however, and some of the music found its way into his *Second Symphony*. His teaching duties at the Academy increased in 1872 with the institution of courses in medicine for women, and he only resumed work on *Prince Igor* and its famous *Polovtsian Dances* two years later. Progress on the work was slow, and Borodin broke off again in 1881 to write the *Second String Quartet*, dedicated to his wife. The slow movement ('Nocturne') became very popular, with its haunting, nostalgic main theme introduced on Borodin's own instrument, the cello. His admiration for Mendelssohn, as well as a similar skill with melody, is clearly demonstrated in this work.

Borodin's fame in Europe was helped by Liszt, who arranged for a performance of the *First Symphony* in Baden-Baden in 1880, the same year in which Borodin completed his evocative tone-poem *In the Steppes of Central Asia*. His popularity increased throughout the mid-1880's, but in 1885, he suffered an attack of cholera, which left him severely weakened. He died two years later from a heart attack at a fancy-dress ball. His beloved Ekaterina followed him only five months later.

Prince Igor was finished, after Borodin's death, by Glazunov and Rimsky-Korsakov. Borodin's failure to complete it resulted in part from a badly planned libretto; certain individual numbers, such as the rousing, folk-based *Polovtsian Dances*, are markedly better than the whole. However, his symphonies and string quartets, as well as the memorable *In the Steppes of Central Asia*, have guaranteed Borodin's popularity during the century since his death.

After Igor's Battle with the Polovtsi by Vasnetsov
A scene from Borodin's only opera, Prince Igor, completed after the composer's death by Rimsky-Korsakov and Glazunov, and first performed in St. Petersburg in 1890.

Bizet

Georges Bizet 1838–1875

RECOMMENDED WORK

Carmen
Erato 2292-45207-2
Julia Migenes (mez) Carmen; Plácido Domingo
(ten) Don José; Faith Esham (sop) Micaëla;
Ruggero Raimondi (bass) Escamillo; Lilian Watson
(sop) Frasquita; Susan Daniel (mez) Mercédès;
Jean-Philip Lafont (bar) Dancairo; French Radio
Chorus; French Radio Children's Chorus; French
National Orchestra/Lorin Maazel
*With Plácido Domingo magnificent in the role of Don
José, Maazel's lively rendering will be familiar to many
through its use on the soundtrack of Francesco Rosi's
popular film.*

REPRESENTATIVE WORKS
Symphony in C
L'Arlésienne: Suites Nos. 1 & 2
Jeux d'enfants
Les pêcheurs de perles

Photograph of Celestine Galli as Carmen
**Galli was the first-ever Carmen, at the
opera's original staging in 1875.**

Sketch of Bizet by Paul Gavarni, 1860/65

Bizet was born in Paris in 1838, the son of
a pianist and a singing teacher. He was
quick to master the rudiments of music,
and his father had great hopes that he
would become a composer. At the age of
ten he entered the Paris Conservatoire and
studied with Charles Gounod and Jacques
Halévy, whose daughter Bizet was later to
marry. An exceptional student, Bizet won
many prizes, initially for his piano playing
and later for composition. Chief among
these was the prestigious Prix de Rome,
won when he was 18 and resulting in a
five-year pension. One of his notable early
works is the *Symphony in C* from 1855.
The score was lost for many years, and the
piece was not performed until 1935.

Bizet's first mature opera was the love
story *Les pêcheurs de perles* (The Pearl
Fishers), performed at the Théâtre Lyrique
in Paris in 1863. It drew the attention of
other composers, Berlioz being a particular admirer; but it failed to gain widespread
acceptance by audiences and ran for only
18 performances. Other, equally unsuccessful operas — including the unjustly
neglected *La jolie fille de Perth* (The Fair
Maid of Perth) — appeared during the
next few years, leaving Bizet's future as a
composer uncertain.

At the same time that his musical activities failed to live up to the promise of earlier years, Bizet's personal life also took an
unhappy turn. In 1867 his engagement to
Geneviève Halévy was broken off, and

although they did in fact marry two years
later, she showed signs of increasing
mental instability and suffered a breakdown a year before the birth of their only
child in 1872.

In 1872, Bizet wrote *L'Arlésienne*, the
incidental music for a play by Daudet.
Scored for 26 instruments, including a saxophone, the music was greeted coolly,
although when rescored for full orchestra,
it gained the attention and audience appreciation it deserved.

Without a doubt Bizet's greatest
achievement, however, was the opera
Carmen, which he wrote toward the end of
his short life. Despite being termed an
opéra comique, due to its inclusion of spoken
dialogue, it hardly amounts to a humorous
evening's entertainment. Based on
Prosper Merimée's story of the life, love
affairs, and tragic death of the gypsy
Carmen, it did not achieve immediate success. Critics claimed that it was too sensational, the story 'obscene,' and that it had
no tunes, and audiences were outraged at
the sight of women smoking on stage.

Today *Carmen* is one of the best-loved
operas in the repertoire, and songs such as
'Habañera' and 'The Toreador's Song'
remain consistently popular. The opera
reached a wider audience through *Carmen
Jones*, in which the story was updated by
Oscar Hammerstein to 1940's America.
Unaware of how hugely successful his creation would become, Bizet died near Paris
in 1875 a bitterly disappointed man.

Still from the film *Carmen Jones*, 1954
**Dorothy Dandridge and Harry Belafonte
in an updated version of Carmen.**

Brahms

Johannes Brahms 1833–1897

RECOMMENDED WORKS

Symphony No. 4 in E minor, Op. 98
Sony Classical SK48398
Cleveland Orchestra/George Szell
This mighty performance should serve as an object lesson for all aspiring Brahmsians, conductors and listeners. The recording is not new, but it is beautifully balanced and transfers well to CD.

Ein Deutsches Requiem, Op. 45
Angel CDC7 47238-2
Elisabeth Schwarzkopf (sop); Dietrich Fischer-Dieskau (bar); Philharmonia Chorus and Orchestra/Otto Klemperer
Stoical, patient, and magnificently sung, Klemperer's German Requiem continues to provide a deeply moving musical experience. The sound is true to the conductor's matchless ear for detail.

REPRESENTATIVE WORKS
Symphonies Nos. 1–3
Piano Concertos Nos. 1 & 2
Violin Concerto
Double Concerto for violin and cello
String Sextets No. 1 in B flat; No. 2 in G
Piano Quartets No. 1 in G minor; No. 2 in A; No. 3 in C minor
Piano Quintet
Clarinet Quintet
Violin Sonatas Nos. 1–3
Song of Destiny

Sketches of Brahms by Will von Beckerath, c.1880
Brahms was a better pianist than conductor, but in the 1860's and 1870's he held a number of conducting posts.

The works of Johannes Brahms are among the most consistent of any composer. His style matured early and then changed little, and his meticulous, self-critical approach never allowed publication of any work less than excellent.

Born in Hamburg, he learned the piano from the age of six, first with his father (a double-bass player), then with Otto Cossel and Eduard Marxsen, who also taught him composition and gave an all-round musical training. In his teens Brahms began to compose and performed regularly, earning money (at the cost of his innocence) in a sailors' bar.

In 1853 he was invited to tour with the violinist Eduard Reményi. In Hanover he was introduced to the violin virtuoso Joseph Joachim, who was to become a significant figure in Brahms's life. Joachim arranged for him to meet Liszt in Weimar, where Brahms embarrassed himself by falling asleep during the great pianist's performance of his *Piano Sonata* in B minor. Brahms quickly won a deserved reputation for the frank, even rude manner in which he expressed his opinions. He was never very taken with the 'New German School' and later supported the critic Eduard Hanslick in his campaign against Liszt, Wagner, and Bruckner.

On a visit to Robert and Clara Schumann in Düsseldorf, he met with great enthusiasm for his piano music. Shortly afterward, Schumann broke a ten-year critical silence to announce in the *New Musical Journal* in 1853 that Germany's musical 'Messiah' had arrived: at the age of 20, Brahms became instantly famous. After Schumann's suicide attempt in 1854 and committal to an asylum, Brahms stayed with Clara Schumann. Although he was in love with her, they did not marry after Schumann's death two years later, but became lifelong friends.

During the next few years Brahms often stayed with Joachim, who encouraged his composing; he also traveled frequently with Clara. He had a number of love affairs, but never married.

He was employed as a choral conductor in Hamburg and Vienna, and settled in the Austrian capital in 1869, the year after the triumphant premiere at Bremen of his famous choral work *Ein Deutsches Requiem*. Vienna remained his home for the rest of his life. Early fame had meant early publication; the proceeds spared him from taking court appointments or undertaking too many hectic concert tours.

The great things that had been forecast for him by Schumann were turning into something of a burden, however, and Brahms deliberated for many years over his first orchestral works. He began work on a symphony as early as 1854. Like many other composers, Brahms was awed by the symphonic masterpieces of Beethoven and uncertain about producing examples of his own. After five years it emerged in a revised form as the *First Piano Concerto*. Eventually he completed his *First Symphony* in 1876, 14 years after it was begun. With its broad, abstract Classical form, its emotional progression from tragedy to triumph, and the nobility of its hymnlike finale theme, it was quickly dubbed 'Beethoven's Tenth.'

Brahms had by now mastered orchestral writing: the *Violin Concerto* and *Second Piano Concerto* in addition to three more outstanding symphonies followed within nine years. Brahms's last orchestral work, the *Double Concerto* of 1887 for violin and

cello, was written for Joseph Joachim and marked a reconciliation with him. This followed a seven-year rift, after Brahms had taken the side of Joachim's wife, Amalie, in their divorce proceedings.

Beginning in 1880, Brahms often visited the resort of Bad Ischl, accompanied on two ocassions by Johann Strauss II, whose *Blue Danube* waltz he declared he wished he had composed. He also had a long association with the Meiningen Court Orchestra, which toured with many of his works. In 1891, clarinetist Richard Mühlfeld so impressed Brahms that he wrote four works for the instrument. One of these was the *Clarinet Quintet* (for clarinet and string quartet), which ranks among his finest works.

Brahms created Classical musical structures in a Romantic age. His writing is notable for its rich textures resulting from a dense fabric of interwoven melodies. It gives his music an emotional depth quite different from the passionate intensity of Tchaikovsky, for example; in the *Clarinet Quintet* he beautifully conveys a sense of autumnal melancholy.

Clara Schumann died in 1896 and Brahms undertook a 40-hour journey to attend her funeral, which caused his own health, then precarious, to worsen dramatically. After a short stay at the spa at Karlsbad he struggled back to Vienna to attend Bruckner's funeral, and the following year Brahms himself died, succumbing to cancer of the liver.

Mussorgsky

Modest Mussorgsky 1839–1881

RECOMMENDED WORK
Boris Godunov
Philips 412 281-2
Alexander Vedernikov (bass) Boris Godunov; Vladislav Piavko (ten) False Dmitri; Irina Arkhipova (mez) Marina; Vladimir Matorin (bass) Pimen; Spring Studio Children's Chorus; USSR TV and Radio Large Chorus and Symphony Orchestra/Vladimir Fedoseyev
Rightly opting for the composer's own 1872 revision instead of Rimsky-Korsakov's colorful reworking, Fedoseyev directs a compellingly powerful account.

REPRESENTATIVE WORKS
Night on a Bare Mountain
Pictures at an Exhibition
Kovantschina

Mussorgsky was the most innovative of the group of nationalist Russian composers known as 'The Five.' His parents — cultured, wealthy landowners — sent him to the Guards' cadet school in St. Petersburg, where he met the composer Dargomijsky, and later the other future members of The Five — Balakirev, Borodin, Cui, and Rimsky-Korsakov.

In 1858 he resigned his commission to take up composition and started lessons with Balakirev. In 1863, however, increasing money problems forced him to take a relatively low-ranking civil service position, in which he remained almost until the time of his death.

In this situation he produced his first significant compositions, the songs of 1864. His progress was temporarily halted the following year as he battled against the alcoholism that would plague him throughout his life. He recovered to complete his best orchestral piece — *Night on a Bare Mountain* — in 1867. Despite his justified satisfaction with the work, it was not published or performed until after his death, in a drastically revised version by Rimsky-Korsakov.

Mussorgsky encountered similar difficulties with his opera *Boris Godunov*, based on Pushkin's tragedy, which was rejected in 1869 by the Imperial Opera because it had no lead soprano, no lead tenor, and no central love scene. He revised the work, but it was again rejected and was not performed until 1874. The premiere was a public success but a critical failure, even drawing harsh comments from other members of The Five. The opera was withdrawn after 25 performances.

Mussorgsky's music was simply too unconventional. He avoided the influence of other composers and previous musical traditions, seeking instead to distill the basic elements of music and use them to express his ideas in his own way. If there were influences, they tended to be from spheres other than music. One of these was the painter and architect Victor Hartmann, whose memorial exhibition in 1874 inspired Mussorgsky's *Pictures at an Exhibition* — a collection of piano pieces that reflect ten of Hartmann's paintings. This work came to be very influential and was later orchestrated by several composers, most notably Ravel.

At the end of his life, Mussorgsky enjoyed some fame as a pianist and the composer of *Boris Godunov*, but most of his work was in fact published posthumously, completed or drastically revised by Rimsky-Korsakov. With the restoration in the twentieth century of his original scores, his innovative qualities have now received the recognition they deserve.

Portrait of Mussorgsky by Ilya Repin

Rimsky-Korsakov

Nikolai Rimsky-Korsakov 1844–1908

RECOMMENDED WORK

Sheherazade
Telarc Conifer CD80208
London Symphony Orchestra/Charles Mackerras
Some resplendent Telarc engineering does full justice to perhaps the finest Sheherazade of recent times. Mackerras's conducting has marvelous fire and character, and the LSO responds with great virtuosity.

REPRESENTATIVE WORKS
Capriccio espagnol
Russian Easter Festival Overture
The Snow Maiden
The Golden Cockerel
Sadko

Nikolai Rimsky-Korsakov was born in Tikhvin in Russia. There he first heard the simple folk songs that left an indelible impression. His early ambitions lay not in music, however, but in a burning desire to become a naval officer. He joined the Corps of Naval Cadets in 1856 and while at sea composed a symphony, completed in 1865 with the encouragement of the composer Balakirev. The work showed great promise, especially in its orchestration; subsequently he was offered the professorship of composition at the St. Petersburg Conservatory. He was 27 years old.

Although unqualified for the position, he accepted and immediately became one of the most assiduous pupils, secretly studying harmony and counterpoint. Shortly afterward he married Nadezhda Purgold, also a composer, and at that time a musician far superior to her husband.

During his self-imposed program of study he produced compositions that were dry and academic; but in 1882 his opera *The Snow Maiden* revealed a new, more personal voice with its clever intertwining of fantasy and comedy. Surprisingly, the next few years yielded no new compositions. Finally 1887 ushered in an era of fresh creativity, inaugurated with the *Capriccio espagnol*. This fantastically virtuosic work was interrupted at its rehearsals by applause from the orchestra itself, and was encored in full at its premiere. There followed the *Russian Easter Festival Overture* and then the exotic *Sheherazade*, derived from the classic tale the *Thousand and One Nights*. All three works demonstrate Rimsky's mastery of orchestration

In 1888, Rimsky heard the first performances in Russia of Wagner's *Ring* cycle, and was so overwhelmed that he resolved in future only to write operas. Over the next 20 years he composed 12, including *Christmas Eve*, *Mozart and Salieri* (based on Pushkin's play) and one of his finest works, *Sadko*. A setting of Russian folk legends, this work contains the well-known 'Hindu' song and marks the high point of Rimsky's love affair with the fantastic.

Rimsky's last completed opera, *The Golden Cockerel* (1907), based on Pushkin's satire about a bumbling autocracy, was banned by the Russian censor and remained unperformed during the composer's lifetime. His gift for lively and colorful orchestration is as alive in this work as throughout his entire output.

Costume of the Red Sultan in *Sheherazade*
Diaghilev's Ballets Russes company produced Sheherazade in 1910.

Tchaikovsky

Pyotr Ilyich Tchaikovsky 1840–1893

RECOMMENDED WORKS

Symphony No. 6 in B minor, Op. 74, 'Pathétique'
Erato 2292-45756-2
Leningrad Philharmonic Orchestra/Evgeny Mravinsky
The century's greatest Tchaikovsky conductor captured live during the twilight of his career in a performance that combines ardent lyricism and searing intensity. Raw but impressive sound.

The Sleeping Beauty
Philharmonia Orchestra/George Weldon
Classics for Pleasure CD-CFPD4458
A tasteful, expertly played interpretation of Tchaikovsky's great ballet score, beautifully remastered from early stereo originals.

REPRESENTATIVE WORKS
Symphonies Nos. 4 & 5
Piano Concerto No. 1
Violin Concerto
The Nutcracker
Swan Lake
Romeo and Juliet
Serenade for strings
Eugene Onegin

Tchaikovsky grew up in a family both upper class and unmusical. His father was a government mining official in St. Petersburg, where the family moved when Tchaikovsky was eight. He developed a love of music largely by improvising at the piano, but he was sent to school to prepare for training in law.

At the age of 19 he obtained a position in the Ministry of Justice in St. Petersburg, continuing musical studies in his spare time at the St. Petersburg Conservatory. Its director, Anton Rubinstein, commented that Tchaikovsky, though careless, was 'definitely talented.' With this encouragement Tchaikovsky gave up his job in order to study full time, and in 1865 he was appointed professor of harmony at the new Moscow Conservatory.

Portrait of Tchaikovsky by Nikolai Kusnezoff, 1893

Original advertisement for *The Queen of Spades*

Like Eugene Onegin, The Queen of Spades was inspired by Pushkin.

In 1866 he suffered his first nervous breakdown, brought on by the stress of overwork on his *First Symphony*. Tchaikovsky's 'abnormally neurotic tendency' (in his brother's words) and lifelong unhappiness apparently stemmed in large part from feelings of guilt about his homosexuality and his attempts to repress it.

About this time he met Balakirev — one of the group of Russian composers known as 'The Five' — and out of their friendship came the suggestion for Tchaikovsky's fantasy overture *Romeo and Juliet*. Tchaikovsky's attitude to The Five later soured as he grew to dislike their use of exotic oriental folk melodies (which he parodied in the dances of his ballet *The Nutcracker* in 1892) in the name of a Russian nationalist style.

In 1877 he began to receive love letters from a woman he had never met, Antonina Milyukova. She threatened suicide unless he would meet her. At the time Tchaikovsky was working on his opera *Eugene Onegin*, based on Pushkin's poem, in which the hero rebuffs the love letter sent to him by the heroine, Tatiana. Tchaikovsky had no wish to stoop to such behavior and was trapped into marrying Antonina, with disastrous consequences. She turned out to be mentally unstable and, far from 'curing' his homosexuality, the experience drove him to attempt suicide. He fled to St. Petersburg in a state of nervous collapse. He never saw her again, and she eventually died in an asylum.

By this time Tchaikovsky had begun corresponding with a wealthy widow, Nadezhda von Meck, who confessed to an admiration for his music and gave him an annual pension of 6,000 rubles. It was enough to allow him to compose and tour freely in Europe, and he resigned from his Moscow professorship in 1878. Their letters were intense and passionate, but even though they actually met on her estate once by chance, they never exchanged a spoken word. The relationship lasted for 13 years, until she broke it off suddenly without any explanation.

He completed *Eugene Onegin* in 1878, together with the *Fourth Symphony* (dedicated to his 'best friend,' Nadezhda von Meck) and the *Violin Concerto*. His credentials as a master of melodic invention were already established, but never before in such overtly Romantic material as these two orchestral works were lyrical themes tautly organized into a framework of such sustained dramatic impact.

Tchaikovsky had traveled in Europe almost every year since 1870, but toured as a conductor for the first time in 1888, and again in 1889. He met Brahms, Dvořák, Grieg, and others, visited London, and completed his *Fifth Symphony* and his great ballet score *The Sleeping Beauty*. In his last year he traveled again to England, this time to receive an honorary doctorate in music at Cambridge University in the distinguished company of Boito, Bruch, Saint-Saëns, and Grieg.

He returned to complete the *Pathétique Symphony*, of which he wrote, 'I love it as I have never loved any one of my musical offspring.' Its many innovative features include a 'waltz' movement in 5/4 time and a slow, sorrowful finale. It stands as a fitting end to the career of a tragic man who displayed his deepest feelings in music, often with tremendous emotional power. He died of cholera after drinking contaminated water — possibly deliberately, according to recent research — just nine days after the premiere.

Verdi

Giuseppe Verdi 1813–1901

RECOMMENDED WORK

Otello

London 433 669-2

Luciano Pavarotti (ten) Otello; Kiri Te Kanawa (sop) Desdemona; Leo Nucci (bar) Iago; Anthony Rolfe Johnson (ten) Cassio; Metropolitan Opera Children's Chorus; Chicago Symphony Orchestra/Georg Solti

Verdi's operatic masterpiece as interpreted by some of the finest singers of the day and conducted by a maestro whose experience in the opera pit lends unrivaled authority to his interpretation. A fabulous recording, too.

REPRESENTATIVE WORKS

Rigoletto
La traviata
Un ballo in maschera
La forza del destino
Don Carlos
Falstaff
Requiem

Photograph of Verdi in middle age

After the Masked Ball by J. L. Gérôme, 1857

The picture inspired Verdi to request the libretto for Un ballo in maschera.

Giuseppe Verdi was born into a poor family near Parma in Italy. When he showed early musical promise, his father made sacrifices to buy him a secondhand spinet, on which Verdi learned the basics of music.

At the age of 12, Verdi became the local organist; despite talent as a composer, however, he was denied entrance to the Milan Conservatory in favor of better-trained young musicians. Undeterred by this rejection, Verdi persisted and was rewarded when a patron enabled him to study privately in Milan. At 20, Verdi was by all accounts badly dressed, with a wasted figure and a face that could have been chiseled from a block of wood; nonetheless, his patron's daughter, to whom he was giving singing and piano lessons, fell in love with him. The two were married in 1836.

Verdi had by this time penned his first opera, *Oberto*; with the help of friends it was produced at La Scala opera house. Its moderate success led to a commission to write three more. The first, a comedy, was a failure. *Nabucco* soon followed and was an instant success. Its plot, concerning the conflict between Assyrians and Jews, immediately fired the imaginations of the Italian audience. They empathized with the plight of the Jews, sensing similarities with their own struggle against Austrian oppression, and the famous *Slaves' Chorus* 'Va pensiero,' was encored at its premiere despite a rule to the contrary. The production of *Nabucco* took place during a time of great emotional upheaval for Verdi: in quick succession he lost his two children and then his wife. Only the support of friends got him through what was the most difficult period of his life. The opera's success helped restore a temporary lack of faith in himself, and Verdi threw himself into his work, striving for new heights of achievement.

Italian opera up to this time had been dominated by Rossini, Donizetti, and Bellini, whose approach allowed singers to demonstrate their talents in showpiece arias. Verdi was more concerned with the dramatic aspects of opera. In fact he asked for a 'rough, hoarse, and gloomy voice, with something diabolical about it' for the role of Lady Macbeth in *Macbeth* (1847), rather than the soprano already chosen, who could merely sing 'to perfection.'

After *Macbeth* there followed three of Verdi's most famous operas: *Rigoletto* in 1851, *La traviata* in 1853 — both using libretti by Francesco Maria Piave, with whom Verdi collaborated on nine operas — and *Il trovatore*, also in 1853. *La traviata* treats the theme of selfless love, whereas the other two are highly emotional, centering on the darker side of human nature and involving hatred, murder, torture, dishonor, and seduction. More operas rapidly followed, showing a maturing of style and

enlargement of vision: *Les vêpres siciliennes* was written for Paris, *Un ballo in maschera* for Rome, *La forza del destino* for St. Petersburg, *Don Carlo* again for Paris, and *Aida* for Cairo. Verdi spent more and more time traveling; in London he met his second wife, Giuseppa Strepponi, whom he married in 1859.

For 15 years after *Aida* in 1871, Verdi wrote no more operas; but in 1874 his masterly *Requiem*, written to commemorate his friend the poet and novelist Manzoni, was first performed in Milan. The mixture of religious devotion with highly dramatic music may have offended the purists, but this choral work was nonetheless another triumph.

By now in his seventies, Verdi composed his two last operas, *Otello* and *Falstaff*, performed in 1887 and 1893 respectively. Both were unqualified successes. Verdi was nervous about the reception that would be accorded *Falstaff*, perhaps mindful of the failure of his earlier comedy. But this time he had a brilliant librettist in Arrigo Boito, and Verdi drew on a lifetime's experience to create an opera in which plot, orchestra, music, and singers are perfectly balanced.

Verdi died in Milan in 1901 at the grand age of 87. Two hundred thousand people watched his funeral procession pass by, and although he had requested that no music be played, a member of the crowd began to sing 'Va pensiero' and the refrain was taken up by the multitude.

Bruckner

Anton Bruckner 1824–1896

RECOMMENDED WORK
Symphony No. 8 in C minor
Deutsche Grammophon 427 611-2
Vienna Philharmonic Orchestra/Herbert von Karajan
Karajan is widely considered one of the greatest Bruckner conductors of all, and this, one of his last recordings, amply justifies that view. It is quite simply overwhelming.

REPRESENTATIVE WORKS
Symphonies Nos. 4, 5, 7, & 9

Photograph of Bruckner, 1880

Bruckner was born in Ansfelden, in the rural heartland of Austria. Despite showing great musical promise as a child, he chose to follow in his father's footsteps and train as a schoolteacher. He entered upon a musical career by adding organ playing to his teaching duties during ten years' employment at the St. Florian monastery near Linz, where he had been a pupil.

He used his spare time to study with almost fanatical determination in various musical disciplines; yet when the post of cathedral organist at Linz became free in 1855, it was only with the greatest difficulty that he was persuaded to apply. Though very busy at Linz, Bruckner

found time to take a correspondence course in harmony and counterpoint with Simon Sechter at the Vienna Conservatory. He received his diploma with distinction in 1861 — one of the panel remarked, 'He should have examined us.' In 1868, he once again needed considerable inducement to leave the security of his Linz position and take up a professorship at the Conservatory, complete with salary increase.

Until 1863, Bruckner had written mainly meticulously crafted, anonymous church music, but his encounter with the works of Wagner provided the impulse to break free from all the rules and theory and to develop his own startlingly original voice. His first full symphony soon followed (1865–66) and then four more during the period 1871 to 1876.

He then met with various difficulties, starting with the reluctance of the Vienna Philharmonic Orchestra to perform what they regarded as wild and unplayable works. In response, Bruckner was persuaded, against his better judgment, to allow revisions and cuts to these gigantic symphonies, only to be attacked by the famous music critic Eduard Hanslick for formal inconsistencies. They are now increasingly played in their original form.

Wagner, however, supported Bruckner, praising him as the 'only composer who measures up to Beethoven.' Bruckner reciprocated by dedicating the sublime, funereal *Adagio* of his *Seventh Symphony* (1884) to Wagner's memory. With this work he finally achieved widespread recognition, and his symphonies were performed as far afield as the United States. His *Eighth Symphony*, however, was at first rejected and the consequent revisions took so much time that Bruckner died before finishing his *Ninth Symphony*. The three movements he completed are in many ways his crowning achievement.

Wagner and Bruckner in Bayreuth by Otto Bohler, c.1870

Wagner was a consistent champion of Bruckner's work.

Wagner

Richard Wagner 1813–1883

RECOMMENDED WORKS

Götterdämmerung
London 414 115-2
Birgit Nilsson (sop) Brünnhilde; Wolfgang
Windgassen (ten) Siegfried; Gottlob Frick (bass)
Hagen; Gustav Neidlinger (bass-bar) Alberich;
Dietrich Fischer-Dieskau (bar) Gunther; Vienna
State Opera Chorus; Vienna Philharmonic
Orchestra/Georg Solti
*Always among the most striking of stereo
spectaculars, Solti's high-powered Götterdämmerung
amounts to a sonic experience of Spielbergian
proportions. Vocally, it represented the final flowering
of a Wagnerian Golden Age.*

Tristan und Isolde
Deutsche Grammophon 413 315-2GH4
René Kollo (ten) Tristan; Margaret Price (sop)
Isolde; Brigitte Fassbaender (sop) Brangäne; Kurt
Moll (bass) King Marke; Dietrich Fischer-Dieskau
(bar) Kurwenal; Werner Götz (ten) Melot; Leipzig
Radio Chorus; Staatskapelle Dresden/Carlos
Kleiber
*The greatest of all musical love stories and a
veritable hothouse of unstoppable passion. Kleiber is
magnificent — swift, impulsive, and stylish — while
Price and Kollo make compelling stage lovers.*

REPRESENTATIVE WORKS

Tannhäuser
Lohengrin
Das Rheingold
Die Walküre
Siegfried
Die Meistersinger von Nürnberg
Parsifal

Richard Wagner was born in Leipzig but
brought up in Dresden, where his family
moved soon after his birth. Though he
developed early passions for philosophy
and literature, it was music he went to
study at Leipzig University in 1831. His
early pieces include a symphony and two
concert overtures. In 1833 he began his
first opera, *Die Feen*, but the work was
never performed during his lifetime.

Wagner's first work in the opera world
was as a choral conductor at Würzburg,
followed a year later by an appointment as

Richard Wagner photographed in 1868

musical director of Magdeburg Opera.
There he saw *Das Liebesverbot* (Forbidden
Love) performed, his first opera to gain a
hearing. In 1836 he married a singer and
actress, Minna Planer, a union that lasted
30 years, although Wagner's frequent
affairs were the cause of much unhappiness
for Minna.

Desperately wanting to compose rather
than conduct, Wagner embarked on a
series of travels. In Paris he was reduced to
arranging dance music and writing songs
and articles. The Wagners returned to
Germany in 1842 almost destitute, but not
before Richard had composed two valuable opera scores: *Rienzi*, a grand historical
opera influenced by both Italian and
French opera, and *The Flying Dutchman*,
the first of Wagner's operas that points the
way ahead to his own mature style.

The two operas were great successes
when first performed in Dresden in 1842
and 1843 respectively and led to Wagner's
being appointed Court Opera conductor
in the city. During his time there he wrote
Tannhäuser and *Lohengrin*, both addressing
themes of spiritual and sensual love. As
with all Wagner's operas, the librettos are
his own, *Tannhäuser* adapted from a thirteenth-century German poem and *Lohengrin* from an anonymous epic.

In 1849, Wagner was forced to flee
Saxony when a warrant was issued for his
arrest following his support for revolutionary causes. He spent most of his 12-year
exile in Switzerland. There he wrote
books on subjects such as race, vegetarian-
ism, and hygiene, as well as two influential
volumes on music and art.

It was also during this period that he
began his monumental masterpiece *Der
Ring des Nibelungen* (The Ring of the
Nibelung). This huge work consists of
four full-length operas — *Rheingold*, *Die
Walküre* (The Valkyrie), *Siegfried,* and
Götterdämmerung (Twilight of the Gods)
— and occupied Wagner intermittently
until 1874. He found the source for his
libretto in the ancient Nibelung saga,
which explores the theme (among many
others) of the conflict between love and
money. *The Ring* exemplifies Wagner's
revolutionary approach to opera, which
dispensed with recitative and individual
numbers in favor of long stretches of continuous music. Also distinctive is Wagner's
use of 'leitmotifs' — tunes or phrases that
represent a character or an idea, and are
used to evoke or chart some development
in the thing they represent.

Wagner broke off from writing
Siegfried to work on *Tristan und Isolde*,
inspired in part by his affair with Mathilde
Wesendonck, the impetus too for the
songs known as *Wesendonck Lieder*. *Tristan*
deals with the theme of an all-embracing
love, denied on earth and attainable only
in death. Its startling harmonies foreshadowed the work of Schoenberg and Berg
half a century later and resulted in an opera
of great passion and beauty so difficult to

Women from the cast of *Die Walküre*, 1896

**The photograph gives eloquent evidence
of the robust type of soprano required
for Wagnerian roles.**

Parsifal at the Castle of the Grail by Hermann Heinrich

Parsifal, Wagner's final opera, was written over five years and first produced at Bayreuth in 1882.

stage that the original production was abandoned after 77 rehearsals.

One of Wagner's few purely instrumental pieces is *Siegfried Idyll*, composed as a birthday present for his new wife, Cosima, whom he married in 1870 following Minna's death. It was performed outside Cosima's bedroom on Christmas morning 1870, with Wagner conducting.

During a respite from *The Ring*, Wagner also composed his only comic opera, *Die Meistersinger von Nürnberg* (The Master-singers of Nuremberg), produced in Munich in 1868. During its composition Wagner's desperate financial difficulties were relieved by the young King of Bavaria, Ludwig II, a fanatical admirer of Wagner's music. His funds enabled Wagner to pursue his dream of establishing a festival devoted to his own operas. At an opera house built at Bayreuth in southern Germany, the festival was inaugurated in 1876 with a production of *The Ring*. Despite interruptions during the World

Wars, the festival continues; to this day the opera house has never been used to stage an opera not written by Wagner.

For his final masterpiece, *Parsifal*, Wagner drew on the ancient legend of the Holy Grail, advancing the themes of love, renunciation, and redemption explored in earlier works. Because of the work's sacred nature Wagner wished it to be performed only at Bayreuth, but when the copyright lapsed in 1913, his heirs could not prevent performances elsewhere.

A year after the completion of *Parsifal* in 1882, Wagner suffered a fatal heart attack in Venice. His operas and forceful personality had dominated German music in the second half of the nineteenth century, a powerful influence that has not waned in the intervening hundred years.

Additional Composers

Romanticism was above all a movement that encouraged individuality, and there is enormous character to be found even in the music of many of the lesser figures.

Anton Reicha (1770–1836) wrote mellifluous wind quintets and entertainingly quirky fugues for piano. In addition to his importance as a teacher and theorist, **Carl Loewe** (1796–1869) carved a small but significant niche in the *Lieder* repertoire with ballads such as *Archibald Douglas, Erlkönig,* and *Tom der Reimer*. The Spaniard **Juan Arriaga** (1806–1826) in his brief life wrote a *Symphony* and three *String Quartets* in which the influence of Beethoven does not preclude a delightfully inventive originality.

Two German composers stand at the gateway to full-blooded nineteenth-century Romanticism, **Louis Spohr** (1784–1859) and **Carl Maria von Weber** (1786–1826). Spohr's reputation, enhanced by his career as a violin virtuoso, dwindled after his death; his instrumental works (represented, for example, by the deservedly popular *Octet* and *Nonet*) take a Mozartian elegance and sensitivity as their starting-points, whereas largely forgotten operas such as *Faust* and *Jessonda* look forward, albeit distantly, to Wagner. Infinitely greater, however, was the impact of Weber's opera *Der Freischütz*. The heady mixture of vividly drawn village and forest scenes inspired by folk elements, with stunningly original music and a heroine, Agathe, with an ecstatically lyrical role, all ensured a triumphant reception for a work in which Germany sensed that it had found its own operatic voice. An operatic or dramatic inspiration is found in most of Weber's finest instrumental works: the scintillating and programmatic *Konzertstück* for piano and orchestra, the two *Clarinet Concertos*, the *Grand Duo* for clarinet and piano, and the four large-scale and evocative *Piano Sonatas*.

Later in the century **Jacques Offenbach** (1819–1880), a composer of popular and tuneful music, became a household name. The Frenchman's operettas were inspiration for the later works of waltz-king Johann Strauss II in Vienna. The melodic appeal and wit of *Orpheus in the Underworld*, *La Belle Hélène,* and *La vie parisienne* have proved enduring. At least two of the lyrical if sentimental operas of **Jules Massenet** (1842–1912), *Manon* and *Werther*, also retain a place in the repertoire. Massenet was the most successful French opera composer of the generation after Gounod, and he inherited much of that composer's melodic facility; the popular *Méditations* from the opera *Thaïs* is an appealing example of this quality.

The Romantic Legacy
mid-19th to early 20th century

In the 1880's, imperialism became the costly preoccupation of western nations. Europe's governments expanded their colonial grip overseas and divided much of tropical Africa among them. They also established Asian colonies — at the expense of the Chinese empire — drawing the United States into the expansionist tide. Britain fought a bitter war with the Boer republics, and a newly industrialized Japan inflicted a harsh defeat on Russia and provoked Russia's revolution of 1905. European tensions continued. Russia and Austria-Hungary engaged in ancient rivalries under the watchful eye of the ambitious Germany. The assassination of Archduke Ferdinand by a Serbian patriot sparked a conflict that swiftly engulfed the continent.

It was also an era of artistic change. In France, Impressionist painters made major advances in the use of color and technique to capture light and atmosphere. The challenges to traditional forms were profound, and by the early 1900's, abstract art had made its appearance.

Remarkable scientific discoveries were in progress — the beginnings of atomic physics, the discovery of X-rays, and Pasteur's work on micro-organisms, as well as Einstein's theories of relativity. In a short time, a wide array of inventions — from the phonograph and the electric light bulb to the automobile and telephone — changed the way people lived.

In music, nationalism remained a potent source of inspiration; British, Czech, and Russian composers drew on native folk music, as did Grieg in Norway and Bartók in Hungary. From the United States came ragtime, highly popular and lively music that had its roots firmly in native soil.

Featured Composers

Bayswater Omnibus by George William Joy, 1895
One of the first motorized buses in London, this form of public transportation was used by a mixture of social classes, both women and men, and carried advertisements: a picture of very early modern society.

By the late 1870's the revolutionary and nationalistic fervor so closely associated with the Romantic movement had transformed the map of Europe. The new German Empire maintained a fragile balance of power, upholding the resolutions that had been agreed upon at the Congress of Berlin. Nationalism was by no means a spent force, but in the later years of the century, it assumed a different character. While the unification of Germany and Italy had been essentially constructive processes, as disparate states were built up to form new nations, similar forces in central and eastern Europe tended more to destruction, leading to the break-up of long-established empires.

Romanticism played a lesser part in this second strain of nationalism. In literature and the visual arts the movement was supplanted in the mid-nineteenth century, giving way to the Realist school. In music, Romanticism had a longer life. One of its foremost exponents, Wagner, was still a dominant figure at the end of the century. Increasingly, however, it became a mark of tradition, rather than an instrument for change. In a musical context realism's nearest equivalent was VERISMO (true to life) opera, inspired by Bizet's *Carmen* (1875), which shocked Parisian audiences with its portrayal of lust and savagery. Even so, it helped create a demand for operas concentrating on the seamier aspects of life, a demand that was readily supplied by composers such as Puccini and Mascagni.

The influence of Impressionism and the East

Meanwhile, a veritable revolution was taking place in the art world. In 1874 a group of French painters banded together to stage the first Impressionist show in Paris. In total, they would mount eight exhibitions, all in open defiance of the academic establishment. These artists sought to capture on canvas the effects of light and of changing patterns of weather, as well as the immediacy of Parisian life. Rejecting the carefully composed artifices of their predecessors, they tried to paint pictures that were like 'snapshots.' The Impressionists' emphasis on the fleeting moment had slight Romantic overtones, but their overall approach was more scientific — Monet painted more than 20 versions of Rouen cathedral to illustrate how its appearance altered under different light conditions — and they fiercely opposed the emotionalism of Romantic art.

The evocative style of the Impressionists translated well into musical terms. Manuel de Falla described his *Nights in the Gardens of Spain* (1916) as a series of 'symphonic impressions' for piano and orchestra; some of Ravel's pieces, such as *Miroirs* (1905), could be called impressionistic; and Debussy was greatly attracted to the work of the Impressionists. Indeed, striking parallels exist between the effects created by Impressionist paintings and Debussy's use of subtle textures of harmony and tone to evoke images of misty, atmospheric scenes, as in his *Nuages* (the first part of *Nocturnes*). The understatement and restraint characterizing such works distanced them from the passion and storytelling typical of Romanticism.

From the Universal Exhibition in Paris in 1889 Debussy carried away deep impressions of the sound of the Javanese gamelan orchestra. He incorporated its exotic flavor into works such as *Pagodas* and his *String Quartet* in G minor. Other composers followed suit, similarly seduced by the mystique of the East. Puccini's *Madama Butterfly* centered on the plight of a Japanese geisha girl; Mahler based his *Song of the Earth* on a cycle of Chinese poems; and Gilbert and Sullivan scored one of their biggest successes with *The Mikado*, based on an Eastern theme. This vogue for things oriental swept through most branches of the arts. Blue and white porcelain and Japanese prints became collector's items, and the latter profoundly influenced painters such as Van Gogh and Gauguin. The higher profile of the East, in part due to the beauty of its culture, was all the more exaggerated as the rush for imperial possessions gathered pace in the final years of the nineteenth century.

Portrait of 'Père' Tanguy by Van Gogh, 1887

Composers and artists alike were influenced by the East. Van Gogh admired the boldness and clarity of Japanese prints, seen here in the background.

MUSICAL DEFINITIONS

VERISMO Italian, 'realism.' A type of Italian opera current in the late 19th and early 20th centuries. Aiming at social and psychological realism, verismo operas depicted the lives of ordinary people and addressed contemporary themes.

Rouen Cathedral, Evening by Claude Monet, 1894

Monet produced a sequence of paintings running from dawn to dusk to show how the changing light transformed the appearance of the cathedral.

Colonial expansion and conflict

Russia, thwarted in its advance toward Constantinople, next turned its attention to the moribund Chinese empire and annexed Manchuria. The other European powers soon followed the Russian example. Germany established bases in northern China, Britain consolidated its position in Hong Kong, the French extended their influence over Indochina, and even a comparatively weak state like Portugal managed to take possession of Macão. This involvement in Asian affairs reached a peak in 1900 when a combined force of European, Japanese, and American troops looted and occupied Peking, on the pretext of suppressing the Boxer Rebellion.

The spread of imperialism was not confined to Asia. In every corner of the globe, European governments hastened to stake their claims. Britain led the way, making great gains in central and southern Africa, as well as in the Pacific, where Fiji, New Guinea, and North Borneo were added to the list of new acquisitions. At the same time France tightened its grip on the Ivory Coast and Madagascar, while German forces occupied southwest Africa and the Solomon Islands. In the Congo, King Leopold II of Belgium carved out a personal empire for himself, which he eventually bequeathed to his country.

Even the United States joined this expansionist tide. Hawaii was annexed in 1897, and Puerto Rico, the Philippines, and Guam were taken from Spain the following year. In 1903 the United States encouraged a 'revolution' in Panama in order to bring into American jurisdiction the transcontinental canal that was then under construction.

The race to establish overseas colonies made the great powers less inclined to wage war at home, and as a result, Europe enjoyed a period of comparative peace around the turn of the century. Instead, the major conflicts tended to occur outside the continent, when and where imperial interests were threatened. Britain, for example, became embroiled in a bitter struggle against the Boer Republics in South Africa. It had been thought that the Afrikaners would put up little resistance against the might of the British army, but their forces inflicted heavy losses at the sieges of Mafeking and Kimberley, and the war lasted for three years (1899–1902).

Russia in turmoil

Russia encountered similar problems in its new eastern territories. Early in 1904 the Japanese launched an attack, destroying part of the Vladivostok fleet near the Korean Straits and laying siege to Port Arthur. This vital Manchurian stronghold finally fell in January 1905, and Japanese victory was assured after Admiral Togo's triumph at Tsushima in May of that year.

The Red Funeral by Ilya Repin, 1905–6
Tensions within Russia increased markedly after 'Red Sunday,' when government forces opened fire on demonstrators.

These reverses had serious consequences inside Russia itself, triggering a wave of social unrest. A government minister was assassinated, and strikes multiplied throughout the country. On January 22, 1905 — known as 'Red Sunday' — nearly 1,000 demonstrators were butchered by Tsarist troops as they were attempting to deliver a petition at the Winter Palace in St. Petersburg. Then, in June of the same year, sailors on the battleship *Potemkin* mutinied and put their officers to death. Order was ultimately restored, but the signs of future unrest were ominously clear.

Nationalism and imperialism

The ferment within Russia seemed to vindicate the views of Cecil Rhodes (the founder of Rhodesia), who declared that nations should become imperialist if they wished to avoid civil war. Many European governments shared this opinion, recognizing that colonial success not only would bring economic benefits but also could deflect social discontent at home.

Natives being taught embroidery in the Belgian Congo, c.1890
In spite of education programs, some of the worst imperial excesses occurred in the Belgian Congo, where brutality and forced labor made the colony a paying proposition.

This brought about a significant shift in the nature of nationalist feeling. Whereas in the earlier part of the nineteenth century nationalism had usually been associated with liberalism or with the radical tradition of the French Revolution, it was now also used as a political tool by conservative elements. They sought to awaken a pride in national values and a patriotic sense of duty in order to draw attention away from domestic economic uncertainties.

This proved to be a double-edged sword. While greater national pride had its uses, it also led to an increase in xenophobia, which in turn added to the risk of war. For example, the long-running Dreyfus affair, a case of treason that scandalized France for over a decade, was inflamed by the fact that the army officer in question was Jewish. Captain Dreyfus was wrongly convicted in 1894; his sentence would not be quashed until 1906. Similarly, in England, the hostility to foreigners reached such a pitch that the royal family followed the prudent course of masking their German origins by adopting the name Windsor.

Nationalism and music

In the latter half of the nineteenth century, nationalism proved a potent source of inspiration for many composers. In Czech music the groundwork had been laid by František Skroup, who in 1826 had produced the first home-grown opera, *Dratenik* (The Tinker). He also wrote the song that would many years later be chosen as the national anthem. He was followed by Smetana, whose nationalist sympathies had been stirred by the 1848 uprising. In 1866 his most famous opera, *The Bartered Bride*, a lively evocation of rural life in a Bohemian village, was first produced. Smetana continued to celebrate his homeland with operas such as *Libuše* and with his cycle of symphonic poems, *Má Vlast*.

This patriotic flavor was maintained in the work of Smetana's compatriot Antonín Dvořák, who had played under his direction as a violinist in the national orchestra. Dvořák made particular use of native dance forms such as the dumka and the furiant, and his two collections of *Slavonic Dances* won him international acclaim.

The Czech experience was replicated in other parts of the continent as composers looked to their musical roots for inspiration. However, the political dimensions of this trend varied considerably. Some composers used folk elements as a colorful and exotic feature of an otherwise cosmopolitan style. Liszt's *Hungarian Rhapsodies*, for instance, mostly published in the

Dreyfus escorted from prison to court, 1894

The Dreyfus scandal polarized French opinion. Support for the captain was led by the novelist Émile Zola.

1850's, were not based on true traditional forms, but rather derived from the gypsy music that could be heard in the restaurants and cafés of Budapest. The genuine folk music of Hungary was not appreciated until many years later.

Nationalism also prompted some nations to re-examine their own heritage. In France the National Society for French Music, founded in 1871, attempted to revive the country's musical fortunes by commissioning new editions and performances of works by earlier French masters. This, together with the Schola Cantorum (another educational body, founded in 1904), helped to restore the nation to its prominent position in the musical world.

The British emphasized the creation of a new native school. One mischievous German critic had described England as 'the land without music,' but after the turn of the century, this jibe had lost its sting. Edward Elgar captured the patriotic mood of the country with his *Pomp and Circumstance* marches, while Henry Wood's Promenade Concerts (beginning in 1895) provided the nation with an enduring musical tradition. Their efforts were consolidated by that most English of composers, Ralph Vaughan Williams. His work benefited from his experience as editor of the *New English Hymnal* — he later wrote that his 'close association with some of the best (as well as some of the worst) tunes in the world was a better musical education than any amount of sonatas and fugues' — and from his links with the English Folk Song Society, founded in 1898. Together with Gustav Holst, another folk enthusiast, he made field trips into the English countryside, noting down the songs and dances that he heard. Excursions of this kind into East Anglia provided the raw material for his three *Norfolk Rhapsodies* and *In the Fen Country*.

The importance of folk music

The collecting of folk songs had begun in earnest in England in 1843 with the publication of the Reverend John Broadwood's *Old English Songs*. This led to a series of similar anthologies, culminating in the work of Cecil Sharp (1859–1924), who collected some three thousand songs during his travels. Francis Child, a professor at Harvard University, performed an equally mountainous task in the United States. The motives of most of these collectors were either curatorial — preserving an aspect of culture that was in danger of dying out — or educational.

Flamenco dancing in a bar in Seville, 1890

In Spain, as elsewhere, traditional dances provided a fertile source of inspiration for composers.

In Germany, Brahms used arrangements of folk songs as the basis of many of his *Lieder*. Elsewhere, the use of folk material represented a reaction against the dominance of German culture, whose influence had been so far-reaching that many talented young musicians believed it was necessary for them to study in a German conservatory, if their music was to gain wide acceptance.

One such composer was Edvard Grieg, who trained in Leipzig but returned to his native Norway determined to break away from his foreign musical education. He helped found the Norwegian Academy of Music (1867) and produced scintillating piano arrangements of peasant dances. Debussy might have described some of his pieces as 'bonbons stuffed with snow,' but Grieg's fellow-countrymen considered them a perfect evocation of their misty Nordic homeland. In Finland, Sibelius struck a similarly patriotic note, using the *Kalevala*, the Finnish national epic, as source material for many of his compositions. Equally, composers such as Albéniz and Falla in Spain used traditional sources as a basis for much of their music.

In England the next crucial stage in the collecting of folk songs was undertaken by an Australian musician, Percy Grainger, who had been inspired by Grieg to take an interest in folk music. In 1908 he journeyed through Lincolnshire, using a phonograph to record any tunes he came across. His research was echoed independently in the studies of Kodály and Bartók. They, too, employed a phonograph, amassing some 16,000 recordings of peasant songs and dances during their travels in Hungary, Slovakia, and Romania.

The conditions under which this kind of research was conducted were arduous and painstaking. The machines themselves were barely portable, while the wax cylinders they used ran for only two and a half minutes, which meant interrupting the flow of the performance. Even so, the recordings allowed musicians to study the material more closely and accurately and this, in turn, altered the way in which folk sources were applied. Whereas the earlier Romantics had tended to smooth out the irregularities they found in traditional songs or had simply composed in a folk idiom, later musicians used their discoveries as a departure point for creating newer and more original forms. This was especially true of Bartók, who developed a very personal musical language that stretched tonality — the conventional method of composing a piece around one particular key — to its limits.

Scientific developments

The phonograph, invented by Edison in 1877, was just one of the products of the technological revolution that transformed society in the years leading up to World War I. In 1895 the Lumière brothers had presented the first cinematograph performance in Paris. Four years later Marconi set up wireless communications between England and France and just two years after that managed to establish similar links between Cornwall and Newfoundland. The same period also saw the appearance of such diverse advances as the electric light bulb, the safety razor, and the vacuum cleaner. Just as these symbols of progress were being invented, other scientists were casting doubt on the very foundations of contemporary belief. In 1900, Max Planck postulated his Quantum Theory, and five years later, Albert Einstein published his first Theory of Relativity. In 1904, Sir Ernest Rutherford's book on radioactivity challenged the concept of the indestructibility of matter, taking the study of physics along a new and dangerous path.

Equally influential, though in an entirely different way, was Sigmund Freud's work in psychoanalysis. Gustav Mahler was one of his patients, seeking relief from the agonized soul-searching that permeates so much of his music.

The last years of the nineteenth century also witnessed enormous advances in the fields of transportation and communications. The automobile, which had been pioneered by Daimler and Benz in the 1880's, became an increasingly common sight. London introduced its first taxicabs in 1903 and, four years later, the Model T Ford went into production in Detroit. Even as these developments were taking place, the Wright brothers were hard at work on the next mechanical marvel. In 1903 they achieved the first series of successful airplane flights in North Carolina, the longest of these lasting for just 59 seconds.

New trends in music and art

The vast improvements in communications helped to speed up the transmission of artistic currents. A series of 'crazes' swept across Europe, as musical innovations from the New World made their mark. John Philip Sousa took his band on several well-attended tours of Europe, winning great acclaim for marches like *The Washington Post* and *The Stars and Stripes Forever*. He gave his name to the sousaphone, a type of tuba, and became an international bestselling author with his biography, *Marching Along*.

Another — far less respectable — import was the tango, which had evolved in the brothel quarter of Buenos Aires. Eyebrows were raised at the popularity of this 'immodest' dance. At the same time, and with far greater impact, ragtime burst upon the London scene in 1912. In that year a revue called *Hullo Rag-time* opened at the Hippodrome Theatre in London and ran for 451 performances, giving British audiences their first taste of modern American music.

The undisputed center of artistic developments at this time was Paris. Painters from all over Europe gravitated toward the city. The Russian impresario Sergei Diaghilev chose the city as the home for his Ballets Russes company. Indeed, it was a measure of the city's cosmopolitan appeal that the 'School of Paris' — the group of artists who pioneered modern art at the start of the twentieth century — included two Spaniards (Picasso and Gris), three Russians (Chagall, Soutine, and Lipchitz), an Italian (Modigliani), a Romanian (Brancuși), and a Dutchman (Van Dongen).

If the geographical barriers between the arts were shrinking, so too were the aesthetic ones. Many painters of the period consciously sought to endow their pictures with musical qualities. James Whistler went one stage further, giving his canvases musical titles such as 'Nocturnes' and 'Symphonies.' Accordingly, he dubbed his celebrated portrait of his mother *An Arrangement in Grey and Black*. Conversely, the composer Alexander Scriabin aimed at a marriage of sight and sound through his music. He wanted performances of his symphonic poem *Prometheus* to be accompanied by a display of colored

Above, top: An early airplane above Berlin, 1905
Above: Karl Benz with his son Eugen in an 1893 car at a motor rally in 1925
Below: Edison's phonograph, invented in 1877

Manned flight, the automobile, and the advent of recorded sound transformed the nineteenth-century world.

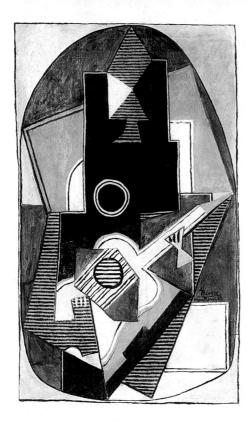

The Guitar Player by Pablo Picasso, 1918

Picasso and Braque led the Cubist movement in the prewar years, laying the basis for abstract art.

lights flashed onto a screen. Each note was to be represented by a different color: 'E,' for example, he visualized as 'pearly white and shimmer of moonlight.'

If nothing else, these experiments demonstrated the feverish spirit of creativity that prevailed in prewar Europe. Post-Impressionism, Art Nouveau, Fauvism, Symbolism, Cubism, and Expressionism were all spawned within a matter of years. The specifics of these new styles differed greatly, but in general they marked the diminishing influence of the official academies that had controlled the arts for so long.

The Suffragette movement

A similar questioning of established order appeared in other sectors of society. The Trade Union and Socialist movements that had taken root in the nineteenth century continued to grow, and these were now joined by the new cause of female emancipation. The United States took the lead in this field, with some states granting women the vote before the turn of the century. In Europe the struggle started later and lasted longer. Women in Finland were granted electoral equality in 1906, with Norway following suit in 1908. In Britain the suffragette campaign began in earnest in 1906. It was cut short

Below: The funeral of Emily Davison, June 14, 1913

Emily Davison became a suffragette martyr when she threw herself under the king's horse at the Epsom Derby. Mass demonstrations accompanied her funeral service in London.

when war broke out, and it was not until 1928 that emancipation became universal, giving all British women the vote.

The road to war

The shadow of war had loomed over Europe since an uneasy peace emerged from the 1878 Congress of Berlin. By 1893 the continent had divided into two camps: the Dual Alliance of France and Russia, and the Triple Alliance of Germany, Italy, and Austria-Hungary. The situation became more complicated in 1904 as France and Britain entered into their Entente Cordiale. On the surface this was little more than an imperialist pact by which France recognized British claims to Egypt, in return for support of its own activities in Morocco. However, the agreement also placed an extra strain on the delicate balance of power. German leaders voiced their fears about encirclement by their enemies, while the opposing powers were equally concerned at the mounting threat of Pan-Germanism. France's lingering bitterness over the loss of Alsace and Lorraine after the Franco-Prussian War rubbed more salt into this wound.

Once again it was the strength of nationalist feeling in the Balkans that tilted the balance toward chaos. In 1908, Austria-Hungary annexed Bosnia and Herzegovina. These provinces, under the nominal control of Turkey, had in reality been administered by the Austrians ever since the Berlin conference. Their annexation now was meant to stem the ambitions of Serbia, which hoped to unite all the Slav nations under its banner. Inevitably, the Serbs protested vociferously at the annexations, supported in this move by Russia. However, the Austro-German commitment to the seizures proved too powerful to contest, and Russia was forced to back down.

The Serbs gained their revenge in June 1914 when the heir to the Austrian throne, the Archduke Ferdinand, was murdered in Sarajevo. The Serbian press boasted that the assassination had been plotted in Belgrade, and pressure on the Austrian government to retaliate was overwhelming. However, in the years that had elapsed since the Bosnian crisis, attitudes had hardened. This time there was to be no backing down. Once Serbia and Austria had begun hostilities, the complex system of alliances came into play, and within a week the continent was at war.

Below left (inset): Archduke Ferdinand and his wife Sophie, June 28, 1914
Below: The arrest of Gavrilo Princip, June 28, 1914

Archduke Ferdinand and his wife photographed in Sarajevo, only moments before their assassination. Below, the chaos that ensued: Gavrilo Princip is arrested after firing the shots that triggered World War I.

Featured Composers

Smetana

Bedřich Smetana 1824–1884

RECOMMENDED WORK

Má Vlast
Supraphon 11 1208-2
Czech Philharmonic Orchestra/Rafael Kubelík
Recorded live in 1990 on the occasion of this great conductor-in-exile's long-awaited return to his homeland. A performance of great majesty and blazing intensity.

REPRESENTATIVE WORKS
String Quartet No. 1, 'From my life'
The Bartered Bride

Smetana, often regarded as the founder of Czech classical music, was born in Litomyšl in Bohemia. Although his parents' eleventh child, he was the first son to survive infancy, and his father, an avid amateur violinist, lavished attention on his musical education. By the age of six he had played in a string quartet and given his first piano recital; two years later he was writing music. When the family moved to Německy Brod — a center of political and cultural thought — Smetana developed an interest in philosophy and literature.

Smetana photographed late in life

In 1843 he settled in Prague and earned a living as tutor to an aristocratic family, at the same time studying composition and piano privately. His diary records his early ambition: 'By the grace of God and with His help I shall one day be a Liszt in technique and a Mozart in composition.'

After taking part in the fighting at the barricades during the abortive 1848 nationalist uprising in Prague, he visited Sweden in 1856, taking up the post of director to the Göteborg Philharmonic Society. His friendship with Liszt (whom he had met several years earlier) led in

The house at Jabkenice, by Smetana's wife Bettina
Smetana retired to this country house to write some of his fine late works.

1858 to an invitation to visit Leipzig, where he attended concerts of contemporary music by composers such as Wagner.

In 1866, Smetana conducted a performance of his first successful large-scale composition, *The Bartered Bride*, one of his most popular works. Its overriding mood is uncharacteristically one of joyous optimism, and Smetana later related how many of the delightful melodies were inspired by his habitual evening walks along the banks of the Vltava river. Also in 1866 he was appointed to the coveted post of principal conductor of the Prague Provisional Theater orchestra (Dvořák was principal violist). This allowed him to promote new works by fellow Czech composers as well as to include more French and Italian music, rather than the almost exclusive diet of Austrian and German music performed in most Czech concert halls.

Smetana's massive orchestral work *Má Vlast* (My Fatherland) occupied the composer for seven years. Completed in 1879, this cycle of six tone poems soon became one of his best-loved pieces, and was performed frequently throughout Europe and America. It represents the struggles of the politically and culturally oppressed Czech people, expressing in music their long-held desire for independence.

During these years, Smetana's health began to deteriorate seriously. The onset of venereal disease brought increasing deafness and badly affected his ability to concentrate. Over the next few years, living in virtual isolation, he composed two operas — *The Kiss* (1876), an attractive blend of serious, romantic, and comic elements, and *The Secret* (1877). The autobiographical string quartet, *From my life*, also composed during these years, includes a piercing whistling sound in the last movement that graphically depicts the effects of Smetana's deafness.

Throughout his last years Smetana's mental health degenerated as well, and in 1884 he was committed to a Prague lunatic asylum. With his death two months later, Czechoslovakia lost its first truly nationalist composer, one who would provide a source of inspiration for generations of artists to come.

Key to Recommended Works

arr. arrangement (by)	**contr** contralto	**hpd** harpsichord	**Op., Opp.** Opus(es)	**pno** piano	**ten** tenor	**vcl** violoncello ('cello)
bar baritone	**gtr** guitar	**mez** mezzo-soprano	**org** organ	**sop** soprano	**treb** treble	**vln** violin

Lalo

Edouard Lalo 1823–1892

RECOMMENDED WORK

Symphonie espagnole
London 411 952-2
Kyung-Wha Chung (vln); Montreal Symphony
Orchestra/Charles Dutoit
*A winning combination of elegance and virtuosity,
stylishly accompanied and brilliantly recorded.*

REPRESENTATIVE WORKS

Cello Concerto
Violin Concerto
Symphony in G minor
Le Roi d'Ys

Violin made in 1863

**Lalo wrote music for the violin with a
marked Spanish feel.**

Photographic portrait of the composer

A letter in Lalo's hand, dated March 19, 1882
**The letter shows a musical quotation
from Lalo's ballet Namouna.**

Lalo was born in Lille in France. He studied the violin and cello at the local conservatory. His parents, although initially happy to foster his interest, strongly disapproved of his intention to make a career in music; at the age of 16 he left home. He enrolled at the Paris Conservatoire, studied composition privately, and while earning a living as a teacher, produced many chamber works that contributed to a revival of interest in chamber music in Paris. In 1855 he formed a string quartet (he played the violin) with the express purpose of promoting the chamber music of Mozart, Haydn, and Beethoven, whose music was until then rarely played in Paris.

A lack of response to his own music disappointed and embittered Lalo, and he composed little in the 1860's. However, during the following decade he began to produce orchestral works that caused audiences to sit up and listen. The *Symphonie espagnole* (1873) for violin and orchestra and the *Cello Concerto* (1876) particularly caught the attention of the public. Both works have a pronounced Spanish character that, coupled with melodic and rhythmic drive, resulted in exciting and accessible music.

By the end of the 1870's, Lalo had gained the respect and support of a number of leading musicians in Paris, including the virtuoso violinist Pablo Sarasate, for whom the *Symphonie espagnole* had been written. Sarasate also gave the first performance of Lalo's *Violin Concerto*. Despite success as an orchestral composer — consolidated by the lively *Symphony in G minor* in 1886 — Lalo stopped writing for this medium, concentrating instead on the theater. From 1875 to 1887 he worked on an opera, *Le Roi d'Ys*, which became recognized as his masterpiece. Having at first failed to excite interest, the work was eventually accepted by the Paris Opéra and performed in 1888. It was an overwhelming success, and in the final years of his life Lalo basked in public recognition. *Le Roi d'Ys* is energetic and colorful, with dramatic orches- tration, and is one of the first French operas of note to display the unmistakable influence of Wagner.

Lalo's music embodies the French characteristics of clarity and logic. Although clearly bound to the great Romantic tradition represented by composers such as Mendelssohn and Schumann, Lalo was one of the first composers who successfully incorporated ideas and colors derived from folk tunes. The result is warm, vibrant, extroverted music that carries the listener inexorably along with it.

Delibes

Léo Delibes 1836–1891

RECOMMENDED WORK

Coppélia

London 414 502-2
National Philharmonic Orchestra/Richard
Bonynge
*A lively, expertly turned rendition, extremely well
recorded, with Bonynge providing a listening
experience shot through with thrilling effects.
Particularly worth attention are the Boléro and the
Valse des heures.*

REPRESENTATIVE WORKS
Lakmé
Sylvia
Le roi l'a dit

Léo Delibes was born in St. Germain-du-Val in France. After his father's death in 1838, he was educated by his mother and uncle, learning both to sing and to play the organ. He entered the Paris Conservatoire at the age of 12 and won a first prize two years later. In 1853, aged 17, he became organist of St. Pierre de Chaillot in Paris, and obtained his first professional appointment as an accompanist at the Théâtre Lyrique. His duties included playing the piano for rehearsals and conducting some rehearsals to lighten the burden of the principal conductor. He held the post at the Théâtre Lyrique for ten years. Although he continued his organist's duties until 1871, he was clearly more drawn to the exciting and changeable life of the theater.

Delibes's first stage work, *Deux sous de charbon*, was premiered in 1856. It was the first of many light operettas, which he produced at the rate of one a year for the next 14 years. The second of these, *Deux vieilles grades*, caught the imagination of the theater-going public. It became an enormous success, praised for its witty presentation, tuneful melodies, and generally light touch.

Léo Delibes photographed c.1880

Marcella Sembrich playing the title role in Delibes's
opera *Lakmé*

**The music from this perennially popular
opera includes the 'Flower Duet,' sung
by two sopranos.**

Delibes was appointed chorus master at the Paris Opéra in 1864, a position presenting many new opportunities and experiences. His last operetta, *La source* (1869), he wrote jointly with the little-known composer Louis Minkus. Delibes's contribution conspicuously outshone that of his colleague, and served to consolidate an already flourishing reputation as one of Paris's leading theater composers.

In 1870, Delibes produced what many believe to be his finest work, the ballet *Coppélia*. It was an immediate success and has remained one of the best loved of all classical ballets. The sheer spectacle of the work and the natural grace and vivacity it contains show the composer's natural affinity for the medium.

The following year Delibes left his employment at the Opéra to concentrate more fully on composition. From this point on his output decreased in quantity; at the same time it was generally conceived on a larger scale and is of a more complex nature. In 1877 he completed his second full-length ballet, *Sylvia*. Based on a mythological subject, *Sylvia* is full of the composer's characteristic melodic charm, although it has never achieved the popularity of *Coppélia*.

In 1881, Delibes was made professor of composition at the Paris Conservatoire. Two years later, inspired by the vogue for all things Asian, he wrote his most famous opera, *Lakmé*, about the doomed love of an Indian temple-priestess for an English soldier. The exotic and melodic music — including the still popular 'Flower Duet' sung by Lakmé and her friend as they prepare to bathe — is supported by a well-constructed libretto that ensured a splendid first production at the Opéra. The star role (for soprano) allows the performer ample opportunity to show off her accomplishments, while the colorful orchestration contributes to a compelling and dramatic work that displays stylistic similarity to *Carmen*, by Delibes's compatriot Bizet.

Above all, Delibes's great gift was for the lightness and humor demanded by the theater of his time. The natural spontaneity of his music continues to captivate audiences today.

Saint-Saëns

Camille Saint-Saëns 1835–1921

RECOMMENDED WORK

Symphony No. 3 in C minor, 'Organ'
RCA 09026 61500-2
Berj Zamkochian (org); Boston Symphony Orchestra/Charles Munch
A stunning sonic refurbishment of a thrilling 1959 production, magnificently played and conducted with panache and sensitivity.

REPRESENTATIVE WORKS
Piano Concertos No. 2 in G minor & No. 4 in C minor
Cello Concerto No. 1
Le Carnaval des animaux
Samson et Dalila

Camille Saint-Saëns was born in Paris and brought up by his mother. He began music lessons early. By the age of three he had already composed his first piano piece. At the age of seven he began taking composition lessons and soon gained a reputation in Paris as a child prodigy. In 1846, aged 11, he gave a recital of Mozart and Beethoven piano concertos; for an encore

Saint-Saëns taking the solo part in a Mozart piano concerto, 1913

he offered to play any one of Beethoven's piano sonatas from memory.

He entered the Paris Conservatoire in 1848, and over the next five years his dazzling gifts won both the friendship and patronage of composers Rossini, Gounod, Liszt, and Berlioz. His mentors feared only that his chameleonlike ability to absorb information and musical styles, while in

A scene from *Samson et Dalila*
Saint-Saëns's best-known opera was first produced at Weimar in 1877.

one sense an advantage, might inhibit some originality of expression in his own compositions.

The 1860's were probably the most contented and stable years of Saint-Saëns's life. During this time he quickly acquired a formidable reputation as a composer and a virtuoso pianist. In 1868 his *Piano Concerto No. 2*, written in just 17 days, received warm praise from Liszt. He went on to produce a total of five concertos for piano, ranging in mood from the graceful, capricious, and lyrical to the heroic and, in the case of *No. 4* — untypically for Saint-Saëns — the tragic.

At the École Niedermeyer between 1861 and 1865, in Saint-Saëns's only professional teaching appointment, his pupils included the composer Gabriel Fauré, who became a close friend. In 1871, Saint-Saëns co-founded the Société Nationale de Musique, an institution designed to promote the works of French composers. The Société gave important premieres of works by Debussy, Ravel, Saint-Saëns himself, and many others. In 1875 he married a young woman half his age. The marriage lasted only five years, probably due in part to Saint-Saëns's high-strung temperament and the couple's frustrated desire to start a family (two children died in infancy).

The 1870's and 1880's saw the composition of some of Saint-Saëns's best, most characteristic works, including the opera *Samson et Dalila* (1877), the *Symphony No. 3* ('The Organ'), and in 1886 *Le Carnaval des animaux* (The Carnival of the Animals). The last consists of musical portraits of various animals — including such species as 'Fossils' and 'Pianists,' among the more conventional animals, such as the famous 'Swan' music for cello. *The Carnival of the Animals* was written as a private joke. Saint-Saëns did not allow a performance during his lifetime. It is ironic that this piece more than any other has secured his fame in the present day.

Saint-Saëns spent his final years traveling in Europe and the United States. On his death in 1921 he left a legacy of music that revealed a passion for order, clarity, and precision, as well as an always attractive, and very French, melodic charm.

Grieg

Edvard Grieg 1843–1907

RECOMMENDED WORK

Piano Concerto in A minor
Philips 412 923-2
Stephen Kovacevich (pno); BBC Symphony
Orchestra/Colin Davis
*A warm and dramatic re-enactment of this most
endearing of Scandinavian concertos, sensitively
conducted and beautifully recorded.*

REPRESENTATIVE WORKS
Peer Gynt: Suites Nos. 1 & 2
Holberg Suite
Lyric Suite
Lyric Pieces
Norwegian Folk Tunes
Wedding Day at Troldhaugen
Sketches of Norwegian Life
Haugtussa

Hallingen by August Schneider, 1869
***Folk music and dances, such as the
halling, influenced Grieg's compositions.***

Grieg at the piano, photographed with his wife Nina
***Piano music made up a significant part
of Grieg's output, most notably in the
various collections of Lyric Pieces.***

Edvard Grieg, born in Bergen, Norway, received music lessons from his mother at the age of six. In 1853 he was sent to the Leipzig Conservatory, where he studied piano and composition. He did not enjoy life at the Conservatory; in 1860 he had to take time off after suffering a violent attack of pleurisy that left him with recurring respiratory troubles. He returned to Norway in 1862 and the following year traveled to Copenhagen to begin a career as a pianist. There he met his cousin and future wife, Nina Hayerup.

At this time Norwegian culture was heavily overshadowed by Danish influence. As Grieg grew older, however, he became increasingly conscious of the musical potential of his own country's folk culture and began to promote Norwegian nationalism by writing pieces based on traditional popular music.

In 1867 he produced his first set of miniature pieces for piano, the *Lyric Pieces*, which consists of eight short movements in contrasting moods. He wrote nine further collections under the same title, each gathering together six to eight short but beautifully constructed movements of an individual character. The following year Grieg finished what has become one of his best-known pieces, the *Piano Concerto* in A minor. It is a striking and technically demanding work that retains much of its original freshness even today.

Grieg started work on the suite *Peer Gynt* when the playwright Henrik Ibsen asked him to provide music for his play of that name. The first performance in 1876 was a resounding success and made Grieg into a national figure overnight. In the same year he attended and thoroughly enjoyed the first performance of Wagner's cycle of four operas, *Der Ring des Nibelungen* (The Ring Cycle). Yet musically the two composers could not be further apart. Wagner produced colossal pieces lasting over four hours, while Grieg concentrated on writing concise and beautiful miniatures.

In 1884, Grieg accepted a commission to write a piece to commemorate the bicentennial of the birth of the Norwegian philosopher and playwright Ludvig Holberg. The resulting *Holberg Suite* is a five-movement piece for piano written in the manner of an eighteenth-century dance suite. Several months later he arranged it for string orchestra, in which form the highly lyrical and graceful music has become popular.

By 1885, Grieg had established a considerable reputation. He built himself a house at Troldhaugen, where he lived for the rest of his life. Over the next 20 years he managed to establish a pattern of composing in the spring and early summer, fitting in a walking vacation in late summer, and then spending the autumn and winter on lengthy concert tours. The impulse to travel never left him, and in his final years he continued with grueling concert schedules around Europe. In the last year of his life he visited Berlin and Kiel; he was making plans to leave for England when he was taken ill and died. He was buried near his house in the wall of a cliff that overhangs a fjord.

Grieg shied away from the larger forms of musical expression, such as the symphony and the opera, but in his preferred field — as a miniaturist — he is without equal. His music, accessible, highly individual and nationalist in flavor, has almost universal appeal.

Dvořák

Antonín Dvořák 1841–1904

RECOMMENDED WORK

Symphony No. 9, 'From the New World'

Deutsche Grammophon 427 202-2
Berlin Philharmonic Orchestra/Rafael Kubelík
A glamorous orchestra in full cry, a master Dvořák conductor at the very height of his powers, and first-class recorded sound.

REPRESENTATIVE WORKS

Symphonies Nos. 7 & 8
Cello Concerto
Violin Concerto
Slavonic Dances
Serenade for strings
String Quartet No. 12, 'The American'
Rusalka

Dvořák was born in a small village on the banks of the river Vltava, approximately 45 miles north of Prague. He left school at age 11 to become an apprentice butcher, and the following year was sent to Zlonce to learn German. Most of his time, however, he spent on music lessons, learning the organ, viola, piano, and basic composition. His interest in music was such that, despite misgivings, his father allowed him to enroll at the Prague Organ School in 1857. There Dvořák received the strict training of a church musician. But after classes he attended as many orchestral concerts as he could, enjoying especially the music of contemporary composers such as Wagner and Schumann.

After graduating in 1859, Dvořák became principal violist in the new Provisional Theater orchestra, conducted after 1866 by Smetana. The need to supplement his income by teaching left Dvořák with limited free time, and in 1871 he gave up the orchestra in order to compose. He fell in love with one of his pupils and wrote a song cycle, *Cypress Trees*, expressing his anguish at her marriage to another man. He soon overcame

Dvořák photographed in 1882

his despondency, however, and in 1873 he married her sister Anna Cermakova.

In 1874, Dvořák entered no fewer than 15 works — including his *Third Symphony* — for the Austrian National prize. He won and received a welcome cash prize and, perhaps more important, the admiration and support of Brahms, who was one of the judges. Brahms put Dvořák in touch with his own publisher, Simrock, who commissioned the popular first set of *Slavonic Dances* in 1878. These robust pieces, notable for sudden mood switches from exuberant dance tunes to dark and melancholy melodies, were played not only in the musical centers of Europe but also in the United States and England.

From this point on Dvořák's fame escalated. In 1884 he received a warm welcome in London, the first of nine visits. Several of his major works, including the *Seventh* and *Eighth Symphonies*, were written for performance in England. Often regarded as Dvořák's greatest work, the *Seventh Symphony* powerfully expresses a mood of tragedy through solemn music overlaid with ominous and foreboding overtones. In contrast, the more relaxed *Eighth Symphony* makes use of folk melodies, conveyed with rhythmic verve and colorful orchestration.

Dvořák was appointed professor of composition at the Prague Conservatory in 1891, but soon after took up the offer of Directorship of the National

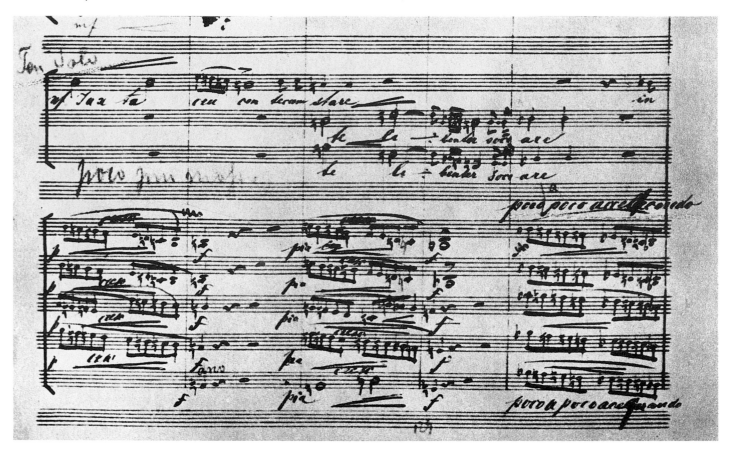

Conservatory of Music in New York. He stayed for three years in the United States, spending summer holidays in Spillville, a Czech-speaking community in Iowa. It is from this period that some of his best-loved music comes, notably the *Symphony No. 9* ('From the New World') and the *American String Quartet*. Both these works make use of themes influenced by Native American folk melodies and Negro spirituals. As Dvořák later admitted, something of their melancholy can be attributed to the homesickness he felt during his time in America. Just before leaving in 1895, he produced his last major symphonic work, the remarkable *Cello Concerto*, which in its expressive power and melodic beauty rivals even the *Seventh Symphony*.

Returning to Prague, Dvořák resumed his post at the Prague Conservatory and in 1901 became its director. For the last three years of his life he devoted the greater part of his creative energies to working on symphonic poems and operas. He died in 1904.

Dvořák's importance lies partly in his nationalist outlook. During the latter half of the nineteenth century, Bohemia (later part of the Czech Republic) — long suppressed under German rule — fought for its political and cultural independence.

Dvořák, like Smetana and Janáček, consciously looked to Bohemian folklore for artistic inspiration, imitating traditional melodies, as in the *Slavonic Dances*, or using traditional legends, as in his best-known opera, *Rusalka*, composed in 1900. Dvořák exercised a great gift for absorbing folk styles and reproducing them in the context of the Classical tradition.

Above: Manuscript of Dvořák's *Stabat Mater*, 1876
This early choral work was commissioned by the London Musical Society.

Below: Bartholdi supervising work on the Statue of Liberty, 1883
During his sojourn in the United States, Dvořák took a keen interest in Native American music.

Wolf

Hugo Wolf 1860–1903

RECOMMENDED WORK

Italienisches Liederbuch
Angel CDM7 63732-2
Elisabeth Schwarzkopf (sop); Dietrich Fischer-
Dieskau (bar); Gerald Moore (pno)
*Two of the century's greatest Lieder singers, both
combining matchless characterization and profound
musical perception, with a supremely supportive
accompaniment from the inimitable Gerald Moore.*

REPRESENTATIVE WORKS
Goethe-Lieder
Mörike-Lieder
Spanisches Liederbuch
Italian Serenade
Der Corregidor

Born in Austria, Hugo Wolf was the fourth of six children. At the age of eight he was taken to see his first opera, Donizetti's *Belisaro*, an important event in his formative years. Overwhelmed, the young boy was afterward able to repeat substantial chunks of it from memory at the piano. However, a willful and stubborn nature inherited from his father did not make him ideal teaching material, and he attended a succession of schools, rarely managing to stay out of trouble for long.

In 1875 he entered the Vienna Conservatory and formed a friendship with the young Gustav Mahler. He regularly went to the opera and developed a passion for Wagner's works. Unfortunately, Wolf's unpredictable temperament again let him down and by March 1877 he was back at home in disgrace after being expelled. He returned to Vienna later that year in order to teach and was adopted by a cultured and intelligent circle of men. Wolf was probably with them when he visited a brothel and contracted the venereal disease that would later drive him insane.

Unable to settle down to composing, he took work as a critic with a respected

Photograph of Wolf's study, c.1905
The composer's workplace, showing the piano at which he composed.

Sunday paper in 1884, producing polemical and often offensive articles — most notably directed against Brahms, for whom Wolf reserved his most vitriolic language. In 1887 his fortunes as a composer began to change, and he wrote the *Italian Serenade* for string quartet, whose lyrical beauty has ensured that it remains his most popular instrumental piece. He also began to compose songs, sometimes at a rate of three a day, and compiled a book of settings of the many-faceted poems of Eduard Mörike known as the *Mörike-Lieder* (1888). These songs were well received by audiences in Vienna and reveal a particularly sensitive and sympathetic

Hugo Wolf photographed in 1889

response to the varying moods of the text. Heartened, Wolf started work on the *Spanish Songbook*, giving the first indication of his passion for Spanish literature and culture, which would culminate in the opera *Der Corregidor* (The Magistrate).

Wolf began *Der Corregidor* in 1895 and finished the first draft in just 14 weeks. The highly dramatic, expressive music proved a great success at its first performance in 1896, but gradually attendances dropped and the work never regained its popularity. In the same year Wolf completed the *Italienisches Liederbuch* (Italian Songbook). The songs in this volume are undoubtedly some of the most perfect ever written, showing a level of refinement uncommon in earlier works and exhibiting at the same time great freshness and charm.

Wolf's health had been deteriorating sharply for some time as his illness took hold. After increasingly debilitating bouts of mental instability, he was committed to an asylum in 1897. When he died six years later he left some of the finest songs ever written, always lyrical and expressive, and constantly searching for profound psychological insight. During his extremely short creative maturity (little more than nine years in all) Wolf proved himself to be, like Schubert and Schumann before him, a song composer of genius.

Leoncavallo

Ruggero Leoncavallo 1857–1919

RECOMMENDED WORK

I Pagliacci
Angel CMS7 63967-2
Franco Corelli (ten) Canio; Lucine Amara (sop)
Nedda; Tito Gobbi (bar) Tonio; Mario Zanasi
(bar) Silvio; Mario Spina (ten) Beppe; Chorus and
Orchestra of La Scala, Milan/Lovro von Matačíc
*Some of the most dramatically potent singing on
record, especially from the incomparable Franco
Corelli. Masterfully conducted by von Matačíc.*

REPRESENTATIVE WORKS

Zazà
Edipo Re
Mattinata

The son of a police magistrate, Leoncavallo was born in Naples and entered the conservatory there in 1866. He remained for ten years before moving on to Bologna University in order to broaden his education, and received a degree in literature two years later.

In 1876, Leoncavallo arranged to have his first opera, *Chatterton*, performed, raising the money himself. His efforts failed when the impresario organizing the venture absconded, taking the funds with him. The composer spent the next few years in poverty, earning a living by playing piano in cafés while traveling across Europe. His fortunes appeared to improve when he was introduced to the publisher Giulio Ricordi, but after several abortive projects Leoncavallo lost patience. Over the next five months he wrote the poem and music of his opera *I Pagliacci*.

In 1892 he took the score to a rival publisher, who immediately arranged a performance in Milan. The opera, based on the experiences of Leoncavallo's father as a judge, makes good use of a plot in which a middle-aged actor murders his young and unfaithful wife. The work was a resounding success, mainly due to the coupling of a melodramatic plot with intensely passionate music: moments of great excitement follow in quick succession, forging a powerful and colorful impression.

In 1893 both Leoncavallo and Puccini independently began setting the text of the popular novel, *La Bohème*, but Leoncavallo's version reached the stage a year after Puccini's and was unable to compete with his rival's already highly popular work. After this he turned to a French subject for his next opera, *Zazà*. This picturesque work is unashamedly sentimental. The emotional and lyrical music requires a skilled soprano with a forceful stage presence if it is to succeed. Although *Zazà* was enthusiastically received at its first performance in 1900, it failed to surpass *Pagliacci*, which remains his most popular opera.

At this time the phonograph record was coming into use, and Leoncavallo was one of the first composers to grasp the opportunities it offered. In 1904 he recorded his best-known song, *Mattinata*, and three years later became the first man to record an entire opera when he conducted *Pagliacci* in the studio. He spent his final years traveling widely to promote his music, and his last opera, *Edipo Re*, was performed posthumously in Chicago in 1920, the year after its composer's death.

Although Leoncavallo never achieved the universal recognition he felt should be his, he was an accomplished musician and his best work has a dramatic appeal that has guaranteed continuing popularity.

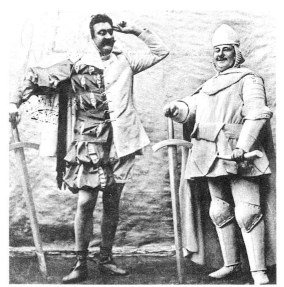
Comic postcard of Leoncavallo (left) posing in theatrical costume, c.1905

Puccini

Giacomo Puccini 1858–1924

RECOMMENDED WORK

Tosca
Angel mono CDS7 47175-8
Maria Callas (sop) Tosca; Giuseppe di Stefano
(ten) Cavaradossi; Tito Gobbi (bar) Scarpia;
Franco Calabrese (bass) Angelotti; Angelo
Mercuriali (ten) Spoletta; Melchiorre Luise (bass)
Sacristan; Dario Caselli (bass) Sciarrone, Gaoler;
Alvaro Cordova (treb) Shepherd Boy; Chorus and
Orchestra of La Scala, Milan/Victor de Sabata
*Although a vintage rendition (1953), this heart-
rending and searingly dramatic performance remains
the yardstick by which all others are judged. The CD
transfer is extremely lifelike.*

REPRESENTATIVE WORKS

Manon Lescaut
La Bohème
Madama Butterfly
La fanciulla del West
La rondine
Gianni Schicchi
Turandot

Born in the Italian town of Lucca into a family with a strong musical tradition, Puccini was encouraged to develop an interest in music from a very early age. His father started him playing the organ, reportedly by placing shiny coins on the keyboard, which tempted the young boy to grasp them and thus push the keys down. At school he showed little promise or dedication, preferring the company of friends and indulging a taste for practical jokes that were often both complicated and theatrical.

After he moved to the local music conservatory, the Pacini Institute, Puccini's academic record began to improve, and by the age of 16 he was showing an increasing interest in composing and improvising at the organ. In 1876 he walked for seven hours to the town of Pisa in order to attend a performance of Verdi's *Aida*, despite not possessing the price of a ticket. The opera awoke in Puccini a sense of the power of

Puccini with his wife Elvira, 1905

The composer and his wife are pictured about to set sail for Buenos Aires.

Poster advertising *Tosca*, 1900

Tosca was criticized for its violent undercurrents, but the public loved it.

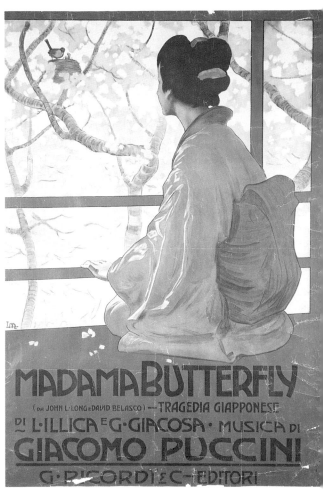

Frontispiece to a score of *Madama Butterfly*, 1904

Puccini followed Tosca with another huge success.

theatrical music, and with the help of a scholarship endowed by none other than the queen of Italy, he was able to enroll at the Milan Conservatory in 1880, at that time the country's biggest and most prestigious music college.

Puccini's first opera, *Le villi*, was produced in 1884, but it was not until *Manon Lescaut* in 1893 that he had a major success. This work set the tone for his later works by concentrating on the psychology of its female heroine. It was followed in 1896 by one of Puccini's best-loved works, *La Bohème* (1896), which was produced in Turin. This tale of the exploits of aspiring artists in the bohemian world of mid-nineteenth-century Paris reflects Puccini's experiences in Milan, and subtly marries sentiment with comedy and tragedy. These qualities, along with its masterly characterization and what Debussy called the 'sheer verve of the music,' have guaranteed its place over the years as one of the most popular operas.

The string of successes continued with his next two operas, *Tosca* (1900) and *Madama Butterfly* (1904). *Tosca* was first performed in Rome in an atmosphere of high tension. The work's anti-authoritarian stance and disrespectful portrait of the clergy fueled rumors that a bomb was to be set off. The premiere passed peacefully, however, and *Tosca* achieved great success with the public, who enjoyed the melodramatic, even sadistic, plot and the composer's unerring sense of timing. In *Butterfly*, which rivals *La Bohème* and *Tosca* in popularity, Puccini achieved his most successful psychological characterization. The part of the heroine — the Japanese geisha who kills herself for love of callous American Lieutenant Pinkerton — requires exceptional vocal and acting skill from the soprano singing the title role.

Puccini's next opera was *La fanciulla del West* (The Girl of the Golden West), first produced in New York in 1910. A rip-roaring drama set in the Wild West, it was

a triumphant success under the guidance of conductor Arturo Toscanini. *La fanciulla* was followed by *La rondine* (The Swallow) and a trio of varied one-act operas — *Il tabarro* (The Overcoat), *Suor Angelica* (Sister Angelica), and *Gianni Schicchi*, known collectively as *Il trittico* — before the composer started work on his final opera, *Turandot*.

Puccini died of cancer before he was able to complete this work, the gruesome story of the wooing of Turandot, Princess of Peking, by an unknown prince who wins her through his courage and persistence. It is performed in a version completed by Franco Alfano. In *Turandot*, as in all the composer's operas, drama laden with erotic passion, tenderness, pathos, and despair is combined with music of breathtaking melodic invention. The mixture has ensured that the works of Puccini, the true successor to Verdi, continue to occupy a place at the center of the operatic repertoire.

Albéniz

Isaac Albéniz 1860–1909

RECOMMENDED WORK
Iberia
London 433 926-2
Alicia de Larrocha (pno)
Albéniz's rich panoramic survey of Spanish life presents de Larrocha with the opportunity to display her pianistic subtlety and charm for the masterwork of her fellow-countryman.

REPRESENTATIVE WORKS
Suite española
España
Cantos de España
Navarra

Born in Catalonia, Isaac Albéniz was a colorful character who showed almost unnatural musical talent; he gave his first piano recital at the age of four. His father, sensing the financial potential of such a prodigy, took him to Paris in 1867, hoping to enroll him at the Conservatoire. After exciting great admiration at his audition, the high-spirited boy spoiled the impression by throwing a ball through the window, whereupon the authorities refused to accept him. Two years later, he entered the conservatory in Madrid, but soon tired of the discipline and ran away, traveling around Spain and giving recitals. After stowing away on a ship bound for South America, he continued his itinerant musical life, giving performances in Argentina, Uruguay, Brazil, Cuba, Puerto Rico, and the United States before finally returning to Spain in 1873.

His youthful energies diminished somewhat, Albéniz embarked upon a period of intense study in Paris, Leipzig, and Brussels. He realized a long-standing ambition in 1878 when he was offered the opportunity to work with his childhood idol, Liszt. Albéniz, a pianist of phenomenal capabilities, toured Europe and, again, South America and became

Photographic portrait of Isaac Albéniz

renowned for performing works by Chopin, Liszt, and Schumann, as well as his own compositions.

In 1883 he married and settled down. He met the Spanish nationalist composer and musicologist Felipe Pedrell, who played a great part in encouraging Albéniz's interest in Spanish folk culture; in 1886 he produced the piano piece *Suite española*, in which Pedrell's influence is evident. Albéniz spent three years in London from 1890 to 1893, then moved to Paris, where he became acquainted with a circle of well-known composers, including Fauré, Debussy, and Dukas. While there he wrote his popular piece for piano, *Cantos de España*, which combines the dazzling virtuosity typical of Liszt with the rhythmic verve of Spanish folk dances.

The years from 1906 until his death in 1909 were spent composing a colorful and exotic suite for the piano titled *Iberia*. It consists of 12 pieces of astounding technical difficulty and has become immensely popular. Invigorating and passionate, the music indisputably stands as Albéniz's crowning achievement as a composer. Like his other works, *Iberia* presents a refreshingly individual view of the central European Romantic tradition by combining it with the panache and vitality of Spanish popular music.

Fauré

Gabriel Fauré 1845–1924

RECOMMENDED WORK
Requiem
London 421 440-2
Kiri Te Kanawa (sop); Sherrill Milnes (bar); Montreal Symphony Choir and Orchestra/Charles Dutoit
The refined timbres of Dutoit's Montreal Orchestra help facilitate a reading of great warmth and piety, luminously recorded and with particularly beautiful solo singing.

REPRESENTATIVE WORKS
Pelléas et Mélisande
Masques et Bergamasques
Pavane
Violin Sonata No. 1
Piano Quartet No. 1
La Bonne Chanson
Nocturnes
Dolly suite
Pénélope

Gabriel Fauré was born in Ariège, in the south of France, the son of a village schoolteacher. Recognizing his son's musical talent, his father sent him to the École Niedermeyer (run by Swiss composer Louis Niedermeyer) in Paris. There the young composer received training as a church musician. But in 1861, Saint-Saëns took over the piano class at the school and introduced Fauré to the music of the great Romantic composers, including Schumann, Liszt, and Wagner. Fauré began writing his own music under the guidance of Saint-Saëns, and in 1865 he left the school, taking with him a first prize for composition.

His first job was as an organist in Rennes, but provincial life did not suit him and he returned to Paris in 1870. He enlisted in the army and took part in raising the siege of Paris during the Franco-Prussian War. After being discharged, he remained in Paris, where he resumed his career as an organist, becoming closely acquainted with the composers Lalo,

During World War I, Fauré remained in Paris and produced some of his most celebrated chamber works, including the *Violin Sonata No. 2* and the *Cello Sonata No. 1*. In general, his music from these years is reflective and introverted, perhaps due to an increasing sense of isolation caused by encroaching deafness. He retired from the Conservatoire in 1920 and died four years later.

In spite of the popularity of his *Requiem*, Fauré excelled above all in 'mood' pieces such as the *Nocturnes* for piano. Over the course of his life he wrote 13 of these beautiful and subtle pieces, which display a melodious and graceful manner derived from Chopin. Most of Fauré's output is on a small scale, but of the few pieces written on a larger scale, the energetic orchestral suite *Masques et Bergamasques* (1919) has remained popular. Although by no means a radical composer, Fauré imbued his music with an elegance and melodic style that are entirely his own.

Fauré (foreground, left) relaxing with members of his family after the premiere of *Prométhée*, 1900

Fauré's first opera is little known today and rarely played.

Duparc, and Chabrier. Together they formed the Société Nationale de Musique, dedicated to the promotion of modern French composers.

In 1887, Fauré started work on what has become his most famous piece, the *Requiem* for choir and orchestra. Its gentle melodic beauty and serene atmosphere contrast starkly with the depression under which Fauré was laboring at the time of its composition. The 1890's brought a series of changes in Fauré's life, however, and his spirits began to revive. In 1896, his growing reputation was recognized when he was appointed professor of composition at the Paris Conservatoire, and the resulting improvement in his financial and social status allowed him to devote more time to composing.

In 1905 he accepted the post of Director of the Conservatoire, and initiated a set of radical reforms that led to a number of resignations among the more conservative-minded staff. Now aged 60, Fauré was finally receiving long-deserved recognition as a composer. His opera *Pénélope* was first performed in 1913.

Unfortunately the theater went bankrupt after only a few weeks, and the remaining performances were canceled. The piece — regarded by many as a masterpiece — never recovered its initial popularity with audiences, despite great melodic charm and vivid characterization.

Autograph sketch for the *String Quartet* in E minor, Opus 121, 1923–34

Fauré was a profound composer of chamber music such as this string quartet.

Mahler

Gustav Mahler 1860–1911

RECOMMENDED WORK

Symphony No. 9
Deutsche Grammophon 427 250-2
Berlin Philharmonic Orchestra/Herbert von
Karajan
*Intensity of expression that reaches almost unbearable
heights in the closing Adagio. A scintillating live
recording from 1983.*

REPRESENTATIVE WORKS

Symphonies Nos. 1–8
Das Lied von der Erde
Lieder eines fahrenden Gesellen

Mahler photographed c.1905

At this time Mahler was director of the Vienna Court Opera.

Poster for performances of the *Eighth Symphony*

Mahler conducted these concerts in the new Festhalle in Munich in 1910.

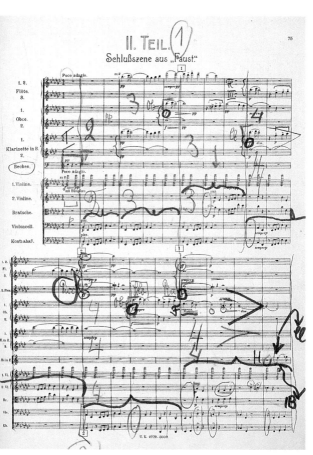

Manuscript of Mahler's *Eighth Symphony*, 1906–7

A page from the second part of the symphony, which is based on the end of Goethe's Faust.

Gustav Mahler was born to Jewish parents in Kališt, Bohemia. He began piano lessons at the age of six, and gave his first public recital four years later. He suffered a traumatic childhood at the hands of a strict father, growing up to be a neurotic and temperamental young man. In 1875 he entered the Vienna Conservatory, where he studied the piano, harmony, and composition. He also developed what was to be a lifelong interest in political and philosophical ideas, which led him to enroll at the university in 1878. The same year he composed his first substantial work, *Das klagende Lied* (The Song of Sorrow), a cantata for four voices, chorus, and orchestra to a text by the composer himself.

Throughout his life, Mahler earned most of his income as a conductor. In 1880 he was appointed to his first conducting post in Upper Austria. During the next few years he moved around from opera house to opera house, gaining vital experience of the standard repertory. While he was at Kassel (1883–85), an unhappy love affair provided the inspiration for his first masterpiece, the song-cycle *Lieder eines fahrenden Gesellen* (Songs of a Wayfarer). He moved to Prague in 1885, and after spells at Leipzig, as second conductor to

Artur Nikisch, and then Budapest, he went to Hamburg in 1891, undertaking the heaviest schedule of his life — conducting as many as 19 operas a month.

By 1894, Mahler had finished his gigantic *Symphony No. 2* in five movements (*Resurrection Symphony*), which lasts for 80 minutes. He had encountered many problems during its composition, and for a long time he was unable to begin the last movement. Then, early in 1894, Mahler attended the funeral of a friend. At the climax of the service the choir intoned the *Resurrection Ode* by eighteenth-century German poet Friedrich Klopstock; Mahler rushed home and immediately set to work using this as the basis for the missing movement. As well as its choral finale, the *Resurrection Symphony* includes a setting for alto voice of texts from a collection of folk poetry titled *Des Knaben Wunderhorn*, which Mahler returned to for his *Third* and *Fourth Symphonies*.

By 1893, Mahler had established his lifelong pattern of composing in the summer and conducting in the winter. In 1897 he renounced his Jewish faith in order to gain the coveted post of Director of the Vienna Court Opera. His achievements there marked one of the most glorious decades in the Opera House's prestigious history. In 1898 he became conductor of the Vienna Philharmonic. He attracted large audiences, but his authoritarian manner and unconventional musical views antagonized players and administrators alike. In 1902 he married Alma Schindler, with whom he had two daughters. The marriage did not always run smoothly, as Mahler demanded that his wife arrange her life entirely around his. The problems between them came to a head in 1910 when Alma's affair with the architect Walter Gropius led Mahler to consult Sigmund Freud.

During his time in Vienna, Mahler composed five symphonies (Nos. 4–8) and a song cycle, *Kindertotenlieder* (Children's Death Songs). The *Sixth Symphony* in particular is enormously powerful and includes three massive chords that represent three hammerblows of fate, the last being fatal. The music affected Mahler so profoundly at the first performance that he was incapable of conducting properly and deleted the third blow, fearful of its prophecy of death. The *Eighth Symphony* surpasses anything written before it in terms of the forces required, using such a massive orchestra, choir, and cast of soloists that it acquired the nickname 'Symphony of a Thousand.'

Despite these successes, Mahler left Vienna in the face of an increasingly virulent anti-Semitic smear campaign initiated by the press. He accepted an offer by the New York Metropolitan Opera and left for the United States at the end of 1907. One of his daughters died that year, and at the same time his health began to suffer seriously, a result of the constant strain he had imposed upon himself all his life. He returned to Europe and died in 1911, leaving three unperformed masterpieces — the *Ninth Symphony*, a work clearly preoccupied with the shadow of death; the beautiful symphonic song cycle *Das Lied von der Erde* (Song of the Earth); and an unfinished *Tenth Symphony*.

Mahler's works fell from favor after his death, but his symphonies, longer and more complex than anyone had dared write before, are now recognized as works of genius.

Nielsen

Carl Nielsen 1865–1931

RECOMMENDED WORK
Symphony No. 5
Sony SMK47598
New York Philharmonic Orchestra/Leonard Bernstein
A towering interpretation that releases the full voltage of Nielsen's electrifying musical vision.

REPRESENTATIVE WORKS
Symphony No. 4, 'The Inextinguishable'
Violin Concerto
Clarinet Concerto

Carl Nielsen, the central figure in late Romantic Danish music, was born into a poor family of 14 children. During school vacations he supplemented the family income by looking after geese. Music was an early interest, and the boy used to bang out tunes on different lengths of firewood. His education, although basic, awakened a respect for learning, and throughout his life he studied literature, philosophy, art, and languages. After receiving funding from a wealthy benefactor, he was able to study the violin, piano, history, and composition at Copenhagen Conservatory from 1884 to 1886, and in 1889 he joined the orchestra of the Royal Chapel as a violinist. He took part in a number of productions of Wagner operas, followed by a trip to Berlin specifically to study Wagner's works.

In 1892, Nielsen completed the first of his six symphonies, a work revealing knowledge of both Brahms and Dvořák and one of the earliest pieces to begin in one key and end in another. His growing reputation as a composer was recognized officially in 1901, when he was awarded a state pension to relieve his precarious financial situation. Nielsen's preoccupation with depicting human emotions — seen in his opera *Saul and David* (1902) — is echoed in a more abstract manner in his

Second Symphony (1901–2), which illustrates a different temperament in each of its four movements — Choleric, Phlegmatic, Melancholic, and Sanguine.

In 1908 he became music director of the Royal Theater in Copenhagen, strengthening his position within Danish musical life. At the height of his powers, Nielsen completed two major works in 1911: the *Sinfonia espansiva*, a powerful work expressing the warm and sunny aspect of his character, and the *Violin Concerto*. The war years saw a period of intense productivity, and in 1916 he finished his *Fourth Symphony* (*The Inextinguishable*), a tough and dramatic work that includes a 'battle' between two sets of timpani in the final movement.

The deterioration of Nielsen's marriage imposed a strain that combined with feverish musical activities to affect his health. Despite this he composed two more symphonies — his fifth (1922) and sixth, the *Sinfonia semplice* (Simple Symphony, 1925). In 1928 he wrote the *Clarinet Concerto*, an angry work lightened by flashes of humor that have ensured its lasting popularity. Nielsen died in 1931, revered in his home country almost as a national institution.

Royal Theatre, Copenhagen, Denmark, c.1900
The city of Copenhagen has been an important musical center since the sixteenth century.

Debussy

Claude Debussy 1862–1918

RECOMMENDED WORK

La Mer

Deutsche Grammophon 427 250-2
Berlin Philharmonic Orchestra/Herbert von
Karajan
*Refinement of execution and a genuine sense of
maritime atmosphere — the sea, the sky, the crying
gulls, and the swell of the waves.*

REPRESENTATIVE WORKS

Prélude à l'après-midi d'un faune
Images
Jeux
String Quartet
Préludes, Book 1
Suite bergamasque — Clair de lune
Children's Corner
Pelléas et Mélisande

Costume design by Léon Bakst, 1912
*This costume was worn by Nijinsky in the
scandalous ballet version of Prélude à
l'après-midi d'un faune.*

Debussy with his daughter Chouchou, 1916
*Chouchou brought stability to the
composer's stormy private life. She was
the dedicatee of Children's Corner.*

Claude Debussy was born in St. Germain-
en-Laye and was encouraged to take up
music at an early age. He entered the Paris
Conservatoire at the age of ten, and
quickly learned to play a considerable
repertoire of very difficult piano works.
However, he abandoned his planned
career as a virtuoso pianist when he joined
the Conservatoire's composition class in
1880 and won the coveted Prix de Rome
competition twice. He traveled extensively in these early years, visiting Italy,
Vienna, and Russia. He also spent two
unhappy years studying in Rome. He was
known as a moody, unsociable youth who
found it difficult to endure the company of
strangers even temporarily.

Debussy returned from Rome in 1887,
and in 1888 and 1889 followed the well-
worn path to Bayreuth in order to sample
Wagner's genius. In 1889, he also attended
the World Exhibition in Paris, where,
like Ravel, he was enthralled by the
Javanese gamelan music. During this time
he set up house with a girlfriend, Gabrielle
Dupont, with whom he would live in
poverty for six years.

In 1892 he began one of his best-
known orchestral works, *Prélude à l'après-
midi d'un faune*. At the first performance it
was enthusiastically received and accorded
an immediate encore, and the work is now
recognized as breaking new musical
ground with its unconventional and
'impressionistic' harmonies. Based on a
poem by Stéphane Mallarmé that
describes the dreams and desires of a faun
basking in the afternoon heat, the music
consists of a beautiful and sensual mosaic of
sound graphically depicting the erotic
content of the poem.

In 1893, Debussy began work on his
only completed opera, *Pelléas et Mélisande*.
It took the composer almost ten years to
finish and was premiered at the Opéra-
Comique in 1902. The music turns away
from the drama and thunderous passion of
Wagnerian opera, remaining for the most
part subdued and always allowing the
words to be clearly audible. The trance-
like quality of the score almost hypnotizes
the listener with a new and beautiful world

of sound. For many *Pelléas et Mélisande* is Debussy's finest creation.

The years 1904 and 1905 were especially fertile for Debussy. He completed the first book of *Images* for piano and the popular orchestral work *La Mer* (The Sea), which makes full use of the impressionistic techniques developed in previous works. At the same time, Debussy's personal life was in tumult. In 1904 he left his wife, Lily, whom he had married barely five years before, to move in with a wealthy woman, Emma Bardac, who was later to become his second wife. Distraught, his first wife shot herself; she was badly wounded and taken to a nursing home. An enormous scandal ensued, fueled by comments from the press. Many of the composer's friends held him to blame and broke with him in disgust. During this time he was also plagued by a series of lawsuits, a result of debts that continued to plague him until his death.

Debussy was now well established and his music increasingly performed, although controversy attended nearly every new work at its first performance. A second book of *Images* for piano was followed in 1908 by the delightful collection of piano pieces *Children's Corner*, dedicated to his daughter, Chouchou. From this set the *Golliwogg's Cakewalk* is especially well known, featuring a playful skit on the opening of Wagner's opera *Tristan und Isolde*. He completed two sets of *Préludes* in 1910 and 1913 and a book of *Etudes* in 1915 — also for the piano. Debussy's last major orchestral work, the ballet score *Jeux*, has been described as 'a beautiful nightmare.' Commissioned by Diaghilev, it was premiered in 1912.

In 1909, Debussy was diagnosed as having cancer, and by 1915 the illness was so serious that he had to undergo surgery. He died in 1918, internationally recognized as the foremost French composer of his time. The use of exotic and unconventional harmonies, together with the delicate coloring that characterizes his work, have revealed Debussy as an innovator who has inspired generations of subsequent composers, and have ensured him a position among the greatest of twentieth-century composers.

Satie

Erik Satie 1866–1925

RECOMMENDED WORK
3 Gymnopédies
London 417 768-2
Pascal Rogé (pno)
Calm and controlled, yet beautifully shaped and full of feeling, Pascal Rogé's readings reach the heart of these poignant and affectingly simple pieces.

REPRESENTATIVE WORKS
6 Gnossiennes
Trois Morceaux en forme de poire
Sports et divertissements
Parade
Socrate

Satie was born in the northern French town of Honfleur to a French father and a Scottish mother. He studied at the Paris Conservatoire but, although gifted, was not an instant success as a musician and gained a reputation for laziness and unreliability. In 1888, however, while working as a pianist in the Montmartre quarter of Paris, he wrote his three famous piano pieces, the *Gymnopédies*. These are constructed from short but perfectly formed melodic phrases that are repeated and juxtaposed but never transformed and developed in the German style.

In 1890, Satie met Claude Debussy, with whom he would maintain a lifelong friendship. The same year, he wrote three exotic piano pieces titled *Gnossiennes*, which are strongly influenced by oriental music. At this time he was frequenting the cafés in Montmartre where artists met to discuss and argue; for Satie, this world was a revelation after his middle-class upbringing, and he turned to bohemianism with increasing enthusiasm. Relations with his family became strained, and he lived in a series of progressively shabbier flats as his funds dwindled. At the same time Satie happily continued to promote a reputation as an outrageous exhibitionist.

In 1898, conscious of his lack of musical education, he moved out of the area and shed his bohemian image. He returned to student life in 1905, studying basic compositional technique with d'Indy and trying to forge a more mature musical style. In 1911 his fortunes finally began to change, and the assiduous promotion of his music by friends such as Ravel brought him to the forefront of public attention. Four years later he met the playwright and poet Jean Cocteau, with whom he produced a ballet, *Parade*. This caused great scandal in the musical world with its prodigious use of slapstick comedy. The orchestral forces require unusual instruments: a typewriter, a steamboat whistle, and a pistol.

By now well established, Satie began work on a cantata, *Socrate*. After the succession of musical jokes to which the public had grown accustomed, the seriousness and intensity of this piece surprised and puzzled audiences. At the time of its premiere in 1920, Satie was at the height of his fame and enjoying a hectic social life. But his heavy drinking proved to be his downfall, and in his last years he grew increasingly taciturn and moody. In 1925, he died in Paris. The first French composer of his generation to free himself from the pervasive influence of Wagner, Satie left a body of music that was of the utmost originality and a source of inspiration for many composers wanting to steer away from the dominance of the Austro-German musical tradition.

Caricature of Satie by A. Frueh, c.1915

Scriabin

Alexander Scriabin 1872–1915

RECOMMENDED WORK
La Poème de l'estase
Deutsche Grammophon 427 324-2
New York Philharmonic Orchestra/Giuseppe Sinopoli
A kaleidoscopic arena of orchestral sound — from the gentle mists of the Poème's opening pages to the massive sonorities of its final full-throated climax.

REPRESENTATIVE WORKS
Symphony No. 3
Preludes

Scriabin at the piano, drawing by L. Pasternak, 1909

Alexander Scriabin was born into an aristocratic family in Moscow and grew up a precocious and egocentric child. After spending nine years in the Moscow Cadet Corps, where music played a significant part in the curriculum, he entered the Moscow Conservatory at the age of 16. There he met Rachmaninov; they were to remain firm friends despite attempts by the press to create a rivalry between them.

Scriabin left the Conservatory in 1892 to pursue a career as a concert pianist. He became renowned for his interpretations

of works by composers such as Chopin, Liszt, and Schumann. In 1894 he met the Russian publisher Belyayev, who took complete control of Scriabin's musical affairs and immediately published his first *Piano sonata*, a work clearly influenced by Chopin's music.

The years 1895 and 1896 were taken up with extensive concert tours in Europe. He composed prolifically, mainly concentrating on short but dramatic pieces such as the set of 24 *Preludes* (Opus 11) for the piano. On returning to Moscow, he joined the staff at the Conservatory and married a gifted piano student.

Scriabin's first major success as an orchestral composer came in 1900 when his *First Symphony* was performed. Consisting of six movements, it includes a choral finale that sets to music a text praising art and written by Scriabin. By 1902 he was becoming increasingly preoccupied with philosophical and mystical ideas. A deeply serious man, he now gained a reputation for indulging in prolonged intellectual debate. His thirst for inner knowledge made him ever more isolated from everyday reality and increased his egocentricity. But if his personality was adversely affected, his compositions became less derivative, more adventurous, and increasingly complex and dissonant.

Star Sonata, Allegro, 1908, by Mikolajus Ciurlionis
Like Ciurlionis, who gave musical titles to his paintings, Scriabin sought to unify visual and musical forms in his works.

During this period he wrote the *Third Symphony*, completed in 1903, which takes the form of one gigantic movement and juxtaposes lyrical passages with moments of great violence.

In 1904 he again left Russia and traveled to Italy, Switzerland, and Belgium. He did not take his wife, having become involved with a much younger woman. His new companion provided the admiration bordering on hero worship that Scriabin demanded, and the relationship stimulated another period of intense activity. He wrote a lengthy text titled *La Poème de l'estase* (Poem of Ecstasy) that formed the basis for several future compositions, including the *Fifth Piano Sonata* and a complex orchestral work bearing the name of the text.

The following year Scriabin returned to Russia and composed his last five sonatas for piano, all of which are extraordinarily dense and dramatic in impact. Although he died at the age of 43, his music achieved enormous popularity during his final years, and he enjoyed international fame and recognition.

Busoni

Ferruccio Busoni 1866–1924

RECOMMENDED WORK
Piano Concerto
Angel CDC7 49996-2
Peter Donohoe (pno); BBC Singers; BBC
Symphony Orchestra/Mark Elder
A thinker's rendition of this most epic and 'philosophical' of piano concertos: powerful, expansive, but never indulgent.

REPRESENTATIVE WORKS
Fantasia contrappuntistica
Doktor Faust

Photograph of Busoni, c.1905

Busoni was born to musical parents near Florence in Italy. He showed much early promise and at the age of 12 conducted one of his own compositions. In 1881 he went to the Reale Accademia Filarmonica at Bologna, where his prodigious talents were quickly noticed. He composed intensively during his youth and in 1883 produced an oratorio, *Il sabato de villaggio*, that received great acclaim. As he matured he became more self-critical, and his output diminished as he subjected many works to substantial revision.

In 1886, Busoni studied with Carl Reinecke in Leipzig. There he met a host of important musicians, including Tchaikovsky, Grieg, Mahler, and Delius. The following year he visited Helsinki, where he met Sibelius. Shortly afterward he toured the United States, solidifying his reputation as a virtuoso pianist.

In 1894, Busoni settled in Berlin, which except for during World War I was his home for the rest of his life. He absorbed and contributed to the progressive spirit of this city, renowned as a center of artistic excellence. In 1902 he organized a series of orchestral concerts designed to promote the work of modern composers; he premiered pieces by Bartók, Debussy, Delius, and Sibelius, as well as his own works.

The following year he started work on a *Piano Concerto*, which clearly shows the influence of Liszt. The difficult piano part does not rely on displays of virtuosity and frequently takes a subordinate role to the orchestra. The music's intensity becomes frenzied and culminates in the introduction of a male voice choir in the final movement.

In 1907, Busoni published a forward-looking treatise titled *Outline of a New Aesthetic of Music*, in which he propounded his idea of a modern but understandable style of composition. His own work, unfortunately, was often badly received and denounced by Berlin critics for its use of Italian rather than German traditions.

In the closing days of 1909 he once more set sail for the United States, where he undertook a hectic schedule of concerts. Despite this he found time to write another large-scale piano work, *Fantasia contrappuntistica*. This takes the form of a gigantic fugue (a highly structured musical form requiring great compositional skill) modeled on Bach's *Art of Fugue*.

In his last years Busoni became increasingly interested in the stage and began work on a setting of Goethe's *Faust*. The resulting intensely expressive and concentrated work, *Doktor Faust*, attained a degree of spirituality and mysticism unique in opera. The work remained unfinished on his death. But in 1925, a posthumous performance of a version completed by Philipp Jarnach was seen to embody the struggle between tradition and innovation that epitomized Busoni's life's work.

Scene from Busoni's *Arlecchino*, Darmstadt, 1925
Composed in 1916, Arlecchino drew on the traditions of commedia dell'arte.

Sibelius

Jean Sibelius 1865–1957

RECOMMENDED WORK
Symphony No. 5
London 430 749-2
Philharmonia Orchestra/Vladimir Ashkenazy
With superlative sound and gloriously full-bodied playing from the Philharmonia, Ashkenazy's recording adds weight and substance to Sibelius's predominantly desolate musical landscape.

REPRESENTATIVE WORKS
Symphonies Nos. 2 & 7
Finlandia
Tapiola
Violin Concerto
String Quartet in D minor, 'Voces intimae'

Watercolor portrait by Axel Gallen-Kallela, 1894

Renowned as Finland's greatest composer, Jean Sibelius showed early musical ability as a violinist and composer. He attained a thorough knowledge of Viennese classics through playing in his family's string trio. In 1885 he enrolled in a law course at the University of Helsinki, but it was soon clear that his ambitions lay in music. The following year, he moved to the Conservatory, where he developed a friendship with the composer Busoni, a member of the teaching staff. In 1889,

Sibelius made a two-year trip abroad to study in Berlin and Vienna. He formed a taste for high society during this period: heavy drinking and extravagance led to the beginning of financial problems that would beset him for some time to come.

Sibelius returned to Finland in 1892 and married Aino Järnefelt, a member of an aristocratic Finnish family. Their marriage survived until Sibelius's death in 1957, despite his debts and drinking. A visit to Bayreuth, the home of Wagnerian opera, in 1894 had a profound effect on the young Sibelius. He abandoned an early opera, perhaps feeling unable to compete with Wagner, and concentrated instead on symphonic music. The result was heard in 1899, when both the *First Symphony* and *Finlandia* were performed to great acclaim. The latter was composed for a pageant that became a rallying point for Finnish nationalists at a time when Russian domination of the country was increasing.

The first decade of the twentieth century saw a massive growth in Sibelius's international reputation. He traveled extensively, and was received warmly in England and the United States. In 1901 he met Dvořák in Prague and spent the rest of the year working on the *Second Symphony*, which takes a more overtly nationalist stance than his other symphonies. One of his most frequently performed works, the

Part of the manuscript of the *Violin Concerto*, 1903
Sibelius had hopes of becoming a virtuoso violinist.

Violin Concerto, was composed in 1903 and became immediately successful.

This was also a period of extravagance and mounting debt. In 1908, Sibelius became seriously ill and was forced to give up smoking and drinking for some years. The threat to his life posed by a suspected cancer may well account for a renewed concentration and depth in the works that followed. His symphonies are notable for their organic growth, subtly achieved forms, and refined instrumentation.

The *Fifth Symphony*, his most popular, was composed during World War I. Heroic in mood, it is accessible and contains some of his most colorful music. The postwar years saw only four major new works by Sibelius: the final symphonies (Nos. 6 and 7), incidental music to Shakespeare's *The Tempest*, and finally the tone poem *Tapiola* in 1925.

Despite rumors of an eighth symphony, Sibelius lived out his remaining 30 years in musical silence. Many reasons have been suggested for this, his drinking and disillusionment with modern music being most often cited. Whatever the reason, Sibelius had already proven himself a composer of the highest rank.

Falla

Manuel de Falla 1876–1946

RECOMMENDED WORK

El amor brujo
Deutsche Grammophon 429 181-2
Teresa Berganza (mez); London Symphony
Orchestra/Garcia Navarro
*Fiery singing and orchestral playing that combines
passion, strong rhythms, and vivid tonal color.*

REPRESENTATIVE WORKS
Nights in the Gardens of Spain
The Three-Cornered Hat
Harpsichord Concerto
Siete canciones populares españolas
El Retablo de Maese Pedro
La vida breve — Danse espagnole No. I

Spanish dancers and musicians, Seville, 1900
*Falla's Andalusian roots are always
reflected in his music.*

Falla and the choreographer Massine at the
Alhambra, Granada, 1919

Manuel de Falla was Spain's first major nationalist composer. Born in Cádiz, Andalusia, he received his first piano lessons from his mother. He was torn between a literary and a musical career, but having decided on music, he proceeded to work hard at both the piano and composition. In 1902 he went to study with the Spanish composer and musicologist Felipe Pedrell, who was known for his belief that a country's music should draw on its native folk culture, and who impressed this on his pupils. He found a kindred spirit in Falla, whose first major work, the opera *La vida breve* (The Short Life; 1905), made copious use of local folklore.

In 1907, Falla traveled to Paris, where he was befriended by musicians such as Debussy and Ravel. At the outbreak of World War I, he returned to Spain and entered his most creative period. In 1915 he composed *El amor brujo* (Love the Magician), a ballet inspired by Spanish folk art, and the following year wrote one of his most beautiful and moving works, *Noches en los jardines de España* (Nights in the Gardens of Spain). This suite of three symphonic impressions for piano and orchestra integrates Spanish folk music with colorful orchestration reminiscent of Rimsky-Korsakov. Of the three movements the first is the most atmospheric and makes use of shimmering, drifting harmonies, while the second and third are more exuberant and dancelike.

Falla's reputation was firmly established in 1919 with the ballet *El sombrero de tres picos* (The Three-Cornered Hat). Full of humor and panache, it was well-received at its premiere in London. The enthrallingly vital and dramatic last movement can hardly fail to excite as the music sweeps the listener along. It is Falla's music at its most witty and ebullient, rhythmical and lyrical, treating the orchestra almost as a giant guitar.

Given his interest in Spanish nationalism, it is not surprising that Falla chose to set parts of Cervantes' *Don Quixote*. The resulting chamber opera, *El Retablo de Maese Pedro* (Master Peter's Puppet Show), was first performed in 1923 and consolidated Falla's reputation as a composer of flair and dexterity. His last major work was a *Harpsichord Concerto*, written in 1926 for the Polish virtuoso Wanda Landowska. After this Falla became less productive musically. The traumas of the Spanish Civil War (1936–39) nearly crushed him, so delicate was his state of health. In 1939 he accepted an invitation to Argentina, where he lived until his death in 1946.

Although no revolutionary, Falla successfully shaped elements of traditional Spanish music and created a colorful musical style distinctly his own.

Elgar

Edward Elgar 1857–1934

RECOMMENDED WORKS

Enigma Variations
Deutsche Grammophon 429 713-2
Royal Philharmonic Orchestra/Norman Del Mar
A deeply felt, supremely idiomatic account of Elgar's masterpiece. The sumptuous Guildford Cathedral acoustic lends a most beguiling bloom to proceedings.

Cello Concerto
EMI CDC7 47329-2
Jacqueline Du Pré (vcl); London Symphony Orchestra/John Barbirolli
Still one of the best loved of all classical recordings. Du Pré plays with consummate virtuosity and enormous poignancy; Barbirolli's accompaniment positively glows.

REPRESENTATIVE WORKS
Symphonies Nos. 1 & 2
Cockaigne
Pomp and Circumstance March No.1
Falstaff
Introduction and Allegro
Violin Concerto
The Dream of Gerontius

Edward Elgar was born in an area of beautiful English countryside near Malvern in Worcestershire and spent his formative years in Worcester living above his father's music shop. There he had unlimited access to music scores and painstakingly taught himself the rudiments of composition. His lack of a formal musical education, except for lessons from a local violin teacher, and the social stigma attached to being a tradesman's son left deep marks in his psyche, and he never fully acquired the confidence to match his talent.

At the age of 15 he left school and began to earn a living in a solicitor's office. However, he soon realized his true vocation and left to pursue the career of a freelance musician. Taking advantage of an abundance of local work, he taught himself to play many instruments, developing a prowess on the violin and a working knowledge of the piano, double-bass,

cello, bassoon, and trombone. In 1882 he took his first job outside Worcester. As a violinist in a Birmingham orchestra conducted by W. C. Stockley, he saw some of his earliest compositions first performed. Three years later he succeeded his father as organist at a local church.

In 1889, Elgar married into a family far superior to his own in social status. Alice, daughter of Major-General Sir Henry Gee Roberts, KCB, provided the temperamental composer with firm support through the bouts of depression that periodically assailed him. The following year they moved to London to broaden Elgar's career prospects, but the venture proved

Elgar conducting a recording session, London, 1914
This early orchestral recording took place at the Gramophone Company's studio.

The coronation procession of Edward VII, 1902
Some of Elgar's best music was in a ceremonial or patriotic vein, such as the **Pomp and Circumstance March No. 1.**

a failure. The couple returned to Worcestershire in 1891. He returned to his old life and took pupils in order to earn a living. Even so, he was truly happy only when composing — he once said that teaching was akin to turning a grindstone with a dislocated shoulder!

The 1890's saw Elgar's first successes as a composer. In 1899 the performance in London of his orchestral work *Variations on an Original Theme (Enigma)* brought national prominence. Each variation depicts one of his friends and shows his consummate skill in catching and musically portraying different moods. It is a

warm, intimate, and indisputably great work that still sounds fresh today. The 'enigma' is the hidden tune that Elgar said the music was based on. Ever since its composition debate has continued over the identity of the theme, suggestions ranging from 'Auld Lang Syne' to 'God Save the Queen.' Recently a new solution was proposed, that the enigma is in fact a theme from the slow movement of Mozart's *Prague Symphony* (No. 38). Because his publisher only paid royalties on non-orchestral compositions, Elgar reckoned that by 1904 he had made a grand total of £8 ($15) from what is probably his most often performed work.

In 1900, Elgar completed his masterpiece, *The Dream of Gerontius*, based on Cardinal Newman's long poem. Despite a disastrous first performance, the work gained widespread acclaim. This extremely emotional and expressive statement amply justifies Elgar's message to his audience written on the final pages of the score: 'This is the best of me; for the rest I ate and drank and slept, loved and hated like another . . . this, if anything of mine, is worth your memory.'

His reputation was assured in 1901 when his *Pomp and Circumstance Marches* were first performed. The ceremonial glory of the five marches, particularly the first of the set, have proven that good music can also be truly popular. Elgar was knighted in 1904; the following year he composed the *Introduction and Allegro*, a lyrical and profound piece for string orchestra. He also finished two symphonies (1908 and 1911) that show the composer at his most powerful and moody — the music is noble, exuberant, melancholy, warmly emotional, and frenetic. His changeable and passionate temperament is again seen in the *Violin Concerto* (1909–10) and in the *Cello Concerto* (1918–19). This last work is practically his final utterance. After Alice's death in 1920 and until his own death fourteen years later, he produced only works derived from earlier sketches. However, his reputation, both national and international, was unshakably established by this time and he remains one of England's greatest composers.

Strauss

Richard Strauss 1864–1949

Also sprach Zarathustra
RCA 09026 61494-2
Chicago Symphony Orchestra/Fritz Reiner
Master Straussian Fritz Reiner presides over a fabulous account, aided by some stunningly eloquent orchestral playing. You would never guess the recording was 40 years old.

Four Last Songs
Deutsche Grammophon 423 888-2
Gundula Janowitz (sop); Berlin Philharmonic Orchestra/Herbert von Karajan
With Janowitz in glorious voice and orchestral playing that is the stuff of dreams, the seductive glow of this performance is impossible to resist.

REPRESENTATIVE WORKS
Don Juan
Death and Transfiguration
Don Quixote
Ein Heldenleben
Salome
Der Rosenkavalier
Metamorphosen

The son of a brilliant horn player, Strauss came to music early in life. His first piano lessons began at the age of four, and by six he was composing. In 1881, his first symphony and string quartet, both written when Strauss was 16, were performed in Munich. He entered the University of Munich in 1882, studying philosophy, aesthetics, and the history of art while continuing his music studies privately. He benefited immensely from being able to attend the rehearsals of the Munich Court Orchestra where his father worked. By 1884 he had found his vocation and left the university to concentrate on music. Composition came easily to him, and even at this early stage he wrote many fine works, including the vivacious *Horn Concerto No. 1.*

In 1885 he was appointed assistant conductor at Meiningen, rising to principal

Photograph of Strauss with his wife and son, *c.*1915

conductor a few months later. However, he had his sights set firmly on greater things and moved on quickly to the Munich Court Opera, gathering valuable experience in the operatic repertoire. Like Mahler, throughout his life he earned a living by conducting, using his free time to compose. He later met Mahler and, though wary of one another, they became friends.

In 1889, Strauss began work at the Weimar Opera House and gained his first compositional success with the symphonic poem *Don Juan*, rapidly establishing a reputation as the most significant German composer since Wagner. The period from 1894 to 1902 was one of intense activity, during which Strauss continued his series of symphonic tone poems (works that refer to an external 'program' — often a book — and use instruments to tell a story or illustrate a theme). Among these, *Also sprach Zarathustra* (Thus Spake Zarathustra, 1896) is one of the grandest in design: based on the text by Nietzsche, it uses huge orchestral forces to depict the evolution of the human race. *Don Quixote* (1897–98) is a portrayal of scenes from the classic novel by Cervantes, in which the

Title page of a piano score of *Salome*, 1905

This controversial opera was based on Oscar Wilde's play about the death of John the Baptist.

Title page of a piano score of *Elektra*, 1909

Elektra was first in a series of successful collaborations between Strauss and librettist Hugo von Hofmannsthal.

cello represents the knight and the viola his servant, Sancho Panza. *Symphonia Domestica* (1902–3) describes in music a day in the life of Strauss's own household.

Strauss accepted the post of chief conductor at the Royal Court Opera at Berlin in 1898 and during his first season conducted 71 performances of 25 different operas. The next decade was also one of frenetic compositional activity. His third opera, *Salome*, from Oscar Wilde's play, caused massive controversy when performed in 1905. This sensual and erotic work was received with such enthusiasm at the first performance that Strauss had to make 38 curtain calls. Despite dealing with a biblical subject, the music is dramatic and sexual in a manner that had never before been heard, and the scandal it provoked led to huge attendances across Germany.

In 1909, Strauss produced *Elektra*, his first opera to a libretto by German poet Hugo von Hofmannsthal. The emotionally charged music and the story of vengeance and burning resentment again attracted media attention: opera houses were packed with audiences wanting to

hear the 'decadent' and 'immoral' music. Hofmannsthal would be Strauss's regular collaborator until his death in 1929.

Strauss's next opera, *Der Rosenkavalier*, was a shock of a different nature. Without warning, Strauss renounced his reputation as a 'progressive' composer, and produced a Mozartian opera full of memorable tunes and Viennese waltzes. It is a warm, human work, received with an almost universal acclaim that has never abated. It is a measure of Strauss's prominence that special *Rosenkavalier* trains ran from Berlin to Dresden for the first performance. He followed the work with the delightful *Ariadne auf Naxos*, a subtle combination of the comic and the romantic.

Immediately after World War I, Strauss signed a five-year contract with the Vienna Opera House, then perhaps the most prestigious position in Europe. His magnificence as a conductor was incontrovertible, but he was forced to resign in 1924 due to antagonism with the management, who regarded his infamous financial extravagance as unacceptable. The rest of the interwar period was less happy. His compositions met with diminishing success, and rumors of connections with the Nazis led to difficulties; the extent of his involvement with Hitler's government is still a shadowy and controversial subject.

Undoubtedly his true concern was music, but his conducting of Wagner's *Parsifal* in 1933, after the previous conductor had resigned in protest at the Nazi regime, lost him much respect outside Germany.

Among Strauss's late works is the conversation piece *Capriccio*, which discusses the relative importance in opera of words and music. He continued to compose thoughout World War II, and was stimulated by its horrors to a final outpouring of compositions. *Metamorphosen* (1945), for 23 strings, is an elegy for the pre-war German musical life shattered beyond recognition by the conflict. In 1945 he moved to Switzerland while being investigated by the denazification board; he returned to Berlin a free citizen three years later. He died in 1949, a year after completing the serenely beautiful *Four Last Songs*, settings of poems by Hesse and Eichendorff for soprano and orchestra.

Termed by many the last of the great Romantics, Strauss left an extraordinary catalogue of works, whose power and warmth have earned them an unassailable position in musical life today.

Ravel

Maurice Ravel 1875–1937

RECOMMENDED WORK
Daphnis et Chloé
Erato 4509-91712-2
London Symphony Orchestra and Chorus/Kent Nagano
A genuine sense of fantasy and theater, and a recording that captures even the subtlest detail in Ravel's multi-colored scoring.

REPRESENTATIVE WORKS
Piano Concerto in G
Piano Concerto for Left Hand
Rapsodie espagnole
Boléro
Pavane pour une infante défunte
Gaspard de la nuit

Renowned for its eclectic, individual style and rebellious nature, Ravel's music is the product of scrupulous craftsmanship. Ravel was born in the Pyrenees but brought up in Paris. He began piano lessons at the age of seven and entered the Paris Conservatoire in 1889. As a child he was easily distracted from his studies, and his mother resorted to offering him bribes for each hour of work completed. A tutor's nightmare, he refused to obey musical conventions in his compositions and took mischievous delight in hunting down similar examples in the works of established masters.

One of the most important events of his formative years was his attendance at the Paris World Exhibition of 1889. There he responded with great excitement to his first contact with oriental harmonies, performances on the Javanese gamelan. He also attended many concerts of Russian music. Rimsky-Korsakov was an immediate favorite, and later in life Ravel's orchestration of Mussorgsky's *Pictures at an Exhibition* established the work in the orchestral repertoire.

Ravel left the Conservatoire in 1895 but returned two years later to study with

Above: Costume design for *L'Enfant et les sortilèges*, 1949

Above: Costume design for *Boléro*, 1941

Ravel at the piano, 1928
Ravel is pictured here on his American tour of 1927–28. George Gershwin appears on the right.

Fauré, whose sympathetic and liberal-minded encouragement did much to develop his style. This is seen in the lyrical *String Quartet in F major* (1903), whose silky and charming character emulates Fauré's own style. Despite the success of this work, Ravel could not satisfy the Conservatoire authorities when it came to harmony exercises. In 1905, after he failed to pass the first stage in the coveted *Prix de Rome* competition, the press took up his cause and a heated debate ensued. The furor was so great that Théodore Dubois, Director of the Conservatoire, resigned his post to be replaced by Fauré. The only person who appeared indifferent to these events was Ravel himself: he was happily yachting in the Netherlands at the time.

In 1908 he completed a three-part work for piano, *Gaspard de la nuit*, in which the dazzling, virtuosic writing serves to remind the listener of Ravel's lifelong admiration for Liszt. The following year he began his most ambitious stage work — the ballet *Daphnis et Chloé*. It contains some of his most remarkable and beautiful music and was highly successful both in the theater and as an orchestral piece in the concert hall.

The outbreak of World War I had a profound effect on Ravel. He clearly believed that he had a duty to serve his country, and although he was classified unfit for military service, he managed to

195

secure a job as a driver in the motor transport corps. He fell dangerously ill in 1916 and returned to Paris only to find his mother on her deathbed. After her funeral he went into a deep depression: he had never married, and she was the only focus of his love. However, he was soon composing again and, in common with several French artists during this period, turned his attentions to reviving past national glories. This is most clearly demonstrated in *Le Tombeau de Couperin*, a suite based on Baroque dance forms. Each of the work's six movements is dedicated to a victim of the war and written in a beautifully clear and pure style that has ensured lasting popularity with concert audiences.

With the death of Debussy in 1918, Ravel became generally recognized as the leading light of French music, although he continued to view the establishment with suspicion and tried to minimize his contact with it. The last 17 years of his life were dogged by gradually worsening health, which adversely affected the quantity, but not the quality, of his output. Despite suffering increasingly from insomnia and nervous debility, he traveled extensively to receive warm welcomes in both Europe and the United States. In 1924 he wrote his short opera *L'Enfant et les sortilèges*, followed in 1928 by his best-known work, *Boléro*, which incited even more scandal in the Paris press. It was conceived as a musical joke, and consists of a single theme repeated with increasing intensity and density of orchestration. His final works, the two piano concertos, both composed in 1931, mark the end of his creative career. Both pieces overflow with Ravelian drive and panache, although the *Piano Concerto for Left Hand*, written for the pianist Paul Wittgenstein, who had lost his arm in the war, is considerably more serious in outlook.

The year 1932 marks the beginning of Ravel's tragic final period, during which he gradually succumbed to a progressively incapacitating illness. With his death, French music lost one of its dazzling innovators in terms of both his development of pianistic technique and his colorful orchestral writing.

Set design for Daphnis et Chloé, *by Léon Bakst, 1912*
Diaghilev commissioned this hour-long ballet, which tells the story of the Sicilian shepherd who invented pastoral poetry.

Vaughan Williams

Ralph Vaughan Williams 1872–1958

RECOMMENDED WORK
Symphony No. 3, 'Pastoral'
Angel Eminence CD-EMX2192
Alison Barlow (sop); Royal Liverpool Philharmonic Orchestra/Vernon Handley
A profoundly insightful, superbly engineered rendition that realizes both the music's serenity and its more mysterious, darker aspect.

REPRESENTATIVE WORKS
The Lark Ascending
Fantasia on a Theme by Thomas Tallis
Fantasia on Greensleeves
Symphonies Nos. 2 ('London'), 4, & 6

The foremost English composer of his generation, Ralph Vaughan Williams was born in Gloucestershire but brought up in Surrey. He studied music theory, piano, and violin before the age of nine and went to Trinity College, Cambridge, in 1892. After graduating with a degree in history he entered the Royal College of Music, where he met the composer Gustav Holst, with whom he formed a lifelong friendship. In 1897, Vaughan Williams married and also spent three months in Berlin studying with Max Bruch.

On returning to London, he obtained a post as a church organist and began to form a reputation as a writer, lecturer, and music editor. At the forefront of the revival of interest in English folksong at the turn of the century, he collected more than 800 examples. A late developer musically, he began to find his personal voice as a composer only toward the end of the first decade of the twentieth century.

In 1910, Vaughan Williams completed what has become one of his best-loved works, the *Fantasia on a Theme by Thomas Tallis*. Its luscious, rich texture and song-like melodies complement the original sixteenth-century theme, and have ensured the lasting popularity of the piece.

Vaughan Williams (left) at a rehearsal of *The Pilgrim's Progress*, 1951

The composer mused over the theme of this opera for 30 years.

The following year he produced his first large-scale work, the *Sea Symphony*, which was immediately acclaimed as a dramatic, expansive, and impressive piece that makes good use of a large orchestra and choir. In 1914 he completed the *London Symphony*, a warm and human testimony to the composer's love for that noisy and bustling city.

After serving in the Royal Army Medical Corps during World War I, Vaughan Williams joined the staff at the Royal College of Music and for the rest of his life devoted himself to composing. *The Lark Ascending*, a romance for solo violin and orchestra, was first performed in 1920. It quickly proved to be one of his most popular works, describing the flight of the lark with beautiful, soaring melodies on the solo violin.

In 1935 Vaughan Williams' leadership of the English school of composers was confirmed with the performance of his *Fourth Symphony*, a loud and uncharacteristically aggressive work. Four years later his music was banned in Germany as a result of his work on behalf of refugees seeking shelter from the Nazis, against whom he continued to campaign vigorously for the duration of the war.

A new departure came in 1940–41 when Vaughan Williams composed music for a film, *The Forty-Ninth Parallel*. His melodious and dramatic style was ideally suited to this medium, and he went on to provide music for ten more, including *Scott of the Antarctic*, which formed the basis for his *Seventh Symphony*. In 1951 the last of his six operas, *The Pilgrim's Progress*, was produced at Covent Garden. Like the others, however, it has failed to hold a place in the repertory.

Vaughan Williams remained in good health in old age, and in 1954 he undertook an extensive tour of the United States, lecturing and conducting to widespread public acclaim. With his death in 1958, England lost not only a fine individual musician but a statesman as well, one who spent much time trying to help others. He believed that a composer should 'make his art an expression of the whole life of the community,' and the warmth and popularity of his music indicate clearly how well he succeeded.

Additional composers

Composers in the latter half of the nineteenth century were affected in varying degrees by nationalism. In Russia the most fiery spokesman for the cause was **Mily Balakirev** (1837–1910), whose work is best represented by the oriental fantasy for piano, *Islamey*. In Poland, the violin virtuoso **Henryk Wieniawski** (1835–1880) favored the national dance forms of mazurka and polonaise, although his fine *Second Violin Concerto* has a more international flavor. The Spaniard **Enrique Granados** (1867–1916) showed an affinity with Spanish art of earlier periods; his masterpiece is the suite of piano pieces *Goyescas*. The cosmopolitan **Max Bruch** (1838–1920) was quite at home using Russian, Swedish, Scottish, and Hebrew melodies (the last in the *Scotch Fantasy* and the beautiful *Kol Nidrei*). He never recaptured the richly memorable invention of the popular *First Violin Concerto* in G minor.

In France, **Emmanuel Chabrier** (1841–1894) and **Ernest Chausson** (1855–1899) were consummate artists who wrote music of great character and polish. Chabrier's wit and colorful orchestration are at their finest in the rhapsody *España*, but the *Dix pièces pittoresques* for piano have more delicate sensitivity. The opera *Gwendoline* shows his interest in Wagner, who also influenced Chausson, sometimes stiflingly. However, Chausson's *Symphony* is an outstandingly graceful vision, superior in every way to César Franck's bombastic though more popular example. In *Poème* (Opus 25) Chausson achieved a masterpiece whose ecstatic lyricism is enhanced by its succinctness. Although psychosomatic illness led **Henri Duparc** (1848–1933) to abandon composition, his output of 13 songs, composed between 1868 and 1884, is one of the most moving utterances in French music.

In Italy the predominance of opera produced bolder, even crude music: the *verismo* movement of violent naturalism was anticipated by **Amilcare Ponchielli** (1834–1886) in *La Gioconda* (1876), and later exemplified by **Pietro Mascagni** (1863–1945) in *Cavalleria rusticana*, whose emotional effectiveness produced a sensational overnight success.

In the United States, the virtuoso piano music of **Louis Gottschalk** (1829–1869), though often brash, had a delightfully exotic feel in works such as *Le bananier* and *Le banjo*. The piano pieces of **Edward MacDowell** (1860–1908), the *Woodland Sketches*, were closer in spirit to Grieg. His fine *Second Piano Concerto* well deserves its occasional airing.

The Early Twentieth Century

In 1914 a social order that had changed little since the middle of the nineteenth century was shattered beyond repair. When Austria declared war on Serbia, a web of alliances brought all the great nations of Europe into the conflict. British and French armies faced the Germans across trenches that stretched from the English Channel to the Swiss frontier. In Eastern Europe the long war demoralized the Russian army; the tsar abdicated, and a provisional government was formed, only to be overthrown by a Communist revolution. America's entry into the war ensured the defeat of Germany, but the peace treaties that followed sowed the seeds of future conflict. The Great Depression of the late 1920's created mass unemployment throughout the industrial world. Hitler brought the Nazis to power in Germany, establishing a ruthless dictatorship equaled only by the Stalinist regime in the Soviet Union. Hitler's territorial ambitions led to the outbreak of hostilities in Europe in 1939; as the Soviet Union, the United States, and Japan entered the war, the conflict became truly global. It ended in 1945 with the defeat of Germany and Japan, but at a dreadful cost in human suffering. The atomic bomb changed forever the concept of warfare.

In the early twentieth century the notion of art as an imitation of nature was overturned by the Cubism of Picasso and Braque. Dada artists stressed the irrational and the absurd, and Surrealists explored the subconscious mind with dreamscapes. In Germany the Bauhaus school architects created a functional design that became quite popular during the interwar years.

English music achieved world stature through Elgar, and in the United States, Ives produced music of great originality. Meanwhile, Schoenberg and his successors rejected traditional ideas of harmony and melody to create music that came to characterize the art of the twentieth century.

Featured Composers

Pedestrians looking up at planes over Bilbao in air raid, May 1937 by Robert Capa
Capa's photograph captured a potent image of the fear and unease that were rife during the first half of the twentieth century.

The early twentieth century was a time of rapid and dramatic transformation in the arts, just as it was in science and so many other fields of human endeavor. A person in 1900 looking back to his or her youth in 1850 would have remembered a world that had undergone momentous developments; 50 years later, a person looking back to 1900 would remember a time that seemed in many fundamental ways part of an entirely different era.

In 1900 the horse was still the major form of transportation in even the most highly developed countries, agriculture was the principal industry, and domestic service was by far the most common form of employment for women (especially in Europe). In the United States, the latter half of the nineteenth century had been marked by the Civil War, followed by the period of Reconstruction that, despite the recession, was largely a peaceful time. The Austrian, Chinese, Russian, and Turkish empires were still intact and in Britain, Queen Victoria — that supreme symbol of stability — was on the throne she had occupied since 1837. For most people the rhythm and texture of daily life had scarcely altered during her reign. All this would be lost on the fields of Flanders; the remorseless butchery of World War I would drain the strength of the contending nations, laying them open to radical change.

The war to end all wars

In June 1914, the Austrian Archduke Franz Ferdinand and his wife were assassinated in Sarajevo, the capital of Serbia. Austria soon declared war on Serbia, an act of aggression that brought into play a complex system of political and military alliances — Russia massed troops on the German border, prompting Germany to declare war on Russia and then on its ally, France. Germany invaded Belgium, provoking Britain to declare war on Germany on August 4. At the outbreak of hostilities there was genuine optimism that the war would be over by Christmas. This hope soon evaporated as the soldiers on the Western front became trapped in a lethal stalemate, in trenches that extended from the Belgian coast to Verdun, in northeastern France. At the third Battle of Ypres, in 1917, for example, the British line advanced five miles in four months, at a cost of 400,000 casualties.

Inevitably, the wholesale slaughter undermined morale and created a dangerous unrest. In 1916 the 'Easter Rising' in Dublin threatened British interests in Ireland. It was swiftly

Australian soldiers at Château Wood, Ypres, October 29, 1917

Ypres, in northern France, was the scene of some of the costliest trench warfare of World War I.

Lenin attending a parade in Moscow's Red Square

The appalling hardships suffered by Russia during World War I were one cause of the uprising that put Lenin in power.

quashed, but the violence only increased popular support for the republican cause.

In Russia, the situation was even more serious. By March 1917, there were strikes and food riots in Moscow and Petrograd (St. Petersburg). Tsar Nicholas II was forced to abdicate, and a provisional government was formed under a moderate socialist revolutionary, Alexander Kerensky. Meanwhile Vladimir Lenin, a professional revolutionary who had been living in western Europe since 1907, returned to Russia in April 1917, seeing the war as the opportunity for a worldwide socialist uprising. In November 1917 (October, according to the calendar then in use in Russia) he led the Bolsheviks (Communists) in overthrowing Kerensky and became in effect dictator of the country. In theory the October Revolution established the rule of the people, but in practice it was the Communist Party that ruled. Civil War between Communist (Red) forces, led by Leon Trotsky, and anti-Communist (White) forces followed. The Communists eventually prevailed, but at the cost of enormous devastation to the country.

The immediate effect of the Revolution was to take Russia out of the war. This would have strengthened the position of Germany and her allies, had they not been facing similar internal crises. In Vienna, the Dual Monarchy (of Austria and Hungary) was dissolved in 1918 and the old Hapsburg empire began to break up. In the Near East, Turkish influence continued to wane as Colonel T. E. Lawrence ('Lawrence of Arabia') spearheaded the Arab revolt and assisted in the capture of Damascus in 1918. Germany, too, was racked with disorder. There were mutinies at Kiel and other major ports, while Bavaria declared itself a republic. These factors, combined with the arrival of American forces in Europe, finally persuaded the German authorities to sue for peace in November 1918.

201

The Treaty of Versailles

American involvement in the war had been crucial to the Allied cause, and President Woodrow Wilson's 'Fourteen Points,' which included suggestions for a League of Nations, offered the best chance of a lasting peace. However, the settlement that emerged from the Treaty of Versailles in 1919 was far less satisfactory. Wilson was defeated at the polls in November 1920, and his Republican successor backtracked on the United States' commitments in Europe, keeping it out of the League of Nations. Meanwhile, the other victorious powers placed the full blame for the war on Germany and tried to exact huge reparations, which were the cause of terrible hardships among its people. The injustice of this left Germans simmering with resentment and paved the way for a new conflict. It was no accident that 1919 witnessed both Mussolini's foundation of the Fascist Party in Italy and the creation of the National Socialist (Nazi) Party in Germany.

Music in the early twentieth century

In addition to the strains it placed on political and economic institutions, the war disrupted the cultural upsurge that had taken place in the early years of the century. Nowhere had this rebirth been more startling than in Britain, which had endured a long fallow period since Tudor and Stuart times, when it was justly famed for music. In 1899 came the successful premiere of Edward Elgar's *Enigma Variations*, the work that established his reputation, followed a year later by his *Dream of Gerontius*. Together these works ushered in a period when British music once again achieved world stature — Gustav Holst and Vaughan Williams being among the leaders of the revival.

The musical blossoming of the United States in the twentieth century was just as sudden and exciting, with Charles Ives the composer who marked the country's coming of age. Ives's first major works, such as the cantata *Celestial City*, were composed around the turn of the century. Other areas that became major centers of musical creativity during this period include Scandinavia (where Sibelius was the towering figure), central Europe (notably Bartók in Hungary and Janáček in Czechoslovakia), and Latin America (in particular Villa-Lobos).

MUSICAL DEFINITIONS

ATONALITY Atonality defies the convention of tonalism by not being centered on any one key. Instead of there being a 'home base' to which the music must return, all notes have equal validity, as do all possible sequences of notes and all possible combinations of notes in chords.

12-NOTE or 12-TONE SYSTEM Developed by Schoenberg in the early 1920's; the original and simplest type of 'serialism' (see below). 12-note pieces are based on a 'row' of 12 notes (the seven white and five black notes of the chromatic scale on the piano) — not necessarily in the same octave — arranged in whatever order the composer chooses, and not repeating any note. As no single note dominates, there is no home key.

SERIALISM A form of atonalism. Often synonymous with the 12-note system, but can apply to a row of any number of notes (up to 12).

A musical revolution

The two musical giants of the period were Arnold Schoenberg and Igor Stravinsky, who created a new musical language for the twentieth century. The key word is tonality, for in 1908 Schoenberg had started to write ATONAL music, that is, music not centered on any key. Schoenberg preferred the term 'pantonal,' meaning that the music embraced all tonalities, but the more negative 'atonal' became the established term. Whatever it was called, to most ears (even musically trained ears) it sounded like chaos, as the reactions to it show. 'A cat walking down the keyboard of a piano could evolve a melody more lovely than any which came from this Viennese composer's consciousness,' wrote the critic of the *Chicago Record Herald* of Schoenberg's *Five Orchestral Pieces* in November 1913. Earlier that year, at the premiere of Stravinsky's ballet *The Rite of Spring* in Paris, the savage dissonance of the music brought a hostile reaction from large sections of the audience and the performance eventually degenerated into a riot.

Stravinsky was a friend of Picasso, and they are often seen as the prime revolutionaries in their respective arts in the dazzling period leading up to World War I, a period that has never been matched for experimental fervor. In painting, a series of movements, beginning with Fauvism in 1905, undermined and eventually overthrew the idea that art was essentially the imitation of nature — an idea that had not been seriously

Above: *Grosstadt — urban debauchery*, triptych by Otto Dix, 1927–28

Dix portrayed the decadent values caused by the harsh conditions in Germany after World War I. Here he juxtaposes misfortune and poverty with the frantic gaiety of the jazz club.

King Oliver's Creole Jazz Band, *c.*1920

In a similar way to folk music, jazz made its influence felt in the world of classical music, as composers incorporated its innovative idioms into their pieces.

challenged since the Renaissance. Cubism, which Picasso created with Georges Braque in 1907, was the most radical of these 'isms.' By showing objects from several viewpoints simultaneously — as the mind knows them to be rather than as the eye sees them — they broke drastically with tradition, paving the way for abstraction. Music critics never found an 'ism' that could be made to stick to Stravinsky's music, although they applied labels like 'barbarism,' 'dynamism,' and 'primitivism.'

Some critics saw atonality more positively — as a kind of musical equivalent of the Expressionism that was such a powerful force in the visual arts at this time. (Schoenberg himself was a talented Expressionist painter.) But the heyday of atonal music came in the early 1920's, when Schoenberg developed the 12-NOTE (or 12-TONE) SYSTEM, which uses all 12 notes of the chromatic scale arranged in any order as a 'row' or theme in a composition. Sometimes the term SERIALISM is used as a synonym for 12-note music, although in fact the 12-note system is just one — the simplest — type of serialism.

Schoenberg's ideas came to have worldwide influence, but initially his chief followers were his pupils Alban Berg and Anton Webern. Together these three are sometimes known as the 'Second Viennese School.' The 12-note system that links them is a method and not a style, so their music is often dissimilar. Webern's tends to be concentrated and intense (some of his pieces last less than a minute, and his entire published output amounts only to about four hours' listening), whereas Berg's is more approachable and sometimes lyrical in feeling.

In contrast to this subjective and emotional spirit, there was the order and clarity of neoclassical music. As the name suggests, neoclassicism looked back to the music of the past, specifically that of the eighteenth century, but it was not simply a pastiche. There was an added rhythmic strength that marked out such music as clearly of the twentieth century, and often a spirit of affectionate parody. Stravinsky's *Pulcinella* (1919–20) is sometimes cited as the first full-blown neoclassical work, although Prokofiev's *Classical Symphony* (1916–17) has some claim to the title. Other composers who worked in the vein were Paul Hindemith and (in his later work) Bartók. French composers such as Francis Poulenc and Jacques Ibert showed a strongly neoclassical inspiration. Even Schoenberg was influenced by neoclassicism, just as Stravinsky was influenced by serialism toward the end of his career. Neoclassicism was to some extent a reaction against the lushness of Romanticism and it often has a playful spirit, as if aiming to deflate pomposity.

Certainly, there was nothing pompous about the age that spawned it. The jazz era possessed a genuine exuberance that affected most branches of the arts. In the world of *haute couture*, Chanel and Poiret produced bright, streamlined fashions that complemented perfectly the contemporary taste for Art Deco. It was during the 1920's, too, that the radio and phonograph brought jazz and dance music within reach of most people — one of the most significant developments in the twentieth century — and the influence of the new popular music can be heard in the work of such diverse composers as Stravinsky, William Walton, Maurice Ravel, and Darius Milhaud. At the same time, Kurt Weill's harsh, jazzy style, brilliantly combining the idiom of popular music with avant-garde techniques, provided a striking evocation of the brittle, decadent atmosphere of postwar Germany.

The partition of Ireland

The glamorous aspects of the age could not disguise the underlying tensions on the political scene. In Ireland, the republican question surfaced once again, following the election victory of the Sinn Fein Party in 1918. A Home Rule Bill was swiftly rushed through Parliament, and Ireland was divided into the independent Irish Free State and the Province of Ulster, which remained part of the United Kingdom. This deferred the problem rather than solving it; the Republicans regarded the partition as a temporary compromise, while the Ulster Unionists saw it as a permanent arrangement.

Stalinism

In the Soviet Union, the peace was threatened by the death of Lenin in 1924. A power struggle ensued between Trotsky and Stalin, which the latter eventually won (Trotsky was exiled in 1929). Stalin's priority was to turn the Soviet Republic into a major industrial force. In 1928, he introduced his first 'Five-

The dust storm, Cimarron County, Oklahoma, 1936, photo by Arthur Rothstein

The Wall Street Crash of 1929 led to the Great Depression in the United States. John Steinbeck's novel The Grapes of Wrath captured the spirit of the Depression, depicting a family driven by poverty to flee the Oklahoma dust bowl.

Year Plan,' entailing 'collectivization' (the creation of large, communal farms) and the liquidation of the kulak (peasant proprietor) class. Stalin's purges proceeded ruthlessly during the 1930's, rivaling the outrages committed by the Nazis.

The Great Depression

The West, meanwhile, was still suffering from the economic aftermath of the war. In Germany, there was hyperinflation — in 1923, the cost of a bus ticket soared to an extraordinary 150,000 million Marks. In Britain, the General Strike of 1926 brought the country to a virtual standstill for nine days. The crisis had been sparked by a demand by mine owners for longer working hours and lower wages, and although public support for the strike was considerable, the miners were eventually forced to comply with their employers' wishes.

Even the United States did not remain exempt from such problems. From 1927 to 1929 the American economy experienced an artificial boom, with share prices soaring amid rash speculation. In September 1929, confidence began to falter, and on October 24 came the Great Crash — known as 'Black Thursday' — with waves of panic selling. Many businesses collapsed, and when American banks called in foreign loans, the panic spread outside the United States. The most devastating

consequence of the Great Depression that followed was mass unemployment. By 1932 there were about 14 million unemployed in the United States, and the figures in Germany and Britain were about 5.6 million and 2.8 million respectively. There had been recessions before, but this 'world slump' was worse than anything ever experienced.

In the United States the government created various schemes to help artists through the worst times. Collectively known as the Federal Arts Projects, the programs dealt separately with music, theater, writing, and visual arts. An enormous amount of work appeared under the auspices of the projects — artists were paid regular salaries and employed, for example, in the decoration of public buildings — but little of it attained distinction. The work that perhaps best captures the spirit of the Depression years is John Steinbeck's novel *The Grapes of Wrath* (1939), which deals with the problems faced by a family trying to find a better life in California after fleeing Oklahoma's dust bowl.

The Depression swept the Republicans out of office, bringing Franklin Roosevelt a landslide victory in 1932. His 'New Deal' — a recovery program that involved massive spending on public projects in order to stimulate employment — gradually turned the economic tide. Even so, the slump had inflicted long-term damage on many economies and produced a strong political swing to the right in several European countries. It is not surprising that at such a time many people could succumb to the promise of strong leadership without thinking too hard about how it was to be put into practice; Adolf Hitler's rise to power in Germany must be seen in this context.

The rise of Hitler

Hitler, an Austrian by birth, fought for Germany in World War I and believed the country was betrayed by the politicians who signed the humiliating Treaty of Versailles. By the Treaty, Germany admitted guilt for the war and agreed to severe restrictions on the size of its armed forces; the economic and trade restrictions imposed upon it by the Allies led to severe shortages; and the country was crippled by soaring inflation. Hitler joined the National Socialist Party in 1919 and exploited the prevailing mood of discontent, becoming notorious as an orator in tirades against the Treaty as well as against the Jews, whom he cast as a convenient scapegoat for the country's troubles. Although he failed in an attempt to take over the government of Bavaria in 1923 (the Munich Putsch) and spent 13 months in prison, support for the Nazi party was growing, aided by the formidable propaganda skills of one of Hitler's henchmen, Joseph Goebbels. After the political failure of three successive chancellors, Hitler was appointed to the post in January 1933. When President Hindenburg died in August 1934, Hitler became sole leader (*Führer*) of the country.

The arts under dictatorship

Hitler's ruthless dictatorship extended to the arts, which were harnessed to promote the cult of his own personality and the Nazi philosophy of Aryan supremacy. Any art that conflicted with his ideology was ridiculed, repressed, and eventually destroyed. One of the first artistic casualties of Hitler's regime was the Bauhaus, a school of architecture and applied arts that had become world famous in the years since its foundation in 1919. Its teaching staff constituted one of the finest arrays of artistic talent ever assembled in one place, and it had enormous influence on design, promoting a functional style that became extremely popular in the interwar years. The Nazis shut the school down in April 1933.

Other branches of the arts soon suffered a similar fate. The Fascists coined the term *entartete Kunst* (degenerate art) for any art they disapproved of (which meant the work of most of the best painters and sculptors of the day). In 1937 an infamous exhibition of so-called degenerate art was held in Munich and then went on tour. Works by artists of the caliber of Picasso and Paul Klee were mocked by being shown alongside pictures painted by the inmates of lunatic asylums. 'Degenerate' works were confiscated from museums; some were sold, others burned. Similarly, *entartete Musik* (which included all atonal music) was banned, and by the outbreak of war, about 200 composers (including Schoenberg and Webern, the surviving members of the Second Viennese School) had been deprived of their livelihoods.

Having consolidated his position at home, Hitler looked to extend his influence abroad. In defiance of the terms of the Treaty of Versailles, he began to rearm the country, and in March 1936, he occupied the demilitarized zone in the Rhineland. In the same year he also formed an alliance (the Rome–Berlin Axis) with the Italian Fascist leader, Benito

Mussolini, whose earlier rise to power had also been based on exploiting economic discontent and nationalistic feelings.

Hitler also aided General Francisco Franco in establishing a dictatorship in Spain by giving him material support during the country's civil war (1936–39). In 1931 the unpopular King Alfonso XIII had been driven out of Spain and the country had become a republic. Among conservatives there was resentment at the socialist and anticlerical measures of the republican authorities, and disturbances continued throughout the early 1930's. In 1936, following the election of a left-wing Popular Front government, a military revolt broke out in Spanish Morocco, which spread to Spain itself, igniting the civil war. The rebels, under the leadership of Franco, were aided by Italy as well as by Germany. The beleaguered republican government received assistance from sympathizers in other countries — indeed the war turned Spain into an ideological battleground for all Europe. Many liberal-minded artists supported the republicans, among them the English writer George Orwell, who fought with the 'International Brigades' and was wounded, later writing *Homage to Catalonia* about his experiences. The bombing of the Basque town of Guernica by German planes in 1937 inspired one of the most famous paintings of the twentieth century, Pablo Picasso's *Guernica*. About a million people are thought to have been killed in the war before Franco emerged victorious when he captured Madrid in March 1939, after a siege lasting more than two years.

The war in Spain provided a dress rehearsal for the wider conflict that was to come, and Franco's success undoubtedly encouraged Hitler in his ambitions. Austria and Czechoslovakia were annexed in 1938, as the Western powers persisted with their disastrous policy of appeasement. Only when Poland was overrun in September 1939 did Britain and France bow to the inevitable and declare war on Germany. Hitler was surprised but undaunted by the news. He continued his advance, occupying Norway and Denmark, and prepared his forces for the westward push. However, despite the declaration of war, there was no armed conflict. This 'phony war' became all too real in May 1940, when German troops swept through the Netherlands and Belgium into France. The surviving Allied forces were evacuated to Britain from Dunkirk, and in the ensuing months, London was subjected to an intensive bombing campaign. It seemed a German invasion was imminent.

Amazingly, this attack never came. In 1941, the fortunes of war began to shift. Russia had signed a nonaggression pact with Germany in 1939, enabling the latter to make substantial territorial gains in Finland and Poland. However, the two powers quarreled over the fate of Bulgaria, and German forces invaded Russia in June 1941. Ultimately Hitler's campaign proved as ill-fated as Napoleon's had done, foundering during the debilitating siege of Stalingrad over the winter of 1942 to 1943. Meanwhile, Hitler continued to pursue his goal of Aryan supremacy, using concentration camps as a means of implementing a horrific policy of genocide against the Jewish race and groups such as Gypsies, homosexuals, and the disabled.

The United States entered the war in December 1941, following the surprise attack by the Japanese air force on the American naval base at Pearl Harbor. Their economic and military might helped turn the tide against the Axis powers. The conquest of Italy began in the summer of 1943, while the Normandy landings of June 6, 1944, marked the start of the Liberation in the north. In the east, the struggle showed signs of lingering on until the United States devastated Hiroshima and Nagasaki with the new atomic bomb. At great cost, peace was achieved, but no one could feel secure about the future.

Right: Hitler at the Nuremberg rally of 1936
The annual gatherings of the Nazi faithful at Nuremberg were highly orchestrated displays of military might.

Below: Children in a concentration camp at Litauen, after liberation by Soviet troops in 1944
The full horror of the atrocities committed at the concentration camps was not fully realized until liberation.

Featured Composers

Prokofiev

Sergei Prokofiev 1891–1953

RECOMMENDED WORKS

Peter and the Wolf
London Headline Classics 433 612-2
Ralph Richardson, London Symphony Orchestra/
Malcolm Sargent
Ralph Richardson's Peter and the Wolf *has long
been a favorite. Sargent's good-humored contribution
(with a vintage, late 1950's LSO) positively twinkles
at you.*

Romeo and Juliet
London 417 510-2
Cleveland Orchestra/Lorin Maazel
*Immaculate poise and breathtaking virtuosity are the
order of the day in Maazel's exciting theatrical
conception. The 1973 analog recording remains
among the best of its era.*

REPRESENTATIVE WORKS
Lieutenant Kijé
Classical Symphony
Symphony No. 5
Piano Concerto No. 3
Violin Concerto No. 1
Alexander Nevsky

Sketch of Ballets Russes rehearsal, M. Larionov, 1921
**Prokofiev is seated between Diaghilev
(right) and Larionov himself, who
produced stage designs for the Ballet.**

A scene from *Alexander Nevsky*, 1939
**Nevsky was a national hero and
Prokofiev's majestic film score endeared
him to the Soviet authorities.**

Prokofiev was born in Sontsovka in the Ukraine, the son of a well-to-do agricultural engineer. Encouraged by his pianist mother, he made rapid musical strides. He was a gifted pianist himself, and his earliest piano piece dates from his fifth year; by the age of 11 he had written two operas.

In 1904 he entered the St. Petersburg Conservatory, but the somewhat willful and arrogant young Prokofiev found the lessons from Liadov and Rimsky-Korsakov dull and old-fashioned: he gained more stimulation from his friendships with the composers Nikolai Myaskovsky and Boris Asafyev. Lessons with Anna Esipova increased the expressive range of Prokofiev's already strong and brilliant playing.

Recognition came steadily, and in 1911 Prokofiev saw his first works in print and his first public orchestral performance. Many critics of the time were bewildered by the unusual sonorities of his music, and the premiere of his *First Piano Concerto*, performed by the composer himself in 1912, caused a furor, giving rise to his rep-

utation as the *enfant terrible* of Russian music — something hard to understand now when one listens to this sparkling and attractive work.

On graduating from the conservatory in 1914, Prokofiev immediately traveled to London, where he met the Russian ballet impresario Sergei Diaghilev and was greatly impressed by Stravinsky's ballets. The impact of *The Rite of Spring* is evident in the music Prokofiev intended for a ballet for Diaghilev, *Ala and Lolli*, but which found its way instead into the savage *Scythian Suite*. A second work, *Chout*, was also aimed at Diaghilev, but was not mounted until 1921 in Paris.

Returning to Russia, Prokofiev spent the greater part of the World War I period in St. Petersburg. There an operatic commission, *The Gambler*, foundered at the rehearsal stage, but his *First Violin Concerto* and the *First Symphony* (the 'Classical') had happier outcomes; the latter — a conscious re-creation of the wit and clarity of Haydn's style — brought him international success.

Key to Recommended Works

arr. arrangement (by)	**contr** contralto	**hpd** harpsichord	**Op., Opp.** Opus(es)	**pno** piano	**ten** tenor	**vcl** violoncello ('cello)
bar baritone	**gtr** guitar	**mez** mezzo-soprano	**org** organ	**sop** soprano	**treb** treble	**vln** violin

In the turmoil that followed the Russian revolution in 1917, Prokofiev moved to the United States, where his vivid fantasy opera *The Love for Three Oranges* was commissioned by the Chicago Opera. However, it was Paris that increasingly attracted Prokofiev, and he moved there in 1920 to revise his ballet *Chout* for Diaghilev. While living in France he also completed the superb *Third Piano Concerto*, a virtuoso work whose combination of glittering ebullience alongside wistful melancholy is totally characteristic of its composer.

Prokofiev's works of the next decade include the controversial machine-age *Second Symphony* and two further ballets for Diaghilev — *Le pas d'acier*, about Soviet industrialization, and *L'enfant prodigue.*

In 1933, Prokofiev returned to the Soviet Union, and in the next three years re-established links with his homeland. The Kirov Theater in Leningrad commissioned the ballet *Romeo and Juliet* in 1934, and in 1936 Prokofiev, his wife — a Spanish singer — and their two sons took up residence in Moscow. *Romeo and Juliet* was not popular with the Soviet authorities, who at the same time condemned Shostakovich's opera *Lady Macbeth of Mtsensk.* Prokofiev responded by turning his hand to utilitarian and patriotic music, including the score for Sergei Eisenstein's film *Alexander Nevsky*, re-arranged in 1939 as a cantata. His operas fared less well in Soviet Russia: *Semyon Kotko* was swiftly dropped; performance of the second, *The Duenna*, was postponed for several years; and his third, *War and Peace*, a project particularly dear to him, remained unperformed at his death.

During the 1940's Prokofiev's health underwent a gradual decline. His imposing *Fifth Symphony* of 1945 struck a renewed note of heroic assurance, but continuing difficulties with the authorities culminated in bitter attacks on him in 1948 and the banning of many of his earlier works. His spirit was broken, and the works of his final years have the air of feeble sops to the dominant Soviet ideologies. He died in 1953, ironically on exactly the same day as his chief persecutor, Joseph Stalin.

Rachmaninov

Sergei Rachmaninov 1873–1943

RECOMMENDED WORK
Piano Concerto No. 2
Deutsche Grammophon 415 119-2
Sviatoslav Richter, Warsaw Philharmonic Orchestra/Stanislaw Wislocki
Richter's virtuosity is staggering, his keyboard presence magnetic: you may not agree with everything he does, but what an astonishingly accomplished brand of pianism he displays!

REPRESENTATIVE WORKS
Symphony No. 2
Symphony No. 3
The Isle of the Dead
Rhapsody on a Theme of Paganini
Piano Concerto No. 3
Symphonic Dances
24 Preludes
The Bells
All-Night Vigil

Sergei Rachmaninov was not only one of the greatest pianists of the twentieth century but also the last great representative of the Russian Romantic tradition, exemplified especially by Tchaikovsky and Rimsky-Korsakov.

Originally wealthy, Rachmaninov's family was reduced to straitened circumstances by his father's extravagance, the resulting strain eventually leading to his parents' separation. In 1885, after an initial period of study at the St. Petersburg Conservatory, Rachmaninov was sent to study the piano with the strict teacher Nikolai Zverev, whose regimen required that the boy's piano practice begin every morning at six o'clock. Living at Zverev's also gave the young Rachmaninov the opportunity to meet such impressive musicians as Anton Rubinstein, Anton Arensky, and most crucially, Tchaikovsky, at Sunday afternoon gatherings.

In 1888, Rachmaninov started taking composition lessons with Taneyev and Arensky, and the increasing importance to him of composing led to a breach with the piano-oriented Zverev. Before his graduation he wrote such successful works as the warmly emotional *First Piano Concerto*,

Rachmaninov at the Piano, by Leonid Pasternak, 1916
Rachmaninov spent some time as a concert pianist after the Revolution.

Religious procession, *Illustrated London News*, 1906

Russian priests celebrating the name day of a saint. Rachmaninov's music was influenced by Russian Orthodox chants.

the *Trio élégiaque No. 1*, and the very Russian, Tchaikovsky-influenced one-act opera *Aleko* — his graduation exercise — for which he was awarded the highest grade possible.

Rachmaninov seemed to be about to launch on an assured career, and in 1892 he wrote one of his most popular pieces, the *Prelude in C sharp minor*, the performance of which as an encore was to become a resented chore for the composer. But five years later the premiere of his ambitious *First Symphony* met with disaster, possibly because of the inadequacies of Glazunov's conducting, and Rachmaninov sank into three years of compositional inactivity. His depression was eventually cured by treatment under hypnosis, and the result of his rediscovered confidence was the immediately successful and enduringly popular *Second Piano Concerto*. The momentum and excitement engendered by the build-up to the finale's climax in this work became a model for the conclusions of Rachmaninov's subsequent pieces.

The next 15 years were highly productive, and saw such large-scale fruits of his maturity as the *Second Symphony* (1906–07), the *Third Piano Concerto* in 1909, and in 1913 *The Bells*, a choral symphony based

on a poem by Edgar Allan Poe. Rachmaninov again abandoned composition when he and his family left Russia for the United States following the revolution in 1917, and the necessities of supporting a household forced him into a career as an international concert pianist.

When Rachmaninov returned to composition in 1926 with the *Fourth Piano Concerto*, its negative critical reception suggested he may have lost his flair. But in the 1930's he recaptured former glories with the *Variations on a Theme of Corelli* (his last solo piano work); the *Rhapsody on a Theme of Paganini*, for piano and orchestra, in which he achieved a new leanness and concision of expression; and the *Third Symphony*, completed in 1936.

His last work, completed three years before his death from cancer in March 1943, was the *Symphonic Dances*, which not only shows his interest in instrumental sonorities — illustrated by the use of an alto saxophone — but also reaches back to evoke the beloved Russian Orthodox chants of his homeland.

Janáček

Leoš Janáček 1854–1928

RECOMMENDED WORK

Sinfonietta
Deutsche Grammophon Galleria 437 254-2
Bavarian Radio Symphony Orchestra/Rafael Kubelík
The blazing fervor and intensity of this reading are something to savor. The veteran Kubelík remains perhaps the most unsung and sheerly musical conductor of his generation.

REPRESENTATIVE WORKS
Taras Bulba
Jenůfa
Katya Kabanova
The Cunning Little Vixen
Glagolitic Mass

Leoš Janáček's long and rich creative life is a story of slowly and patiently acquired mastery, an achievement crowned above all by a sequence of operas whose warm and vivid originality is unparalleled among the music of his peers.

The son of a village schoolmaster in Moravia (later Czechoslovakia), Janáček received his formative musical experience

Leoš Janáček, c.1920

Stage design for *The Makropoulos Case*, 1926

This late opera was based on Karel Capek's unusual play about a singer who lives for 200 years. The stage design was the work of Karel Capek's brother.

as a chorister in the Augustinian monastery in Brno. The sound of the human voice, either solo or in a choir, was always to remain an inspiration to him. He trained and qualified as a general teacher and between 1874 and 1880 led an active musical life in Brno, centered on teaching and choral conducting, alternating with short, and not wholly satisfactory, periods of study in Prague, Leipzig, and Vienna.

Janáček was recognized as a full teacher of music in 1880, and the following year he married his piano pupil, the 15-year-old Zdenka Schulzová. Over time, this proved a stressful liaison, the tensions between the fiery, patriotic Czech and the stubborn, very young Germanic girl never really resolved.

Although the 1880's were for Janáček a period of intense musical activity as conductor, teacher, and musical administrator, his personality as a composer was slow to take shape. His earlier works show a debt to the nineteenth-century world of Dvořák and Smetana: he also became greatly interested in Moravian folk music, and spent time editing and performing it.

After one or two initial attempts at operatic composition, he spent the years between 1894 and 1901 writing his first great opera, *Jenůfa*, and with it he began to establish a type of opera that integrated elements of folk song with colorfully dramatic effects, in which the music followed inflections of speech to produce a direct and realistic impact far removed from the high-flown sentiments of much nineteenth-century opera.

The success of the Brno premiere of *Jenůfa*, when Janáček was aged 50, enabled him to devote more of his time to composition over the following ten years; the operas *Osud* and *Mr. Brouček's Excursion to the Moon* were written during this time. However, it was the enormous success of the premiere of *Jenůfa*, in the town of Písek in 1916, that opened the floodgates of the 62-year-old composer's last, extraordinary period of creativity.

A catalyst for this amazing outpouring was the composer's passionate, though unreciprocated and unconsummated, love for Kamila Stösslová, the wife of an antiques dealer and 38 years younger than Janáček. The emotional heights and depths of this affair of the imagination were graphically portrayed in such works as the song cycle *The Diary of One Who Disappeared* and the *Second String Quartet* ('Intimate Letters'). At the same time, operas such as *Katya Kabanova* and *The Cunning Little Vixen* were immediately successful, and the 1920's performances of these works in Berlin, London, and New York began to establish Janáček's international reputation.

In his seventies the composer wrote two of his most communicative and popular scores, the *Sinfonietta* in 1926 (inspired in part by the sound of a brass band playing in a Prague park) and the *Glagolitic Mass* in 1927. His last opera, *From the House of the Dead*, was practically complete at his death in 1928. It closed an astonishing late harvest of works, reminiscent in their vitality and originality of the last creative outpourings of Haydn and Verdi.

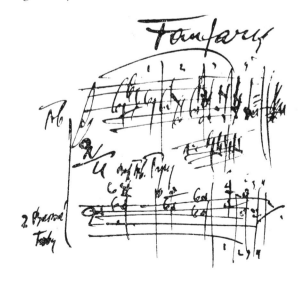

Manuscript score for *Sinfonietta*, 1926

Janáček's Sinfonietta was a lively evocation of his early days in the Moravian city of Brno.

Bartók

Béla Bartók 1881–1945

RECOMMENDED WORK

Concerto for Orchestra
Deutsche Grammophon Galleria 437 247-2
Boston Symphony Orchestra/Rafael Kubelík
A performance of towering humanity. Kubelík's wonderfully wise and witty direction strikes to the emotional heart of this great score with unerring perception.

REPRESENTATIVE WORKS
**Music for Strings, Percussion, and Celesta
Violin Concerto No. 2
Piano Concerto No. 3
Dance Suite
Bluebeard's Castle
String Quartet No. 6**

Photograph of the composer playing the hurdy-gurdy, c.1919

Béla Bartók not only is the greatest composer Hungary has produced, but his music — a unique synthesis of the Western Classical tradition with mid-European folk music — is one of the outstanding musical achievements of the twentieth century.

Bartók was born in Nagyszentmiklós, a small town now in Romania. His father, a teacher and amateur musician, died when Bartók was young, and his mother, Paula, had to support her family by teaching the piano. Paula Bartók was fully aware of her son's musical gifts — his earliest compositions date from his ninth year — and she finally managed to find a permanent teaching position in Poszony (now Bratislava), where she found excellent piano and harmony teachers for the young composer.

In 1899, Bartók had to decide where to continue his studies, and although the Vienna Conservatory was the obvious choice, Bartók followed the advice of his schoolmate, Ernö Dohnányi, and went to the Budapest Academy. There he was considered a virtuoso pianist of outstanding potential. As a composer, like Dohnányi he initially took Brahms as a model. But in 1902 and 1903 he was profoundly affected by two new preoccupations: the music of Richard Strauss and the rising tide of Hungarian nationalism. Both influences found expression in 1903 in the symphonic poem *Kossuth*, based on the life of the leader of Hungary's 1848 uprising.

Bartók found a further and more enduring outlet for his nationalist sentiments in Hungarian folk songs, which he started collecting in 1904. This led to a lifelong collaboration with Zoltán Kodály, a pioneer in the field. From 1906, Bartók made annual trips, using an Edison phonograph as recording equipment, to collect songs not only in Hungary but also in Romania, Slovakia, and Transylvania.

Also through Kodály, Bartók was introduced to the music of Debussy, which was a revelation to him. The twin influences of Debussy and folk song formed the background to the composition of his first mature works, the *First String Quartet* of 1908 and various short piano pieces, including the *14 Bagatelles*. In 1909 he married his teenage pupil, Márta Ziegler, to whom he dedicated his one-act opera

Bluebeard's Castle, an allegorical study of the individual's ultimate isolation from the rest of humanity.

Starting in 1907, Bartók served as a professor of piano at the Budapest Academy, a position that gave him a degree of security and enabled him to continue his research into folklore, including a visit to northern Africa in 1913. His health was too frail for active participation in World War I; during the period 1914 to 1917 he wrote the ballet *The Wooden Prince* and his *Second String Quartet*, works that show the impression made by Stravinsky's rhythmic innovations in *The Rite of Spring* and Schoenberg's experiments with tonality. In the pantomime *The Miraculous Mandarin*, Bartók pushed to an audacious extreme these tendencies toward driving rhythmic exuberance and unusual orchestral colors (variations, or shades, of tone).

The 1920's saw the consolidation of Bartók's international reputation as composer and pianist, both in solo music and partnering the great Hungarian violinists of the time, such as Joseph Szigeti. He wrote virtuoso works to perform himself in the 1920's and 1930's, including the *First* and *Second Piano Concertos*, the *Piano Sonata*, and the *Sonata for Two Pianos and Percussion*. The last was written for himself and his second wife, Ditta Pásztory, whom

Set for a 1942 production of *The Miraculous Mandarin*
This mime drama told the story of a Chinese man lured to a Western city.

Kodály

Zoltán Kodály 1882–1967

RECOMMENDED WORK
Háry János Suite
Deutsche Grammophon 427 408-2
Berlin Radio Symphony Orchestra/Ferenc Fricsay
Immensely characterful music-making. Hungarian-born Fricsay brings boundless affection and zest to his compatriot's marvelously colorful score.

REPRESENTATIVE WORKS
Peacock Variations
Dances from Galánta
Psalmus Hungaricus

he had married in 1923 following his divorce from Márta. Its journey from primeval darkness to searing light makes for a gripping aural experience.

The *Music for Strings, Percussion, and Celesta* of 1937, one of many classic commissions by the Swiss conductor Paul Sacher, is also impressive. This work creates the sense of an odyssey, enhanced by the telling return of the first movement's tortuous, mysterious fugue theme toward the end of the fourth and final movement. The slow movement contains a favorite Bartók device, a 'night music' section, where, in an atmosphere of hushed expectancy, a tapestry is woven of the tiny sounds of nocturnal animals and insects.

In 1940 the Bartóks moved to New York to escape the political situation in Hungary. The declining health, periods of depression, and financial worries that clouded Bartók's American years did not prevent him from completing such masterpieces as the *Concerto for Orchestra* and the *Sixth String Quartet*. The delicate *Third Piano Concerto* was practically finished when Bartók died in New York in September 1945.

The son of a stationmaster, Zoltán Kodály spent his early years living in rural Hungary, where he taught himself to play the piano, violin, viola, and cello and had his first contact with folk music. At the age of 18 he went to Budapest University to study Hungarian and German; he also studied at the Academy of Music. While studying in Berlin and Paris in 1906 and 1907, Kodály discovered the music of Claude Debussy.

His interest in folk songs led to a close collaboration and friendship with Bartók, of which he later remarked: 'The vision of an educated Hungary, reborn from the people, rose before us. We decided to devote our lives to its realization.'

Kodály was appointed professor at the Budapest Academy in 1907, and over the next decade produced chamber and vocal music, and continued research into folklore. He fell afoul of the authorities after the short-lived bourgeois revolution of 1919, but his fortunes improved with the great success of his *Psalmus Hungaricus*, premiered in 1923 to mark the fiftieth anniversary of the founding of Budapest.

The opera *Háry János*, and the suite derived from it, further established Kodály's international reputation. With these pieces, as well as the *Dances of Marosszék* from 1927, the *Dances of Galánta*

of 1933, and the orchestral variations on the Hungarian folk song *The Peacock*, Kodály extended his use of folk material and resources: the *Háry János* suite introduced the cimbalom, a unique Hungarian instrument; the *Dances of Galánta* evoked the sounds of the gypsy bands Kodály remembered from his boyhood.

This international success did not diminish the energy and intensity of Kodály's efforts to guide the Hungarian populace toward musical literacy. He regarded singing rather than instrumental performance as the key to musicianship, and composed innumerable choruses and choral exercises based on folk song that he presented to choirs all over the country.

Kodály's public esteem was sometimes overshadowed by tension with the authorities, and his *Missa Brevis* was completed in 1944 in the basement of a convent where he and his wife were seeking refuge. In the years following the war, he made triumphant conducting trips to Britain, the United States, and the Soviet Union, and received a constant stream of honors in recognition of the breadth of his musical activities. Kodály's energies as both composer and musical ambassador continued undiminished through the latter years of his long life. He lived to see two of his long-standing ambitions under way: the publication of a scholarly edition of Hungarian folk music and the introduction of elementary music education in schools, following his principles.

Kodály with a phonograph, c.1950

Delius

Frederick Delius 1862–1934

RECOMMENDED WORK
Sea Drift
Chandos CHAN9214
Bryn Terfel (bass-bar); Bournemouth Symphony
Orchestra and Chorus/Richard Hickox
Hickox's fluent, supersensitive direction makes for a
sympathetic realization of this glorious score; Terfel's
memorable contribution is the icing on the cake.

REPRESENTATIVE WORKS
Appalachia
Brigg Fair
Song of the High Hills
A Village Romeo and Juliet

Painting of Rue Lafayette by Edvard Munch, 1891
Delius met this Norwegian painter when
moving in avant-garde circles in Paris.

Portrait of Delius by Sir Herbert Gunn, c.1930

Born into a family of Bradford wool-merchants, Frederick Delius led a more cosmopolitan life than most of his English contemporaries. Early piano and violin lessons were a strictly amateur pursuit, and on leaving school Delius entered the family firm. Though he showed little aptitude for business, related trips to Paris and Norway produced links that would have lifelong importance to his music.

In 1884 he persuaded his father to help set him up as an orange grower in Florida. There Delius at last had the time and freedom to devote himself to composition, aided by lessons from Thomas Ward, a fine local musician. The subtropical surroundings, the sense of isolation and exile, and the songs of the black plantation workers had a potent influence on the young man.

In 1886, Delius returned to Europe, where his father supported him during a course at the Leipzig Conservatory. Although the rather dry, academic teaching was of little benefit to his instinctive talent, his stay did produce a momentous meeting with Norwegian composer Edvard Grieg. Grieg not only befriended and encouraged Delius but also convinced Delius's father to support his son as a composer.

Delius then moved to Paris, where he led a bohemian life, composing prolifically and moving in artistic circles; friends included Gauguin, Strindberg, and Munch. In 1896 he met Jelka Rosen, a young artist, whom he married in 1897. They settled in the village of Grez-sur-Loing in France, where, apart from a brief wartime spell in England, Delius remained until his death.

His life gradually became more settled and peaceful. He had labored hard to establish his style, and he now started to compose his first masterpieces: *Paris* in 1899 and above all *A Village Romeo and Juliet*, finished in 1902, which epitomizes essential Delius qualities — a sense of the transience of love and passion, an aching nostalgia, and a feeling for the consolation provided by the eternal cycles of nature.

In 1907, Delius met the English conductor Thomas Beecham, who became his most devoted interpreter, and his reputation started to spread back to his native land. The compositions now pouring from his pen included large-scale choral and orchestral pieces — *Appalachia*, *Sea Drift*, and *A Mass of Life* — as well as the English rhapsody *Brigg Fair* (based on a folk song) and such exquisite orchestral miniatures as *On Hearing the First Cuckoo in Spring*. It is touching and appropriate that this last work uses a Norwegian folk tune arranged for piano by Delius's mentor, Grieg.

After 1918, Delius slowly succumbed to syphilis, becoming blind and paralyzed. He stopped composing, but when a young Yorkshireman, Eric Fenby, offered his services as an amanuensis, with painstaking difficulty and slowness Delius was able to dictate a sequence of final works, including *Song of Summer* and *Song of Farewell*.

Holst

Gustav Holst 1874–1934

RECOMMENDED WORK

The Planets
Angel CDC7 47160-2
London Symphony Orchestra/André Previn
*Still one of the highlights of the LSO/Previn era. Here
is a set of* Planets *that has retained all its sense of
freshness and spontaneity over the years.*

REPRESENTATIVE WORKS
Savitri
The Perfect Fool
St. Paul's Suite
Egdon Heath
The Hymn of Jesus

Gustav Holst had a striking originality as a
composer and breadth of interest as a
thinker. He was born in Cheltenham to
musical parents of Scandinavian and German extraction, and studied at the Royal
College of Music in London. There his
friendship with Ralph Vaughan Williams
was considerably more stimulating to him
than composition lessons with the ultra-
traditional composer Charles Stanford. He
conceived as well a passion for Wagner,
whose style looms large in Holst's apprentice works, and an interest in Hindu philosophy and literature.

After a few early years playing orchestral trombone, Holst turned to teaching as
his mainstay. From 1905 until his death he
was director of music at St. Paul's Girls'
School in London, and the *St. Paul's Suite*
for strings of 1912 is only the best known
of many works that he wrote for amateur
music-making, in which his involvement
was serious and wholehearted. The folk
song collecting of Vaughan Williams and
Cecil Sharp also excited Holst; in 1906 to
1907 he wrote *A Somerset Rhapsody*, based
on traditional tunes.

The most notable of many works
springing from Holst's preoccupation with
Hinduism was the chamber opera *Savitri*
dating from 1908, based on an episode
from the epic poem *Mahabharata*: its economy and intensity are exemplified in the
arresting and dramatic opening, where
Death sings, offstage and unaccompanied.

Holst's heavy teaching schedule meant
that composing was confined to weekends
and vacations: the orchestral suite *The
Planets* consequently took him from 1914
to 1916 to write. It achieved almost
overnight success for its bewildered composer, who never considered it his best
work. One can imagine, however, the
impact of the terrifying martial music of
'Mars' on audiences immersed in the
horror of World War I. He evoked a different but equally imaginative sense of
timelessness in the offstage women's chorus dying away at the end of 'Neptune.'

The Hymn of Jesus of 1917, for choir and
orchestra, also met with success. Quite distinct from the traditional English oratorio,
Holst's setting of his own translation of
part of the apocryphal Acts of St. John
evoked, by means of dancing rhythms and
clashes of harmony, an exultant and mystical experience.

Success gave Holst more time to compose, but his works of the 1920's puzzled
audiences and critics alike: even the loyal
Vaughan Williams felt unable to summon
up more than 'cold admiration' for the
ambitious *Choral Symphony* (1923–24).
One of the best pieces from this later,
introverted period is the orchestral tone
poem *Egdon Heath*, based on a passage
from Thomas Hardy's novel *The Return of
the Native*. Hardy's description of the heath
as 'like man, slighted and enduring; and
withal singularly colossal and mysterious in
its swarthy monotony' accords well with
the quiet power and lean textures of this
restrained and hypnotic music.

Holst received numerous awards during his last years and was appointed a visiting lecturer at Harvard University. He died
in May 1934.

Bampton Morris Dancers, Whit Monday, 1897
**Holst was fascinated by English folk
traditions, such as this celebration.**

Portrait photograph taken in 1911

Signed photograph dedicated to Clive Carey, 1926

Grainger

Percy Grainger 1882–1961

RECOMMENDED WORK

Country Gardens
Mercury 434 330-2
Eastman-Rochester Orchestra/Frederick
Fennell
An infectiously bouncy rendering of Country
Gardens — *just one item from a sparkling edition of
Grainger orchestral favorites on this disc.*

REPRESENTATIVE WORKS

The Warriors
Danish Folk Song Suite
Lincolnshire Posy
Shepherd's Hey

The zany and genially subversive presence of the Australian-American pianist and composer Percy Grainger on the sidelines of twentieth-century music was largely disregarded until recently, when his enormous though chaotic and somewhat eccentric output came to be seen as significant as well as colorful.

Born in Melbourne, Grainger was largely educated by his mother, a dominant and obsessive influence on his life, whose suicide when Grainger was 40 left him devastated. He studied piano and composition in Frankfurt, and in 1901 settled in London, establishing a reputation as an international concert pianist of fiery temperament and flair. As a composer he was unsympathetic to the central Classical tradition, and was haunted by a conception of 'free music' unfettered by fixed meter and pitch, which would imitate the inflections of such natural phenomena as waves or the wind.

While in London, Grainger became infected with the enthusiasm for collecting English folk songs initiated by Cecil Sharp and Vaughan Williams, although he later

came to despise the prettified, drawing-room arrangements purveyed by Sharp. He was an energetic pioneer in the use of the wax-cylinder phonograph for field recording, and his arrangements of such tunes as *Shallow Brown*, *Molly on the Shore*, *Country Gardens*, and *Shepherd's Hey* have a raw energy and intensity, and sometimes a searing pathos, that show a true empathy with the world of village singers from whom the tunes were collected. This empathy led very naturally to powerful friendships with Grieg and Delius, whom Grainger met in 1906 and 1907.

In 1914, Grainger moved to New York, where he wrote the hugely ambitious orchestral work *The Warriors*, with an instrumentation including massed pianos. Grainger typically wrote several versions of his works, often as a result of the laudably democratic desire to make music available to as great a diversity of ensembles as possible.

In 1926 he married a Swedish poet and artist, Ella Ström. Their relationship seems to have involved an extensive and obsessive sado-masochism. Indeed, Grainger displayed a streak of cruelty elsewhere as well. His basic liberalism was tainted with an unpleasant tinge of racism, particularly against Latin cultures; he eschewed the use of Italian musical terms, discarding 'crescendo' in favor of 'louden lots.' Nevertheless, his basic humanity is shown in the studies of the music of different cultures and races that increasingly took the place of composition as he grew older.

Grainger spent his last years trying to build 'free music' machines that would liberate music from conventional scales and pitches; he and his wife scoured the neighborhood garbage cans searching for useful components. By the time he died, he was an isolated and largely forgotten man. Over his life he had built up an archive of manuscripts and memorabilia, which was divided between the museum he founded at the University of Melbourne, his library in White Plains, New York, and the Library of Congress. Although scholars have not yet made sense of this vast and ramshackle legacy, Grainger's reputation as a major creative figure increases as more of his larger pieces are brought to light.

Elsie Avril and dancers, Stratford, 1912

In common with several other composers of the period, Grainger was a keen collector of folk material such as the music played to accompany these dancers.

Ives

Charles Ives 1874–1954

RECOMMENDED WORK
Three Places in New England
Deutsche Grammophon 423 243-2
Boston Symphony Orchestra/Michael Tilson
Thomas
*With the great Boston orchestra in immaculate form,
this is a perceptive and atmospheric presentation of
some compelling music.*

REPRESENTATIVE WORKS
The Unanswered Question
Symphony No. 3
Central Park in the Dark
Piano Sonata No. 2, 'Concord'

Charles Ives is the true father of twentieth-century American music; his works combine an audacious experimentation in compositional techniques with a deeply felt nostalgia for the music and culture of his boyhood. He was born in Danbury, Connecticut, the son of the local bandmaster. His father was an extraordinary man whose principles of musical education were anything but conventional.

The variety of experience to be found in a small American town entered the young Ives's memory and sensibility at a profound level, and re-creations of this world pervade his music — of religious

Portrait photograph by Eugene Smith, c.1950

meetings, holidays (with the clashing dissonances of simultaneously heard marching bands), natural scenery and landscape, even of sports (Ives was a talented athlete, and his piano piece *Some Southpaw Pitching* gives the performer's left hand some healthy exercise!).

At 14, Ives became organist at the local Baptist Church, for which he wrote often daring psalm settings and organ music. Such experimentation had to be suppressed during the period from 1894 to 1898, when Ives attended Yale University and took lessons from the conservative Horatio Parker; there he wrote such comparatively decorous works as the *First Symphony*, the *First String Quartet*, and the cantata *The Celestial Country*.

On leaving Yale, Ives decided not to embark on a professional career in music but instead went into the insurance business, which he approached with characteristic idealism. Although he was left with only evenings and weekends to compose, he produced in the first 15 years of the century a huge body of radical and remarkable music, most of it unperformed for years. This included orchestral works such as *The Unanswered Question* and *Central Park in the Dark*, which required huge forces and two conductors. It also included a large number of songs covering a range of moods from nostalgic sentiment (*At the River*) to humorous portraits of American life (*The Circus Band*, *The Side*

The town center of Woodstock, Vermont, 1940
In his compositions, Ives created musical landscapes of small-town America, especially his native New England.

Show) to dissonant experimental modernism (*Majority*).

In 1908, Ives married Harmony Twichell, a nurse described as 'the most beautiful girl in Hartford.' The following year he began work on his vast *Piano Sonata No. 2*, the 'Concord,' in which he attempted to portray the spirit of the Transcendentalists, whose ideas and beliefs influenced Ives's own Utopianism. The orchestral *Three Places in New England*, completed in 1914, is one of the most vivid and haunting evocations of Ives's youth. The three movements consist of a meditation on Stephen Foster's song *Old Black Joe*, a re-creation of a festive band meeting, and the impression of hearing a church service from across a river.

In 1918, Ives suffered a heart attack, and with the period of subsequent convalescence, his flow of music gradually dried up until, one day in 1926, in his wife's words, 'he came downstairs with tears in his eyes and said he couldn't seem to compose any more — nothing went well — nothing sounded right.' Ives lived for another 28 years and had the satisfaction of witnessing performers gradually take up his works and make him a model for a whole generation of younger composers.

Placard at the 44th Street Theater, New York, 1934

This popular opera married the words of Stein with hymn tunes and marches.

Thomson

Virgil Thomson 1896–1989

RECOMMENDED WORK

The Plow That Broke the Plains — Suite
Angel CDM7 64306-2
Los Angeles Chamber Orchestra/Neville Marriner
An idiomatically perky, beautifully prepared account of the 1942 suite from Thomson's best-known film score. Light fare, but appealing.

REPRESENTATIVE WORKS
**Symphony on a Hymn Tune
Arcadian Songs and Dances
Four Saints in Three Acts**

An eloquent critic and lifelong promoter of American composers, Virgil Thomson composed music that steered an unusual and enigmatic course. Born in Kansas City, Missouri, his most formative early influences were the Baptist hymns he accompanied as a church organist. At Harvard, he developed a strong interest in French music, particularly that of Erik Satie, whose simplicity, clarity, and humor greatly appealed to him. In 1921 and 1922 a traveling scholarship enabled Thomson to study with Nadia Boulanger in Paris, where he met Satie as well as the composers of the radical group known as *Les Six*; back at Harvard, he gave the American premiere of Satie's *Socrate*.

The charms of Paris proved irresistible, and Thomson returned there to live from 1925 to 1940. Works from the beginning of this period include the *Sonata da chiesa*, whose neoclassical style pays obvious homage to Stravinsky, and which contrasts with the homespun Americana of *Variations and Fugues on Sunday-School Tunes*. In

A performance of *Four Saints in Three Acts*, 1934
A scene with angels and chorus from Act I of the opera.

1926 he met the writer Gertrude Stein, with whom he planned an operatic collaboration. Although ostensibly concerning Spanish saints, Stein's libretto turned out to be a mystifying assemblage of nonsense texts, chosen more for sound than for meaning. Thomson matched them with the music for a full-length opera, *Four Saints in Three Acts*. The characteristics of this piece were to become familiar hallmarks of his subsequent works — a direct, unassuming style, frequent quotations from well-known American melodies, and popular dance forms such as the tango and waltz. The opera was premiered in Hartford, Connecticut, in 1934 amid widespread publicity.

From this point Thomson entered on a period of largely abstract instrumental pieces, including a series of *Portraits*. He followed these in the late 1930's with a return to nationalist themes in scores for the films *The Plow That Broke the Plains* and *The River*, in which he used spirituals and cowboy songs. In 1940, Thomson returned to the United States to become music critic of the *New York Herald Tribune*. For 14 years his articulate, provocative, and opinionated pieces for the newspaper made him a major critical writer and arbiter of taste.

A further collaboration with Gertrude Stein resulted in 1947 in the opera *The Mother of Us All*, in which a less outrageous, though still unconventional libretto about the women's suffrage movement gave Thomson the opportunity to evoke nineteenth-century America through a collage of waltzes, hymn tunes, and marches. Another film score, *Louisiana Story*, in 1948 furnished the material for two widely performed suites, *Arcadian Songs and Dances* and *Louisiana Story*.

Thomson continued composing energetically throughout his later years. Between 1961 and 1968 he was absorbed in his most ambitious project yet, the opera *Lord Byron*, in which he attempted an emotional range not hinted at in the childlike naïveté of his earlier works. However, the *Cantata on Poems of Edward Lear* of 1973, showed that the world of childhood humor retained a perennial fascination for him.

Gershwin

George Gershwin 1898–1937

RECOMMENDED WORKS

Rhapsody in Blue
Sony Classical Royal Edition SMK437529
Columbia Symphony Orchestra/Leonard
Bernstein (pno)
*There's no missing the freewheeling spontaneity of
Lenny's famous 1960 account; the sheer chutzpah of
it all is both exhilarating and totally disarming.*

Porgy and Bess
Angel CDS7 49568-2
Willard White (bass) Porgy; Cynthia Haymon
(sop) Bess; Harolyn Blackwell (sop) Clara; Cynthia
Clarey (sop) Serena; Damon Evans (bar) Sportin'
Life; Marietta Simpson (mez) Maria; Gregg Baker
(bar) Crown; Glyndebourne Chorus; London
Philharmonic Orchestra/Simon Rattle
*Rattle at his most inspired. The whole performance
possesses a dramatic flair and overwhelming
emotional thrust that are all too rarely encountered
on record.*

REPRESENTATIVE WORKS
An American in Paris
Piano Concerto in F
Gershwin Songbook
Girl Crazy

Gershwin at the piano, c.1935

George Gershwin brought American popular music into the concert hall, writing as well a wealth of standard popular songs. Predominantly accompanied by lyrics by his brother, Ira, these remain unsurpassed in the twentieth century for melodic invention and memorability.

Gershwin was born to poor Jewish parents in Manhattan and had little exposure to music in his childhood. Initially self-taught as a pianist, he took piano and music theory lessons but never became fluent at reading music. In 1914, Gershwin left school to work for Remick's, a Tin Pan Alley publisher. He was soon having his own songs published and in 1919 wrote his first musical, *La La Lucille*. This was also the year of his first big hit, the song 'Swanee,' which became very popular in a recording by Al Jolson.

Gershwin's aspirations toward serious composition were never far from the surface. In 1919 he wrote *Lullaby* for string quartet; a one-act jazz opera, *Blue Monday Blues*, followed in 1922. But when the bandleader Paul Whiteman commissioned *Rhapsody in Blue* in 1924, Gershwin came of age as a concert composer. Gershwin himself was the first soloist in this brilliant conception, a one-movement concerto for piano and jazz band. Whiteman entrusted the work's orchestration, however, to his arranger, Ferde Grofé, because Gershwin lacked experience with instrumentation. Like all of the composer's large-scale works, *Rhapsody in Blue* can be criticized for its rather primitive sense of structure; but this has never stopped an adoring public from warming to its haunting melodies and the effective brilliance of its piano writing. One of the work's most famous features, the opening glissando for clarinet, was in fact an afterthought: Gershwin had originally written a 17-note scale, but when the band's clarinettist played a glissando in rehearsal as a joke, the composer so liked the effect that he incorporated it into the score.

Following the success of *Rhapsody in Blue*, Gershwin was commissioned to write further large concert works: the *Piano Concerto in F*, from 1925, and *An American in Paris* from 1928. He continued to compose songs, and from 1924 the

Detail of advertising poster for *Porgy and Bess*, 1959
**The film version of Gershwin's opera
starred Pearl Bailey and Sidney Poitier.**

lyrics for almost all of them were written by his brother, Ira, whose deft and witty words contributed to making the brothers one of the most successful songwriting teams on Broadway, responsible for such works as *Girl Crazy* and *Strike Up the Band*, recently revived on CD in authentic editions. With a fortune by then matching his fame, Gershwin in the late 1920's began to collect paintings by artists such as Braque and Chagall; he also devoted more and more time to painting his own pictures.

Between 1934 and 1935, Gershwin fulfilled a long-standing ambition to compose a Negro folk opera. The result was *Porgy and Bess*, written in part while Gershwin was living on the island near Charleston, South Carolina, where the opera is set: songs such as 'Summertime' and 'I Got Plenty of Nuttin'' were influenced by the speech and music of the local black community.

In 1937, Gershwin started to experience spells of dizziness; in July of that year he died, tragically young, of a brain tumor. The synthesis of jazz and serious music he achieved not only is remarkable in its own right but also stands as a unique reflection of American society between the wars.

Barber

Samuel Barber 1910–1981

RECOMMENDED WORK
Adagio for Strings
Argo 436 288-2
Baltimore Symphony Orchestra/David Zinman
An affectingly noble, beautifully refined presentation of Barber's poignant essay. Part of a superb all-Barber anthology from this underrated conductor.

REPRESENTATIVE WORKS
Violin Concerto
Piano Concerto
Dover Beach

The American Samuel Barber continued to fly the flag of musical Romanticism in a century when it was unfashionable. The melodic appeal and unbridled emotional content of his finest works won acclaim with concert audiences. But critics, were not as comfortable with him, reacting negatively to the more ambitious works, particularly the opera *Antony and Cleopatra*.

Born in Pennsylvania, Barber was early influenced by his aunt and uncle, Louise and Sidney Homer: she was a famous contralto, he a composer of songs. Samuel's affinity with the voice showed itself not only in a large output of vocal music but also in his fine baritone voice. From 1924 to 1932 he studied at the Curtis Institute in Philadelphia, taking lessons in both voice and composition. For a while he even contemplated a career as a singer, and made a famous and moving recording of one of his earliest successes, the intensely somber setting of Matthew Arnold's poem *Dover Beach* for voice and string quartet, written in 1931.

After his graduation Barber won a succession of prizes and awards that enabled him to travel in Europe, where he forged important links with Italy. His traveling companion, and lifelong friend, was his fellow student and composer, Gian Carlo Menotti. Works such as his *First Symphony* (1936) were immediately performed in Rome as well as New York, and in 1938 the great Italian conductor Arturo Toscanini premiered what was to become Barber's popular classic, the *Adagio for Strings*. This lyrical elegy was arranged from the central movement of his *First String Quartet*, but the additional richness and intensity of the orchestral string sound brought it such huge success that the composer was induced to make a third arrangement of it in 1967, as a choral 'Agnus Dei.'

Apart from a brief spell in the United States Air Force from 1943 to 1945, Barber settled down to a steady and often spectacular compositional career, including such works as the appealing *Violin Concerto* (1939–40) and the *Piano Sonata* (1949), the latter commissioned by the legendary pianist Vladimir Horowitz. The airy delicacy of its scherzo and audacious complexity of its final fugue were clearly inspired by his skill. In the 1950's Barber produced the *Hermit Songs* — settings of medieval Irish monastic texts, sacred and profane — and in 1957 the opera *Vanessa*, to a libretto by Menotti. But his instinctive talent now seemed suffused with effort, and despite the success of the assertive *Piano Concerto* in 1962, with its self-conscious adoption of a more contemporary idiom, the failure of *Antony and Cleopatra* cast a shadow over Barber's later years.

Perhaps the best summary of Barber's approach came from the composer himself in 1971: 'It is said that I have no style at all but that doesn't matter. I just go on doing, as they say, my thing. I believe this takes a certain courage.'

Photograph of Samuel Barber, 1966

Walton

William Walton 1902–1983

RECOMMENDED WORK
Symphony No. 1
RCA Gold Seal GD87830
London Symphony Orchestra/André Previn
Surely Prévin's finest hour in the studio. Since this classic performance first appeared in 1966, no other version has quite matched its blistering power and ferocious intensity.

REPRESENTATIVE WORKS
Façade
Viola Concerto
Violin Concerto
Belshazzar's Feast

Walton won an early reputation as a bright young *enfant terrible* of the 1920's. When his real personality emerged, however, he showed himself as essentially a late Romantic, primarily orchestral composer, in the mold of Elgar and Sibelius. A very personal strain of bittersweet nostalgia permeates much of his work.

Born in Oldham, Lancashire, he showed no particular signs of precocious talent, but his natural singing ability enabled him to become a chorister at Christ Church Cathedral, Oxford, at the age of ten. He became a music undergraduate at the unusually early age of 16, but left Oxford without a degree in 1920.

The rigors of earning a living were kept at bay thanks to his friendship with the aristocratic and literary Sitwell family. He lived with the Sitwells in Chelsea and abroad for the next decade, becoming especially close to the brothers Osbert and Sacheverell. In 1921 and 1922, Walton set to music some of Edith Sitwell's poetry: the result, *Façade*, was an early, if not entirely characteristic masterpiece. Conceived originally as a drawing-room entertainment, it features quirky and often surrealistic poems declaimed by a narrator over music for a small ensemble,

Portrait photograph, c.1930

in a style similar to the Parisian frivolities of *Les Six* (see pages 228 and 229).

Walton withdrew a *String Quartet* of the same era because he felt it leaned too heavily on Berg and Schoenberg; but with his *Portsmouth Point* overture of 1925, Walton created an impression of high spirits and ebullience that would often recur in his scherzo movements. The *Viola Concerto*, completed in 1929, was written for the English violist Lionel Tertis, but was actually first performed by Paul Hindemith, a fine violist as well as a composer. Displaying absolute mastery and assurance, it was the first work to give full expression to the strain of restless melancholy that so characterizes the composer.

The oratorio *Belshazzar's Feast* (1929-31) gave Walton the opportunity to challenge the complacency into which the English chorale had fallen. While the glitter and imagination of the work were widely recognized, its 'pagan' modernism was controversial. Walton next started work on his *First Symphony*, which gave him much trouble and was first performed in 1934 without its final movement. Birth pangs notwithstanding, it is a formidable achievement. The expansive build-ups owe much to Sibelius, and the breadth of canvas and pageantry of the Finale look back to Elgar; but few if any of Walton's British contemporaries could approach the excitement and authority with which the large form is handled.

In the 1930's, Walton began to write music for films, culminating in his scores for three of Laurence Olivier's Shakespeare films, *Henry V* (1944), *Hamlet* (1947), and *Richard III* (1955). His style remained fundamentally unchanged for the rest of his career. Large-scale works such as the *Violin Concerto*, the *Cello Concerto*, and the *Second Symphony* explored familiar terrain with a warmth and ease that perhaps lacked only the frisson of adventure. The sumptuous operatic score *Troilus and Cressida* (1950–54) reflected the Mediterranean warmth of the island of Ischia, where Walton had recently settled with his wife, Susana, and which remained his home for the rest of his life.

Recording the score of *The Battle of Britain*, 1969
Walton is seated between Malcolm Arnold on the left and the film's director, Guy Hamilton.

Respighi

Ottorino Respighi 1879–1936

RECOMMENDED WORK
Pines of Rome
London 410 145-2
Montreal Symphony Orchestra/Charles Dutoit
Ever the wizard of orchestral color, Charles Dutoit coaxes some ravishing sounds from his virtuoso Montreal band. Spectacular recording.

REPRESENTATIVE WORKS
Fountains of Rome
The Birds
Three Botticelli Pictures
Ancient Airs and Dances
La Boutique fantasque
Lauda per la Natività del Signore

Born in Bologna in Italy, Ottorino Respighi studied violin and composition at the city's Liceo Musicale from 1891 to 1901. Toward the end of this period, and again in 1902–03, he visited St. Petersburg in Russia, where lessons from the great master of orchestration Nikolai Rimsky-Korsakov deeply influenced him. In the first decade of the century, living in Bologna, Respighi was active as a pianist, string player, conductor, and teacher, but he was slow to find a characteristic voice as a composer. A setting from 1910 of Shelley's poem 'Aretusa' does show a certain amount of individuality, but the shadow of Richard Strauss is all too visible over the huge and unwieldy *Sinfonia drammatica* of 1913–14.

In 1913, Respighi settled in Rome to take up a post as professor of composition at the conservatory. With his four orchestral impressions of Roman scenes at different times of day, *Fontane di Roma* (Fountains of Rome, 1914–16), Respighi at last found the perfect vehicle to suit his talent. Without attempting to plumb emotional or intellectual depths, the music evokes glittering and colorful scenes with great success.

Respighi's international reputation was assured when conductors of the caliber of Arturo Toscanini took *Fontane di Roma* and its successor, *Pini di Roma* (Pines of Rome), into their repertories. In *Pini di Roma*, Respighi displays vivid powers of observation as he imitates children's songs in the opening piece, 'Pines of Villa Borghese.' The night evocation of 'Pines of the Janiculum' even uses a phonograph recording of a nightingale's song. Had he been born a generation later, Respighi would have had obvious credentials for a career in film music.

His later attempts to repeat the formula were not always so happy. In *Feste Romane* (Roman Festivals), for example, the naïveté of earlier works turned into boisterous and superficial brashness. But Respighi's explorations into the Italian music of the past, which he had conducted for 20 years, also bore extensive fruit. In the 1919 production of his ballet *La Boutique fantasque* (The Magical Toyshop), he arranged for orchestra piano pieces by Rossini with ideal wit and verve; and in 1927 he composed the suite for chamber orchestra *Gli Uccelli* (The Birds), skillful and affectionate arrangements of short harpsichord pieces by seventeenth- and eighteenth-century composers such as Rameau and Pasquini.

Respighi's interest in the musical language of pre-Classical composers led him to create a series of more austere and abstract instrumental works, such as the *Concerto gregoriano* of 1921 for violin and orchestra and the *Quartetto dorico* of 1924. The most attractive and endearing result of these 'archaic' interests was the delightful Christmas cantata *Lauda per la Natività del Signore*, clearly inspired in part by the works of Monteverdi.

During Respighi's final years he turned his attentions increasingly to opera, but none of the resultant works entered the general repertory, although the charming children's opera *La bella dormente nel bosco* (The Sleeping Beauty in the Wood) is worthy of revival. His reputation rests to a large extent on his brilliant and attractive use of orchestral color and timber to evoke scenes and places, particularly Rome, where he died in 1936.

Schoenberg

Arnold Schoenberg 1874–1951

RECOMMENDED WORK
Verklärte Nacht
Deutsche Grammophon 415 326-2
Berlin Philharmonic Orchestra/Herbert von Karajan
Schoenberg's youthful masterpiece has never sounded more headily beautiful. The Berlin strings surpass themselves in terms of tonal opulence and sensitivity to nuance; the overall effect is at once ravishing and powerful.

REPRESENTATIVE WORKS
Gurrelieder
Pelleas und Melisande
5 Pieces for Orchestra
Pierrot Lunaire
Erwartung
Moses und Aron

Schoenberg was born in Vienna into an orthodox Jewish family. After his father's death, he was obliged to work in a bank from 1891 to 1895, but found time to pursue his musical development through amateur chamber music performance and composition lessons with Alexander von Zemlinsky. The early *String Quartet in D* from 1897 shows the influence of Dvořák and Brahms, and was performed with success. But his next work initiated the controversy that followed Schoenberg throughout his career. The string sextet *Verklärte Nacht* (Transfigured Night) — whose Romantic character and impassioned richness of harmony and color are reminiscent of Wagner and Richard Strauss — was turned down by the Vienna Music Association because of some unacceptably dissonant chords.

Schoenberg married Zemlinsky's sister in 1901 and moved to Berlin, where he subsidized composition of the symphonic poem *Pelleas und Melisande* by orchestrating operettas in a cabaret theater. He was rescued from such drudgery when on

Drawing of Schoenberg by Egon Schiele, 1917
An accomplished painter himself, Schoenberg knew several Expressionist artists, including Schiele, Wassily Kandinsky, and Franz Marc.

Engraving by Felix Muller of *Pierrot Lunaire*, 1912
The songs of Pierrot Lunaire evoked a world of madness and despair.

Richard Strauss's recommendation he was appointed to teach at Berlin's Stern Academy. This was the start of Schoenberg's long career as a great teacher. In 1903 he returned to Vienna to teach privately. Alban Berg and Anton Webern — who would, with Schoenberg, form the 'Second Viennese School' — became his pupils the following year.

This atmosphere of creative stimulation produced bold and rapid developments in Schoenberg's style, with the *First Chamber Symphony* pushing and the *Second String Quartet* breaking the limits of tonality (the traditional method of composing a piece of music in one particular key). The soprano that Schoenberg added to the quartet sings words that appear symbolic and significant: 'I breathe the air from another planet.'

Schoenberg returned to Berlin in 1912 to conduct the premiere of *Pierrot Lunaire*, a setting of 21 poems for speaker and chamber ensemble. In this piece, a key work of the twentieth century, the composer drew on the surrealist poems of Albert Giraud, which express the worlds of subconscious violence, madness, and desperate nostalgia that were implicit in the musical worlds Schoenberg was exploring. The work makes a feature of *Sprechgesang*, a type of vocal production between singing and speech. Schoenberg's compositional experiments culminated in the technique of serialism, an atonal method in which the 12 notes of the chromatic scale are used with equal emphasis. His first works in this style date from 1923, two early examples being the *Piano Suite* and the *Suite for Eight Instruments*.

In 1923, Schoenberg's wife died; ten months later he remarried. From 1925 he taught at the Prussian Academy of Arts in Berlin, where he wrote the first two acts of the opera *Moses und Aron*, as well as a number of instrumental works that re-established links with composers of the Classical period. In 1933, with the coming to power of the Nazi Party, his Jewishness made his position in Germany untenable and he left the country, eventually to settle in Los Angeles. He spent the rest of his life there, teaching for some time at the University of Southern California. His later works show an enriching of his style to encompass both tonal and serial techniques, as well as a renewed concentration on Jewish elements in works such as *A Survivor from Warsaw* (1947). During the last year of his life he worked on meditative, religious works. He died in Los Angeles in July 1951.

Schoenberg stands alongside Stravinsky as one of two giant figures unsurpassed in their influence on twentieth-century music. Although Schoenberg was the more overtly revolutionary, he regarded his innovations as the continuation of a direct Classical lineage, where originality first required the framework of Classical forms in order to communicate coherently to the listener.

Berg

Alban Berg 1885–1935

RECOMMENDED WORK
Violin Concerto
Deutsche Grammophon 437 093-2
Anne-Sophie Mutter (vln); Chicago Symphony
Orchestra/James Levine
*Anne-Sophie Mutter and James Levine form an
inspired partnership, assured and marvelously
eloquent. A splendid achievement, including state-of-
the-art engineering.*

REPRESENTATIVE WORKS
Wozzeck
Lulu
Lyric Suite
Seven early songs

Alban Berg, along with Anton Webern
and their teacher Arnold Schoenberg,
formed a triumvirate known as the
'Second Viennese School.' The explorations of this trio into the craft of musical
composition would revolutionize the
whole of twentieth-century music.

Photographic portrait of Berg, c.1920

Berg lived his whole life in Vienna,
although the family of minor gentry into
which he was born had an estate in the
Alps that he frequented in the summer.
As a young man he moved in the artistic
circles — including painters such as Klimt
and Kokoschka and writers such as the
poet Altenberg — that were challenging
the snobbish complacency of Viennese
culture at that time.

He had almost no formal musical training before his lessons with Schoenberg
started in 1904. Berg regarded the older
composer (in fact only 11 years his senior)
as a friend and father figure, as well as a
musical ideal. Four years into the lessons
he wrote his Opus 1, the one-movement
Piano Sonata. Although certainly paying
homage to the styles of Schoenberg and
Mahler in its darkly hued, late Romantic
gloom, the *Piano Sonata* shows the hand of
a master in its richness of material and formal confidence. The *String Quartet* of 1910
was the last work Berg wrote directly
under Schoenberg's tutelage, and with it
he loosed the final ties with tonality and
the notion that a piece is linked to one specific key. The music of this period is colored also by Berg's love for Helene
Nahowski, whom he married in 1911.
The *Altenberg Songs* of 1912, for soprano
and orchestra, show a sultry and bitter
eroticism that would find more extended
outlets in Berg's two operas. Schoenberg
disapproved of the *Altenberg Songs*, and in
his *Three Pieces for Orchestra*, Berg
attempted far longer, more highly developed structures (heavily influenced by
Mahler's *Ninth Symphony*) in a deliberate
effort to appease his teacher, to whom he
dedicated the work.

From 1915 to 1917, Berg served in the
Austrian army, and he wrote his superbly
powerful opera *Wozzeck* (adapted from
the play by Georg Büchner) between 1917
and 1922. His humane and sympathetic
treatment of the soldier Wozzeck, as well
as an almost unbearable dramatic intensity
and angst, cut right through the complex
surface of the music to communicate with
immense power to audiences

In the *Chamber Concerto*, for piano, violin, and 13 wind instruments, finished in
1925, Berg celebrated the threesome of

The front cover of the score of *Wozzeck*, published
by Universal Edition, 1925

**Wozzeck tells the story of a low-ranking
soldier who is bullied and mistreated by
all around him.**

Schoenberg, Webern, and himself in a
work whose complex and highly mathematical structure is based on the number
three. The *Lyric Suite* for string quartet
(1925–26) was similarly influenced by an
external event, woven into the music by
means of codes and cryptograms. This was
Berg's love affair with Hanna Fuchs-
Robettin, which also found expression in
the overt and highly charged sexuality of
Berg's last opera, *Lulu.*

In 1935, Berg was commissioned to
compose a *Violin Concerto* as a memorial
for Manon Gropius, the 18-year-old
daughter of Mahler's widow, Alma, and
the architect Walter Gropius. Completing
the work quickly, Berg wove Bach's
chorale *Es ist genug* into the final movement to create an intensely moving elegy.
He never heard the work played; in
December 1935 he died of general sep-
ticemia, and the posthumous premiere
became his own requiem.

Hindemith

Paul Hindemith 1895–1963

RECOMMENDED WORK

Symphonic Metamorphosis on Themes of Carl Maria von Weber
Sony Essential Classics SBK53258
Cleveland Orchestra/George Szell
Under Szell's meticulous, dynamic guidance, Hindemith's superbly witty orchestral showpiece receives the performance of a lifetime. Don't let the cumbersome title put you off.

REPRESENTATIVE WORKS
Mathis der Maler
Die Harmonie der Welt
Konzertmusik, Op. 50, for brass and strings
Nobilissima Visione
Organ Sonata No. 2
Trauermusik

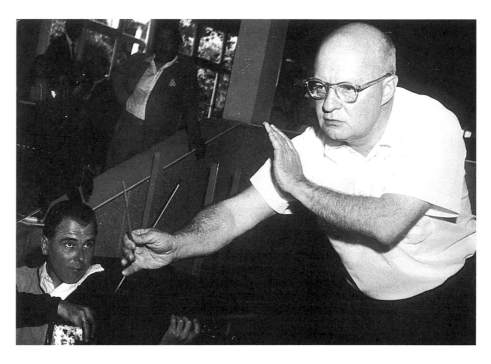

Hindemith conducting Beethoven's *Ninth Symphony* in Bayreuth, 1953

Hindemith believed composers should be proficient in all aspects of their craft and mastered several instruments himself.

Born near Frankfurt, the prolific composer Paul Hindemith studied at the Frankfurt Conservatory, where he proved himself a versatile instrumentalist, demonstrating proficiency on the violin, viola, piano, and clarinet. At the age of 19 he became leader of the Frankfurt Opera orchestra, and also second violin in the Rebner String Quartet. Work at the opera was interrupted by a period of military service between 1917 and 1919, during which Hindemith played in a regimental band and an army string quartet.

Hindemith's early works attracted immediate attention and even notoriety: their sensational elements included violence and sexuality in the one-act operas *Mörder* (Murder), of 1919, and *Sancta Susanna*, of 1921; and jazz and sleazy nightclub music in the piano suite *1922* and the *Kammermusik No. 1*, whose instrumentation includes a siren. Despite its air of boisterous parody, the *Kammermusik* was the first of many works by Hindemith to use Baroque models such as Bach's *Brandenburg Concertos* for form, texture, and rhythmic drive.

In 1923 the success of the Amar Quartet, in which Hindemith was now violist, enabled him to relinquish his Frankfurt Opera post. He abandoned his musical shock tactics, and moved toward a style distinguished by its energy and objectivity. The opera *Cardillac*, for example, deals with a goldsmith who murders his customers, but the horrific aspects of the story are mitigated by the formal structure and unemotional clarity of the music.

Hindemith next turned increasingly to the composition of works for amateurs, such as the *Lehrstück* of 1929 with texts by Bertolt Brecht, which encouraged directness and simplicity of expression in his work. The *Trauermusik* for viola and strings emphasized Hindemith's desire for immediacy in his music. It was composed the day after the death in 1936 of the English king, George V, and premiered the day after that.

A much larger-scale summing-up of Hindemith's ideas had come earlier in the 1930's with the completion of the opera *Mathis der Maler* (Mathis the Artist) and the symphony based on it. The German painter Matthias Grünewald symbolized for Hindemith the dilemma of all artists caught up in political upheavals: Hindemith had himself been attacked by the Nazis, and in 1937 was forced to leave Germany. The three movements of the symphony *Mathis der Maler* each represent one of the panels of Grünewald's altarpiece at Isenheim, and the warmth and humanity of the work show the composer coming to terms with his Classical and Romantic heritage, and with his innate respect for tradition.

Hindemith found refuge from the Nazis in the United States, where he taught at Yale University and gained U. S. citizenship in 1946. A series of orchestral commissions included the *Symphonic Metamorphosis on Themes of Carl Maria von Weber*, whose wordy title conceals a work of the most deft and delightful humor, an antidote to the common view of the mature Hindemith as a composer of unbending Teutonic seriousness. In 1953 he moved to Switzerland, and there, in his last years, completed *Die Harmonie der Welt* (The Harmony of the World), a mystical opera about the astronomer Johan Kepler.

Hindemith is today recognized as the leading German composer of his generation, whose music, carefully formulated philosophy, and dynamism as a performer were an inspiration to his contemporaries.

Villa-Lobos

Heitor Villa-Lobos 1887–1959

RECOMMENDED WORK
Bachianas Brasileiras No. 5
Hyperion CDA66257
Jill Gomez (sop); Pleeth Cello Octet
Jill Gomez brings a real understanding to Bachianas Brasileiras No. 5, a fusion of the forms and ideals of Bach with more contemporary Brazilian moods; her rendition of 'Cantilena' is especially seductive. Well-balanced digital sound adds to making this a must.

REPRESENTATIVE WORKS
Bachianas Brasileiras No. 9
Chôros No. 6
Concerto for Guitar and Orchestra
Distribução de flores
Prole do bebê

A prolific composer and a man of exuberant energy, Heitor Villa-Lobos transformed the musical life of his native Brazil and put the country on the international musical map.

His musical education was anything but academic. From an early age he learned the cello with his father, and it was always an instrument close to his heart. He also gained a virtuosic command of the guitar, on which he improvised with popular musicians in his home city, Rio de Janeiro.

Between the ages of 18 and 25, Villa-Lobos traveled all over Brazil exploring various forms of Brazilian music and collecting materials. He later entertained Parisian circles with tales of being captured by cannibal Indians, who released him unharmed only because of his musical abilities. On his return to Rio, his attempts at formal training in composition proved uncongenial to his fiery and impatient temperament, but he did study the works of the great masters while earning his living playing in cafés. He composed continuously, gaining increasing recognition, and in 1922 received an official commission for a work about World War I — his *Third Symphony* 'A guerra' (To War).

Villa-Lobos, photographed c.1935

With the help and encouragement of the pianist Arthur Rubinstein, Villa-Lobos was able in the late 1920's to go to Paris, where he was influenced by Satie and Milhaud. He caused a sensation with the exotic brilliance and vitality of his *Chôros*, a series of works for forces varying from solo guitar to chorus, band, and orchestra, all re-creating the sounds and forms of Brazilian popular music. Villa-Lobos lived mainly in Paris until 1930, and was much admired by fellow musicians, including Edgard Varèse and Olivier Messiaen.

His return to Brazil coincided with the arrival of the new nationalist regime, under which Villa-Lobos was put in charge of organizing the musical life of the country: his energy and imagination in the educational reforms he carried out are comparable only to the achievements of Kodály in Hungary. The works that best encapsulate his thinking during these years are the *Bachianas Brasileiras*, which abandon the wildness of much of his earlier music in favor of a Classical serenity. He paid homage to his beloved Bach by pointing to the parallels between Bach's counterpoint and the independent lines of much Brazilian folk music. *No. 5* of the *Bachianas*, for wordless soprano and eight cellos, is a haunting example of this.

In 1945, Villa-Lobos founded the Brazilian Academy of Music and nominated its first 50 members. The works of his last years include some virtuosic concertos, as well as a large proportion of his 17 string quartets. He died in 1959 and was accorded the honor of a state funeral.

Stravinsky

Igor Stravinsky 1882–1971

RECOMMENDED WORKS
The Rite of Spring
Angel Eminence CD EMX 2188
London Philharmonic Orchestra/Charles Mackerras
Mackerras turns in a wonderfully fresh account, with countless textural revelations. An enthusiastic LPO respond as if their very lives depended on it.

Petrushka
Deutsche Grammophon 437 022-2
London Symphony Orchestra/Claudio Abbado
This memorable and engrossing performance shows the LSO-Abbado partnership at the peak of its accomplishment. With superb engineering to match, this is hard to beat.

REPRESENTATIVE WORKS
The Firebird
Pulcinella
The Soldier's Tale
Apollon musagète
Symphony of Psalms
Symphony in Three Movements
The Rake's Progress

Stravinsky's long, varied life is mirrored by a rich and diverse musical output, whose inner strength and consistency survived extreme outward changes of style. He was born at Oranienbaum in Russia, the son of a bass singer at the St. Petersburg Opera: Russian opera and ballet were the musical backdrop to his childhood. He studied law at St. Petersburg University from 1901 to 1905, but focused his main attention on composing, taking private lessons from Rimsky-Korsakov. In 1906 he married his cousin, Katerina, and over the next couple of years they had a son and daughter.

Two works from this period, *Scherzo fantastique* and *Fireworks*, impressed the impresario Diaghilev, who commissioned a large-scale ballet, *The Firebird*, premiered in Paris in 1910. Although Stravinsky's score for this Russian fairy tale is a direct descendant of the music familiar from his

After the war, Diaghilev was again the catalyst for a major change in Stravinsky's style. He suggested that Stravinsky adapt some short pieces by the Baroque composer Pergolesi, and Stravinsky's enthusiasm for the project not only produced a sparkling masterpiece in the ballet *Pulcinella* but also initiated a long period of 'neoclassical' works that revived musical models and precepts from the past, often in a spirit of ironic affection — Bach's *Brandenburg Concertos* in the concerto *Dumbarton Oaks*, Mozartian comic opera in *The Rake's Progress*, and the oratorios of Handel in *Oedipus Rex*.

From 1920 to 1939, Stravinsky lived in France. Russian themes still influenced such works as the short opera *Mavra* (1921–22), based on Pushkin, and the *Symphony of Psalms* (1930), with its echoes of Russian Orthodox ritual. Meanwhile, Stravinsky's growing careers as conductor and pianist were reflected in works such as the *Concerto for Piano and Wind Instruments* and the *Capriccio for Piano and Orchestra*, both written for himself to play.

Oedipus Rex and *Perséphone*, both novel variations on the cantata form, were premiered in Paris in 1927 and 1934; but commissions increasingly came from the States. Following the deaths of his wife and mother in 1939, Stravinsky embarked for New York, and the United States became his home for the rest of his life. He was joined in 1940 by his longtime mistress, Vera Sudeikina; they married and settled in Hollywood.

Apart from such bizarre initial commissions as a ballet for young elephants (*Circus Polka*), the 1940's saw the magisterial *Symphony in Three Movements*, the ballet *Orpheus*, and the opera *The Rake's Progress*. In the 1950's, Stravinsky's style underwent a final transformation, precipitated by a rediscovery of Webern's music and the techniques of Schoenberg: *Agon*, *Canticum Sacrum*, and *Threni* show this change of direction. His last works are short and austere, culminating in the *Requiem Canticles* of 1966. Stravinsky's health eventually failed; he died in New York in 1971 and was buried in Venice, near the grave of his collaborator and the commissioner of some of his greatest works, Diaghilev.

early years, especially that of Rimsky-Korsakov, its unmistakable brilliance won the composer international renown. Stravinsky took his family to Western Europe and enhanced his reputation with two further ballets for Diaghilev. In the first, *Petrushka*, set during St. Petersburg's Shrovetide Fair, the composer brought to the misfortunes of the central character, a puppet, a new acerbic brittleness that he pushed further still in *The Rite of Spring*. One of the most momentous and uncompromising works of the twentieth century, this portrayal of sacrificial rituals of pagan Russia introduced a level of dissonance and rhythmic innovation that outraged the

Photograph of Stravinsky, c.1932

The composer captured deep in concentration as he studies a score.

first-night audience in Paris in 1913, provoking wild protest and disorder.

Switzerland, a frequent haunt of the Stravinskys, became their home during World War I. Russian folk material continued to inspire Stravinsky in such works as *Les Noces* (The Wedding) and *Renard* (Fox), but an increasing leanness and economy of style appear in *The Soldier's Tale* of 1918, echoing the straitened circumstances of the time. The work uses only a handful of performers.

Honegger

Arthur Honegger. 1892–1955

RECOMMENDED WORK
Pacific 231
Supraphon 11 0667-2
Czech Philharmonic Orchestra/Serge Baudo
The Czech Philharmonic Orchestra have a distinguished tradition in French repertoire, and this sympathetic, wonderfully graphic realization of Honegger's celebrated portrait in sound is as compelling as any available.

REPRESENTATIVE WORKS
Symphony No. 3, 'Liturgique'
Le Roi David
Jeanne d'Arc au bûcher
Pastorale d'été
Rugby

Honegger in front of 'Pacific 231,' 1923

Pacific 231 *is an orchestral tone poem in which Honegger sought to capture the flavor of a steam locomotive in action.*

The Swiss composer Arthur Honegger was an unsensational artist of great integrity, whose best work combines a French sensibility with a German seriousness of approach.

He was born not in Switzerland but in northern France, and initially French influences prevailed, his years at the Paris Conservatoire (1911–14) overshadowing an earlier period of study in Zurich. As an adolescent he had been profoundly moved by performances of Bach's cantatas and chorales, and this influence resurfaced later on in Honegger's own oratorios. Beethoven too provided a lifelong influence, as did the contrasting but vivid impressions made by the music of Stravinsky and Prokofiev that Honegger heard later in Paris.

It was in Paris that Honegger became a member of *Les Six*, the group of composers formed under the guidance of Jean Cocteau. The group included Poulenc and Milhaud, and aimed primarily to deflate pomposity and grandiosity in music with a wittily subversive simplicity and modernism. In this loosely aligned group, Honegger proved to have very little in common with the others.

More representative of Honegger than the group identity of *Les Six* was one of his earliest Parisian successes, the oratorio *Le Roi David* of 1921. This work employs a narrator — a device borrowed from the Bach Passions — and shows imaginative and graphic use of the chorus. Paris was also the scene in 1921 of the premiere of Honegger's *Pastorale d'été* for small orchestra. In 1923 the orchestral work *Pacific 231*, a programmatic description of a steam locomotive, was even more successful as one of the earliest examples of 'machine music.' In *Rugby* of 1928, the composer used his favorite sport as similarly unlikely subject matter, although Honegger himself decried this illustrative side to his talent: despite producing large numbers of film and radio scores throughout his career, he preferred that his pieces be listened to as pure music.

Le Roi David was followed throughout the 1920's and 1930's by a succession of large-scale oratorio and operatic projects, which can be seen as moral pageants relating to the social and political conflicts that preoccupied Honegger at the time. *Jeanne d'Arc au bûcher* (Joan of Arc at the Stake; 1934–35), described as a 'stage oratorio,' with a libretto by Paul Claudel, is perhaps the most striking of these.

Honegger's cycle of five symphonies, composed between 1930 and 1951, constituted a more enduring achievement. He composed the *Second Symphony* in wartime Paris. This dark work for string orchestra includes a moving and surprising conclusion in which a solo trumpet plays a blazingly optimistic chorale; Bach again provided the inspiration. Honegger wrote no finer work than his *Third Symphony*, known as the 'Liturgical' (1945–46). Each of its three movements draws its subtitle from the Requiem Mass. The first and last movements are 'dances of death,' with woodwind shrieks portraying souls in agony; but in the final section Honegger achieves a moving sense of release and liberation, and the closing flute melody (foreshadowed at the ends of the first and second movements) has the effect of a benediction.

In Honegger's last years he developed close relationships with Switzerland and the United States. He also taught in Paris for several years despite ill health, and died there of heart disease in 1955.

Poulenc

Francis Poulenc 1899–1963

RECOMMENDED WORK

Les Biches
Angel Rouge et Noir CZS7 62690-2
Ambrosian Singers, Philharmonia Orchestra/
Georges Prêtre
Irresistible! Supremely elegant Philharmonia playing;
life-enhancing direction from Georges Prêtre; wonderful
engineering. Miss at your peril!

REPRESENTATIVE WORKS
Concert champêtre
Concerto for organ, strings, and timpani
Flute Sonata
Gloria

The Gallic wit and chic of much of Poulenc's music epitomize the spirit of Paris in the 1920's; but strains of pathos, irony, and religious contemplation also run through his work and reveal the composer as a more complex and ambiguous figure, aptly described by one critic as 'at once monk and playboy.'

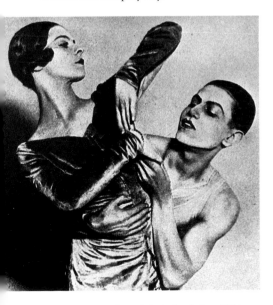

Alice Nikitina and Serge Lifar in *Les Biches*, 1924
Poulenc intended to shock audiences
with the blatant eroticism of this ballet.

Poulenc's mother, herself a fine pianist, provided her son with his first piano lessons. At the age of 14, Poulenc first heard Stravinsky's *The Rite of Spring*; Stravinsky remained a model and inspiration throughout Poulenc's life.

He published his first composition, the *Rapsodie nègre*, in 1917 and dedicated it to Erik Satie. Satie's subversive humor and aversion to pomposity made him a natural father figure to the group known as *Les Six*, which in addition to Poulenc included Milhaud, Honegger, Tailleferre, Durey, and Auric. Poulenc was perhaps the most naturally disposed to the aims of the group, laid down by the guiding aesthetic hand of Jean Cocteau as simplicity, elegance, and a sophisticated modernity.

In Poulenc's settings of animal poems by Apollinaire, *Le Bestiaire*, dating from 1918–19, he already showed an astonishing assurance and freshness, and an understanding of poetry that would make him a superb songwriter. Nonetheless, Poulenc felt the need for further formal training, and found a helpful teacher in Charles Koechlin. The ballet *Les Biches* (The Hinds, or The Little Darlings) followed, written for Diaghilev in 1924. It established Poulenc's reputation internationally; the suite he made from the music has become one of his most popular works, overflowing with memorable melodies.

In 1935 Poulenc's friend Pierre-Octave Ferroud was killed in a car accident. Poulenc subsequently rediscovered his Catholic faith and composed a long series of sacred works, including the *Litanies à la vierge noire* and the *Quatre motets pour un temps de pénitence*. Also in 1935, Poulenc gave his first recital playing piano accompaniment to the baritone Pierre Bearnac; this artistic partnership would last the rest of his life, and for it he composed many song cycles and individual songs. A few years later the *Concerto for organ, strings, and timpani* of 1938 appeared, a superb example of Poulenc's ambivalence, in which moments of Bach-like austerity rub shoulders with passages of bustling razzmatazz.

Poulenc remained in occupied France during the war, articulating its mood of grief and desolation in the haunting song titled simply *C*. After the war, he

Portrait including members of *Les Six* by Jacques-Emile Blanche, c.1921

Poulenc is pictured top right, between
singer Jane Bathori and Jean Cocteau.

alternated between concert tours with Bearnac and quiet periods of work at his large country home at Noizay, where he gained fame as a host. His first opera, *Les mamelles de Tirésias* (The Breasts of Tiresias), was a great success in Paris and was followed by two more. *Les Dialogues des carmélites*, probably his masterpiece, tells in moving terms of the heroism of nuns in a convent during the French Revolution; *La voix humaine* appeared in 1958. Poulenc also composed a large-scale *Gloria* for soprano, chorus, and orchestra, and the first three of a projected series of six woodwind sonatas (for flute, clarinet, and oboe). He was at work on a fourth opera when he died of a heart attack, shortly after his sixty-fourth birthday.

Weill

Kurt Weill 1900–1950

RECOMMENDED WORK
The Threepenny Opera
CBS MK42637
Soloists, Chorus, and Dance Orchestra of Radio
Free Berlin/Wilhelm Brückner-Rüggeberg
*With the composer's widow, Lotte Lenya, uniquely
authoritative in the role of Jenny, this account, dating
from 1958, remains unrivaled to this day. A classic
recording.*

REPRESENTATIVE WORKS
The Seven Deadly Sins
The Rise and Fall of the Town of Mahagonny
Symphony No. 2

Weill was born in Dessau in Germany, the
son of a cantor and composer of Jewish
liturgical music. By the age of 12, when he
started composing, Weill's wide musical
experiences included trips to the local
opera house, where he later worked as a
coach. He studied in Berlin between 1918
and 1923, under Humperdinck, Busoni,
and the latter's pupil, Philipp Jarnach. It
was to Jarnach that Weill dedicated his
Sinfonia Sacra of 1922, one of four works of
his premiered in the 1922–23 season, two
by the Berlin Philharmonic.

In his first opera, *Der Protagonist*, Weill
collaborated with the leading expressionist
playwright Georg Kaiser, and its Dresden
premiere in 1926 brought him wide

Lotte Lenya and Kurt Weill, 1929

renown. His fame increased in 1928 with
Die Dreigroschenoper (The Threepenny
Opera), a modern version of John Gay's
The Beggar's Opera, in which Weill's wife,
Lotte Lenya, sang the role of Jenny. The
work's most striking feature, the inclusion
of jazz and cabaret music in its memorable
and tuneful numbers, combined with
librettist Bertolt Brecht's biting social crit-
icsm to produce a huge success.

Weill continued his collaboration with
Brecht to produce *Happy End* and *The Rise
and Fall of the Town of Mahagonny*, but in
1930 riots disrupted the Leipzig premiere
of the latter work — a hard-hitting, cynical look at society — and when the Nazis
came to power in 1933, Weill was forced
to flee to Paris. There his last joint venture
with Brecht and one of his most powerful
scores, *The Seven Deadly Sins*, was premiered but received a lackluster reception.

Weill's gift for popular styles led him
naturally to New York, where he settled in
1935. He found a new librettist in the
highly regarded Maxwell Anderson, and
together they produced the political satire
Knickerbocker Holiday; its hit number,
'September Song,' found particular success with the public. From 1939 on, Weill
devoted himself to Broadway musicals,
convinced that this was the correct and
necessary means of addressing and serving
society — he no longer had any interest in
what he regarded as the cerebral experimentation of European 'art music.' *Lady in
the Dark* and *One Touch of Venus* were great
commercial hits, but *Street Scene*, *Love Life*,
and *Lost in the Stars* were regarded as dubious investments, and reached performance
only with a great deal of idealistic support.
However, in recent years, *Street Scene*
has been successfully revived and re-
evaluated as one of his most cogent and
moving works.

The strains of Broadway life eventually
proved too much for Weill, and shortly
after starting an adaptation of *Huckleberry
Finn* he died of a chronic heart disorder. It
is above all as an innovative theater composer that Weill's reputation stands. His
career was diverse, encompassing everything from serious concert works to
Broadway musicals, but his motives and
principles remained pure and idealistic.

Shostakovich

Dmitri Shostakovich 1906–1975

RECOMMENDED WORK
Symphony No. 10
Deutsche Grammophon Galleria 429 716-2
Berlin Philharmonic Orchestra/Herbert von
Karajan
*Karajan's 1981 digital remake never quite matched
the untrammeled eloquence and sheer grip of this
superb 1966 reading of the Tenth Symphony.
Unquestionably one of this conductor's finest
achievements on record.*

REPRESENTATIVE WORKS
Symphony No. 1
Symphony No. 4
Lady Macbeth of Mtsensk
Symphony No. 5
String Quartet No. 8
Concerto for piano, trumpet, and strings
Piano Concerto No. 2

Critics generally agree that Shostakovich,
in his 15 symphonies and 15 string quartets, exhibits remarkable stature and range
of expression. The influence of Mahler is
particularly visible in the epic scale of the
symphonies, with their frequent juxtaposition of tragedy and savage irony.

The listener discovers a far more
ambiguous distance, however, between
Shostakovich as the foremost Soviet

Shostakovich at work, 1943

The siege of Stalingrad, 1941–42

Russians remained resilient during the harsh siege: above, cabbages are being grown in the grounds of St. Isaac's Cathedral. Shostakovich's wartime music was patriotic in sentiment.

composer of his time — with a long list of optimistic and affirmative 'official' works to his name — and the private man, whose bleak depression appears at its most extreme in such late works as the *String Quartet No. 15*, made up of six *Adagio* movements.

The young Shostakovich studied at the St. Petersburg Conservatory, taking time off from his studies to play the piano in silent-movie theaters to support his sisters and widowed mother. He was outstanding as both a pianist and a composer, and in 1927 won a prize at the Warsaw Chopin Competition for his playing. His *Symphony No. 1*, a precociously assured masterpiece written in 1924 and 1925, soon gained a place in the international repertoire, which it has retained to this day.

Incidental music for film and stage suited Shostakovich's fluent abilities, and in an opera, *The Nose*, he explored his gift for satire. He employed satire in the opera *Lady Macbeth of Mtsensk* to heighten the tragic emotional world of the central char-

acter, a frustrated wife who murders her husband. The opera was at first a great success, performed 83 times in St. Petersburg and 97 in Moscow between 1934 and 1936. In 1936, however, the composer suffered a dramatic reversal of fortune when an article in *Pravda* titled 'Chaos Instead of Music' viciously attacked the modernist tendencies of his score.

Shostakovich's *Symphony No. 5* in 1937 was subtitled by the composer 'the creative reply of a Soviet artist to justified criticism.' While it reinstated the composer in official favor — and remains popular — one can detect a subtext of irony in its heroics. Shostakovich followed with his *Symphony No. 7*, 'Leningrad,' a straightforward and widely performed symbol of wartime patriotism, then with the more ambiguous *Eighth Symphony*. His increasing exploration of chamber music and its capacity for expressing more private utterances resulted in his again being condemned, along with fellow Soviets Prokofiev and Aram Khachaturian, in the cultural purge of 1948.

Shostakovich resorted to writing vacuous, optimistic trivia, holding back works such as the *Violin Concerto No. 1* that might annoy Stalin. Stalin's death in 1953 gradually ushered in a period of official relaxation: Shostakovich's *Symphony No. 10* of that year has the air of a personal statement, with its ubiquitous use of a figure derived from letters of the composer's name, and its slow progression from darkness to guarded optimism. By the 1960's sufficient liberalization had occurred for *Lady Macbeth* to be performed again, and the *Symphony No. 13*, though ostensibly dealing with Nazi atrocities against the Jews, was widely interpreted as a condemnation of Stalin.

Shostakovich suffered from ill health during his last decade, and much of the lean music dating from that period is concerned with death. Of his *Symphony No. 14* he said, 'The entire symphony is my protest against death': a song cycle for soprano, bass, and string orchestra, it is a striking instance of possibly the greatest symphonist of his time redefining what the symphony can do.

Additional Composers

Two tendencies dominated this period in music: a pioneering exploration into new tonal (or atonal) territories and a nostalgic attachment to Romanticism. Nowhere is this split seen more clearly than in Vienna. **Franz Schmidt** (1874–1939) found stimulation from the symphonic tradition of Brahms and Bruckner in his *Fourth Symphony*, while **Franz Lehár** (1870–1948) wrote operettas (such as *The Merry Widow*) in the Strauss tradition. At the same time, **Anton Webern** (1883–1945), Schoenberg's most radical pupil, distilled the sound and fury of Mahlerian symphonic movements into miniatures: the third of the *Three Little Pieces* for cello and piano, Op. 11, contains just 20 notes. The mysticism and jewel-like concentration of his mature style are shown in such works as the *Variations*, Op. 30.

In Germany, **Hanns Eisler** (1898–1962) expressed his political convictions in collaborations with Brecht such as *Die Massnahme* and a large output of bitingly observant songs and theatrical music.

Schoenberg's influence reached to the Mediterranean: Spanish **Roberto Gerhard** (1896–1970) brought a superb ear for color to serial techniques in his four symphonies and in chamber works such as *Leo* and *Libra*.

In France, the huge but uneven output of **Darius Milhaud** (1892–1974) is best shown in the jazz-influenced ballets *Le boeuf sur le toit* and *La création du monde*. **Albert Roussel** (1869–1937) produced a more sustained and serious output, including *Bacchus et Ariane* and the *Third* and *Fourth Symphonies*. Comparably serious and perhaps more impressive is Swiss **Frank Martin** (1890–1974), who added the bite of Bartók to French refinement in pieces such as the *Petite symphonie concertante*.

Roussel's example was important to Czech **Bohuslav Martinů** (1890–1959), whose six symphonies combine neoclassicism and Czech folk music. The Polish **Karol Szymanowski** (1882–1937), in his *Third Symphony* and opera *King Roger*, and Armenian **Aram Khachaturian,** in his ballets *Gayane* and *Spartacus*, explored more unusual themes.

In England, insularity still allowed for originality. **Arnold Bax** (1883–1953) created lush orchestral soundscapes such as *Tintagel*; **Frank Bridge** (1879–1941) progressed to using bold dissonance and rich expressionism in his *Third* and *Fourth Quartets*.

Tradition and experiment were found in the United States with **Roy Harris** (1898–1979), who wrote ruggedly impressive, very American symphonies, and **Henry Cowell** (1897–1965), whose experiments with the piano produced music of unexpected charm.

The Late Twentieth Century

With the end of World War II, relations between the United States and the Soviet Union deteriorated. Stalin absorbed the Eastern European countries into the Soviet Bloc, and tensions were increased by the Korean War. Adding to the climate of fear, the world powers raced to accumulate nuclear weapons. Elsewhere the world was being reshaped: India, Pakistan, Indonesia, and Burma achieved independence; the state of Israel was created; and a Communist government took power in China. Europe took its first steps toward unity with the Treaty of Rome, while in Africa, black nationalists fought to free their nations from colonial powers. In the United States, the Civil Rights movement gained strength, and throughout the Western world, people were becoming alarmed about environmental issues. By the 1970's, the United States had withdrawn from Vietnam's civil war. In the 1980's, while Islamic fundamentalism grew, Soviet Communism collapsed, once again transforming the map of Eastern Europe and awakening ancient antagonisms, particularly in Yugoslavia. The Middle East remained a potent source of potential conflict.

As world powers ebbed and flowed, and international boundaries shifted, technology advanced. With computers came a level of micro-invention that has launched the world on an adventure whose limits lie far in the future. The youth culture that took hold in the 1960's engendered a mood of rebellion reflected in current literature, fashion, and popular music.

Experimentation in the arts led to the music of Boulez, Stockhausen, and Cage, using principles that do not begin with recognizable melodies or grand themes. While some listeners and performers appreciate the random and discordant elements in modern music, others have reacted with styles that use electronic synthesizers or reproductions of ancient instruments to return to simpler and more accessible sounds. Tradition survives in the operatic work of Britten, Tippett, and Henze.

Featured Composers

V-yramid by Nam June Paik, 1982

In the late twentieth century, life has become more and more influenced by mass media. As well as the written word, television, cable, and satellite have made communications instantaneous and truly global.

233

United Nations building, New York City

The United Nations offered hope for lasting peace; its charter gave it power to discuss all matters of international security.

The end of hostilities in 1945 was greeted by many Europeans with a mixture of relief and despair. Peace brought with it the realization that the continent faced political and economic ruin. Indeed, as the horrors of the concentration camps were revealed, it seemed that the moral foundations of European civilization had been undermined.

The reconstruction process was slow and painful, and nowhere more so than in the political arena. The first steps toward a settlement were taken at the Yalta Conference in February 1945, a few months before the end of the war. The Allies made plans for the creation of the United Nations, which it was hoped would prevent the outbreak of any further global conflicts. At the same time, the Allied leaders (Churchill, Roosevelt, and Stalin) also discussed the shape of postwar Europe. Their decisions, it later transpired, were over generous to the Soviet Union.

The beginning of the Cold War

After the war, Europe rapidly divided into two camps. As early as March 1946, Churchill delivered his prophetic speech at Fulton, Missouri, in which he talked about an 'Iron Curtain' partitioning the continent between the Baltic and the Adriatic. The Soviet Union had made huge territorial gains as a result of the peace settlement and soon filled the power vacuum that had been created by the dismemberment of Nazi Germany. Satellite Communist governments were installed in Poland, Romania, Hungary, Bulgaria, and Albania, with a coup in Prague in February 1948 adding Czechoslovakia to their number. Meanwhile, civil war raged in Greece, raising the possibility that it, too, might be swallowed up by the Eastern bloc.

The extent of Russian ambitions was fully exposed by the blockade of Berlin in June 1948. Though situated on East German soil, Berlin remained under the administration of the four major powers (the United States, Britain, France, and the Soviet Union). Now, as Soviet forces severed road and rail links, the West was left with two options: either abandon the city or supply all its needs by air. The Allies adopted the second course of action, and the subsequent 'Berlin airlift' continued for almost a year, until the Communist authorities relented. This blatant brinkmanship had been successfully dealt with, but no one could now be in any doubt that a 'Cold War' between East and West had begun. The invasion of South Korea by Communist North Korea in 1950, leading to military confrontation between the United States and Communist China, heightened East–West tension even further.

One of the immediate causes of the Berlin blockade was West German monetary reform, which successfully stabilized the Mark. This, along with much of the recovery of Western Europe, was stimulated by the generous aid package proposed by George Marshall, the U.S. Secretary of State. The 'Marshall Plan' enabled Western economies to grow much more quickly than their Eastern counterparts, further highlighting the differences between the two Europes.

Western recovery entailed widespread state intervention and nationalization. In France the government took control of the services and industries that had been seized by the Nazis, while Britain nationalized the coal mines, railroads, and the Bank of England between 1946 and 1949. The Western nations also tried to break down the trade barriers between them. In April 1948, the Organization for European Economic Cooperation was set up, carrying within it the seeds of the European Economic Community. The latter was eventually established in 1957 by the Treaty of Rome.

Music in the postwar world

Moves to rebuild the economies of Western Europe were echoed in the cultural field. At the center of these initiatives, Germany made efforts to counter the censorship that had prevailed under the Nazi regime. Immediately after the war, Karl-Amadeus Hartmann began the 'Musica Viva' series of concerts in Munich, which reintroduced to German audiences the work of Stravinsky, Bartók, and the Second Viennese School. Building on this, in 1946 Wolfgang Steinecke founded the International Summer School in Darmstadt, using it as a vehicle to promote new music. The teachers at Darmstadt resumed their prewar preoccupation with serialism, although they showed less interest in the work of its pioneer, Arnold Schoenberg, than in that of one of his pupils, Anton Webern. This was all the more remarkable in that most of Webern's output was not available on record before 1957.

However, the true value of the Darmstadt School was its scope. Olivier Messiaen taught there from 1949 to 1951, composing his *Mode de valeurs et d'intensités* during one of the courses. This was a key piece in the development of 'total serialism,' a form of 12-note composition that extended beyond pitch to cover such areas as rhythm and dynamics. Pierre Boulez and Karlheinz Stockhausen, both students of Messiaen's, also began lecturing at Darmstadt in the 1950's, while the same period witnessed the very different approach of John Cage, who gave a series of classes in 1958.

The Darmstadt courses were not an isolated phenomenon. In 1937, a similar summer school — known as the Berkshire Festival — was held at the Berkshire Music Center at Tanglewood, Massachusetts. Like Darmstadt, this would become an annual phenomenon. At Tanglewood, the most prominent lecturer was Aaron Copland, who held the post of chairman of the faculty until his retirement.

During the late 1940's in Paris, Pierre Schaeffer and others pioneered *musique concrète*, an experimental technique using prerecorded natural sounds on tape as raw material for a musical composition. Edgard Varèse, the Franco-American composer, would become a noted exponent. *Musique concrète* was the forerunner of electronic music, in whose development Stockhausen was to play such a prominent part.

Nuclear power, the space age, and the threat of war

The early postwar period has been characterized as an age of austerity, but it was also a time of great technological advances. At the forefront of these was the harnessing of nuclear power. The American bombing of Hiroshima and Nagasaki in 1945 had imposed the subject of atomic energy on the public consciousness in the most forcible way possible, adding to the climate of fear during the Cold War. Apprehensions increased still further when it became clear that both the United States and Soviet governments had developed the hydrogen bomb, which was 500 times more powerful than the bombs that had been dropped on Japan. This resulted in the formation of groups such as CND (Campaign for Nuclear Disarmament) in Britain, which organized protest marches and campaigns.

While the arms race was the most worrying aspect of the Cold War, the conquest of space became another, equally potent, symbol of East–West rivalry. Here, the Soviet Union won most of the early plaudits. In 1957 a dog named Laika became the first living creature to be propelled into space. Four years later, Yuri Gagarin orbited the earth in the spaceship *Vostok I*, and in 1963 Valentina Tereshkova achieved fame as the first female astronaut. This ever-quickening contest reached its climax at the end of the decade when the Americans Armstrong, Aldrin, and Collins succeeded in setting foot on the moon in 1969.

The space race produced many beneficial side effects. The need for highly sophisticated yet also highly compact, computerized equipment stimulated research into the whole field of miniaturization. In the musical world this hastened the appearance of both the transistor radio and the tape cassette machine. Music became a portable commodity.

The Cold War continued unabated into the 1960's, and tension reached a peak in the early years of the decade, when a series of incidents threatened to bring the United States and the Soviet Union into direct conflict. In May 1960 an American U-2 pilot was shot down while flying over Soviet territory. Then, in the following year, the United States supported an abortive invasion attempt by Cuban exiles against the Soviet-backed regime in Cuba, one that foundered dangerously in the Bay of Pigs. Cuba was at the center of world attention once again in 1962, when President Kennedy set up a naval blockade of the island following the discovery that Soviet missile

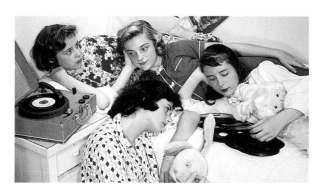

Teenagers at a slumber party, c.1958

By the 1950's, popular music was a well-established part of home life.

bases had been installed there. For six days the prospect of war loomed ominously, until the Khrushchev administration agreed to dismantle the weapons.

The new youth culture

In spite of these crises, indications grew that the repressive atmosphere of the postwar era was ending. In Britain, the production of John Osborne's play *Look Back in Anger* in 1956 signaled the arrival of the 'Angry Young Men,' a group of dramatists and novelists who challenged the moral and social values of the older generation. Their anger was fueled by the disastrous Anglo-French military assault on Egypt in November of that year and the subsequent humiliating withdrawal.

In the United States, this air of rebellion fostered the growth of a new youth culture. The word 'teenager' had been in use since the 1920's, but not until the 1950's did the spending power of young adults enable them to develop a life-style that was quite different from that of their parents. Their heroes repudiated the spirit of discipline and self-sacrifice that had been necessary in wartime. Jack Kerouac's novel *On the Road* (1957) inspired the bohemian attitudes of the 'Beat Generation.' Meanwhile, teenagers could also admire the blend of rebelliousness and overt sexuality in movie stars such as Marlon Brando and James Dean, or in singers such as Elvis Presley and Little Richard.

The new youth movement expressed itself through pop records and fashion, and both these fields enjoyed a period of intense creativity in the 1960's. Britain was in the vanguard of these experiments. In Liverpool the Beatles created the 'Mersey sound,' which helped to transform the music industry. The boutiques of Carnaby Street and the King's Road briefly focused the attention of the fashion world on London.

The young were not alone in having more money at their disposal. Standards of living in the West rose dramatically, creating a genuine consumer boom. People spent their money on luxury electrical equipment, on newly affordable foreign travel (the tourist industry achieved spectacular growth), and on cars. Their spending was encouraged by advertising that appeared on the new, fast-developing medium, television.

The mass-produced imagery that accompanied the rise of consumerism was itself the inspiration for Pop Art, a movement that flourished in the United States and Britain between the late 1950's and the early 1970's. Roy Liechtenstein painted large-scale reproductions of comic strips, Claes Oldenburg produced giant replicas of hamburgers and chocolates, while Andy Warhol exhibited silk-screen depictions of soup cans, Coca-Cola bottles, and press reports about road accidents. By translating these everyday objects and mass-media images into the language of 'serious' art, Pop artists deliberately blurred the distinctions between commercial and fine art, bringing into question the role of art itself.

New developments in music

This interest in radical experimentation had its parallels in the musical world. At Black Mountain College in North Carolina, John Cage lectured for several summers. Cage reacted against the mathematical precision that had turned serial music into a straitjacket for composers. Instead, his personal interest in Zen Buddhism and the *I Ching* led him to introduce an element of chance into his compositions (he once indicated that his purpose was to eliminate purpose). His *Imaginary Landscape No. 4*

MUSICAL DEFINITIONS

MINIMALISM Compositions in which one basic pattern is repeated again and again, providing a static, mesmeric quality reminiscent of Eastern forms.

---

of 1951 entailed the manipulation of the frequency and volume controls on 12 radio sets. The composer's directions to the 'performers' who turned the knobs were quite specific but, of course, the resulting cocktail of sound varied according to the programs that were on the air.

Amid other new trends in music in the 1960's and 1970's came the growth of MINIMALISM, in which one basic pattern is repeated again and again, providing a static, mesmeric quality reminiscent of Eastern forms. Noted exponents of this kind of music were Philip Glass and Steve Reich. At the same time, a more orthodox tradition survived in the work of Benjamin Britten, Michael Tippett, and Hans Werner Henze, whose operas achieved considerable success on the postwar scene.

The break-up of the European empires

These artistic experiments took place against a backdrop of rapid social and political change. For the European nations nothing symbolized the dismantling of the old order more emphatically than the break-up of their empires. The war had stirred up discontent in many of their overseas possessions, and both the United States and Soviet governments exerted further pressure in favor of decolonization.

The process began shortly after the war. India and Pakistan gained their independence in 1947, with Ceylon (Sri Lanka) and Burma following suit a year later. In 1949, the Dutch

Freedom march in Michigan, June 23, 1963

Dr. Martin Luther King, Jr., (fifth from left) leading an estimated 125,000 civil rights protesters through the heart of Detroit.

agreed to relinquish most of their territories in Southeast Asia to the newly created republic of Indonesia. In Africa, moves toward independence were sometimes hampered by conflicting loyalties, as European administrations were torn between a desire to free themselves from their former commitments and a lingering sympathy for the plight of white settlers. In the French colony of Algeria, for example, the transition was achieved in 1962 after eight years of violent unrest, which at times threatened to unseat the government in Paris.

These problems were echoed in British colonies with substantial white minorities. In Kenya the Mau Mau guerrillas engaged in an armed struggle during the 1950's; the rebellion was suppressed but hastened the country's move to independence in 1963. In southern Africa, resistance to change proved even more stubborn. The white administration in Southern Rhodesia withdrew from the Commonwealth in 1965 and did not accept full democratic rule as Zimbabwe until 1980, after prolonged civil strife. The neighboring government of South Africa pursued an equally isolationist path, declaring itself a republic in 1961 and maintaining white supremacy through the system of apartheid. Not until the early 1990's did the South African regime begin to demolish the structure of apartheid in moves toward multiparty democracy.

Probably the bloodiest of all these post-colonial conflicts occurred in Vietnam, where the independence process became entangled with the West's long-running battle against Communism. The area had been under French control until the fall of the stronghold at Dien Bien Phu in 1954, after which United States forces gradually replaced the French presence. An attempt to partition the country only led to an escalation in the fighting, and throughout the 1960's and early 1970's, the region became a tragic symbol of the ideological differences dividing East and West.

Civil rights, the new technology, and the environment

The United States had no overseas colonies to shed, but it shared some of the racial problems that the old imperial powers had faced. The ugly confrontations in 1957 between blacks and whites at Little Rock, Arkansas, highlighted the evils of segregation and acted as a spur to the burgeoning civil rights movement. Under the leadership of Dr. Martin Luther King, Jr., civil rights activists pressured the government into passing a mass of new legislation, although the most significant reforms did not take place until after King's assassination in 1968.

The message of the civil rights campaign was largely conveyed through mass marches and public demonstrations, and

its eventual success testified to the growing power of the media. The speed with which news and opinion could be transmitted into private homes afforded the citizens living in democracies a greater influence than they had ever wielded through the ballot box. Television brought the horrors of the Vietnam War directly into American sitting rooms, compelling politicians to hasten their search for a solution. Similarly, it dwelt on every detail of the Watergate scandal that forced President Nixon out of office in 1974.

On a more destructive note, the glare of publicity also led to a sharp increase in terrorism after 1970. Atrocities such as the murder of Israeli athletes at the Munich Olympics (1972), the hostage crisis at the United States embassy in Iran (1979–80), and the IRA bomb attacks in Britain in Hyde Park, London (1982), and in Brighton (1984) were all carried out in the sure knowledge that the camera crews of the world's press would flock to record the events.

Qualms about the possible effects of new technology increased still further in the 1980's, when the advent of video recorders, computer graphics, and satellite television brought a new dimension to the media revolution. These advances summoned up the specter of a 'global village,' which threatened to submerge the richness and variety of individual cultures. However, they also presented world issues to the widest possible audience. In 1985, for example, the Live Aid concert, watched by one billion viewers in 152 countries, raised $60 million for the victims of famine in Ethiopia.

Environmental issues also came to the fore in the 1980's, as scientists warned of the dangers of pollution and the depletion of the ozone layer. The need for international cooperation on such matters was illustrated all too clearly by the disaster in the Soviet Union in 1986 at the Chernobyl nuclear plant, which spread high levels of radiation over much of Europe.

The world in the 1990's

Had the Chernobyl accident occurred at the height of the Cold War, the political consequences might have been devastating. However, by the mid-1980's the tension between East and West had begun to ease. The appointment of Mikhail

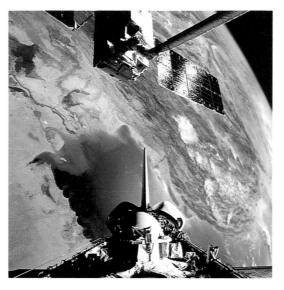

Eureca-I, the first European Retrievable Carrier satellite, 1992

The development of satellite technology has greatly aided global communications. Here, Eureca-I is deployed from the shuttle Atlantis.

Gorbachev as Soviet leader in 1985 ushered in a new era of détente. An important arms control agreement was signed in 1987, and in the following year, Soviet troops began to withdraw from Afghanistan, where they had conducted a fruitless war since 1979.

Since then, the rapid pace of change has astonished even experienced politicians. The liberalization of the Eastern bloc, the reunification of Germany, and the break-up of the old Soviet empire have redrawn the map of Europe; formerly Communist countries rush to compete with the established Western economies. At the same time, the loss of a powerful, centralized regime has reawakened many old nationalist rivalries that had lain dormant since World War I. It is not yet possible to know whether civil strife will be limited to the former territories of Yugoslavia. In the longer term, Europeans remain optimistic that a stronger and more united Europe will emerge from the turmoil, but this is still a distant prospect.

Meanwhile, the Middle East has remained a potent source of unrest since 1945, with the hostility between Israel and its Arab neighbors, the struggle between Iran and Iraq, the long, drawn-out civil war in Lebanon, and the Gulf War of 1991. The agreement in 1993 between Israel and the Palestine Liberation Organization may have brought hopes of a solution to one apparently intractable problem, but many countries in the region continue to be troubled by the rise of Islamic fundamentalism.

Music today

In the modern world, technology has made music more available than ever before. At the flick of a switch, the listener can hear it while driving, sitting at home, or even while walking. The development of digital recording has also ensured that the quality of sound reproduction has never been higher. Even so, composers have had to confront a new set of challenges. With public attention focused overwhelmingly on popular music, and given the complexity of many modern pieces, there is a risk that contemporary classical music will become a minority interest, accessible only to an informed elite.

In recent years, there have been determined attempts to shed this stuffy, academic image. Certain composers, conductors, and performers have successfully marketed themselves along the same lines as rock stars, some actually featuring in the pop charts. If this trend continues, Beethoven's wish — that music be enjoyed by everyone — will surely come to fruition.

Sydney Opera House, Australia

The Opera House, with its dramatic architecture and state-of-the-art facilities, displays an adventurous intention to integrate music into the life of the city and encourage all-comers.

Featured Composers

Scenes from *Rodeo*, the second of Copland's 'cowboy ballets'

Left: The dancer Allyn McLerie (1953). Below: The stage design by Oliver Smith (1973).

Copland

Aaron Copland 1900–1990

RECOMMENDED WORK

Appalachian Spring — suite from the ballet
Deutsche Grammophon 431 048-2
Los Angeles Philharmonic Orchestra/Leonard Bernstein
A delectable mixture of poetry, vivid tone-painting, and swaggering extroversion. Bernstein's (second) recording is among the most compelling ever made.

REPRESENTATIVE WORKS
Billy the Kid
Clarinet Concerto
Piano Concerto
Piano Sonata
Symphony No. 3
El salón México

Copland, 'the Dean of American music,' was born into a Russian-Jewish family in Brooklyn, New York. He learned the piano from the age of three and began theory studies with Goldmark at 17; but he rebelled against the latter's strict traditional approach, taking an interest in Debussy, Scriabin, Mussorgsky, and others.

He spent the years from 1920 to 1924 in Paris, studying with Nadia Boulanger, and

Photograph of Aaron Copland by Clive Barda, 1973

enjoying the city's stimulating cultural atmosphere. At the time Diaghilev's dance company Ballets Russes was performing works by Debussy, Ravel, and Stravinsky, who all clearly influenced Copland's first major work, *Grohg* (1922–25, reworked as the *Dance Symphony* in 1930). Boulanger commissioned his *Organ Symphony* (1924) for her first American tour as an organist, a work that established Copland as a leading American composer.

While in Paris, he became aware of the various emerging European national styles, and resolved to develop an American equivalent. Some early works, such as the *Piano Concerto* of 1926, employ jazz rhythms and blues harmonies. But *Piano Variations* (1931), which Copland described as 'one of the best things I've done,' typified his early mature style of modernist abstraction and economy of expression. Its unmistakable Copland flavor, recognizable throughout all his music, became far more important than jazz elements in defining the new American classical music.

The worsening world economic and political situation in the 1930's led him to seek a more popular, socially relevant style, epitomized by the three 'cowboy ballets,' *Billy the Kid* (1938), *Rodeo* (1942), and the Pulitzer Prize-winning *Appalachian Spring* (1944). These reached large audiences and became the models, along with his own film scores (he won an Oscar for *The Heiress* in 1948), for countless musical backdrops to Hollywood's Wild West. His popular style also reflected a left-wing political stance, or 'Communist leanings' according to the McCarthy Committee, which in 1953 temporarily restricted the availability of his music. The music world, however, united to support him.

Copland's style borrows heavily from American folk songs, but he rarely quoted these exactly, inserting rhythmic idiosyncrasies, and always setting them in the context of his unique, expansive musical landscapes. The final movement of his *Third Symphony* (1944–46) is an extensive fantasia on his own famous folk anthem, *Fanfare for the Common Man* (1942).

Copland never abandoned serious abstract idioms and even belatedly explored 12-note techniques in the two orchestral pieces *Connotations* (1962) and *Inscape* (1967), but by then he was responding to American music rather than shaping it. His inspiration gradually diminished, and he ceased composing in the 1970's.

Regarded universally with affection, Copland encouraged younger colleagues who had been his students at Tanglewood and Harvard, and who now gradually succeeded him. In later years he took great pleasure in conducting, but in 1983 he retired, a victim of Alzheimer's disease. He chose *Appalachian Spring* for his final concert, perhaps for its variations on the Shaker melody *Simple Gifts*, reflecting a contribution in music that reached out to millions during an age of increasing complexity.

Key to Recommended Works

| arr. arrangement (by) | contr contralto | hpd harpsichord | Op., Opp. Opus(es) | pno piano | ten tenor | vcl violoncello ('cello) |
| bar baritone | gtr guitar | mez mezzo-soprano | org organ | sop soprano | treb treble | vln violin |

Carter

Elliott Carter born 1908

Portrait photograph of Elliott Carter

Following the death of Copland, Carter is now generally recognized as America's greatest living composer. He was born in New York, and his musical aspirations were encouraged by Charles Ives, who introduced him from the age of 16 to a range of modernist influences. He accompanied his father on a business trip to Vienna in 1925 and bought all the available scores of the Second Viennese School.

Carter studied at Harvard from 1926 to 1932, and in Paris from 1932 to 1935. Private lessons with Nadia Boulanger brought him into close contact with the neoclassical works of Stravinsky, whose influence can be heard in the ballet suite *Pocahontas* (1938–39), his first major orchestral work. However, reading the work of Austrian psychiatrist Sigmund Freud in the 1940's led Carter to question the expressive limitations of the Stravinskian approach, and he made his last neoclassical gestures in *The Minotaur* (1947).

His new style was already apparent in the *Piano Sonata* (1945–46). Though indebted to Copland's *Sonata* of 1939–41, Carter's piece is arguably the greater, and perhaps marks the point at which he took over from Copland in the further development of American music. Passages of great rhythmic vitality, particularly in the dazzling second-movement fugue, still show the influence of jazz.

Research into medieval, Eastern, and African music and the *Player-Piano Studies* by Conlon Nancarrow (born in 1912) led to his *First String Quartet* (1950–51). Apart from his own new brand of atonalism, Carter took 'polyrhythm' (when, for example, one performer plays three notes in the same time as another plays two) to new extremes, with combinations among four players of, in one instance, three against seven against 15 against 21. He also introduced the related technique of 'metric modulation,' involving successive changes in the basic musical pulse according to such ratios.

Carter's work often explores the interaction or conflict between individual or groups of instruments with disparate rhythms and pulses, making his music at times incomprehensible, at least on first hearing. It also provides new challenges for the performers: in the Pulitzer Prize-winning *Third String Quartet* (1971) the four players, arranged in two opposing duos, can remain coordinated only by listening through headphones to a click machine.

However, Carter maintains that his primary aim is to write good music, regardless of its initial inaccessibility, and that if he can persuade his performers of its value, it will eventually find its public. He has gradually succeeded with the help of such significant figures as Stravinsky, who regarded the *Double Concerto* of 1961 as the first true American masterpiece, and the rock group The Grateful Dead, who were so im-pressed by the *Concerto for Orchestra* (1969) that they sponsored a 1991 London performance and subsequent recording by the London Sinfonietta.

Carter has held several prestigious professorships and has been awarded numerous prizes and honors worldwide. In 1989 he celebrated 50 years of marriage to the sculptress Helen Frost-Jones with the composition *Anniversary* — one of the *Three Occasions* for orchestra. Now in his mid-eighties, he has firmly promised to fulfill commissions until beyond 1996, including a fifth string quartet. His resolve to continue expanding musical language shows no signs of wavering.

Fats Waller at the piano, c.1942

In common with most American composers of his generation, Carter was influenced by the vitality of jazz.

Rodrigo

Joaquin Rodrigo born 1901

RECOMMENDED WORK
Concierto de Aranjuez
London 417 748-2
Carlos Bonell (gtr); Montreal Symphony
Orchestra/Charles Dutoit
*Solo playing of great refinement and character,
sympathetically accompanied and spectacularly well
recorded — all within the context of an admirably
varied program (Falla's* El amor brujo *and* Nights in
the Gardens of Spain*).*

REPRESENTATIVE WORKS
Fantasía para un gentilhombre
Concierto madrigal
3 Piezas españolas
4 Madrigales amatorios

Spain's most eminent composer, Rodrigo, was born in Sagunto in the province of Valencia on November 22, the feast day of St. Cecilia — music's patron saint. Permanently blinded by diphtheria at the age of three, and no doubt sensitized to sound as a result, he learned the piano and violin from the age of eight. Beginning in 1918, he attended composition lessons with Antich at the Conservatory in Valencia and completed his first works around 1923. From the start, he composed first in braille, dictating each completed work to a copyist.

In 1927, following the example of Albéniz, Granados, and Falla, Rodrigo moved to Paris, where he studied with Dukas for five years at the École Normale de Musique. He won recognition as a pianist and composer with encouragement from Ravel and Falla, while Stravinsky's influence gave his music a neoclassical element. In 1929, he met the Turkish pianist Victoria Kamhi and the two were married in 1933.

During a brief return to Spain, he won a scholarship for further studies in musicology at the Paris Conservatoire and at the Sorbonne. The outbreak of civil war in Spain in 1936 cut off the grant, leaving the Rodrigos in Paris in difficult financial circumstances. After the war, in 1939, they returned to Madrid, which has remained their home ever since.

On his return Rodrigo brought with him the recently completed score of the *Concierto de Aranjuez*, for guitar and orchestra, which was premiered the following year and established him immediately as Spain's leading composer. Since then the piece has become internationally famous as the most frequently performed guitar concerto, and remains by far his most popular work. The slow movement in particular has become almost a second national anthem, with its haunting melody evoking distinctly Spanish moods and colors yet without making direct reference to folk sources.

The success of the *Concierto de Aranjuez* led Rodrigo to write a further ten concertos for leading international performers, such as the *Concierto pastoral* (1977) for the flautist James Galway. However, none of the pieces has achieved the success of their precursor, although many of the solo guitar works and the *Fantasía para un gentilhombre* for guitar and orchestra (1954) are widely performed.

In the immediate postwar period Rodrigo was a highly influential force in Spanish music, but his style developed little after *Aranjuez*; indeed, its success has arguably presented an obstacle for younger Spanish composers seeking to continue Falla's work in establishing a more progressive national style.

In 1939, Rodrigo was appointed head of Spanish Radio's music broadcasts; he has also acted as head of the music section of the Spanish National Organization for the Blind. In 1947 the Manuel de Falla Professorship in music at Madrid University was created for him, and in 1954 he became vice-president of the International Society for Contemporary Music. He has toured in North and South America, Europe, Israel, and Japan, and has received numerous awards and honorary doctorates. He continued composing songs and piano and guitar pieces until well into his eighties, although no large-scale works have emerged since 1982.

Messiaen

Olivier Messiaen 1908–1992

RECOMMENDED WORK
**Quatuor pour le fin du temps
(Quartet for the End of Time)**
Delos DE3043
Chamber Music Northwest
*Chamber Music Northwest are more fully in tune than
most with the Quartet's inherent mysticism, and the
sound quality leaves nothing to be desired.*

REPRESENTATIVE WORKS
Turangalîla symphonie
Et exspecto resurrectionem mortuorum
La Nativité du Seigneur
20 Regards sur l'enfant Jésus

Perhaps the most influential composer of the postwar era, Messiaen was born in the French town of Avignon, the son of the poet Cécile Sauvage. From 1919, he spent 11 years at the Paris Conservatoire, where he studied composition with Dukas and organ with Dupré.

Scene from the ballet *Oiseaux exotiques*, 1967
**Choreographer John Cranko transformed
Messiaen's piano concerto into a ballet.**

Photograph of Olivier Messiaen at the organ, taken around 1950

A devout Catholic, Messiaen held the post of church organist at La Sainte Trinité, Paris, for 60 years.

In 1931 he was appointed organist at La Sainte Trinité church in Paris, where he played regularly for 60 years. Messiaen drew lifelong artistic inspiration from his Catholic faith, but was already exploring wider influences in such early religious works as *La Nativité du Seigneur* (1935) for organ, which uses rhythmic patterns based on ancient Indian theory.

Messiaen was conscripted at the outbreak of World War II, but was soon captured and imprisoned in Silesia. There he wrote the *Quatuor pour la fin du temps* (*Quartet for the End of Time*) for piano, clarinet, violin, and cello, premiered at the camp in 1941 by the composer and three fellow internees for an audience of 5,000 prisoners. 'Never,' he later commented, 'was I listened to with such rapt attention and comprehension.'

As the title might suggest, the piece refers extensively to St. John's vision of the Apocalypse (appropriately enough at such a moment in world history), but Messiaen was also announcing the end of musical time. His music is static — no longer developing toward a goal, but simply existing in a timeless musical space.

In 1942, Messiaen was repatriated. He took up a professorship in harmony at the Paris Conservatoire, where his pupils would later include Boulez, Stockhausen, Xenakis, and the pianist Yvonne Loriod. Many important works date from this period, including the gigantic *Turangalîla symphonie* (1946–48), which was premiered in 1949 by the Boston Symphony Orchestra, conducted by Leonard Bernstein. The title comes from an Indian poetic term for a rhythmic love song, and the work is a vibrant and sensual celebration of love. In his program notes in the *Turangalîla* score, Messiaen describes the climactic fifth movement (of ten) as 'the peak of carnal passion expressed in a long and frenetic dance of joy.' As well as a solo piano, the piece features the ondes martenot — an early electronic instrument — and employs, among other effects, 'Hindu rhythms' and birdsong material.

After a brief exploration of 12-note techniques that proved a remarkable inspiration for his pupils, Messiaen spent much of the 1950's transcribing birdsong and composing with it. The transcriptions are not particularly literal, as he sought also to capture a sound equivalent of the birds' colors. In 1956, he wrote the 'piano concerto' *Oiseaux exotiques* (Exotic Birds) for Yvonne Loriod. Messiaen's first wife, Claire, died in 1959 after a long illness, and he and Loriod married three years later.

In his later works he placed his refined birdsongs in a wider context, resulting in such large-scale works as *Des canyons aux étoiles* (From the Canyons to the Stars; 1970–74), inspired by the landscapes of Bryce Canyon in Utah. In 1978, a mountain in Utah was named after him. His only opera, *St. Francis of Assisi* (1975–83), gave him the perfect vehicle for a marriage of his twin interests, birdsong and religion.

Messiaen retired from the Conservatoire in 1978 but continued to compose in his instantly recognizable style until his final year. His penultimate work, *Un Sourire* (A Smile), was written for the Mozart bicentennial in 1991.

A guard's cabin at Struthop slave labor camp, 1944
Messiaen drew inspiration from adversity. His Quartet for the End of Time was composed while he was a prisoner of war during World War II.

Britten

Benjamin Britten 1913–1976

RECOMMENDED WORK

Serenade for tenor, horn, and strings, Op. 31
London 417 153-2
Peter Pears (ten); Barry Tuckwell (horn); English Chamber Orchestra/Benjamin Britten
A deep understanding of the chosen poetic texts combined with insightful conducting from Britten himself, superb solo playing from Tuckwell and the ECO members, and first-rate sound.

REPRESENTATIVE WORKS
Young Person's Guide to the Orchestra
Variations on a Theme of Frank Bridge
War Requiem
Peter Grimes

Benjamin Britten was arguably the leading British composer of the postwar period. Born in Lowestoft in Suffolk, he began composing at the age of five and completed a string quartet within four years. He studied theory with Frank Bridge, who shared his distaste for the prevailing English pastoral style, preferring such Continental figures as Bartók and Schoenberg; later composition studies with John Ireland at the Royal College of Music were therefore disappointing. A project to study with Berg in Vienna in

Britten and Peter Pears at Glyndebourne, 1946

1934 fell through, but the success of his *Variations on a Theme of Frank Bridge* at the 1937 Salzburg Festival established Britten on the international scene.

At the same time, Britten was writing documentary film music for the postal service, as part of a team that included the poet W. H. Auden, with whom he went on to collaborate on other projects. When Auden left for the United States in 1939, Britten followed, together with the singer Peter Pears. Pears became his lifelong companion and lover, and their artistic relationship proved uncommonly fruitful. They were ardent pacifists and conscientious objectors during World War II, and after returning to England in 1942, toured as a duo (with Britten at the piano), giving concerts in hospitals and bombed areas.

A fisherman mending his nets, early 20th century
Britten's love of the Suffolk coast is reflected in his choice of maritime themes.

During the war, Britten worked on his first major opera, *Peter Grimes*, based on George Crabbe's depiction of a rough yet poetic fisherman as an outsider in a closed community. The music shows Britten's huge talent for scene-setting, especially in the four orchestral *Sea Interludes* that capture the austere atmosphere of the Suffolk coast. *Peter Grimes* also reveals a typical sympathy with his main character, the violent and tragically complex Grimes, sung by Pears in the first production in 1945.

The work was an instant success, and Britten's operatic output for the rest of his life was prolific. Several works are chamber operas, among them *The Turn of the Screw* and *The Rape of Lucretia*, for which he formed the English Opera Group in 1946; they were often performed at the Aldeburgh Festival, inaugurated in 1948. He and Pears settled in this Suffolk coastal town, where they remained for the rest of their lives. Britten composed two full-scale operas for Covent Garden, *Billy Budd* (1952) and *Gloriana* (1953), and the ballet *The Prince of the Pagodas* (1956).

Britten's pacifism re-emerged with the *War Requiem*, written in 1962 for the consecration of the rebuilt Coventry Cathedral. Probably his greatest work for the concert hall, it combines the requiem text with the war poems of Wilfred Owen. Here, again, Britten shows his genius for matching significant music to the subject.

Britten and Pears were travelers, visiting Shostakovich and the cellist Rostropovich in the Soviet Union. Their tour of the Far East included Bali, where Britten was deeply impressed by the traditional gamelan music. He used gamelan effects extensively in his final opera, *Death in Venice* (1973), based on Thomas Mann's novella. Again he identified with his main character, Aschenbach, whose one-sided infatuation with the boy Tadzio (played by a dancer) is expressed largely in soliloquy. It was Pears's most demanding role.

By the time *Death in Venice* was completed Britten's health was failing, and he returned to smaller-scale instrumental music with the still forward-looking *Third String Quartet* (1975). In the year of his death, he became the first British musician to receive a peerage in recognition of his achievements.

Tippett

Michael Tippett born 1905

RECOMMENDED WORK

A Child of Our Time
Collins Classics 1339-2
Faye Robinson (sop); Sarah Walker (mez); Jon
Garrison (ten); John Cheek (bass); City of
Birmingham Symphony Chorus and Orchestra/
Michael Tippett
*A beautifully recorded interpretation of a most
moving work, outstandingly well sung, and with the
invaluable bonus of having the composer at the helm.*

REPRESENTATIVE WORKS
The Mask of Time
The Ice Break
Concerto for Double String Orchestra
Symphony No. 4

Although less fêted than his younger
British contemporary, Benjamin Britten,
Michaeil Tippett has emerged as a figure
of comparable importance. He was born in
London but spent his childhood in
Suffolk, southern France, and Italy. He
attended the Royal College of Music in
London from 1923 to 1928, studying
composition and conducting under
Charles Wood and R. O. Morris, and then
taught briefly at a private school.

Michael Tippett, 1975

Dissatisfied with his works of this time,
Tippett withdrew them all and returned to
the Royal College in 1930 for intensive
study of sixteenth-century English music,
Bach, and Beethoven. This formed the
basis for his characteristic contrapuntal
style, already prominent in the *Concerto for
Double String Orchestra* (1938–39).

Tippett responded to the world political situation of the late 1930's with his
early masterpiece, *A Child of Our Time*
(1939–41). The work was prompted by
the assassination in Paris, in 1938, of a Nazi
diplomat by a young Jewish boy, Herschel
Grynspan, an act that triggered a new wave
of anti-Semitic persecution in Germany.
The work is a humanitarian oratorio,
modeled on Bach's Passions, in which
Negro spiritual settings, such as *Deep River*
and *Nobody Knows the Trouble I've Seen*,
take the role of Bach's chorales.

Tippett's pacifist principles led to a
three-month prison sentence in 1943 for
refusing to comply with the conditions
(noncombatant military duties) imposed at
his tribunal for registration as a conscientious objector. In the immediate postwar
period, his work was somewhat eclipsed
by the debate over the comparative merits
of Britten and Vaughan Williams, and did
not achieve real prominence until the
1960's. Perhaps one reason for this was
the length of time he spent on his first
opera, *The Midsummer Marriage* (1947–52),
during which period Britten produced
half a dozen.

The Midsummer Marriage defines a
'world' of dance and lyricism, out of
which came a string of works in the same
vein, including the *Piano Concerto* (1953–
55) and the *Second Symphony* (1956–57).
This pattern, of a large work (often an
opera) forming the fullest expression of the
style of a period, has persisted throughout
his career. Thus his next opera, *King Priam*
(1958–61), defines a new, more static
world of Stravinskian juxtaposed blocks of
music, reflected in the *Concerto for Orchestra*
(1962–63). Further groups of works cluster around the psychological drama *The
Knot Garden* (1966–70) and the *Fourth
Symphony* (1976–77).

Tippett has remained a committed
humanist, frequently drawing on Jungian

Photograph of Herschel Grynspan, 1938
**Grynspan's assassination of Von Rath,
Third Secretary at the German Embassy
in Paris, inspired Tippett to write A
Child of Our Time.**

psychology in his operas, for which he
writes his own librettos. *The Midsummer
Marriage* deals with the reconciliation of
various human opposites in a parable about
the union of a young man and woman,
while in *King Priam* the composer attacks
the false utopias of Marxism and, less
explicitly, Christianity.

He was knighted in 1966, received the
Order of Merit in 1983, and has won
many international awards. His later works
include the *Triple Concerto* (1978–79),
incorporating Balinese influences, and his
fifth opera, *New Year* (1986–88). He celebrated his eighty-fifth birthday in 1990
with a three-month tour of the United
States and Australasia, and published his
autobiography, *Those Twentieth-Century
Blues*, in 1991. As Tippett explained in
Contemporary Composers, he remains committed to creating, 'in an age of mediocrity
and shattered dreams, images of abound-
ing, generous, exuberant beauty.'

Cage

John Cage 1912–1992

RECOMMENDED WORK

Three Dances for Prepared Piano: Dance No. 1

Koch International Classics 37238-2
Patrick Moraz (prepared piano)
Cage's innovative style, using this percussion instrument of his own devising, is interpreted with a sharp, fiercely rhythmic, and compelling expressiveness.

REPRESENTATIVE WORKS

**The Wonderful Widow of Eighteen Springs
Concert for Piano and Orchestra**

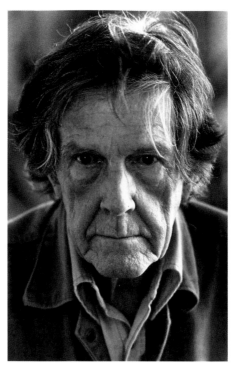

John Cage, photographed in New York, 1986

Scene from *Inventions*, 1989

The Merce Cunningham Dance Company interprets one of Cage's late works.

The son of an inventor, John Cage was born and educated in Los Angeles. He toured the major cities of Europe in 1930 before studying composition with Adolph Weiss and Henry Cowell in New York, and then with Arnold Schoenberg in Los Angeles.

His first appointment, in 1937, was as an accompanist and composer for dance classes at the Cornish School in Seattle. This began a long association with dance, most notably, in later years, with the Merce Cunningham Dance Company, of which he became music director in 1944. In 1942, Cage moved to New York, which became his lifelong base, and soon achieved public prominence with a percussion concert at the Museum of Modern Art, reviewed in *Life* magazine.

Cage's first compositions were 12-note works, but he gradually turned to rhythmically organized percussion pieces. He also introduced a highly flexible percussion instrument in the 'prepared piano' (with various objects placed among the strings), for which he wrote *Sonatas and Interludes* (1946–48), exploring traditional Eastern Indian thought.

From the late 1940's, Cage studied Eastern philosophies, including Zen Buddhism, which led to the introduction of chance elements into the composition process. In *Music of Changes* (1951) the notes and their lengths were determined by the *I Ching* — derived from charts and coin tosses — with the aim of escaping from 'individual taste and memory' and the '"traditions" of the art.'

Then, in 1952, came the notorious work titled *4' 33"*, for any combination of performers and instruments, who sit in silence on stage for the prescribed duration. Presumably a Zen-inspired composition, its 'music' consists of any audible sound from the audience or outside, shifting the emphasis from 'understanding' to 'awareness.'

In these works Cage was seeking to break down the distinctions between 'Life' and 'Art' by presenting 'Life' in a concert hall. In a 1962 performance of his own *0' 0"*, designed 'to be performed in any way to anyone,' Cage chopped and blended vegetables, drank the juice (any 'Life' action would do), and amplified the sounds for the concert audience.

It is perhaps not surprising that these performances often met with ridicule and hostility, both in the United States and in Europe, where he toured in 1954. A New York Philharmonic performance of *Atlas Elipticalis* under Bernstein in 1964 was sabotaged by the orchestra, and many in the audience walked out.

However, Cage gained influence as a teacher, giving classes in Darmstadt from 1958 on, and holding a number of university posts in the late 1960's, when he became something of a cult figure on the campuses. As well as music, he taught mushroom identification, and while working at Berio's studio in Milan in 1958, he successfully answered five weeks' worth of questions on mushrooms on a weekly Italian television quiz show, which won him a large prize.

Cage's later works involved ever more diverse materials and media. *HPSCHD* (1967) employs seven harpsichords playing computer-generated mixtures of music by Mozart, Beethoven, Cage, and others, accompanied by tapes, films, slides, and colored lights. *Branches* (1976) uses amplified plant materials. However, nothing composed in later life compares in importance with the innovations of the 1950's, and it is undoubtedly for these that he will be most remembered.

Lutoslawski

Witold Lutoslawski 1913–1994

RECOMMENDED WORK
Symphony No. 3
Erato 4509-91711-2
Chicago Symphony Orchestra/Daniel
Barenboim
*A combination of textual clarity and visceral
excitement makes for a recording that should win this
fine work many new friends. The sound quality is
remarkably realistic.*

REPRESENTATIVE WORKS
Concerto for Orchestra
Cello Concerto
Funeral Music
Variations on a Theme of Paganini
String Quartet

Witold Lutoslawski, c.1989

Poland's most eminent twentieth-century composer, Witold Lutoslawski was born in Warsaw, studied piano and violin, and began composing at the age of nine. He attended Warsaw Conservatory from 1932 to 1937, but plans to continue his study in Paris were interrupted by the outbreak of World War II.

He was captured by the Germans while commanding a military radio unit near Krakow, but soon escaped to Warsaw, where he led a precarious existence playing piano duets in cafés with fellow composer Andrzej Panufnik. Almost all their arrangements were destroyed in the 1944 Warsaw Uprising, with the exception of Lutoslawski's enduring *Variations on a Theme of Paganini* (1941).

He led a double musical life in the uncertain postwar years. He continued composing 'serious' music for his own artistic ends, only to earn the dubious distinction in 1949 of seeing his *First Symphony* become the first Polish work of art to be banned as 'formalist' under the Stalinist cultural policy of 'social realism.' He was forced to produce 'functional' radio, theater, and film music in order to make a modest living.

However, Lutoslawski's work was not entirely rejected by the Stalinist regime. His use of folk music in composition coincided with the demands of the state for simple works. This interest also led to the grander conception of the *Concerto for Orchestra* (1950–54), a piece clearly influenced by Bartók; indeed, Lutoslawski dedicated his next major work, *Funeral Music* (1954–58), to Bartók's memory. Stalin's death in 1953 began a cultural 'thaw,' and Lutoslawski took the opportunity in this work to reorient his musical language in a more avant-garde direction.

After hearing Cage at Darmstadt in 1961, Lutoslawski introduced a chance element in his next work, *Venetian Games*, a form he continued to explore until his death. He annotated all the material, but allowed certain sections to proceed at the players' chosen speeds, so that the resulting mesh of sound was not predetermined.

He continued to travel and explore new methods in the relatively relaxed cultural climate of the 1960's and 1970's. The *Second Symphony* (1967) was perhaps the best example of a 'two movement' form, employed in a number of works. The first movement, 'Hesitant,' is preparatory and open-ended, while the second, 'Direct,' provides a climax and resolution.

In the late 1970's, political troubles reemerged in Poland with the rise of the pro-democracy movement in Gdansk. In 1981, Lutoslawski spoke out in a lecture titled 'The Role of Truth in Art' at the Polish Congress of Culture, organized by the trade union movement Solidarity. Days later, martial law was imposed and he became *persona non grata* in the Soviet Union for comments on the Stalinist era.

In the 1980's, Lutoslawski completed his *Third Symphony*, which had been commissioned by the Chicago Symphony Orchestra in 1972, and a series of three works titled *Chain*, in which a sequence of notated segments or 'links' overlap one another to form a musical chain.

With successive removals of state restraint on cultural activities, Lutoslawski was described by the late Olivier Messiaen as 'grow[ing] more and more modern.' He died early in 1994, the year after celebrating his eightieth birthday with the Los Angeles premiere of his *Fourth Symphony*, which he conducted himself in several subsequent performances worldwide.

A Solidarity rally, 1981
**Lutoslawski's support for Solidarity
enraged Poland's Communist authorities.**

Bernstein

Leonard Bernstein 1918–1990

RECOMMENDED WORK

West Side Story
Deutsche Grammophon 415 253-2
Kiri Te Kanawa (sop) Nina; José Carreras (ten)
Tony; Tatiana Troyanos (mez) Anita; Kurt
Ollmann (bar) Riff; Marilyn Horne (mez); chorus
and orchestra from 'on and off' Broadway/
Leonard Bernstein
*All the tension, excitement, and spontaneity of a live
event, with top-ranking vocalists galvanized into action
by the master himself. Excellent sound.*

REPRESENTATIVE WORKS
Symphony No. 2, 'The Age of Anxiety'
On the Waterfront – Symphonic Suite
Songfest
On the Town
Candide

Leonard Bernstein at the piano, c.1949

Bernstein's eclectic style bridged the worlds of popular and classical music.

Renowned as a composer, conductor, pianist, and academic, Leonard Bernstein was one of the century's greatest musical all-rounders. Born in Lawrence, Massachusetts, he began to learn the piano at the age of ten. He studied theory at Harvard University and conducting with Fritz Reiner at the Curtis Institute in Philadelphia. After three summers under Serge Koussevitzky at Tanglewood, from 1940 to 1942, he became assistant conductor of the New York Philharmonic Orchestra. His career was launched in 1943 with a sensational début as an eleventh-hour replacement for Bruno Walter.

Bernstein was principal conductor of the New York Philharmonic from 1958 until 1969, when he was appointed conductor laureate for life. During his career he conducted the major orchestras of the world, enjoying particularly close relationships with the Israel Philharmonic, and the Vienna Philharmonic, which collaborated in his series of live releases of the 1980's, issued as part of his protest against overengineered recordings.

Bernstein the composer developed an eclectic style that drew on anything from big-band jazz in the *Prelude, Fugue, and Riffs* (1949) to 12-note techniques in the later *Symphony No. 3 (Kaddish)* of 1963. His *Symphony No. 1 (Jeremiah)* of 1944 was named 'Best New American Orchestral Work' by the New York Music Critics Circle. However, he soon made an even greater impact on the music-theater world with his musicals. His first, *On the Town* (1944), was based on the exploits of three sailors with a day's shore leave in New York, and ran for 463 performances.

In the 1950's he composed mainly for stage and screen, including *West Side Story* (1957), regarded by many as the best musical ever. It was typical of Bernstein's consistent defiance of musical categories that this extrovertly popular work, with its Latin American dances, 'cool jive,' and melting ballads, should also include music of the highest quality and compositional skill, just as his more 'serious' works frequently used 'popular' idioms.

Compositional activity slackened in the 1960's as he toured the world with the New York Philharmonic, but resumed with the theater piece *Mass* in 1971. Two years later he delivered the Charles Eliot Norton Lectures at Harvard, published in 1976 as *The Unanswered Question*, which confirmed his position as an outstanding communicator and ambassador for the cause of music. He also received a number of Emmy awards for his educational broadcasts for children.

But 'Lenny' the consummate popularist was also a complicated and controversial figure. He admitted homosexual promiscuity while remaining devoted to his wife, Felicia, until her death in 1978. His candor in later life, and campaigns on behalf of those suffering from HIV and AIDS, may have been his own kind of penance for concealing his libertarian impulses and bisexuality during the McCarthy era.

Bernstein continued to conduct and compose throughout the 1980's, until his lifetime of chain-smoking caught up with him. After suffering for years with emphysema and eventually lung cancer, he died from cardiac arrest following lung failure, just five days after announcing his retirement. He was mourned the world over like few others in the history of music.

Boulez

Pierre Boulez born 1925

RECOMMENDED WORK
Rituel in memoriam Bruno Maderna
Erato 2292-45493-2
Orchestre de Paris/Daniel Barenboim
An imposingly sonorous re-enactment of Boulez's memorial, and one of the most communicative recordings of the composer's work currently available. The sound is spacious and realistic.

REPRESENTATIVE WORKS
Notations
Le marteau sans maître
Les soleils des caux
Eclat
Piano Sonata No. 2

Photograph of Boulez by Betty Freeman, 1986

Boulez is generally acknowledged as the co-leader, with Stockhausen, of the post-war avant-garde. During childhood he showed great aptitude in mathematics, and was encouraged by his father to prepare for engineering training at the École Polytechnique in Paris. However, on arrival in Paris in 1942, he applied instead to the Conservatoire, failed the piano entrance examination, but attended Messiaen's famous harmony classes for the next three years.

Armed with a formidable intellect, Boulez pursued with revolutionary zeal the idea of composition as a scientific exploration of musical aesthetics, attacking music that he felt was poorly crafted or that merely fed on some personality cult. After studying 12-note methods with Leibowitz, he wrote in *Relèves d'Apprenti* (1966) that 'any musician who has not felt . . . the necessity of the dodecaphonic [12-note] language is OF NO USE.'

With the *Livre pour Quatuor* (1948) he was already moving toward 'total serialism,' which extended serial or mathematical procedures (already applied to pitch, in 12-note music) to the duration, timbre, and intensity of the notes. To obtain the necessary precision, he worked initially in Pierre Schaeffer's studio for *musique concrète*, with natural (rather than electronic) sounds committed to tape. He then modified, cut, and reassembled the sounds into a kind of musical collage. He nevertheless risked using live performers in his last and most successful total serial work, *Structures I* (1952), for two pianos.

Le Marteau sans maître (1954) — Boulez's setting of poems by Char for alto and small ensemble — became the first undisputed masterpiece of the postwar serial language. It marked the evolution of a new, thoroughly logical musical system that nevertheless admitted and even necessitated the freedom of imagination lacking in total serialism. It is this breakthrough that is perhaps his greatest achievement.

His compositional activity slowed as he spent time on theoretical writings, the most important of which, *Musikdenken Heute* (Musical Thought Today), resulted from lectures given at Darmstadt, where he taught for 12 years starting in 1955. Composition also became a protracted process in which he would allow publication of some works as parts of larger 'works in progress.' Thus *Improvisations sur Mallarmé* and *Strophes* (1957) became parts of *Pli selon pli* (1962), and *Éclats* (1965) led to the still 'progressing' *Éclats/Multiples* (begun in 1965).

Composition gradually gave way to conducting in the 1960's, particularly with Boulez's own *'Domaine Musical'* concerts from 1954 to 1967. In 1971 he became principal conductor of both the BBC Symphony Orchestra (until 1975) and the New York Philharmonic (until 1977), succeeding Bernstein. His famously acute sense of hearing has enabled him to bring out previously unheard detail in performances and recordings, particularly in the works of Debussy.

In 1975, Boulez was appointed director of the new Institute for Research and Coordination in Acoustics and Music (IRCAM) in Paris, where he remained until 1991. His work there included *Répons* (1983), which refers subtly to the influence of Debussy. Boulez remains an uncompromising modernist and propagandist for twentieth-century music and composers, especially Debussy, Stravinsky, Webern, and Messiaen.

Monument in the Fertile Land by Paul Klee, 1929
This watercolor by the Swiss painter had a profound effect on Boulez.

Stockhausen

Karlheinz Stockhausen born 1928

RECOMMENDED WORK
Stimmung
Hyperion CDA66115
Songcircle/Gregory Rose
From Gregory Rose and his supremely accomplished band of singers comes a marvelously intense realization, fully conveying the hypnotic power and remarkable concentration of Stockhausen's minimalistic inspiration.

REPRESENTATIVE WORKS
Gesang der Jünglinge
Hymnen
Klavierstücke

Stockhausen in a studio in Cologne, c.1960

Karlheinz Stockhausen made one of the most important contributions to the new music of the 1950's and 1960's. Born near Cologne and orphaned during World War II, he was obliged to work as a stretcher bearer, farm laborer, and pianist in order to finance his schooling and later studies at the Cologne Musikhochschule and university. Although studying composition, musicology, and philosophy, he qualified initially only as a school music teacher.

His encounter with the post-Webern avant-garde at the 1951 summer course at Darmstadt inspired *Kreuzspiel*, from which he dated the start of his compositional career. The following year, he studied with Messiaen in Paris where he also met Boulez and worked in Schaeffer's studio with *musique concrète* (music prepared from recorded sounds).

Kreuzspiel already leans toward total serialism, but could as soon be described as *pointillist* because of a texture based on isolated 'points' of sound. Seeing the expressive limitations of 'points,' Stockhausen formed them into aggregates called 'groups' in *Kontra-Punkte* (Against Points, 1952–53). He took the 'group' method to its most developed form in *Gruppen*

(Groups, 1955–57), which also marks the climax of Stockhausen's total serialism.

Like Boulez, Stockhausen explored electronic methods in developing his serial language. The early electronic masterpiece, *Gesang der Jünglinge* (1955–56) for tape, went further than *musique concrète* by combining an electronically modified recording of a boy's voice, singing the Benedicite text, with purely electronically generated sounds. Later electronic works such as *Mikrophonie I* (1964) dispensed with tapes in favor of generating or modifying sounds 'live' during performance.

His experiments with 'indeterminacy' (inspired by Cage's 1954 and 1958 visits) culminated in works such as *Aus den Sieben Tagen* (1968), whose score contains no musical notation, but poetically expressed directions to be intuitively translated into

music by the performers. As the text explains, 'I do not make my music, but only relay the vibrations I receive.' In this way Stockhausen abdicated as composer, searching instead for a 'music of the whole world' (explored more literally in works using short-wave receivers).

As with Cage, many of these ideas were inspired by Eastern influences such as Japanese Noh dramas and Indian religion. Stockhausen himself acquired guru status in the late 1960's and 1970's with his growing reputation as a teacher — at Darmstadt from 1953 to 1974 and on a number of lecture tours in the United States from 1958. In the mystical, ritualistic *Stimmung* (1968), six singers sit in a circle and vocalize on a single chord for some 75 minutes, gradually shifting the color, intensity, and balance, and occasionally invoking certain 'magic names.'

Since 1977, Stockhausen's entire compositional effort has been devoted to an integration of his various styles and techniques in a seven-opera cycle (each representing one day of the week) titled *LICHT* (Light). Critical opinion remains divided on the merits of the four operas so far completed, despite highly expert performances by Stockhausen's own ensemble, including members of his extensive family. His controversial influence waned markedly during the 1980's and 1990's.

Manuscript from the *Kontakte* (Contacts) series, 1960
Kontakte *explored the interplay of piano, percussion, and electronic sounds.*

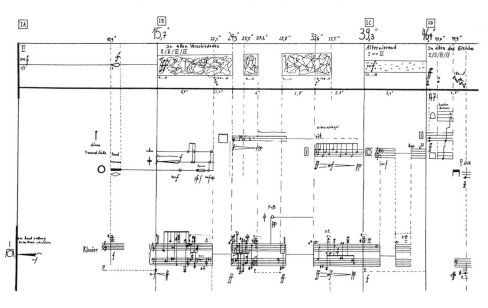

Xenakis

Iannis Xenakis born 1922

RECOMMENDED WORK

Akanthos
Wergo WER6178-2
Penelope Walmsley-Clark (sop); Spectrum/Guy
Protheroe
The participating performers chart the course of this
endlessly inventive and kaleidoscopically varied music
with obvious enthusiasm; the recording is excellent.

REPRESENTATIVE WORKS
Orestia
Metastasis
Naama

Xenakis is credited with the major role in
the early development of computer music.
Born in Romania of Greek parents, he
moved to Greece when he was ten and
studied engineering in Athens. In 1941, he
joined the Greek resistance, which later
came into conflict with the returning,
Allied-backed government-in-exile. Civil
war erupted in 1947. Xenakis was himself
wounded, losing his sight in one eye. He

Photograph of Xenakis by Ralph A. Fassey, 1987

was captured and condemned to death,
but escaped to France in 1947, remaining
there as a political refugee until 1965,
when he gained full French citizenship.

He was largely self-taught in music, but
studied with Messiaen in 1950 and 1951.
He met the celebrated French architect Le
Corbusier, and worked with him on such
projects as the Philips Pavilion at the
Brussels World Fair in 1958. With a growing reputation as a composer he gradually
moved away from architecture, but it continued to influence his musical thought.

Metastasis (1953–54), his first published
musical work, uses 12-note methods but is
also based on the relationship of music to
architecture through mathematics. It is
scored for an orchestra of 60 players —
mainly strings — each with an independent part, and uses glissando effects (sliding
the finger along the string from one note
to the next) to represent straight lines.

His use of mathematics in dealing with
large numbers of musical 'events' led to an
exploration of probability theory, and
hence 'stochastic' music, from the Greek
stochos (meaning 'goal'). In probability theory, an event may be determined by the
nature of previous events, so those at the
beginning of a sequence can be fairly random, but later ones tend toward a goal.

To calculate enough events to make up
a piece of music, Xenakis turned to the
computer — more specifically an IBM
7090 — whose more mundane uses
included market research and planning the
movements of oil shipping. The resulting

Cités cosmiques by Xenakis, 1963
Xenakis described some of his pieces as
aural versions of architectural forms.

music went to extremes of incomprehen-
sibility at a time when even Boulez and
Stockhausen were compromising their
mathematical procedures for greater acces-
sibility to listeners.

Antikthon appeared in 1971, commissioned by George Balanchine for the New
York City Ballet. Working from a
Pythagorean term meaning 'anti-earth,'
Xenakis created a work that uses 'suns' of
brass against 'worlds' of woodwind in the
'architectural' context of the strings.

From 1967, Xenakis composed and
designed a number of sound and light
shows, in line with a general softening of
his approach to the problem of audience
communication. *Persepolis* (1971) was
written for the ruins of the ancient city in
Iran, *Polytope de Mycènes* (1978) for the
ruins at Mycenae in Greece, and *Diatope*
(1978) for the inauguration of the
Pompidou Center in Paris. His music from
the 1970's on has assumed a much simpler,
bolder, melodic style, with rhythmic patterns reminiscent of folk music.

Xenakis has held professorships at City
University in London, at the University of
Indiana, and at the Sorbonne in Paris
(1972–89), where he became Emeritus
Professor in 1990. He has received numerous honors and awards, including, in 1992,
an honorary diploma in architecture from
the Athens Polytechnic.

Berio

Luciano Berio born 1925

RECOMMENDED WORK
Sinfonia
Erato 2292-45228-2
New Swingle Singers; French National Orchestra/
Pierre Boulez
Boulez traces Berio's sundry references and quotations with a clear head and ample imagination, while both performers and engineers support him admirably.

REPRESENTATIVE WORKS
Coro
Folk Songs
Sequenze I–11

Born in the Italian town of Oneglia, Berio is Italy's most important postwar composer. One of a long line of musicians, he studied composition and piano with his father until suffering an accident to his right hand at the age of 19. After World War II he studied law at Milan University, attended composition classes at the conservatory, and worked as an orchestral player and conductor in opera productions.

In 1950, Berio received his composition diploma and married the American

Luciano Berio, photographed in 1966

singer Cathy Berberian. During several trips to the United States he studied 12-note methods under Dallapiccola at Tanglewood and became interested in electronic music. In 1955 he established his own studio at the Milan radio station, where he worked on his early electronic classic, *Thema (Omaggio a Joyce)*, which used a recording of Berberian reading extracts from James Joyce's *Ulysses*.

Between 1956 and 1960 he produced a magazine and organized concerts in Milan under the title *Musical Encounters*, in which Cage and Boulez performed. He regularly visited Darmstadt during this period, mixing with Stockhausen and others. The combination of his nationality, compositional style, and a tendency to use popular elements in his work, in contrast to the esoteric modernism of his colleagues, gave him the title 'Rossini of the avant-garde.' *Folk Songs* (1964), one of his most accessible works, includes arrangements of nine traditional folk songs from around the world; he transcribed the final song by ear from a recording of an Azerbaijani folk band.

Berio taught extensively in the 1960's — at Tanglewood, at Darmstadt, at Dartington in England, and in academic posts in the United States. His composition took two main directions: stage works, such as *Laborintus II*, which won the Italia Prize in 1966, and solo works, notably the *Sequenze* (Sequences). These are highly virtuoso pieces for a solo instrument or voice, the first of which, for flute, was written in 1958 and the latest, for guitar, in 1988.

In 1968 and 1969 he wrote *Sinfonia* for eight voices and large orchestra. The third movement centers on the *Scherzo* from Mahler's *Second Symphony* and flows more or less audibly 'through a constantly changing landscape' of literary and musical quotes — from Samuel Beckett's novel *The Unnameable* to Stravinsky's *Rite of Spring*, Beethoven's *Sixth Symphony*, and Debussy's *La Mer*.

In 1972, Berio returned to Italy, where he has been popularizing his and others' music; in 1981 he founded an institute in Florence, *Tempo Reale*. He won a second Italia Prize in 1975, for *Diario Immaginario*, and in 1989 was awarded the international Ernst von Siemens Music Prize.

Henze

Hans Werner Henze born 1926

RECOMMENDED WORK
Symphony No. 4
Deutsche Grammophon 429 854-2
Berlin Philharmonic Orchestra/Hans Werner Henze
A superb digital transfer of a fine and idiomatic performance, one that liberates the score's inherent sense of melancholy.

REPRESENTATIVE WORKS
Symphony No. 6
The Bassarids

Hans Werner Henze grew up with the rise of Nazism in Germany. He played chamber music with his Jewish neighbors in the 1930's, giving him the notion of music as a subversive activity as he gradually became aware of Hitler's suppression of progressive movements in the arts. He was conscripted in 1944, serving for a short time in Poland and then on a propaganda film team before ending the war as a British prisoner. He worked for a while as a theater pianist but soon moved on to study at the Heidelberg Institute for Church Music with Fortner, at Darmstadt, and with Leibowitz.

In his prolific early output, he developed a free use of 12-note techniques, but only as a means to other ends. His first full opera, *Boulevard Solitude* (1952), is based on the *Manon Lescaut* story; it unites recitative, aria, jazz, and blues by deriving them all from the same 12-note series, based on a sequence from *La Bohème*.

Henze became ballet director at the Wiesbaden State Theater in 1950, but his increasing distaste for Germany led him to move in 1953 to the Bay of Naples. There he worked in seclusion on the operas *König Hirsch* and *Der Prinz von Homburg*.

With his move to Rome in 1961, he gained a higher international profile; he began teaching at the Salzburg Mozarteum

Hans Werner Henze, c. 1975

and wrote his *Fifth Symphony* for the New York Philharmonic, traveling to the United States for the first time in 1963 for its premiere under Bernstein.

During the 1960's Henze became more interested in Marxism and the New Left. His musical commitment to 'man's greatest work of art, the World Revolution' emerged dramatically in 1968 with the oratorio *Das Floss der Medusa* (The Raft of the Medusa), a requiem for Che Guevara, based on the story told in Géricault's painting. At the Hamburg premiere, police arrested students who had draped a red flag across the stage, as well as the librettist, Schnabel, who attempted to intervene.

Henze spent from 1969 to 1970 in Cuba, teaching, researching, and conducting the premiere of his *Sixth Symphony*, a bewilderingly complex, continuous 40-minute movement incorporating Vietnamese and Greek freedom songs. The excursion also bore fruit in collaborations with revolutionary Latin-American writers such as the Cuban Miguel Barnet and the Chilean Gaston Salvatore.

In later works Henze took a less belligerent stance. The opera *We Come to the River* (1974–76), with a libretto by Edward Bond, accepts the dilemma of balancing individual freedom with the needs of society. The music reintroduces all the parody and lyricism of his earlier works, but without diminution of power or ambition.

Henze's love affair with Italy has continued with his establishment of the Montepulciano Festival, but he has also reconciled himself with his native Germany, whose federal premier Richard von Weizsäcker presided when Henze was awarded the international Ernst von Siemens Music Prize in 1990. His output remains as prolific as ever.

Simpson

Robert Simpson born 1921

RECOMMENDED WORK
Symphony No. 9
Hyperion CDA66299
Bournemouth Symphony Orchestra/Vernon Handley
Total identification between composer and conductor, with excellent orchestral playing and superb sound. A landmark in twentieth-century symphonic recording.

REPRESENTATIVE WORKS
Symphony No. 2
Symphony No. 6
String Quartet No. 3

In a fiercely individual approach to composition, Simpson eschews avant-garde techniques and other trends in the belief that 'contact with durable human instincts is more vital than tagging onto fashions.'

He was born in Leamington Spa and educated at Westminster City School in London. He learned the cornet from the age of seven. In accordance with his parents' wishes, he initially studied medicine, but soon gave up and, from 1941 to 1946, took lessons in harmony and counterpoint with Herbert Howells. As a registered conscientious objector during World War II, he fitted his musical studies around duties in a mobile surgical unit.

Simpson's first acknowledged works date from around 1946, when he also began work on his *First Symphony*. Four destroyed attempts predated the final version, for which he received a doctorate from Durham University in 1951. He joined the BBC in 1951, remaining there as a music producer until 1980, when he resigned in protest over the corporation's artistic policies.

He has written a number of critical and theoretical works on music, including books on the symphonies of Nielsen, Sibelius, Bruckner, and Beethoven — the greatest influences on his own symphonies (11 to date), which provide the fullest expression of his compositional style.

In particular he follows Beethoven's example of creating large structures from the inherent tensions and resonances in a germinal melodic idea. The structures are indeed large in his *Ninth Symphony* (1986), reportedly the longest Western work with a single unchanging pulse ever constructed. His music remained stubbornly tonal in an atonal and serial age, and avoided the static forms of Messiaen and others, adhering instead to Nielsen's principle that music is nothing unless it has a 'current.'

Another dominant genre in Simpson's output is the string quartet, of which he has so far written 15, again consciously founded on Beethoven's principles. The *Fourth*, *Fifth*, and *Sixth Quartets* (1973–75) are closely modeled on Beethoven's three *Rasumovsky Quartets*, while the opening of the *Quintet* for clarinet and string quartet (1968) contains an obvious melodic reference to Beethoven's *String Quartet* in C sharp minor, Opus 131.

Since leaving the BBC, Simpson has devoted more time to composition, producing four symphonies and seven string quartets. A recording of his *Ninth Symphony* won *Gramophone* magazine's award for the best contemporary issue of 1989. He has been awarded the Kilenyi Medal of Honor by the Bruckner Society of America, and the Danish Carl Nielsen Gold Medal. Since 1986 he has lived with his second wife in County Kerry, Ireland.

Portrait photograph by Peter Musgrave

Maxwell Davies

Peter Maxwell Davies born 1934

RECOMMENDED WORK

Trumpet Concerto
Collins Classics 1181-2
John Wallace (tpt); Scottish National Orchestra/
Peter Maxwell Davies
*Virtuoso trumpeting of the highest order and yet
notably rich in passages of atmospheric
introspection.*

REPRESENTATIVE WORKS
Symphony No. 4
Solstice of Light
Eight Songs for a Mad King
Ave maris stella

Maxwell Davies was born in Manchester, where he studied at the university and at the Royal Manchester College of Music until 1957. His fellow students included Birtwistle and Goehr, who became collectively known as the 'Manchester School.' They shared a then unusual interest in Schoenberg and the Continental avant-garde, and in medieval and Indian music. Davies attended summer school in Darmstadt in 1956 and studied in Rome from 1957 to 1959, while making arrangements of historical music. His orchestral 'motet,' *Worldes Blis* (1966–69), is based on a thirteenth-century English song.

Conducting the Scottish Chamber Orchestra, 1990

During the 1960's, he studied with Roger Sessions in the United States, after which he toured Europe, Australia, and New Zealand as a lecturer. He founded the Pierrot Players with Birtwistle in 1967, which was re-established as The Fires of London when Birtwistle left in 1970. The group was modeled on the instrumentation of Schoenberg's *Pierrot Lunaire*, whose implied theatricality also inspired many of the music-theater works written for them, notably *Vesalii Icones* and *Eight Songs for a Mad King* (1969).

Along with madness, Davies was interested in religious honesty and doubt; he explores all of these in his major work of the 1960's, the opera *Taverner* (1962–70), which deals with the crisis of faith of the sixteenth-century English composer, who supposedly gave up writing Masses to join Henry VIII's persecution of the Catholics.

In 1970, Maxwell Davies moved to a croft on the island of Hoy in the Scottish Orkneys, and most of his music since then has been written there. His active interest in island life is reflected in collaborations with the Orkney poet George Mackay Browne, such as *Black Pentecost* (1979). Scored for mezzo-soprano, baritone, and orchestra, it protests against the impact of industry on the Orkneys. The opera *The Martyrdom of St. Magnus*, based on a novel by Browne, was written for the inaugural 1977 St. Magnus Festival on the islands.

Since his spell as a school head of music (from 1959 to 1962), Davies has worked to reshape children's music; for young Orkadians he has written an operatic version of *Cinderella* (1979–80) with local references, and *Songs of Hoy* (1981) for voices, recorders, percussion, and piano.

Returning to large-scale orchestral works in the mid-1970's, Davies has tamed the wild expressionism of his 1960's works and replaced it with Orkney land- and seascapes, and occasional echoes of Scottish dances. He has written six symphonies. In 1985 he became Associate Composer/Conductor of the Scottish Chamber Orchestra, which led to a commission for ten 'Strathclyde Concertos' for the orchestra's principal players. The last of these was completed in 1993, the year Maxwell Davies was knighted.

Additional Composers

Bartók, master though he was, seemed to exert surprisingly little influence after his death; but since then two major Hungarian composers have emerged who took him as a springboard. **György Ligeti** (born 1923) is an iconoclastic figure, whose zany sense of humor is shown in the 'comic-strip' opera *Le Grand Macabre*, with its opening of automobile horns. The range of his music is wide, from the almost static soundscape of *Atmosphères*, through the rhythmic mechanisms of the *Second String Quartet*, to the re-examination of Brahms in the *Horn Trio*. **György Kurtág** (born 1926) is more reticent, preferring sets of short, compressed pieces, which can achieve great emotional intensity, as in *Messages of the late Miss R. V. Troussova*.

Henri Pousseur (born 1929) and **Luigi Nono** (born 1924) both moved from the Boulez- and Stockhausen-influenced avant-garde of the 1950's into preoccupations with music in society. Pousseur's opera *Votre Faust* re-examines music of earlier eras, as well as allowing for audience choice regarding the musical discourse. Nono expressed passionate political radicalism in works such as the opera *Intolleranza*, and *Como una ola de fuerza y luz*, inspired by the death of a young leader of the Chilean revolutionary movement.

The Polish **Krzysztof Penderecki** (born 1933) managed in the 1960's to create an emotional impact from avant-garde devices, with works such as *Threnody for the Victims of Hiroshima*. Less sensational but perhaps more enduring is the refined music of the French **Henri Dutilleux** (born 1916), whose style, founded in Ravel, has pursued an independent but observant path, in such works as the cello concerto *Tout un monde lointain*.

In Britain, **Harrison Birtwistle** (born 1934) has explored worlds of violence (*Punch and Judy*) and ritual (*The Triumph of Time*), while **Jonathan Harvey** (born 1939) has used a variety of means, including electronics, to communicate a personal and charismatic spirituality, as in the opera *Inquest of Love*. **Alexander Goehr** (born 1932) (*Little Symphony*; *Sonata about Jerusalem*) and **Hugh Wood** (born 1932) (*Cello Concerto*; *Symphony*) have both been able to reinvigorate the tradition of Schoenberg and Berg with music combining passion and control.

Milton Babbitt (born 1916), in the United States, has continued to develop the serial legacy of Schoenberg and Webern with impressive consistency (*Philomel* for soprano and tape). **Morton Feldman** (1926–87) came under Cage's influence, and composed mainly slow and meditative music, such as the sequence *The Viola in My Life*.

Contemporary Trends

Steve Reich

Philip Glass

A wide variety of musical styles have developed since the start of the twentieth century, dominated in the 1950's and 1960's by the avant-garde movement. Led by Boulez and Stockhausen, avant-garde composers built on the serial techniques developed by Schoenberg in the 1920's. Composition teachers in universities and conservatories focused on these techniques, in which compositions are based on all 12 notes of the chromatic scale, used in an order chosen by the composer. Technically, no note is repeated until all 12 have appeared once. Attending courses at Darmstadt in Germany or Tanglewood in the United States became obligatory for any aspiring composer. Even individualist composers such as Messiaen and Copland flirted with the new serial language.

But many people found serialism inaccessible. By the 1960's, resistance to the form was growing, along with division among the avant-garde themselves. John Cage, in his lectures at Darmstadt in 1958, confronted avant-garde composers with a style radically different from their highly complex, ultra-organized language. He based his work on chance, indeterminacy, Eastern philosophy, and even, in *4' 33"*, silence. Although Stockhausen and others absorbed many of these elements, they remained serialist. A still more significant reaction came from a different quarter.

Minimalism and its developments

During the 1960's and early 1970's, La Monte Young, Terry Riley, Steve Reich, and Philip Glass introduced a new musical style called minimalism. These composers were all born in the United States in the 1930's and attended universities and conservatories there during the heyday of serialism. They knew each other, occasionally worked together, and shared the view that serialist music was both emotionally irrele-

vant and intellectually oppressive. Though the term 'minimalism' could apply to a number of John Cage's works employing limited (or nonexistent) musical means, it was in fact a distinct form.

Riley's *In C* (1964) resulted from work he did with Young, in which they experimented with variations over a single note, or drone. In *In C*, Riley introduced repeated melodic cells or motifs against unchanging harmony. His work became seminal to the minimalist movement, and the features he used — static harmony and repetition of melodic and rhythmic patterns — became the basic materials of minimalism. Everything was clearly audible, the harmony was usually tonal (based around one particular key), and its static quality drew the listener into the nature of sound, rather than presenting a complex structure to be grappled with.

Steve Reich (born 1936)

After writing theater and film music from 1963 to 1965, Reich introduced into minimalism the 'phasing' technique, notably in *Come Out* (1966). He used two or more instruments or voices to repeat the same rhythmic or melodic pattern at minutely different speeds so that they moved successively in and out of phase with each other. In 1970, he spent several months in Ghana at the University of Accra, studying African drumming with a master drummer of the Ewe tribe. Out of his experience, he produced the late minimalist classic *Drumming* (1971).

Since then Reich has outgrown his minimalist label. He pursued his interest in non-Western traditions in the 1970's with studies of Balinese music and the Hebrew cantorial chanting tradition. In *Tehillim* (1981), which uses a text and Hebrew Psalms, Reich needed longer spans of melody than the minimalist form allowed.

Echoes of African music, as well as jazz influences, appear in Reich's *Electric Counterpoint* (1987), written for the rock guitarist Pat Metheny, and *Sextet* (1984–85), composed for the percussion group Nexus. In these works, Reich continues to move away from pure minimalism. His harmonies are no longer as static, though they still remain gentle on the ear, and the fabric he weaves of gradually shifting rhythmic patterns is richer than in his early work. *Different Trains* (1988; recommended CD: Elektra Nonesuch 7559-79176-2), using tape and a string quartet, is an evocative and startling autobiographical recollection of his wartime journeys between New York and Los Angeles.

Reich collaborated with his wife, Beryl Korot, in *The Cave* (1989–93). This reflection on the biblical story of Abraham, from Jewish, Arab, and American perspectives, uses video footage of interviews, and treats the inflections of the recorded speech as a source of melody.

Philip Glass (born 1937)

Glass experimented with 12-note methods at university in Chicago and studied with Nadia Boulanger in Paris. There he was introduced to Indian music when a filmmaker hired him to transcribe the music of Ravi Shankar into Western notation. During the next year, Glass traveled in India and North Africa, then returned to New York in 1967. In the spirit of the 1960's Glass turned to the East in his reaction against the musical complexities of the age.

His contribution to minimalism was summarized in the three-hour *Music in Twelve Parts* (1971–74). But, like Reich, he outgrew the label. From composing incidental music for the theater, Glass moved to opera with *Einstein on the Beach*, which has become a landmark of contemporary music-theater. He went on to write

John Adams

Michael Nyman

Arvo Pärt

the highly successful *Akhnaten* (1984); *The Making of the Representative for Planet 8* (1988), based on Doris Lessing's novel; and *Orphée* (1993), based on Cocteau's film. He has also written instrumental works, music for the 1984 Los Angeles Olympics, and scores for films, including the documentary based on Stephen Hawking's *A Brief History of Time*. In contrast to his longer works, *Itaipú* (1988; recommended CD: Sony Classical SK46352) is a compact and more immediately accessible orchestral essay. It is a portrait of nature (of a hydroelectric dam in Paraguay) combining a full orchestral sound and Guaraní Indian texts.

Unlike Reich, Glass uses simple rhythms and repeated arpeggio figures, that effectively contrast the harmonies in a work. His later music shows greater concern for harmonic progression than for the static minimalist ideal.

John Adams (born 1947)

Adams left postgraduate studies at Harvard University under the combined influence of *Silence* (John Cage's collection of essays) and his first exposure to minimalism. He moved to San Francisco, where he rocketed to international fame in 1987 with the controversial opera *Nixon in China*, presenting contemporary history as high art and the discredited President Nixon and Chairman Mao as operatic heroes.

His music is influenced by homegrown American jazz and rock music, with which he creates a more varied and harmonically flexible offshoot of minimalism. In *Fearful Symmetries* (1988), he combines relentless rhythm with jazz riffs in the music, and adds a saxophone quartet and a synthesized silent-movie organ to the orchestra. Some critics have described his music as irritatingly banal, but Adams regards his banal elements as valid musical

material. At the opposite pole to *Fearful Symmetries* is *The Wound-Dresser* (1989; recommended CD: Elektra Nonesuch 7559-79281-2). This setting of a Walt Whitman poem describing wounded soldiers during the American Civil War is one of Adams's most lyrical and accessible pieces — elegiac, deeply moving, and compassionate.

With his 1993 opera *The Death of Klinghoffer*, Adams attracted accusations of exploitation and anti-Semitism. The opera deals with the tragic events of the 1985 terrorist hijacking of the Italian cruiser *Achille Lauro*. Controversy, it seems, brings marketability: in 1993, Adams became the most performed living American composer.

Michael Nyman (born 1944)

The prevailing serial approach of his teachers at the Royal Academy of Music and King's College, London, initially discouraged Nyman from composing. Instead he wrote articles and books on music, including the still authoritative *Experimental Music — Cage and Beyond*. He claims to have been the first to use the term 'minimalist' with respect to music.

As a composer, Nyman at first became known for his scores to Peter Greenaway's films; in *The Draughtsman's Contract* (1982; recommended CD: Virgin Venture DVEBN55), he innovated with the music of Purcell, and in *Drowning by Numbers* (1987), he based his work on material from the slow movement of Mozart's *Sinfonia Concertante* for violin and viola. He also wrote the music for Jane Campion's film *The Piano* (1993), which won the Cannes Film Festival's Palme d'Or and three Oscars. Nyman has also established a reputation in more conventional fields with a chamber opera, *The Man Who Mistook His Wife for a Hat* (1986), as well as three string quartets (1985, 1988, and 1990).

Spiritual reawakenings

What began with minimalism — a musically limited reaction to the avant-garde — became a diversity of new classical styles. Composers sought to return to clearly audible structures and predominantly tonal harmonies. The same concerns prompted yet another, and quite different, response in independent developments east of the old Iron Curtain.

Arvo Pärt (born 1935)

The Estonian Arvo Pärt scandalized the Soviet musical establishment with his serialist first work, *Necrology* (1959). For many years, official response to his music oscillated between enthusiastic recognition and censorship. Until the late 1960's he worked as a recording director with Estonian Radio in Tallinn, also composing some 50 film scores. He continued to use strict serial techniques in his 'serious' works and experimented with collage techniques, quoting Tchaikovsky in his *Second Symphony* (1966). Then, during a ten-year compositional silence (broken briefly in 1971 by the *Third Symphony*), he turned to an intensive study of Gregorian chant and choral music from Machaut through to Josquin Desprez. The result was his celebrated personal rediscovery of the triad, the simplest basic three-note chord and the foundation of tonal harmony.

A turning point came in 1977 with three works — *Fratres*, *Cantus in Memoriam Benjamin Britten*, and *Tabula Rasa* (recommended CD: ECM 817 764-2) — that attracted musicians and concertgoers alike. Pärt emigrated to the West three years later, and since then his work has explored religious texts such as the *St. John Passion* (1982), *Miserere* (1989), and the *Berliner Mass* (1990–92). This later music is infused with a haunting medieval flavor, combined with a disarming and profound

Henryk Górecki

John Tavener

Toru Takemitsu

simplicity. *Cantus*, for string orchestra and a single bell, is constructed entirely from counterpointed repetitions of a descending minor scale, with the bell decaying into silence at the end.

Henryk Górecki (born 1933)

The Polish composer Górecki achieved phenomenal commercial success when his *Third Symphony* (1976; recommended CD: Elektra Nonesuch 7559-79282-2) became, in 1993, the first ever contemporary classical work to enter the British pop charts. He spent the early part of his career as an avant-gardist in the Darmstadt mold. Then, in the same year that he made his only visit to Darmstadt, he composed *Three Pieces in the Old Style* (1963), drawing on medieval Polish music. Though he continued both threads of musical thought for some years, he finally settled on the 'old style.' The *Third Symphony* disconcerted an avant-garde audience at its 1977 premiere, with its long, slow, melodic outpouring that combines folk material and funeral songs. The work includes a setting for soprano of poetry written by a woman prisoner at Auschwitz.

Górecki's output has since included *Miserere* in 1981 — written in response to police violence against Solidarity and consequently banned until 1987 — and three string quartets.

John Tavener (born 1944)

The individual style of English composer John Tavener emerged from a different musical background, but his interest in mystical Eastern Orthodox philosophy and his conversion to the Russian arm of the church in 1977 reveal striking stylistic parallels with Pärt's music in particular.

He made an immediate impact in Britain in 1968 with the premiere of his first major work, *The Whale* (1965–66),

showing the influence if not the total acceptance of avant-garde methods. But since his religious conversion, his works have a radiant, iconic quality that reflects his beliefs. Based on Orthodox texts and chants, *Ikon of Light* (1984), for chorus and string trio, uses simple melodic formulas to build up rich choral textures which are then juxtaposed with long-held string chords and dramatic punctuating silences. *The Protecting Veil* (1987) for cello and orchestra (recommended CD: Virgin Classics VC7 59052-2) achieved widespread public as well as critical acclaim in a 1992 recording.

New directions

'Serious' composing flourishes, despite competition from pop and other styles of music. In Western and Eastern Europe, the Americas and, increasingly, the Far East, composers continue to extend the boundaries of style and method. As is particularly the case in Scandinavia, they are at times encouraged by state funding.

It is particularly intriguing from a Western point of view to observe the impact of composers from the Far East, who reverse the Western approach by adding Western influences to an Eastern background. The South Korean-born composer Isang Yun (born 1917) settled in Germany in the 1950's and had a close association with the avant-garde. After his 1967 abduction by the South Korean secret police and imprisonment on spying charges, a petition signed by Stravinsky, Stockhausen, Boulez, and others eventually secured his release. He became a German citizen in 1971. He gradually abandoned serialism in the 1970's, and developed his 'central tone' concept, based on the East Asian notion that each note has an individual identity, independent of melodic context. He has also trans-

lated the Chinese yin-and-yang philosophy into opposing yet complementary blocks of strings and brass in a series of five symphonies, composed from 1983 to 1987.

Toru Takemitsu (born 1930)

The Japanese composer Takemitsu became a symbolic cross-cultural figure in the 1960's after he gave a lecture series in 1964 with Cage. Largely self-taught, he absorbed the influences of Debussy, Webern, Stravinsky, Messiaen, and Boulez before gradually drawing more and more on his own cultural heritage. He briefly explored electronic music and, in *Vocalism A-I* (*ai* means 'love' in Japanese), he anticipated Stockhausen's vocalizing techniques in *Stimmung*. In *November Steps* (1967), one of his best works, he featured the traditional Japanese biwa (a kind of lute) and shakuhachi (a bamboo flute) in music that, though adopting a European style, nevertheless uses rhythms and forms derived from Japanese musical tradition. Takemitsu's inspirations often come from painting. In the guitar concerto *To the Edge of Dream* (1983; recommended CD: Sony Classical CD46720), the work of Belgian surrealist Paul Delvaux urges tranquillity and menace from the musical score.

He has also written a number of film scores including *Ran* (1985) — the highly acclaimed Japanese adaptation of the King Lear story — in which the director, Akira Kurosawa, achieved remarkable dreamlike battle sequences by replacing the noise of action with Takemitsu's slow, expansive, and austere music.

Britain's contributions to the contemporary music stream flow in conflicting directions. A new generation of avant-gardists, such as Brian Ferneyhough (born 1943) and Michael Finnissey (born 1946), embraced the serialist tradition. The

Sophia Gubaidulina

Alfred Schnittke

Romantic compositions of George Lloyd (born 1913) resurfaced in the 1970's to much public (if less critical) acclaim, especially works such as *A Symphonic Mass* (1993). Steeped in the traditions of Stravinsky and Varèse, Harrison Birtwistle (born 1934) has continued to provide provocative, individualist scores, from the trumpet concerto *Endless Parade* (1986–87) to operatic works such as *Punch and Judy* (1968) and *Gawain* (1991). Scottish composer James MacMillan (born 1959) has taken another contrary turn in *Búsqueda*, *The Confession of Isobel Gowdie* and more recently *Veni, Veni Emmanuel* (1992), all cast in an emotional and relatively accessible idiom and influenced by his devout Catholicism and socialist beliefs.

Sofia Gubaidulina (born 1931)
One of the most distinctive voices to emerge from the enforced obscurity of the former Soviet Union is Sofia Gubaidulina. She says she has been influenced by Schoenberg and Webern, mainly because they have 'taught me to be myself.' Her diverse and eclectic approach to composition ranges from modernist poetry, as in *Hommage à T. S. Eliot* (1987), to spiritual thinking, with *In Croce* (1987) for cello and organ, and *Rejoice!*, a sonata for cello and violin that embraces both the Ordinary of the Mass and Polish parables. Perhaps her most accomplished work to date is a violin concerto, *Offertorium* (1980; recommended CD: Deutsche Grammophon 427 336-2), which refers back to J. S. Bach.

Alfred Schnittke (born 1934)
Schnittke, preeminent among the ex-Soviet composers, is one of Europe's most performed living composers. Like Gubaidulina, he supported himself under Soviet rule by writing for films, also devoting himself to an intense study of serial methods.

Since the late 1960's, Schnittke has developed a 'polystylistic' approach that in one piece borrows from Mozart and jazz, ranges from rigorously modernist to neo-Romantic, and often includes considerable humor. But there is nothing flippant about his music, and since suffering major strokes in 1985 and 1991, he writes with a new sense of urgency. He completed a thoroughly impassioned orchestral work, the *Cello Concerto No. 1* (1985–86; recommended CD: EMI CDC7 54443-2), after his first near-fatal illness. The first movement of the concerto contains an almost palpable sense of anguished soul-searching. Schnittke's first and so far only opera, *Life with an Idiot* (1990–91), is a rich allegory of life in the Soviet Union, and of human nature in general.

Classical music in the marketplace
Until the twentieth century, classical music depended largely on the patronage of church and aristocracy. In recent times, that supportive role has passed in part to universities and conservatories, where many composers have held teaching posts. But for music to win recognition, it must be performed, and it is there that technological and economic revolutions since 1945 have had a profound effect.

Particularly in capitalist economies, performers have increasingly had to cater to commercial sponsors. Commercial recording companies account for much of the revenue in the music profession, and they must answer to the needs of the market. Music that is more accessible, or seems more relevant to the social concerns of the day, is more marketable, and so producers divert resources toward such music. This has undoubtedly played a major part in the popular success of all the composers so far mentioned. Nevertheless, a number of smaller companies enthusiastically promote music that is less well known and more esoteric. These producers deserve credit for their support of composers whose music is not likely to achieve commercial success. Although avant-garde composers are often ousted from center stage by the commercial expansion in classical music, they have found new ways of promoting their music and retaining their audience. Computers have made it possible for many composers to publish their own music, although getting works performed and marketed remains a struggle.

Stepping into the future
It is appropriate that composers ranging from Reich, Glass, and Adams to Schnittke and Gubaidulina have won recognition in recent years. Classical music now embraces a rich diversity of styles — from the margins of pop to seemingly impenetrable total serialism, and in some cases (for example, Schnittke) combining styles. The geographical spread of composers reaches far and wide — East and West, old worlds and new. Europe is, as ever, a hotbed of compositional activity. In some countries, such as those of Scandinavia, composing is often a state-funded activity, while in others composers have to fight their way into the public view, adding sophisticated marketing to the innate appeal of their music.

Posterity will ultimately decide which composers have the most lasting significance of today's generation. Serialism has been succeeded by a range of styles, with the more accessible early minimalists paving the way, and capturing an audience, for greater experimentation in forms and structures. The stylistic range is such that no one style or composer dominates the field like a latter-day Beethoven, or even a Stravinsky. Composers today do not lead a mainstream, but rather fit their own segments of an ever-widening spectrum.

Pavarotti in Hyde Park, London in 1992

Vast crowds attend an open air performance by celebrated tenor Luciano Pavarotti.

Glossary

Words in SMALL CAPITAL LETTERS within an entry are cross-referenced.

a cappella (Italian, 'in the chapel style') Describing choral music sung without instrumental accompaniment.

acoustics 1) The science of sound and sound waves. 2) The characteristics of a concert hall, auditorium, etc., that determine the quality of the sounds produced in it.

adagio (Italian, 'slowly') 1) An indication that the music is to be performed at a slow pace. 2) A movement or piece to be played at a slow pace.

allegro (Italian, 'lively') 1) An indication that the music is to be performed at a fairly brisk pace. 2) A movement or piece to be played at a brisk pace.

alto 1) The highest male voice; the term is sometimes applied to the female voice usually referred to as CONTRALTO. 2) Describing an instrument with approximately the same range as the alto voice.

anthem A short choral composition for religious services, usually with words taken from the biblical Scriptures.

aria (Italian, 'air') A composition for solo voice and instrumental accompaniment in an OPERA or ORATORIO.

arpeggio (from Italian, 'to play on a harp') The sounding of the NOTES (1) of a CHORD in succession rather than simultaneously.

Ars Antiqua (Latin, 'old art') A term relative to ARS NOVA, describing the music of the school of Notre Dame in Paris in the 12th and 13th centuries, notable for the full development of ORGANUM.

Ars Nova (Latin, 'new art') The music of the 14th century, especially that associated with the French composer Machaut, characterized by greater complexity and more varied RHYTHMIC patterns than previously used.

atonalism, atonality Loyalty to no KEY (1): a system of composition in which no one key is dominant. See also **serialism, twelve-note system**. Compare **tonality**.

Ave Maria (Latin, 'Hail, Mary') A Latin prayer to the Virgin Mary used as the basis of many musical settings by Renaissance composers and later notably by Schubert and Gounod.

ayre A short English song for voice, usually with a lute accompaniment, of the late 16th and early 17th centuries.

bagatelle A short, light musical composition, usually for the piano.

ballad 1) A narrative poem adapted for singing. 2) A type of sentimental song that achieved great popularity in Victorian England.

ballade 1) A medieval secular POLYPHONIC song derived from one of the most common forms of 14th-century French poetry. 2) A composition, usually for solo piano and often lyrical and heroic in tone, which Chopin, Liszt, and others made popular.

bar or (United States) **measure** Metrical unit (see METER) marked by the vertical 'bar' lines in a musical SCORE. Thus 'three beats to the bar,' etc.

barcarolle A boating song derived from the Venetian gondoliers, characterized by a lilting RHYTHM. Mendelssohn, Chopin, and Offenbach wrote notable examples.

baritone A male voice with a range between TENOR and BASS.

bass The deepest range of musical PITCH, applied to the lowest male voice and to musical instruments.

basso continuo or **thorough bass** Shorthand NOTATION of the BASS line, usually written below the STAVE, indicating the CHORDS to be played by the secondary instruments (usually keyboard or lute) accompanying the main melody. It was a common musical convention during the Baroque period.

bel canto (Italian, 'beautiful singing') A style of singing characterized by tonal beauty, pure line, and clarity of enunciation, primarily associated with 19th-century Italian OPERA.

berceuse (from French *bercer*, 'to rock') A cradle song or lullaby; or an instrumental piece, usually for piano, redolent of a lullaby.

broken chord See **chord**.

cadenza Florid, often improvised passage at the close of an instrumental or vocal piece, most often encountered in 19th-century works.

canon A composition in which a voice or PART is followed at fixed intervals by other voices or parts, each taking up the same melody in succession and overlapping each other.

cantata (Italian, 'sung') A work for voices and CHORUS, usually including RECITATIVE and ARIA, and generally with ORCHESTRAL accompaniment. Cantatas, which may be either sacred or secular, were composed chiefly in the Baroque period, notably by J. S. Bach.

cantus firmus (Latin, 'fixed melody') A melody serving as the main theme upon which a CONTRAPUNTAL composition is built.

castrato Male singer castrated before puberty to preserve his SOPRANO or ALTO voice. The power, range, and purity of this voice won castrati immense prestige in Italian OPERA in the 17th and 18th centuries.

chaconne An ancient dance in slow TRIPLE TIME, probably of Spanish origin. Musical examples include works by Purcell and Bach. See also **passacaglia**.

chamber music Music suited to performance in a room or a small concert hall, usually written for two or more instruments, with only one instrument to a PART. The most common combination is the string QUARTET (1).

chanson Secular song flourishing in France in the 15th and 16th centuries.

chorale A simple HYMN tune of the German Protestant Church, often adapted from PLAINCHANT and intended for singing by CHOIR and congregation together.

chord The simultaneous sounding of a group of NOTES (1) of different PITCH. A broken chord is one in which the notes are played one after the other.

chorus 1) A body of people singing in concert, especially in an OPERA, ORATORIO, etc. 2) The refrain of a song in which others join the principal singer or singers.

chromaticism The use of NOTES (1) in a composition that do not form part of the DIATONIC SCALE in which it is written.

chromatic scale A SCALE that progresses in SEMITONES, using all 12 NOTES (1) of an OCTAVE.

clef (French, 'key') A symbol at the beginning of a STAVE fixing the PITCH of the NOTES (1) and their names according to their position on the stave.

coda (Italian, 'tail') The final section of a piece of music, intended to round it off in a satisfactory manner.

coloratura An elaborate, highly ornamented style of singing particularly suited to a light, high, and agile SOPRANO voice.

concerto A composition for one or more solo instruments and ORCHESTRA, usually in three MOVEMENTS.

concerto grosso A composition in which a small group of solo instruments is contrasted with the main body of the ORCHESTRA. The concerto grosso enjoyed great popularity during the Baroque era.

concrete music See *musique concrète*.

conductor The director of an ORCHESTRA, CHORUS, etc., who controls the performance by means of gestures (often with a baton). He or she is responsible for both technical excellence and artistic interpretation of the music.

conservatory or **conservatoire** An institution for training musicians.

consort The name given, in the 16th and 17th centuries, to a small instrumental ENSEMBLE (1). A 'whole consort' consisted of instruments of the same family; a 'broken consort' was a mixed group of various families.

continuo See **basso continuo**.

contralto The lowest of the three ranges of female voice.

counterpoint, contrapuntal Music that combines two or more individual melodic lines to form a harmonious whole.

countertenor Adult male voice higher than the TENOR, similar to the ALTO.

crescendo (Italian, 'growing') An indication for the music to become louder.

diatonic scale The MAJOR and MINOR SCALES of Western classical music. See **scale, chromatic scale**.

diminuendo (Italian, 'diminishing') An indication that the music should become softer.

divertimento An 18th-century ORCHESTRAL form, usually divided into a number of short MOVEMENTS.

duet A composition for two voices or instruments.

dynamics Variations in the loudness and softness of a piece of music.

electronic music Music based on sounds created by electronic means rather than by the use of traditional instruments.

ensemble 1) A small group of players or singers. 2) A set piece in an OPERA for two or more soloists.

étude (French, 'study') A short composition, usually for solo instrument, designed mainly to improve or display the performer's technical ability. Chopin, Debussy, and Scriabin wrote études for concert performance.

falsetto An unnaturally high adult voice, usually a man's, with a PITCH or range above the normal REGISTER.

figured bass A form of musical shorthand in which the BASS PART has numbers added above or below the NOTES (1) to indicate the CHORDS to be played. See also **basso continuo**.

flat 1) A symbol ♭ placed before a NOTE (2) or in a KEY SIGNATURE to indicate that the PITCH is to be reduced by a SEMITONE. 2) Describing a musical sound that is lower in pitch than it should be.

forte, fortissimo The Italian for 'loud' and 'very loud' respectively, represented in SCORES by the abbreviations *f* and *ff*.

fugue A POLYPHONIC composition based on one or more short themes that are taken up by a number of voices or parts in turn and then undergo CONTRAPUNTAL development.

galant See **style galant**.

galliard A lively dance of the 16th and 17th centuries, usually in TRIPLE TIME.

gamelan A traditional kind of Indonesian orchestra, consisting mainly of percussion instruments and characterized by complex RHYTHMS.

gigue (French, 'jig') A dance originating in England. Introduced into France, the English 'jig' evolved into the 'gigue,' often forming the lively final MOVEMENT of the Classical SUITE (2).

glissando (bastard Italian from French *glisser*, 'to slide') The effect achieved by sliding one finger rapidly across the KEYS of a piano or strings of a harp.

grand opera Imprecise term usually referring to 'serious' OPERA as opposed to OPERETTA. French *grand opéra* was on an epic or historical subject and included a ballet.

Gregorian chant See **plainchant**.

harmony, harmonic Music combining sounds in a way considered pleasing, according to a system based on the concept of TONALITY and the MAJOR and MINOR KEYS.

hymn A song or ode in praise of God, a deity, etc. Forming part of the earliest devotional music, the hymn first appeared in the 4th century.

imitation The repetition of a phrase or subject in a different PITCH or KEY (1) or in a different voice part from the original.

impromptu A short instrumental piece designed to convey the impression of IMPROVISATION.

improvisation A piece of music created for a particular performance without any previous preparation. An important element of jazz.

incidental music Music to accompany the action of a film, play, etc.

interlude A short piece of instrumental music played between the acts of a play or between longer pieces of music.

intermedio or **intermezzo** 1) A performance of MADRIGALS and songs as part of Renaissance court entertainment. 2) A piece of music played between the acts or scenes of an OPERA. 3) An interlude. 4) A short 19th-century instrumental piece.

interval The difference in PITCH between two NOTES (1).

jongleur An itinerant musician and entertainer of the Middle Ages who often accompanied or sang the heroic verses written by TROUBADOURS.

Kapellmeister (German, 'chapel master') Originally the musician in charge of a German court chapel, later director of music at a court and, by the 19th century, director of a choir or instrumental ENSEMBLE (1). More recently the term has come to mean the resident conductor of an opera house or an orchestra.

key 1) The DIATONIC SCALE that predominates in a piece of music: a composition in the key of C major will use NOTES (1) close to that scale. 2) A lever on a musical instrument that is operated by a finger to produce a note.

keynote See **tonic**.

key signature The SHARPS (1) and FLATS (1) placed after the CLEF at the beginning of a STAVE to indicate the prevailing KEY (1).

Lamentations A setting of the Old Testament 'Lamentations of Jeremiah' used at the Roman Catholic service of Matins during Holy Week. It inspired various POLYPHONIC settings, notably by Tallis, Byrd, and Couperin.

lay A medieval French verse form intended for singing.

Leitmotiv (German, 'leading motive') A musical theme associated throughout a work with a particular person, idea, or situation, notably in the OPERAS of Wagner.

libretto (Italian, 'little book') The text of an OPERA, ORATORIO, or other extended musical composition.

Lied (German, 'song'; pl. *Lieder*) A traditional German lyric song that by the 15th and 16th centuries had acquired a POLYPHONIC form and was regarded as a distinct genre. In the 19th century, Schubert raised it to new heights, with piano accompaniment providing a counterpart to the voice.

madrigal A form of unaccompanied vocal music that originated in Italy in the 14th century, reaching its fullest development during the 16th and early 17th centuries, when the complexity of five or six voices was used to convey a wide range of emotions, from amorous to comical.

maestro di cappella (Italian, 'chapel master') Italian equal of KAPELLMEISTER.

Magnificat The HYMN of the Virgin Mary (Luke I, 46–55), sung at Evensong or Vespers and found in both PLAINCHANT and POLYPHONIC settings.

major scale A DIATONIC SCALE comprising five INTERVALS of a tone and two of a SEMITONE (between the third and fourth NOTES [1] and between the seventh and eighth).

masque A courtly entertainment, popular in England during the 16th and 17th centuries, in which vocal and instrumental music combined with drama, poetry, and dancing.

Mass The main service of worship of the Roman Catholic Church, of which the Kyrie Eleison, the Gloria, the Credo, the Sanctus and Benedictus, and the Agnus Dei (which includes the Dona nobis pacem) are sung.

mazurka A Polish folk dance in TRIPLE TIME. Chopin wrote a considerable number for the piano.

measure See **bar**.

Meistersinger (German, 'mastersinger(s)') Groups of poets, singers, and musicians who established guilds in German towns for the composing and performing of songs from the 15th to 17th century. Their tradition grew out of the aristocratic MINNESINGER.

meter The regular succession of rhythmic impulses, or beats, in music (and poetry). See also **rhythm**.

mezzo-forte The Italian for 'medium-loud,' represented in SCORES by the abbreviation *mf*.

mezzo-soprano (Italian, 'mid-soprano') The middle voice of the three female voices, with a range between SOPRANO and CONTRALTO. Often abbreviated to 'mezzo.'

minimalism A style of music in which one basic pattern is repeated again and again, providing a static, mesmeric quality reminiscent of Eastern forms of music.

Minnesinger (German, 'singer(s) of love') Type of aristocratic poet-musician that flourished in Germany during the Middle Ages. Similar to the French TROUBADOURS, they sang of courtly love. They were superseded by the merchant-class MEISTERSINGER.

minor scale There are two minor scales: the 'harmonic' is played the same ascending as descending and consists of INTERVALS of a TONE except for a SEMITONE between NOTES (1) 2–3, 5–6, and 7–8. The 'melodic' has semitones between 2–3 and 7–8 ascending, between 6–5 and 3–2 descending.

minstrel In the Middle Ages, one of a class of professional musicians who sang or recited to instrumental accompaniment.

minuet A court dance in TRIPLE TIME of the 17th and 18th centuries. Two minuets together (the second called the TRIO [3]) formed the third MOVEMENT of the Classical SYMPHONY.

Miserere The opening of Psalm 51, of which notable POLYPHONIC settings were made by Josquin and Allegri.

monophony, monophonic (Greek, 'single-sounded') A style of music having a single line of melody with no HARMONIC accompaniment, the dominant style before the development of POLYPHONY.

motet In medieval music, a POLYPHONIC composition in three parts, each part being sung at a different speed and using different words. Usually for unaccompanied voices, it was the sacred counterpart to the MADRIGAL and reached a peak with the *Motets* of J. S. Bach.

movement Self-contained section of a large composition. Each movement of a work usually has a separate TEMPO indication, hence the name.

musique concrète The name given in the late 1940's to the technique of using prerecorded natural sounds on tape as raw material for musical composition.

nocturne A musical composition suggesting the calm of evening or nighttime, which achieved great popularity in the lyrical piano pieces of John Field and Chopin.

notation Any system of recording music using written symbols for individual sounds, so they can be accurately reproduced in performance.

note 1) A single musical sound of specific PITCH and precise duration. 2) A symbol for this in a particular NOTATION. 3) The KEY (2) on a keyboard instrument that produces a note when depressed.

octave 1) An interval of eight NOTES (1) on the DIATONIC SCALE, the upper note having a frequency exactly double that of the lower one. 2) A series of notes or KEYS (2) extending through this interval.

octet 1) A composition for eight voices or instruments. 2) A group of singers or players who perform such a composition.

oeuvre (French, 'work') The complete output of works by a composer (or artist in any medium).

opera A dramatic work in which music forms the predominant part, consisting of ARIAS, RECITATIVES, CHORUSES, and often elaborate and spectacular staging. Opera began in 16th-century Italy as an attempt to re-create the forms of classical Greek drama.

opera-ballet A French theatrical presentation of the 17th and 18th centuries in which the action combines both OPERA and dancing.

opéra bouffe A 19th-century French OPERA of a witty or satirical nature, derived from the OPERA BUFFA.

opera buffa A type of Italian comic OPERA of the 18th century, opposite to OPERA SERIA.

opéra comique A form of French OPERA — not necessarily comic — that contains some spoken dialogue.

opera seria Serious Italian OPERA, the chief operatic genre of the 17th and 18th centuries, with a formal, elaborate structure and often using mythological themes.

operetta (Italian, 'little opera') A usually light OPERA, often containing spoken dialogue.

opus (Latin, 'work') 1) A musical composition. 2) (Commonly abbreviated Op.; pl. Opp.) Followed by a number, denotes a piece by a particular composer, usually in order of publication.

oratorio An extended musical setting of a (usually) religious text with solo voices, CHORUS, and ORCHESTRA. Developed in Rome in the 17th century, the oratorio had a similar structure to an OPERA but was presented in a concert hall rather than being acted out on stage.

orchestra A body of musicians performing on various instruments comprising four main groups: strings, woodwinds, brass, and percussion. The modern orchestra evolved in the 17th century and now includes between 80 and 120 players, although its size and format will vary with the requirements of the composition.

organum A form of early POLYPHONY in which the lower voice retained the basic PLAINCHANT while the other parts moved more freely above it. It was current in church music from the 9th to the 13th centuries.

ornament A NOTE (1) or notes added to vocal or instrumental music as a decoration or embellishment.

overture 1) An ORCHESTRAL composition serving as the introduction to an OPERA, ORATORIO, or stage play. 2) A concert work for orchestra comprising a single MOVEMENT.

part The music written for a particular instrument or voice in an ORCHESTRA, CHOIR, etc.

partita A composite work such as a SUITE of pieces — as, for example, Bach's partitas for unaccompanied violin.

part-song A song with PARTS for several voices, usually without instrumental accompaniment.

passacaglia An instrumental piece, very similar to the CHACONNE, based on a slow dance of Spanish origin and consisting of variations above a short, repeated bass theme.

Passion A musical setting of the Gospel account of the sufferings and death of Christ. From simple medieval passion plays in PLAINCHANT, there developed, during the Renaissance and Baroque periods, increasingly elaborate settings with solo voices, CHORUS, and ORCHESTRAL accompaniment, which culminated in the works of J. S. Bach.

pastoral or **pastorale** 1) A kind of early OPERA with a pastoral theme, popular in France and Italy. 2) A piece of music that evokes pastoral life.

pavan or (French) *pavane* A slow, stately court dance of the 16th and 17th centuries. Popular with Elizabethan composers, it enjoyed a revival in the 19th and 20th centuries.

piano, pianissimo The Italian for 'soft' and 'very soft' respectively, represented in SCORES by the abbreviations *p* and *pp*.

pitch The quality of a musical sound which determines its position on a SCALE and is measured by the frequency of the vibrations that produce it.

pizzicato (Italian, 'pinched') An instruction to pluck the strings of a normally bowed string instrument.

plainchant or **plainsong** The unaccompanied liturgical music used in the Christian church from earliest times. It consisted of a single line of text and melody, sung by a single voice (priest) or several in unison (CHOIR).

polonaise A slow dance in TRIPLE TIME, of Polish origin. It was used by J. S. Bach and later by Beethoven and Schubert, but found its most vigorous expression in Chopin's polonaises for piano.

polyphony, polyphonic (Greek, 'many-sounded') A style of music combining two or more independent melodic lines, thus giving greater depth and complexity than previous, single-line music. It flourished from the 13th to the 16th century. Compare **monophony**.

prelude A piece of music originally intended as an introduction to another, such as a FUGUE or SUITE. In the 19th century the term came to be applied to a relatively short, independent composition, usually for piano.

prima donna (Italian, 'first lady') Main female singer in an OPERA production.

program music Music that is inspired by nonmusical ideas and seeks to convey an impression of scenes, events, people, paintings, ideas, etc. It achieved popularity in the 19th century. See also **symphonic poem**.

quartet 1) A composition for four voices or instruments. 2) A group of four singers or players who perform such a composition.

quintet 1) A composition for five voices or instruments. 2) A group of five singers or players who perform such a composition.

recitative A form of solo singing in OPERA and ORATORIO that adopts the patterns of ordinary speech, inserted between ARIAS as a means of conveying dramatic dialogue to the audience. It may be accompanied by the ORCHESTRA or unaccompanied except for an occasional BROKEN CHORD.

register A part of the compass (range) of a voice or instrument having a distinctive tonal quality — i.e. the lower and higher registers of a voice.

requiem A musical setting of the Roman Catholic MASS for the repose of the dead. Notable examples are those by Mozart, Berlioz, and Verdi.

rhythm The organization of the NOTES (1) of a piece of music in relation to TIME. Its basic structure is determined by the way in which the notes are grouped in BARS, the number of beats in a bar, and the manner in which the beats are accented. See also **meter**.

ripieno (Italian, 'full') The main body of musicians in the ORCHESTRAS of the 17th and 18th centuries. The term is used specifically to refer to the TUTTI group in a CONCERTO GROSSO, the solo group being known as *concertante*.

rondeau A medieval French verse of three or four stanzas intended for singing. In the 14th century, POLYPHONIC settings were made for instruments and several voices.

rondo A form of instrumental music in which an initial theme is repeated while alternating with a series of contrasting themes. The form was widely used in the final MOVEMENTS of SONATAS, SYMPHONIES, and CONCERTOS during the 18th and 19th centuries.

round A PART-SONG in which several unaccompanied voices take up the melody in succession and at equal intervals, each singing a complete melody.

scale A series of NOTES (1) ascending or descending by determined increments. There are various types of scale, depending on the musical system being used. See **chromatic, diatonic, major,** and **minor scales.**

score A book showing the music for all the PARTS of a composition arranged on STAVES, ranged down the page. Conventionally, the woodwind parts are at the top of the page and the strings at the bottom.

semitone Half a TONE; the smallest INTERVAL in Western classical music.

septet 1) A composition for seven voices or instruments. 2) A group of seven singers or players who perform such a composition.

serialism A form of ATONALISM developed in the early 20th century that revolutionized composition. Serial works are based on a systematized arrangement or 'row' of specified NOTES (1), not necessarily in the same OCTAVE, arranged in whatever order the composer chooses, and not repeating any note. As no single note dominates, there is no home KEY. See also **twelve-note system, total serialism.**

sextet 1) A composition for six voices or instruments. 2) A group of six singers or players who perform such a composition.

sharp 1) A symbol ♯ placed before a NOTE (2) or in a KEY SIGNATURE to indicate that the PITCH is to be raised by a SEMITONE. 2) Describes a musical sound that is higher in pitch than it should be.

sinfonia An instrumental composition used as an OVERTURE (1) in early 18th-century OPERA.

sinfonietta A short ORCHESTRAL work in symphonic form (see SYMPHONY).

Singspiel (German, 'song-play') A form of OPERA with extensive use of spoken dialogue in place of RECITATIVE, popular in Germany and Austria in the 18th century.

solo A piece of music intended to be sung or played by one performer alone.

sonata (Italian, 'sounded') Originally a piece of music for instruments as opposed to a CANTATA, which was sung. It evolved into an extended composition in several contrasted but related MOVEMENTS, written for one or more instruments, usually including a keyboard instrument.

sonata form The normal structure of the first MOVEMENT of a SONATA, SYMPHONY, CONCERTO, etc., consisting of the exposition, outlining a musical theme ('first subject') and a contrasting 'second subject'; the development, in which the themes are varied and transformed; and a recapitulation, in which the themes of the exposition are repeated in modified form.

soprano The highest of the three female voices, with a range of more than two OCTAVES.

Stabat Mater A 13th-century Latin HYMN on Mary, the mother of Jesus, before the cross, which was later set to music by a number of composers, including Josquin and Palestrina, and more recently Dvořák and Poulenc.

stave or **staff** NOTATION consisting of five parallel lines and the corresponding spaces between them, on which NOTES (2) are written, their position on the stave determining their relative PITCH.

study See **étude.**

style galant Music of the Rococo period of the mid-18th century, characterized by lightness and elegance.

suite 1) An instrumental composition of the 17th and 18th centuries, consisting of a sequence of stylized dance MOVEMENTS. 2) Any ordered series of instrumental movements.

symphonic poem or **tone poem** A large-scale ORCHESTRAL work, usually in one MOVEMENT, based on a nonmusical subject. A type of PROGRAM MUSIC, drawing inspiration from a variety of literary and artistic sources, it was designed to portray in music a person, a picture, an event, etc.

symphony An instrumental composition in three or four MOVEMENTS having the structure of a SONATA but played by a full ORCHESTRA. The Classical symphony was perfected by Haydn and Mozart, but the form was greatly expanded by Beethoven and later composers, including Brahms and Mahler.

syncopation The shifting of the accent in a BAR to a beat that is normally unaccented, to achieve an irregular RHYTHM, often to dramatic effect.

Te deum laudamus (Latin, 'we praise thee, O God') A Latin HYMN of thanksgiving dating from the 5th century. There are famous settings by Handel, Haydn, Berlioz, and Bruckner.

tempo (Italian, 'time'; pl. tempi) The speed at which a piece of music is played.

Tenebrae (Latin, 'darkness') Music composed for the offices of Matins and Lauds in the Catholic Church during the last three days of Holy Week.

tenor 1) The highest natural male voice, with a range of an OCTAVE either side of middle C. 2) Describing an instrument with a comparable range to this voice.

thorough bass See **basso continuo.**

threnody A song of lamentation for the dead.

timber The characteristic quality of the sound that distinguishes a particular instrument or voice.

time A measure of the general movement of a piece of music with reference to its RHYTHM, metrical structure (see METER), and TEMPO.

tonalism, tonality Use of KEYS (1) as a system of musical composition. In the HARMONIC system used in conventional Western classical music, tonality is the basic principle of organization, using a number of keys, one of which is predominant. Compare **atonality.**

tone The fundamental INTERVAL (for example, from C to D) used to compose SCALES.

tone poem See **symphonic poem.**

tonic or **keynote** The first NOTE (1) of a SCALE, from which the KEY (1) takes its name.

total serialism The application of the principles of SERIALISM to cover all aspects of a composition, including RHYTHM, DYNAMICS, TEMPI, and PITCH.

transcription The arrangement of a composition, originally written for a particular instrument(s), for performance by a different instrument(s).

transposition The shifting of the overall PITCH of a piece of music so that it can be performed in a higher or lower KEY than the original one.

treble 1) The voice of a boy who has not yet reached puberty. 2) The highest PART in a mixed-voice choir. 3) Describing members of various families of high-pitched musical instruments.

triad A CHORD consisting of the first, third, and fifth NOTES (1) of the SCALE.

trio 1) A piece of CHAMBER MUSIC for three voices or instruments. 2) A group of three singers or players. 3) In a symphony, a second MINUET, originally written for three instruments.

trio sonata An early form of CHAMBER MUSIC usually played by two violins and a cello.

triple time The primary division of a piece of music into three beats to a BAR. See **time.**

troubadour Type of poet-musician who flourished in southern France from the 11th to the 13th century, performing songs about courtly love.

twelve-note or **twelve-tone system** The original and simplest form of SERIALISM, developed by Schoenberg in the 1920's. The 12-note system is a method of musical composition based upon a 'note row,' a sequence consisting of each of the 12 NOTES (1) of the CHROMATIC SCALE, arranged in whatever order the composer chooses and not repeating any note. Dispensing with the idea of KEY (1), all notes are treated as equal. See also **atonality, tonality.**

verismo (Italian, 'realism') A type of Italian OPERA of the late 19th and early 20th centuries that addressed contemporary themes in a realistic manner and depicted the sometimes sordid and violent lives of ordinary people.

vibrato A pulsating or throbbing effect designed to enhance the beauty of sound, produced by a slight but rapid change of PITCH of a NOTE (1) in a voice or instrument.

virtuoso A musical performer endowed with outstanding technical skill.

vocalize To sing without words, usually as an exercise in which a vowel sound is sung.

waltz A dance in TRIPLE TIME, based on an Austrian folk dance, which enjoyed great popularity in the early 19th century.

Index of Composers

Allegri, Gregorio **77**
Adams, John **256**
Albéniz, Isaac **182**
Albinoni, Tomaso **87**
Allegri, Gregorio **77**
Arne, Thomas **95**
Auber, Daniel-François-Esprit **117**

Bach, Johann Sebastian **88–89**
Barber, Samuel **220**
Bartók, Béla **212–13**
Beethoven, Ludwig van **136–37**
Bellini, Vincenzo **141**
Berg, Alban **224**
Berio, Luciano **252**
Berlioz, Hector **144–45**
Bernstein, Leonard **248**
Berwald, Franz **119**
Bizet, Georges **153**
Boccherini, Luigi **111**
Borodin, Alexander **152**
Boulez, Pierre **249**
Brahms, Johannes **154–55**
Britten, Benjamin **244**
Bruckner, Anton **159**
Busoni, Ferruccio **189**
Byrd, William **60**

Cage, John **246**
Carissimi, Giacomo **79**
Carter, Elliott **241**
Charpentier, Marc-Antoine **81**
Cherubini, Luigi **115**
Chopin, Frédéric **146–47**
Clementi, Muzio **114**
Copland, Aaron **240**
Corelli, Arcangelo **84**
Couperin, François **85**

Debussy, Claude **186–87**
Delibes, Léo **174**
Delius, Frederick **214**
Donizetti, Gaetano **140**
Dowland, John **61**
Dufay, Guillaume **53**
Dvořák, Antonin **177–78**

Elgar, Edward **192–93**

Falla, Manuel de **191**
Fauré, Gabriel **182–83**
Field, John **116**

Gabrieli, Andrea **62–63**
Gabrieli, Giovanni **62–63**
Gershwin, George **219**
Gesualdo, Carlo **62**
Glass, Philip **255–56**
Glinka, Mikail **142**
Gluck, Christoph Willibald **108**
Górecki, Henryk **257**
Gounod, Charles **145**
Grainger, Percy **216**
Grieg, Edvard **176–77**
Gubaidulina, Sofia **258**

Handel, George Frideric **90–91**
Haydn, Franz Joseph **109–10**
Henze, Hans Werner **252–53**
Hildegard of Bingen **50**
Hindemith, Paul **225**
Holst, Gustav **215**
Honegger, Arthur **228**

Ives, Charles **217**

Janáček, Leoš **210–11**
Josquin Desprez **55**

Kodály, Zoltán **213**

Lalo, Edouard **173**
Lassus, Orlande de **58**
Leoncavallo, Ruggero **180**
Liszt, Franz **148–49**
Lully, Jean-Baptiste **80**
Lutoslawski, Witold **247**

Machaut, Guillaume de **52**
Mahler, Gustav **184–85**
Maxwell Davies, Peter **254**
Mendelssohn, Felix **142–43**
Messiaen, Olivier **242–43**
Meyerbeer, Giacomo **118–19**
Monteverdi, Claudio **76–77**
Mozart, Wolfgang Amadeus **112–13**
Mussorgsky, Modest **155**

Nielsen, Carl **185**
Nyman, Michael **256**

Ockeghem, Johannes **54**

Pachelbel, Johann **82**

Paganini, Niccolò **138**
Palestrina, Giovanni Pierluigi da **57**
Pärt, Arvo **256–57**
Pérotin **51**
Poulenc, Francis **229**
Prokofiev, Sergei **208–9**
Puccini, Giacomo **180–81**
Purcell, Henry **82–83**

Rachmaninov, Sergei **209–10**
Rameau, Jean-Philippe **93**
Ravel, Maurice **195–96**
Reich, Steve **255**
Respighi, Ottorino **222**
Rimsky-Korsakov, Nikolai **156**
Rodrigo, Joaquin **242**
Rossini, Gioacchino **139**

Saint-Saëns, Camille **175**
Satie, Erik **187**
Scarlatti, Domenico **94**
Schnittke, Alfred **258**
Schoenberg, Arnold **222–23**
Schubert, Franz **120–21**
Schumann, Robert **147–48**
Schütz, Heinrich **78**
Scriabin, Alexander **188**
Shostakovich, Dmitri **230–31**
Sibelius, Jean **190**
Simpson, Robert **253**
Smetana, Bedřich **172**
Stockhausen, Karlheinz **250**
Strauss, Johann the Younger **150–51**
Strauss, Richard **193–94**
Stravinsky, Igor **226–27**
Sullivan, Arthur **151**

Takemitsu, Toru **257–58**
Tallis, Thomas **56**
Tavener, John **257**
Tchaikovsky, Pyotr Ilyich **156–57**
Telemann, Georg Philipp **92**
Thomson, Virgil **218**
Tippett, Michael **245**

Vaughan Williams, Ralph **196–97**
Verdi, Giuseppe **158–59**
Victoria, Tomás Luis de **59**
Villa-Lobos, Heitor **226**
Vivaldi, Antonio **86–87**

Wagner, Richard **160–61**
Walton, William **221**
Weill, Kurt **230**
Wolf, Hugo **179**

Xenakis, Iannis **251**

Index

Page numbers in *italic* refer to
the illustrations

Acknowledgments

The publishers would like to thank all those who contributed photographs to this book, particularly Jurgen Raible from Archiv für Kunst und Geschichte, Miranda Dewar from the Bridgeman Art Library, and Leon Myer and Dawn Wyman from the Hulton-Deutsch Collection, Elbie Lebrecht of the Lebrecht Collection, and Paul Collen of the Royal College of Music.

The picture reproduced on page 81 is by courtesy of the Joint Grand Gresham Committee. Fratelli Alinari 44/45; Archiv für Kunst und Geschichte 4 center right, 16/17, 17, 18 top, 19 top, 20/21, 26 right, 27 left, 30/31, 32/33, 33 top right, 34, 34/35, 36/37 bottom, 46/47, 50 top, 50 bottom, 56 right, 73, 75, 76 bottom, 78 bottom, 82, 83 top left, 84 top, 92 left, 105 bottom, 108 bottom, 110, 111 left, 117 top, 129 top, 129 bottom, 135 top, 143 bottom, 144 top, 146 bottom, 149 bottom, 151 top, 157 left, 169 top, 169 center, 173 top right, 174 top, 178 top, 179 bottom, 179 top, 180, 184 bottom, 186 bottom, 187, 188 left, 189 bottom, 190 left, 190 top, 194 left, 206/207, 207 top, 209, 211 bottom, 213, 217 bottom, 219 bottom, 224 bottom, 231, 231, 243 top; Archive Photos 212; Artothek 68/69, 122/123, 126 left, 134, Artothek /© DACS 1994 170 top; Ashmolean Museum, 22 left; Beethoven-Archiv 136, 137 bottom; Bettmann Archive 4 left, 52 bottom, 57 bottom, 79 bottom, 80 bottom, 108 top, 118 top, 153 bottom left; Bibliothèque Nationale 5 center left, 45 top, 52 top; Biblioteca Medicea Laurenziana /Laboratorio Donato Pineider 55 bottom; Bildarchiv Preussischer Kulturbesitz 81, 88 top, 148 bottom; Boosey & Hawkes 257 left; Bibliothèque Royale Albert 1er 54 bottom; Bridgeman Art Library 32 center, 59 top, 66/67, 83 bottom, 88 bottom, 89 bottom, 91 top, 94 bottom, 100, 101, 102 bottom 103, /Bibliothèque Nationale, Paris 186 top, /Bradford Art Galleries & Museums 214 bottom, /British Library 32 top right, 194 right, /Giraudon 53 top, 93 bottom left, 100/101, 104, 115, 183 top, /Giraudon/Bibliothèque du Conservatoire de Musique 183 bottom, /Giraudon/Chateau de Versailles 47, 64/65, /Giraudon/Louvre 146 top, /Giraudon/Musée Condé 158/159, /Historisches Museum der Stadt Wien 109 top, /K. & B. News 55 top, 62/63, /Lauros-Giraudon/DACS 229 top, /Lauros-Giraudon/Louvre 72, /Lauros-Giraudon/Musée Carnavalet 149 top, /Louvre 126 bottom, /Mus_e des Arts Décoratifs 196, /Museo de Arte, Ponce, Puerto Rico 124/125, /Museo di S. Martino 141 top, /Museum of London 162/163, /National Gallery 74, /Private Collection 130/131, 138 top, 181 right, /Pushkin Museum 165, /Staatsbibliothek Preussischer Kulturbesitz 128, /Staatsgalerie Stuttgart /DACS 202/203, /Stapleton Collection 130, /Wakefield Art Gallery 132 top; British Library 18 bottom, 44, 71; British Museum 83 top right; Hanya Chlala 247 top, 257 center; Christie's Images 173 bottom; M. K. Ciurlionis State Museum of Art 188 top; Giancarlo Costa 4 center left, 20, 31 center bottom, 32 top left, 33 top left, 40, 87 top, 93 bottom right, 93 top, 131, 139 bottom center right, 139 top, 139 bottom center, 139 bottom left, 139 bottom right, 141 bottom, 157 right, 161, 169 bottom, 175 bottom, 181 center, 195 center top, 195 center bottom, 212/213, 223 right, 224 top; Czartoryski Foundation 41; Decca /Vivianne Purdom 6; Deutsches Theatermuseum 109 bottom; Melissa Dring, P. S. 8; Antonin Dvorák Museum 177 top; Edinburgh University Collection of Historic Musical Instruments /Antonia Reeve 26 left, 28 center, 28 bottom right, 29 left, 29 right, 30 bottom right, 30 bottom left; English Folk Dance & Song Society 215 right, 216 bottom; English Heritage 4 right; E. T. Archive 65 bottom, 76 top, 86 top, 90, 106 top, 114 top, 120, 129 center, 138

bottom, 145 top, 147 bottom, 150 top, 160 bottom, 200/201; Mary Evans Picture Library 116 bottom; Explorer 23 right, 23 center, 26 center, 80 top,156, 201; Ralph A. Fassy 251 bottom; Finchcocks 114 bottom; Fotomas Index 95; Claudio Garofalo 62; Germanisches Nationalmuseum 92 right; Photographie Giraudon 121, /Musée Rodin 164; Granger Collection 96/97; G. D. Hackett 37; Claus Hansmann 153 top, 159 center; Robert Harding Picture Library 98/99, /Bildagentur Schuster 36 bottom, /FPG International 178 bottom, 235; Herzog Anton Ulrich-Museum 48/49; Historisches Museum der Stadt Wien 15; Hulton Deutsch Collection 36 top left, 56 left, 60 top, 85 bottom, 99, 106 107, 116 top, 117 left, 127, 132 bottom, 133, 135 bottom, 144 bottom, 151 bottom, 152 top, 158 bottom, 160 top, 167, 170 bottom, 171 bottom, 171 top, 172 top, 174 bottom, 182,189 top,192 top, 195 right, 197, 210 bottom, 210 top, 221 bottom, 225, 240 top left, 241 bottom, 242 left, 243 bottom, 244 top, 245 top, 248, 252, /Auerbach Collection 250 top, 253 top, /Linda Stone 254, 255 right, Hulton Deutsch/Bettmann 94 top, 148 top, 176 left, 181 left, 184 top left, 191 bottom,193, 208 left, 215 left, 220; Hannes Kilian 242 left; Kobal Collection 153 bottom right, 208 top, 219 top; Kunsthistorisches Museum 105 top; Kunstmuseum Bern /DACS 249 bottom; Larousse 14, 58 top, 58 bottom, 79 top, 173 top left; Lebrecht Collection 36/37, 119, 142, 143 top, 150 bottom, 154 top,155 top, 159 bottom, 166 right, 184 top right, 192 bottom, 218 top, 218 bottom, 221 top, 226, 228, 230 left, /Betty Freeman 241 top, 249 top, 256 right, 258 right, /Peter Musgrave 253 bottom; Library of Congress 204/205, 217 top; Magnum 227, /Constantine Manos 10/11, /Erich Hartmann 246 top, /Erich Lessing 51, 112 top, 113, /Robert Capa 198/199; Mander & Mitchenson 229 bottom; Mansell Collection 91 bottom; Massachusetts Historical Society 102 top; McNay Art Museum/Collection Robert L. B. Tobin 240 right; Merce Cunningham Dance Company 246 bottom; Metropolitan Museum of Art /Purchase 1924, Joseph Pulitzer Bequest 46, /Robert Lehman Collection, 1975 42/43; Musikverlage Hans Sikorski, Hamburg 258 left; Muzeum české hudby 172 bottom; Národní Muzeum 211 top; Nasjonalgalleriet Oslo /© The Munch Museum /The Munch-Ellingsen Group /DACS 1994 214 top; National Gallery of Victoria /Felton Bequest, 1949–50 19 bottom; National Trust Photographic Library 61 top, /Derrick E. Witty 68 left, /J. Whitaker 24 bottom right, /Jonathon Gibson 25 bottom left; National Gallery of Art /Samuel H. Kress Collection 53 bottom; Peter Newark's American Pictures 203; Novosti 152 bottom,230 right; Deborah O'Grady 256 left; Ordrupgaardsamlingen, Copenhagen – Woldbye 147 left; Performing Arts Library /Clive Barda 240 bottom, 255 left, /Michael Ward 245 bottom; Popperfoto 185; Private collection 137 top, 251 top, /Courtesy Galerie St. Étienne, New York 223 left; Redferns /Malcolm Crowther 257 right, /Colin Streator 256 center; Reed Consumer Books Picture Library 89 top left; Retrograph Archive /Martin Breese 5 center right; Rex Features 259,/Sipa Press 236/237; Rheinisches Bildarchiv Köln 38/39; Rijksmuseum 70/71; Robert-Schumann-Haus 147 right; Roger-Viollet /Collection Viollet 166 left, 168, 191 top; Royal Opera House Archives 140 bottom; Royal College of Music 5 left, 24 left, 27 center, 175 top, 216 top; The Royal Collection /©1994 Her Majesty The Queen 7; Sächsische Landesbibliothek, Abteilung Deutsche Fotothek 78 top; Scala 6/7, 12/13, 25 right, 45 bottom, 54 right, 57 top, 66 left, 86/87, 112 bottom, 140 top, 155 bottom; Science Photo Library /NASA 239; Scottish National Portrait Gallery, by permission of the Earl of Roseberry 69 right; Sotheby's, 84 bottom; Statens Museum for Kunst 61 bottom; © Karlheinz Stockhausen, 51515 Kürten, Germany 250 bottom; Tony Stone Images /Jon Riley 234; Suffolk Record Office 244 bottom; Topham Picture Source 247 bottom; Universitetsbiblioteket Oslo 176 right; V. & A. Picture Library, 22 right, 24 top left, 60 bottom, 85 top, 111 right; Whitney Museum of American Art 232/233; Yale Center for British Art 145 bottom; Zentralbibliothek Zurich 106 bottom.